The Jesus Myth

Books by G.A. Wells

Herder and After (1959)
The Plays of Grillparzer (1969)
The Jesus of the Early Christians (1971)
Did Jesus Exist? (1975; second edition, 1986)
Goethe and the Development of Science (1978)
The Historical Evidence for Jesus (1982)
The Origin of Language: Aspects of the Discussion from Condillac to Wundt (1987)
Religious Postures: Essays on Modern Christian Apologists and Religious Problems (1988)
Who Was Jesus? A Critique of the New Testament Record (1989)
Belief and Make-Believe: Critical Reflections on the Sources of Credulity (1991)
What's in a Name? Reflections on Language, Magic, and Religion (1993)
The Jesus Legend (1996)
The Jesus Myth (1998)

Edited Works

Language: Its Origin and Relation to Thought (co-edited with D.R. Oppenheimer), by F.R.H. Englefield (1977)
The Mind at Work and Play (co-edited with D.R. Oppenheimer), by F.R.H. Englefield (1985)
J.M. Robertson: Liberal, Rationalist, and Scholar (1987)
Critique of Pure Verbiage: Essays on Abuses of Language in Literary, Religious, and Philosophical Writings (co-edited with D.R. Oppenheimer), by F.R.H. Englefield (1990)
The Old Faith and the New, by David Friedrich Strauss (1997)

The Jesus Myth

G.A. Wells

Open Court
Chicago and La Salle, Illinois

To order books from Open Court, call toll-free 1-800-815-2280.

Cover painting reproduced by permission of The Art Institute of Chicago: Guercino (Giovanni Francesco Barbieri), Italian, 1591–1666, *The Entombment of Christ*, oil on canvas, 1656, 146.7 x 221.2 cm, Wilson L. Mead Fund, 1956. 128, photograph © 1996 The Art Institute of Chicago. All Rights Reserved.

Open Court Publishing Company is a division of Carus Publishing Company.

Copyright © 1999 by Carus Publishing Company

First printing 1999

Printed and bound in the United States of America.

Library of Congress Cataloging-in-Publication Data
Wells, George Albert, 1926–
      The Jesus myth / G.A. Wells.
          p.   cm.
      Includes bibliographical references and indexes.
      ISBN 0-8126-9392-2 (pbk. : alk. paper)
      1. Jesus Christ—Historicity.   2. Bible. N.T.—Criticism,
interpretation, etc.   3. Jesus Christ—History of doctrines—Early
church, ca. 30–600.
      I. Title.
      BT303.2.W428   1999   98-27828
      232.9'08—dc21   CIP

To the memory of
Evelyn
(1914–1997)

Contents

Preface

This book has two principal aims: to put before the general reader some fundamental facts about the New Testament (NT) which will help him or her towards an informed opinion concerning its reliability; and to make out a sustainable view of Christian origins, drawing on the extant evidence—Christian, Jewish, and pagan. This involves addressing such questions as: When were the twenty-seven books of the New Testament written? Do they give a substantially consistent portrait of Jesus? If not, are there elements in any one of their portraits that may be taken as reliable? And finally, even if we cannot with any confidence specify what in the gospels is likely to be historically true, do gospels or epistles nevertheless contain acceptable ethical doctrines? Whether or not my readers agree with my evaluations, they will find here the facts on which to base their own conclusions.

Substantial question marks over the Jesus of the gospels are admitted by many—including now even Catholic—theologians, some of whom are prepared to question not only his virgin birth and the miracles he supposedly worked during his ministry, but even the much more fundamental doctrine of the resurrection. Few, however, would go so far as their colleague, Burton Mack, Professor of New Testament Studies at the Claremont School of

Theology in California, who calls the gospels' portrayal of Jesus "fantastic", "the result of a layered history of imaginative embellishments of a founder figure" (1993, p. 247). Nevertheless, I regard this verdict as substantially just, as against the view of apologists who hold that it is merely a series of ephemeral fashions that has put in question much of what the New Testament alleges, and that 'modernist' critical views of the Bible are based on a deplorable tendency to be 'up to date', and not a trustee of tradition.

I have written five earlier books on the origins of Christianity, but there is no need to read any of them before reading *The Jesus Myth*. These six books (four of which are in print and easily available) can be read in any order and emphasize different aspects of the question. My views have naturally undergone some development over the relevant twenty-seven years, and the principal modifications are reflected in *The Jesus Legend* and *The Jesus Myth*. (See, for guidance on this, note 40 on p. 273 below, referring to p. 103 of the text.) One reason for treating the subject from various angles in six books has been to reply to different authors who have defended traditional views of the Jesus of the gospels and who in some cases have attempted to refute my own arguments.

The natural anxiety of scholars to avoid having their work labelled 'out of date' or 'out of touch' all too often leads them to concentrate exclusively on the most recent publications, even though these do not always assimilate what is valuable in relevant work of the past. I have drawn heavily on recent books and articles, without however ignoring somewhat less recent material that is still very much to the point in that it either supports the case that I am myself advancing, or conversely stems from apologists (such as C.S. Lewis and Leslie Weatherhead) who continue to be taken seriously in conservative Christian quarters and therefore still need to be answered.

Acknowledgements

The original spur for the present book was an exchange of letters with Mr. R.N. Tyler, who then (in 1996) published a book criticizing the views I have expressed in earlier books on Jesus and on Christian origins. His book impressed upon me the need for a further work which should attempt to make clear the inadequacies common in many Christian apologetic writings which are highly regarded by clergy and lay people alike. I am grateful to Mr. Tyler for the stimulus of his criticisms, and also for writing some brief comments on this present book which are included as an Afterword on p. 253 below.

I also thank Dr. Douglas Allford, Dr. Derek Banthorpe, Mr. Daniel O'Hara, and Dr. David Ramsay Steele of Open Court for helpful comments on the manuscript of this book which guided me during my rewriting of it.

The staff of Dr. Williams's Library in London have been, as so often before, friendly and helpful. They kept me well supplied with material even when I was not well enough to go to their premises. I can look back over an association with them that has lasted the best part of fifty years.

My wife, Elisabeth, has been as supportive as ever. I am grateful, even more than usual, to my former secretary, Mrs. Evelyn Stone, who persevered with the typing of my manuscript under difficult conditions.

Since I wrote the above, Evelyn Stone has died, succumbing to the heart disease which plagued her in the final year of her life. We had worked closely together for twenty-five years, and I dedicate this book to her memory. I thank Mrs. Elke Wagstaff for completing the task which Evelyn was unable to finish.

Apart from these personal debts, I wish to acknowledge how much I have learnt from the published work of Christian New Testament scholars whom I have never met. One reason why I frequently refer to their arguments is to show that many of my own views are not layman's aberrations, but well-founded in NT scholarship.

Abbreviations

i. Terminology

OT and NT designate the Old and the New Testaments.

I use the terms Matthew, Mark, etc. sometimes to designate the author of the relevant gospel and sometimes to designate that gospel itself. Which meaning is intended will be clear from the context. These traditional names remain convenient, although the authors of all the gospels are in fact unknown.

I follow the usual terminology in calling the first three of the four canonical gospels 'the synoptics'. The term 'synoptic' means 'what can be seen at a glance' and owes its origin to the fact that, if the complete texts of all three are put side by side in parallel columns (as was first done by J.J. Griesbach, who coined the term in 1811), one can see what material has been added, omitted, or adapted in one as compared with another.

ii. Quotations from Scripture

Scripture quotations are (except when otherwise indicated) from the Revised Version (RV), published 1881–85, of the Authorized Version or King James Bible of 1611 (AV). I use the RV because it is now in the public domain. Very occasionally I refer also to the following other English versions:

NEB   *The New English Bible,* copyright of Oxford and Cambridge University Presses.

RSV   *The Revised Standard Version,* copyright of the Division of Christian Education, National Council of the Churches of Christ in the United States.

In some cases brief scriptural phrases have been rendered literally or adapted to the syntax of my sentences.

iii. Other Quotations

In each of my chapters, once details of works have been given, further references to them are normally given simply as page references in my text or notes.

Four of my earlier books on Christian origins or on Jesus are designated as follows:

JEC   *The Jesus of the Early Christians* (1971).

DJE   *Did Jesus Exist?* (1986).

HEJ   *The Historical Evidence for Jesus* (1982).

WWJ   *Who Was Jesus?* (1989).

iv. Abbreviations for Books of the New Testament

Acts	The Acts of the Apostles
Coloss.	Paul's epistle to the Colossians
1 and 2 Cor.	Paul's first and second epistles to the Corinthians
Ephes.	Epistle to the Ephesians (ascribed to Paul in the canon)
Gal.	Paul's epistle to the Galatians
Hebrews	Epistle to the Hebrews
James	The general epistle of James
Jn.	The gospel according to John
1, 2 and 3 Jn.	The three epistles ascribed in the canon to John
Jude	The general epistle of Jude
Lk.	The gospel according to Luke
Mk.	The gospel according to Mark

Mt.	The gospel according to Matthew
1 and 2 Peter	The two epistles ascribed in the canon to Peter
Phil.	Paul's epistle to the Philippians
Rev.	The Revelation of John (The New Testament Apocalypse)
Rom.	Paul's epistle to the Romans
1 and 2 Thess.	Paul's first and second epistles to the Thessalonians

1 and 2 Tim.   { known as 'Pastoral epistles' }   The first and second epistles to Timothy (ascribed in the canon to Paul); the epistle to Titus (ascribed in the canon to Paul)

Titus

Actual Historical Order of Writing of New Testament Books

Dates	Books	
Not later than 60	⎱ Pauline letters: 1 Thessalonians, Romans, 1 and 2 Corinthians, Galatians, Philippians, Philemon	
Possibly earlier than 70	⎱ Epistle to the Hebrews	Early epistles
	Early post Paulines ascribed to Paul ⎱ 2 Thessalonians, Colossians, Ephesians	
Perhaps as late as 90	1, 2 and 3 John	
90–95	James 1 Peter Revelation (the New Testament apocalypse)	
After 70, probably as late as 90	⎱ Mark	Gospels and Acts
90–100	Matthew, Luke, John Acts	
110	Pastoral epistles: 1 and 2 Timothy, Titus	Later epistles
	Jude	
120	2 Peter	

Introduction: The Making of a Myth

The New Testament (NT) comprises twenty-seven books—four gospels and the Acts of the Apostles, followed by twenty-one epistles and the Revelation of St. John the Divine. Many people are aware that the four gospels to some extent clash with each other (particularly the fourth with the other three); but there is little awareness that all four were written relatively late (near the end of the first century) and give a very different portrait of Jesus from what we find in those epistles—and that is the majority of them—which were written earlier (see the table on p. xvi above). The earliest of all are the Pauline letters: today only the most conservative apologists dispute that they antedate the gospels. But the fact that these epistles are earlier is unlikely even to occur to the general reader; for he finds them printed in Bibles *after* the gospels, and addressed to Christian communities who worshipped a Jesus already risen from the dead, whereas the bulk of the gospel material purports to give an account of earlier situations. Hence today the epistles are likely to be read from the supposition that their authors were acquainted with what is said of Jesus in the gospels, although in fact these did not exist when the Pauline epistles were composed, and were clearly not available (even if they already existed in some restricted communities) to the epistle writers who followed in the generation after Paul. Many people will say that, even though the writers of the early epistles did not know the gospels, they did know, and did believe, the stories which came to be incorporated in the gospels. But this is what I dispute.

That Jesus, in the opening decades of the first century, taught and worked miracles, conducted his ministry in Galilee and then died in Jerusalem, and at the behest of the Roman governor Pontius Pilate—all this is what the gospels affirm, and presumably what various traditions on which they drew affirm; but none of it is told of him in the extant Christian epistles which are earlier than the gospels, nor in those documents which are more or less contemporaneous with the gospels but clearly independent of them. This is particularly striking when behaviour or teaching ascribed to him in the gospels has obvious relevance to the concerns being pursued by the writers of these epistles.

It is not just that these epistles are silent on such matters, but that they view Jesus in a quite different way, indeed that their Jesus—a supernatural personage only obscurely on Earth as a man at some unspecified period in the past—is not the same person as the itinerant first-century Galilean preacher whose public activity led to some of the traditions on which the gospels (particularly the first three of them) are based. There is good reason to believe that the Jesus of Paul was constructed largely from musing and reflecting on a supernatural 'Wisdom' figure (amply documented in earlier Jewish literature), who sought an abode on Earth but was there rejected, rather than from information concerning a recently deceased historical individual. Altogether, musing and reflection on earlier sacred texts has been—and often still is—a very significant factor in the formation and development of religious ideas. We meet it again in both Jewish and Christian reflection on the 'Son of man' figure in the book of Daniel—musing which, as I show in chapter 3, was of some importance for the Christian view that the final judgement, bringing the world to a close, is nigh.

Whereas the Jesus of the early epistles does not teach or work miracles, and is not even given a historical context for his life on Earth, the Jesus of the first three gospels is active at specific locations in Galilee and at a specified period of time. Some of the sayings ascribed to him, although absent from Mark, are shared by the gospels of Matthew and Luke. As these two gospels were written independently of each other, these common sayings, with their clear allusions to time and location, will have been drawn from an earlier account of the Galilean Jesus written sufficiently close to his lifetime to include authentic reminiscences, even if exactly what is authentic cannot now be separated out.

The gospels themselves, including the earliest, that of Mark, are sustained attempts to fuse the two Jesus figures. As a result we have a Jesus who no longer lives and dies obscurely in some vaguely considered past, as in the early epistles, but a Jesus who lives prominently as a first century teacher and even miracle-worker, and dies around A.D. 30—for our redemption, as in the epistles, but in a situation which is specified in considerable detail and which involves the authorities (Jewish and Roman) of the day. Why this fusion of the two Jesus figures came about, and particularly why Pontius Pilate came to be linked with Jesus's Passion, needs to be explained.

To counter my proposal that the saviour of the early epistles (Pauline and others) who died to redeem us is not the same person as the Galilean preacher of the gospels, who then suffered under Pilate, my critics may retort that epistles are not gospels, and that we cannot expect to find the substance of mini-biographies in letters. But as I have already indicated, some, indeed much, of this substance is of such relevance to the issues advocated and defended by the epistle writers that they would not have ignored it, had they known of it. Moreover, when we come to epistles (in and outside the canon) which are known to have been written late enough for the gospels (or at any rate some of their underlying traditions) to have been current, then we do find clear allusions to relevant biographical material about Jesus in a way that is earlier unknown. For instance, the letter known as 1 Clement, which commentators date at the very end of the century, states that Jesus taught mercy, forgiveness and reciprocity, and warned against causing the elect to stumble. The author was surely writing when the idea that Jesus had delivered teachings was only beginning to permeate all Christian communities; for he invokes Jesus's words as an absolute authority only twice, as against his more than one hundred references to the Old Testament (OT); and he is still unacquainted with the bulk of the material familiar to us from the gospels.

Even if today there is some awareness of discrepancy between the earlier and the later documents, its significance is not appreciated, but belittled, or at most accepted as a baffling anomaly which can nevertheless be safely ignored. It is really time that theologians faced up to the implications of this fundamental cleavage between the earlier and the later material, instead of trying to represent the NT as basically a unity which testifies to a single staggeringly great event, and to an incomparably great individual person at its centre.

My first chapter addresses this whole question, and its second half includes considerable detail in order to show that the position I am arguing is adequately based on substantial evidence. Although this detail will not obscure the overall thread, I have concluded the chapter with a brief summary review of its principal arguments, and indicated there on which pages the reader will find them stated. My second and third chapters show that much more in the gospels has to be put in question than is generally admitted, and how difficult, if not impossible it is to extract from them any reliable information at all. The discussion of their miracle stories in chapter 2 includes an account of the exorcisms, and this leads to a critical review of the role of exorcisms in the history of the church, and of the recent recrudescence of belief in spirit possession. Chapter 3 shows how arbitrarily the OT often has to be interpreted if it is to be made to yield what the authors of the NT require of it, and how even plausible-seeming incidents in Jesus's life according to the gospels are quite intelligible as constructions of the early church. These will have been made in good faith. Then as now, people constructed in their minds situations in accordance with their convictions about what 'must' be (or have been) the case, and so had no hesitation in affirming that the relevant events had actually occurred.

Chapter 4 is a response to those who find in the Roman and Jewish notices of Jesus welcome assurance that Christian faith has a solid historical foundation. I am particularly concerned with the claim that the Jewish historian Flavius Josephus has put the existence of the Jesus of the gospels beyond reasonable doubt. My fifth chapter deals with attempts to make the confused ethical doctrines of the NT into acceptable guides for behaviour. These two final chapters address their topics differently from the way they are covered in *The Jesus Legend*. In this, as in other respects, the two books complement each other.

1

The Nature of the Evidence

i. The Age of the Manuscripts and of Some Papyrus Fragments

It has been repeatedly claimed that the evidence concerning Jesus is greatly superior to the testimony about other figures of antiquity, whom we nevertheless accept as historical personages. What, it is asked, do we really know about either the lives or the doctrines of Pythagoras, Parmenides, Socrates, and many others, whose existence we nevertheless do not regard as in doubt?

That our information is lamentably incomplete is not in dispute, and little reflection is needed to realize that massive losses have been inevitable. Even today, how little of what happens in any twenty-four hours is recorded, how few of such records survive and, even if they do, are likely to come to the notice of anyone sufficiently interested in their substance to re-record it! In antiquity, records were made mainly on perishable material such as papyrus, which tends to become friable when exposed for long periods to damp conditions. As it was more plentiful than animal skins and easier to manufacture, papyrus did not begin to be displaced by parchment until the fourth century A.D., and was not superseded altogether

1

until the mediaeval period (Gamble 1995, pp. 44–47). Hence except in the driest of climates, papyrus records would need to be copied periodically, and this was expensive and laborious. Nevertheless, even some ancient thinkers who left no writings are well attested. Notices of Socrates were made by contemporaries whose writings are either extant or survive as fragments in later authors. They place him as a teacher at a particular time and place, involved also in specific military and political events of which there is independent evidence. As to what he taught we can be less sure. Aristophanes, as comic poet, caricatures his views, and Plato has been accused of putting his own ideas into his mouth. Xenophon was still a young man when he saw him for the last time, and may have later supplemented his recollections so as to suit his own purposes. Jesus, however, is today hailed as our guide, even our saviour, so in his case we need clear and unambiguous evidence as to what he taught. But in fact we find that the earliest notices of him (many of the NT epistles) do not represent him as a teacher at all, nor say when or where he lived, and that the gospels, written later, ascribe a medley of incompatible doctrines to him.

These are important issues, to which I shall return. Here I am concerned to note the importance of evidence about someone which is contemporary with him. Where this is not forthcoming, we sometimes cannot be sure that the person under discussion even existed. But contemporary evidence does not always mean contemporary documents. Quotations from ancient documents by later inquirers are valuable if there is reason for believing that the later writer was able to consult the earlier documents, and that these latter were either contemporary with the events they describe, or later copies of contemporary documents. This is always a matter of inference.

Two topics are involved here which need to be carefully distinguished, although they are often confused:

1. The time gap between the dates of events alleged in a document and the date when the original of this document was written.

2. The interval between this latter date and the date of the oldest extant copies. In the case of the NT, Sir Frederick Kenyon

(1912, p. 5) put this interval at 250 to 300 years, as against 800 years or more for works by classical authors.

Many play what they regard as a trump by confusing these two topics: the time interval relevant to topic 2 is, for Christian documents, relatively short (Papyrus discoveries since Kenyon wrote have even shortened it further: see below p. 5); and if this interval is not distinguished from the interval relevant to topic 1, then apologists think they can claim not only textual accuracy, but also historicity of a Christian text's contents. Confusion of the two topics is evident when Tyler remarks how scornful unbelievers would be if "the Church's documents . . . were separated by 800 years [or more] from the period which they purport to report" (1996, p. 14). He has hitherto, following Kenyon, adduced the 800 years apropos of topic 2, but here they suddenly figure as relevant to topic 1. If we remain with topic 2, where the 800 or more years belong, we may note in reply that the hypothetical situation envisaged—that a church which has been continuously powerful over the centuries might have flourished for 800 years or more without keeping its foundation documents intact by copying—is not a plausible possibility, and not comparable with copies of, for instance, Tacitus, not being made in the Dark Ages, when interest in pagan literature was minimal. I have noted elsewhere that, if there had been a Tacitus club in every European town for 1,000 or more years with as much influence as the local Christian clergy, sections of the *Annals* would not have been lost. And if, instead of copying orthodox literature repeatedly, Christian scribes had copied works regarded as heretical or even downright hostile to Christianity, we should now have a much clearer picture of what underlay the church's struggle against opposing forces.

Many apologists write of more than a thousand copies of NT books and regard their variant readings as trifling.[1] Parker complains that there is still widespread belief that "the text chosen by the editors of the main current Greek New Testament is virtually certain, and that all variations from it, even those which the edition places at the foot of the page as significant variants, may be ignored" (1997, p. 2). He notes that such optimism is not shared by these editors themselves; and he draws attention to the resentment engendered when large collections of variant readings were made known in the early eighteenth century. The very act of publishing them "was considered by some to be impugning the inspiration and authority of Scripture" (p. 94). He and other textual critics have shown that the variations are in fact considerable, particularly in the case of theologically contentious issues. For instance, whether Luke has a doctrine of atonement depends on which manuscripts of his account of Jesus's words at the Last Supper are to be taken as giving the original reading.[2] Even the Lord's Prayer "contains within its short compass every conceivable problem that could afflict a Gospel saying: it exists in widely divergent forms, it includes a word otherwise unattested whose meaning is unknown, it contains an ambiguity, and its text was altered in the course of its transmission" (p. 49. Parker goes on to justify all these statements). And on the subject of divorce, "the recovery of a single original saying of Jesus is impossible", for "what we have is a collection of interpretative rewritings of a tradition" (pp. 92–93). There is naturally much more manuscript variation in the gospel sayings than in the narrative sections, since it was the sayings that were repeatedly reinterpreted (p. 75). Such variants are to be expected in any text which existed only as different manuscripts for many hundreds of years before it could be printed in the form of thousands of identical copies; for every single manuscript is the artifact of an individual scribe, who could introduce errors or what he—or his patron or his particular religious community—took for improvements (see below, p. 217). This does not unduly worry Parker, as he feels able to appeal to the witness of the Holy Spirit as authenticating essential Christian beliefs: "The definitive text is not essential to Christianity, because the presence of the Spirit is not limited to the inspiration of the written word". He complains that belief in a single authoritative text, which is to be reconstructed from the manuscripts, accords the Spirit "a large role in the formation of Scripture", but "almost none at all in the growth of the tradition" (p. 211).

As for the antiquity of the manuscripts, only two from the third century (P^{45} and P^{75}) contain more than a single chapter of the synoptic gospels, and only four older than A.D. 400 give them in anything like completion. We have no extensive remains of the gospels older than the end of the second century (Parker, p. 208).

The oldest extant NT material consists of papyrus fragments, and apologists naturally try, on palaeographic grounds, to date some of these very early, although Bruce Metzger has urged caution here, noting that "sometimes a scribe took an earlier hand as his model, and consequently his work presents an archaic appearance that is not characteristic of his time". More importantly, "since the style of a person's handwriting may remain more or less constant throughout life, it is unrealistic to seek to fix on a date narrower than a fifty-year spread" (Metzger 1981, p. 50). Hence one needs to allow at least half a century leeway in dating manuscripts on palaeographic evidence. Metzger's book includes a plate and a description (pp. 62–63) of the John Rylands papyrus P[52], very widely accepted as the earliest known manuscript of any identifiable portion of the NT, and "generally assigned to about A.D. 100–150". Ehrman, no doubt with Metzger's cautionary remarks in mind, says that this fragment, comprising five verses from John's gospel "could as easily have been transcribed in 160 as 110" (1995, p. 371 n49).

Palaeographic reasoning came into prominence on the front page of *The Times* of 24 December, 1994, which reports claims that certain fragments are even older than P[52]:

> A papyrus believed to be the oldest extant fragment of the New Testament has been found in an Oxford library. It provides the first material evidence that the Gospel according to St. Matthew is an eyewitness account written by contemporaries of Christ.
>
> In a paper to be published next month, Carsten Thiede, a German papyrologist, will claim that three scraps of Matthew belonging to Magdalen College date from the mid-first century A.D. The fragments, which have been kept at the college since 1901, were thought originally to have been written in the late second century.
>
> Not since the discovery of the Dead Sea Scrolls in 1947 has there been such a potentially important breakthrough in biblical scholarship. The new date is important evidence that Matthew was written a generation after the Crucifixion, or even earlier.

All this refers to three fragments of Matthew on the Magdalen papyrus P[64] (or Magdalen Gr.17). In 1953 the papyrologist Colin Roberts found the hand on them closely paralleled in a fragment from Oxyrhynchus in Egypt which had already been dated around A.D. 200. Roberts showed a photograph of P[64] to three eminent colleagues (Bell, Skeat, and Turner), who "independently and without hesitation pronounced in favour of a date in the later second century", and he concluded that "their verdict can be accepted with confidence" (Roberts 1953, pp. 235–37).

Thiede's article claiming to overturn these findings was published in January 1995 in the Bonn *Zeitschrift für Papyrologie und Epigraphik*, although the article is written in English. It does not make anything like the extravagant claims reported in the *Times*, but suggests, "with all due caution, the possibility of redating the fragments . . . to a period somewhat earlier than the late second century previously assigned to them", even though "certainty will remain elusive, of course" (Thiede 1995, p. 17). This somewhat earlier period is then specified (p. 19) as a date in the "late first century some time after the destruction of the Temple in Jerusalem", but there is no suggestion that Matthew is an eyewitness report; and as everyone now accepts that it is a first-century work, the proved existence of a papyrus fragment of it of late first-century date would hardly be cause for alarm. But a mid-first-century dating, as reported in the *Times*, would be quite another matter. Thiede's article turns out to be what Stanton justly calls "something of a damp squib" in comparison with the newspaper report (1995, p. 13).

Articles published in academic journals such as the Bonn *Zeitschrift* are carefully refereed, and so authors do not find it easy to use these journals as a forum for extravagant claims. In statements to the media, or in publications of their own, they do not have to be so cautious; and so we find the *Church Times* of 30 December 1994 reporting Thiede's claim that the use of the abbreviation 'IS' for Jesus in P[64] is an example of a *nomen sacrum*, suggesting that his divinity was recognized by his contemporaries. The reporter adds, touchingly: "There is much scope for dissent". There is indeed. D.D. Schmidt, reviewing Thiede's publications in the 1996 *Journal of Higher Criticism*, has noted (pp. 316–17) that early Christian manuscripts abbreviate the name Jesus– even when it refers to Joshua (Hebrews 4:8) or Justus (Coloss. 4:11); that they likewise abbreviate half a dozen other 'sacred names', "such as Father, Son, Heaven,

David, Israel and Jerusalem"; and that *kurie*, as a form of address, may be abbreviated whether it means 'Lord' or merely 'Sir' or 'Master', as at Jn. 12:21 when it is addressed to Philip, or even when the noun is used by Jesus in parables about masters and slaves.

The Münster textual critic Klaus Wachtel replied to Thiede's 1995 article in a paper published the same year in a later volume of the same academic journal. He there points out that P[64] and P[67] (which is from the same codex) are late enough to exemplify most of the distinguishing characteristics of the Biblical Uncial style—a style of writing which began from towards the end of the second century and reached its full development in the Biblical codices of the fourth and fifth centuries. It is evidenced as well in non-Christian texts. These characteristics include:

1. A marked tendency towards geometrical forms, in that most letters of the alphabet are written so that their extreme points would touch the sides of a square drawn round them.
2. Consistency in varying the strength of different strokes. Vertical lines drawn downwards are very firm, horizontal lines and gently rising ones are mere threads, while downward sloping strokes are of medium strength.
3. Simplicity, lack of ornamentation of the letters.
4. Certain letters of the alphabet are given less than standard length, while others are extended.

Wachtel finds that the letters of P[64/67] likewise stand isolated from each other, with their proportions governed by the overall square form. The differences in the strength of their different strokes are, he says, obviously oriented towards the Biblical Uncial norm, and the under- and over-lengthenings already correspond mostly to this type. Thiede had adduced, as evidence of writing comparable to that of P[64], a fragment from Qumran which has been dated in the early first century A.D. But he had to admit that its letters are "very close to each other, occasionally even connected (ligatures)." Wachtel comments that this distinction from P[64], where the letters are isolated from each other, is very significant, in that this isolation is one of the characters which approximate P[64] to the Biblical Uncial style. Nor, he adds, is there anything in the Qumran fragment corresponding to the different strength or firmness of the horizontal and vertical strokes of P[64]. It is, then, not surprising that each of the three scholars consulted by Colin Roberts, who first edited P[64], independently confirmed his dating of it.

To all this Thiede has made the unconvincing reply that "there are indeed a number of similarities with second-century hands in the Magdalen fragments, but these are somewhat tenuous, more probably reflecting the partial survival into the second century of much older stylistic traits" (1996, p. 105). He also claims that there is ornamentation on certain letters in the Magdalen papyrus, but admits that it is "less frequent" than in manuscripts which are undoubtedly from the first centuries B.C. and A.D. (p. 108). His overall response to Wachtel's criticisms amounts to contemptuous dismissal of them.[3]

In this 1996 book, co-authored with the journalist Matthew d'Ancona (who was responsible for the extravagant claims in the *Times* of December 1994), Thiede has completely abandoned the caution he had expressed in the academic journal, and even disguises the fact that he had been so cautious.[4] He and his co-author now tell us that "Matthew was written not long after the Crucifixion and certainly before the destruction of the Temple in A.D. 70" (1996, p. 150)—a claim based on reverting to the December 1994 position that the fragments which make up P[64] can be assigned to the first half of the century: they are a "treasure" which "prove(s) how ancient the New Testament scriptures truly are"; and they "cast doubt on the 'secondhand fallacies' of Renan and Strauss" (p. 35. The quoted words within this quotation are those of the original finder of P[64], the clergyman C.B. Huleatt, for whom (Thiede tells us, p. 19) "every sentence in the Gospel was divinely authorized").

This 1996 book also repeats Thiede's earlier advocacy of what has come to be called 'the Qumran Mark'. Fragments from cave 7, which were probably hidden there before Roman forces advanced through the area in A.D. 68, are inscribed with a few Greek letters, and some scholars have taken one of these fragments (classified as 7Q5) for part of Mk. 6:52–53. Thiede defends this interpretation, and is convinced that this piece of papyrus "confirms that a literary tradition about the life of Jesus had begun in scroll form during the first generation of disciples and eyewitnesses" (1996, p. 76). It is interesting to study the manifold assumptions he has to make in order to link this fragment (1½ inches long and 1 inch wide) with Mark. The writing on it is spread over five lines, as follows:

Line 1 has only what Thiede himself admits to be "the bottom curvature" of what could be any one of five Greek letters. Other scholars have found it impossible to say which of these (or other) letters is here partially represented. But if the fragment as reconstructed by him is to be from Mark, the letter must be an *epsilon* (e); and so he decides that "it is perfectly reasonable to assume as much" (p. 68).

Line 2 has a clear *tau* (t) followed by a clear *omega* (ō). If this is from the relevant Markan verse, it would have to be followed by a *nu* (n). What follows on this line does not look like a *nu*, and other scholars have seen it as an *iota* (i) followed by the beginning of an *alpha* (a).

Line 3 has the only complete word on the fragment, the Greek for 'and' (*kai*). It is followed by a *tau* (t), whereas the *kai* in the relevant passage in Mark is followed by a *delta* (d). The next letter would have to be an *iota*, if from Mark. It is too damaged to be identified with certainty, but it comes well below the line (unlike the *iota* in the preceding *kai*), and, in the opinion of the papyrologist T.C. Skeat, is more likely to be a *rho* (r), which often comes below the line (see Elliott 1994a, p. 99).

Line 4 has a clear *nu* and a clear *eta* (ē). If from Mark, these letters would have to be preceded by a further *nu* and followed by a *sigma* (s). In fact only half of the preceding letter is preserved, and is only possibly a *nu*; and there is nothing legible that follows.

Line 5 has one clear letter, an *eta* (ē). If from Mark, a preceding *theta* (th) and a following *sigma* (s) would be required.

Stanton's 1995 book sets all this out clearly, with diagrams and an enlarged photograph of the fragment. His reviewer in *Modern Believing* (volume 37, 1996, p. 58) comments that he has effectively rebutted Thiede's "silly ideas".

Another requirement if the fragment is from Mark is that each of the five lines would need to have 20–23 letters. Thiede simply asserts that this is so (p. 60). Even if it is, three words in all the Greek manuscripts of Mark would have to be missing on line 3 of the fragment, which would otherwise be too long.

It is surely not surprising that the Leeds textual critic J.K. Elliott has called an earlier book by Thiede with these same arguments "a publication cashing in on human gullibility" (Elliott 1994a). Thiede himself attributes the widespread rejection of his proposals to the bias of academic scholars afraid of losing their chances of promotion, should they endorse conservative views (1996, pp. 135,143). "There are", he declares, "virtually no limits to the scholarly acrobatics which some academics will perform to dismiss a thesis that does not fit their intellectual paradigm" (p. 65). It is strange that a man who has constructed such a large glasshouse of his own should throw a stone of this size. It is, however, axiomatic among fundamentalists and those akin to them that their conservative findings result from the purest of pure scholarship, whereas those who reach less reassuring conclusions are merely voicing vested interests.

Thiede warns us that his advocacy of the 'Qumran Mark' and his redating of P^{64} are but the tip of an iceberg, in that more redating which will vindicate traditional Christian claims is forthcoming (p. 150). It is, however, quite clear from what I have said that he does not enjoy the confidence of many workers in the field, and from the evidence I have given it is not hard to understand why. Nevertheless, his 1996 book restates, in popular form, what millions of the faithful are only too glad to hear, and so can count on commercial success.

ii. The Importance of Early and Independent Testimony

A. HOW INDEPENDENT OF EACH OTHER ARE THE GOSPELS?

If we now leave textual transmission and ask how we can know whether what is attested in a text is true, one important factor is the agreement of early testimonies which one has reason to believe are independent of each other. When there are such sources, it is more sensible to account for them by accepting what they say than by supposing some widespread conspiracy to deceive posterity. Absolute agreement is not to be expected, and many discrepancies can be attributed to differing motives, characters or opportunities of the witnesses. The historian tries in this way to make sense of all his evidence, constructing hypotheses which he finds in themselves plausible and which are not inconsistent with each other.

We have four canonical gospels which place Jesus in the period of Pilate's prefecture, which lasted from 26 to 36 A.D. So we now ask: to what extent do they testify independently of each other; how near in time to the events they describe were they written; and what confirmation is forthcoming from documents which can be shown to have been written earlier, nearer in time to the dates the gospels ascribe to Jesus's activities?

A widely agreed answer to the first of these three questions is that Matthew and Luke, although independent of each other, both drew on Mark. The case that Matthew did so has been persuasively restated by Head (1997; see below, p. 20). Also widely agreed is that both evangelists supplemented Mark with a further source (not extant and known as 'Q') common to the two of them, which consisted mainly of sayings of Jesus; that additionally both Matthew and Luke have some material unique to each of them, which they either composed themselves or drew from material available to one or the other but not to both of them; and that John wrote without knowledge of the other three gospels (the so-called synoptics), but at some points used sources similar to theirs. John, says Käsemann, certainly avails himself of a version of the traditions underlying the synoptics, "even if it is one that has run wild" (1964, p. 95).

If Matthew and Luke acted independently of each other in changing Mark, their changes should never agree except by coincidence. But if one looks at printings of the Greek NT, one finds places where they do make identical changes. Some of these so-called 'minor agreements' of Matthew and Luke against Mark are no more than stylistic improvements that might well have occurred to correctors independently. Others cannot be explained in this way, and this is one of the considerations that have led a minority of scholars to suppose that, while Matthew used Mark, Luke used both of them (or alternatively that Luke used Mark and Matthew used both of them). It would then follow that Q never existed, that what overlap exists between Matthew and Luke in their non-Markan material is due either to Matthew having directly copied Luke (a view hardly ever advocated, as Luke's opening verse acknowledges "many" predecessors) or to Luke having directly copied Matthew.

This latter possibility is still defended, although the majority of scholars consider it to be unlikely for various reasons, such as the complete incompatibility of Luke's narrative of Jesus's birth and infancy with Matthew's, and Luke's failure to reproduce any of the material special to Matthew in his passion narrative. Nevertheless the 'minor agreements' have to be accounted for, and one theory is that Matthew and Luke agree against our canonical Mark because they were copying from an earlier edition of Mark (not extant), which was later revised so as to make it into the Mark we now have, manuscripts of which date only from the third century. Another possibility is that, as a result of the known propensity to harmonize manuscripts, all or nearly all manuscripts of one gospel have been changed to be more like the text of the other. Parker insists that this tendency to harmonize gospels must be taken very seriously; for copyists knew them all and felt that they "all told the same story and needed to be cross-referenced, to be supplemented from one another" (1997, p. 119). He also points to the folly of assuming that any modern printing of the Greek NT supplies us with the exact wording either of *the* gospel of Mark which was copied, or of *the* gospel of Matthew or Luke which resulted from the copying. What actually happened is likely to have been much less orderly:

> For example, Matthew copies out bits of Mark in reproducing a tradition; then a later copy of Mark is enriched by some of Matthew's alterations; and next a copy of Matthew (already different from the one we began with) is influenced by something from the also changed Mark. Add in Luke, and oral tradition, and any other sources that might have been available at any points in the development that you please, and you have a process a good deal less recoverable than any [copying from fixed and static originals]. (p. 121)

In any case, there is clearly a literary relationship between the synoptics, even if its nature is complex and not immediately deducible simply from study of a modern Greek edition of them. The hypothesis that Mark was written first and that the other two drew from him independently still remains the best way of making sense of the overall evidence. Working, as most of us must, from a modern printed text, we may then attribute identities among all three to straight copying from Mark, even down to the same Greek particles. (Such identities are more common in the narrative material than in the speeches, where one might expect identities if the actual words of Jesus were there preserved.) And we may attribute the differences between Mark on the one hand and Matthew and Luke on the other, in material shared by all three, to deliberate editing by the later evangelists of what they had read in Mark. We shall be looking at some examples in this chapter.

While few even among conservative apologists deny outright that all this is so, one commonly meets suggestions that both the identities and the discrepancies derive from independent reporting of the same events by different witnesses. Thus France points approvingly to the idea that "we should . . . speak of parallel traditions rather than of Matthew 'using Mark' and so on" (1986, pp. 118f); and Blaiklock holds that the 'seeming' dependence of Matthew's gospel on Mark's indicates "no more than that a second hand was active in [its] final organization", or alternatively that "both writers followed an earlier accepted and approved basic account" (1983, pp. 43f). Such commentators often suppose that the divergencies between the gospels, even the crass ones between the synoptics and John, are due to selective reporting, the synoptics telling what Jesus did at one time, while John records his behaviour at another. In the case of the discourses—totally different in John from what they are in the other gospels—this will lead to the *reductio ad absurdum* spelled out by Sanders, namely that "Jesus spent his short ministry teaching in two such completely different ways, conveying such different contents"; and that what we have are "two traditions, each going back to Jesus, one transmitting 50 percent of what he said and another one the other 50 percent, with almost no overlaps." Rather than accept such an absurd position, scholars have, he adds, almost unanimously concluded that the fourth gospel puts Christian meditations on his person and work into Jesus's own mouth, thus making him himself preach Christolo-

gy in a way unknown to the synoptics (1993a, pp. 70–71). It will not
do to explain the discrepancy by supposing, with Thiede (1996, p.
37), that John preferred to record esoteric teaching ("the more
intimate and personal remarks made by Jesus"), while the synoptics
give his "public speeches". Throughout, for instance, the whole of
chapter 10 of John, Jesus is speaking publicly to "the Jews", in such
a way that some of them understandably concluded (verse 20) that
he was mad.

I turn now to the second of the three questions: how far away in
time are the gospels from the 20s and 30s of the first century?

B. DATES AND SOME TENDENCIES OF THE GOSPELS

α *Mark*

Mark is generally accepted as the oldest of the canonical gospels. It
is anonymous; nothing in it indicates who wrote it, and its title
'According to Mark', is not part of the original, but was added by
what Beare (1964, p. 13) called second-century guesswork. Prominent in this connection is a statement by Papias, Bishop of Hierapolis in about A.D. 130, who tells that he had listened to followers of
presbyters who had themselves been followers of Jesus's disciples,
and that from this (very indirect) channel he had learnt that Mark
compiled his gospel from Peter's preaching. This looks like an
attempt to establish that this gospel is essentially the work of an
apostle and therefore reliable.

I will not here repeat my full discussion of Papias's testimony in
The Jesus Legend (pp. 71–79), especially as very many scholars do
not take Papias seriously.[5] Some, however, still believe, from what
he says, that Mark derived his information from Peter, and also that
it was in Rome that he did so. Whether Peter was ever in Rome at all
has for centuries been the subject of controversy (summarized by
Cullmann, 1962, pp. 72ff). Cullmann himself pleads that he was
there, but allows that "prior to the second half of the second
century, no document asserts [this] explicitly" (p. 113). More
recently, Michael Grant has repeated in full (with acknowledge-
ment) eight arguments I gave in *JEC* against Peter's residence in
Rome, but finds that "they do not add up to anything like a

demonstration" that he never went there (1994, pp. 147ff). I will not cover this whole ground again here, but will note merely that Paul never suggests that Peter had been in Rome, nor does Acts, nor does the epistle known as 1 Clement (written from Rome at a post-apostolic date, yet with no knowledge of the gospels[6]), even though in its chapter 5 it mentions Peter and his "many trials" and tribulations. The idea that Peter was in Rome probably came from 1 Peter, the first of the two canonical epistles ascribed to Peter—a late first-century work which, as Kümmel's standard handbook shows, is "undoubtedly pseudonymous" (1975, pp. 423–24). This epistle conveys greetings from the church in "Babylon" (5:13), this being in some texts (particularly the NT book of Revelation) a code name for Rome. In the same verse greetings are also conveyed from someone whom the author affectionately calls "my son Mark", who is thus represented as with him. Now although Mark was the commonest name in the Roman empire, the early church assumed that all occurrences of a given name in the NT referred to the same individual; and so the 'Mark' of 1 Peter was identified with the (supposed) author of the (originally anonymous) gospel. If this were so, it is amazing that 1 Peter "contains no evidence at all of familiarity with the earthly Jesus", with his "life" or his "teaching" (Kümmel, p. 424).

Whether Papias took 'Babylon' in 1 Peter as meaning Rome, and so located both Peter and Mark there, depends on how a passage in Eusebius's *Ecclesiastical History* is interpreted.[7] Eusebius himself, writing in the fourth century and very much as an apologist,[8] certainly believed that both men were there; and in his *Chronicle* he has Peter arrive in Rome in the second year of Claudius's reign (A.D. 42), and function as bishop there for twenty-five years. J.A.T. Robinson takes this dating seriously, but admits that "the natural reaction of scholars has been to dismiss it as groundless". He adds that "there is obviously much legend" in all this (1976, pp. 111–12). Nevertheless, on this basis conservative apologists continue to believe that Mark could have been written at any time after A.D. 42.

The whole idea of Mark's gospel being even indirectly (via Peter) close to the Jewish origins of Christianity is difficult to reconcile with the defective knowledge of Palestinian geography in this gospel,[9] and with what it says about handwashing as a purity rule kept not only by Pharisees but by "all the Jews" (7:3), which was not in fact the case. (It was required only of priests at this period.) In the following verses Jesus is represented as confuting the Pharisees with a mistranslation of their own scriptures (see below, p. 179), and as allowing the argument to slip from handwashing (a matter of scribal tradition) to unclean foods (something essentially scriptural and included in the Jewish law). All this suggests a very imperfect knowledge of Judaism on the part of an author who was not only writing for gentiles—7:3–4 is an attempt to explain Jewish practices to them—but possibly also a gentile himself, to whom the Jewish law no longer presented an acute problem. Moreover, Mark's account of the Galilean ministry is better understood not as based on an eyewitness report by Peter or anyone else, but as compiled from a series of separate short single stories, each one of which had been originally independently transmitted orally in the preaching and teaching of one or more early Christian communities.[10]

Recognition of these factors has made it difficult to date this gospel earlier than the decade A.D. 65–75, or to link it with a Palestinian author. Even so, apologists cannot divest themselves of hankerings after eyewitness origin. Mitton, for instance, says Mark was writing "only thirty years" later than the events he records, and "for a man of sixty, the events of his life thirty years before, especially outstanding ones such as contact with Jesus must have been, stand out as clearly as yesterday's" (1975, p. 70).

An increasing number of scholars now allow that Mark was written later (if only a little later) than A.D. 70. Christians came to regard the events culminating in the destruction of Jerusalem in that year as a divine punishment of the Jews for their rejection of Jesus; and this theme of Israel's condemnation is set out in the parable of the vineyard tenants in 12:12: because the tenants kill the beloved Son, they will themselves be destroyed.

That the events of A.D. 70 were no longer even very recent is suggested by chapter 13 of Mark, where Jesus sets out the future right up to the time of his second coming. He predicts that Christians will be persecuted by the Roman authorities ("before governors and kings shall ye stand for my sake"), and that the penalty of death is involved (verses 9–13). This is followed by the enigmatic words:

> But when ye see the abomination of desolation standing where he ought not (let him that readeth understand), then let them that are in Judaea [immediately] flee unto the mountains . . .

The phrase 'abomination of desolation' is taken from the book of Daniel, where it is used to allude to the heathen altar which the Syrian Seleucid ruler Antiochus Epiphanes erected in the temple at Jerusalem in 168 B.C. Mark, then, is telling his readers that some event—connected surely with the persecution of Christians foretold in this same context—will fulfil Daniel's 'prophecy', and that then "those in Judaea" are to flee. As Mark was not writing for Judaean Christians, but for gentiles (and, as we saw, doing his best to explain Jewish customs to them) why should he wish to tell Judaeans what to do at a particular moment?

The only convincing explanation of Mark's enigmatic instructions that I have seen is that given by Haenchen (1968a, pp. 444–48), namely that what Mark envisaged was an attempt by a Roman emperor to force pagan worship on Christians, as Antiochus Epiphanes had done on his subjects. Mark did not state this baldly, as open criticism of the imperial power might have been dangerous. Instead, he sounds a note of mystery with the words "let him that readeth understand", clearly calling on readers to apply the 'prophecy' to their own situation: and the circumstances in which Christians faced the threat of persecution by the Roman authorities, from around A.D. 90, could well be the relevant situation.

Whether Mark was written shortly after 70, as many suppose, or some twenty years later, the devastation of Palestine during the Jewish War with Rome from A.D. 66 will have occasioned a break with earlier Palestinian circumstances which will have made it difficult for this evangelist, at a distance from the country, to know them accurately. Those who admit or half-admit that this is so normally suppose that the traditions—oral and written—on which he drew do include reliable reminiscences of a Jesus who ministered in Galilee and was crucified in Jerusalem around A.D. 30. I do not wish to repeat here all the arguments against this view which I have recently given in my account of Mark in chapter 5 of *The Jesus*

Legend; but we shall be seeing, first, that extant Christian literature which predates the gospels portrays a very different Jesus, and, second, that the narrative of all four gospels is so overlain with undoubtedly mythical elements that to disentangle authentic history from them is an extremely daunting task.

Finally, the endings of the gospel of Mark require some comment, as they have been the subject of heated debate. Six different ones are attested, and of these the most important are the 'short ending' (16:1–8), comprising material of undisputed authenticity, and the 'long ending', as printed in the AV, which adds a further twelve verses (16:9–20). This is the ending given in most manuscripts, although these are mainly of mediaeval age. The discovery of other manuscripts and the rise of textual criticism in the nineteenth century has shown that, although both endings already existed in the second century, the short one is the oldest form of the gospel, and the long one is "best read as a . . . pastiche of material gathered from the other Gospels and from other sources" (Parker 1997, p. 138). The short ending states that women visitors to Jesus's tomb were told there that "he is risen; he is not here", whereupon they fled in fear and "said nothing to anyone". No encounters with the risen one are recorded. These are added in the long ending, where Jesus also addresses the disciples with:

> a command to preach the gospel throughout the world;
>
> a statement that baptism is necessary for salvation;
>
> a list of signs which will distinguish believers, namely exorcisms in his name, glossolalia (speaking with tongues), ability to heal the sick and to handle serpents and "drink any deadly thing" without coming to harm.

After this, he is said to have ascended and to have sat at God's right hand; and the disciples went forth and preached everywhere.

Most of this material (except the safe drinking of poison) is found elsewhere in the NT. Even the promise of safe handling of snakes may well have been inspired by Lk. 10:19 ("I have given you authority to tread upon serpents and scorpions") and by Acts 28:3–6, where Paul astonishes onlookers by remaining unharmed after accidentally picking up a viper in a pile of sticks.

The short ending clearly represents a far less triumphant conclusion to the gospel.

β Matthew

Thiede appeals to what he calls "the oldest tradition" about the origin of Matthew's gospel, namely that it is an eyewitness record composed by the former tax collector "Levi-Matthew", whom Jesus summoned to discipleship "while he was sitting at his customs post near Capernaum" (1996, p. 43). In fact, however, our oldest authority for this tradition is Origen (third century), who himself gives no better authority for it than that it reached him "by tradition". What is called 'tradition' in such cases is often merely an original guess that has been uncritically repeated.

Origen also supposed that this tax collector "composed his gospel in the Hebrew language" (Quoted by Eusebius, *Ecclesiastical History*, vi, 25, 4). If Matthew is (as nearly all scholars now agree) the reworking of a Greek gospel of a non-disciple, then any suggestion of Hebraic or eyewitness origin is absurd, and this dependence on Mark is normally and rightly also taken as in itself sufficient to exclude a date of composition earlier than A.D. 70. But Thiede would fain believe that all four gospels are independent eyewitness reports, and that there is no more reason to think that Matthew or Luke was dependent on Mark than there is to suppose that *The Daily Telegraph* copies *The Times* in reporting some current event (pp. 46–48). Any discrepancies between the three synoptic gospels mean no more than that, in one or another of them, "some sermons are omitted or given a different setting" (p. 37). One would not, from this, expect to find that most of the teaching, including Matthew's three-chaptered Sermon on the Mount, is absent from Mark, and is substantially different in Luke (not just given a different venue). Eyewitness reporting is also hard to reconcile with the way the Jesus of Matthew speaks of "the church"—the word occurs in no other gospel. At a time when no church existed, he is represented as saying that irreconcilable differences are to be taken to the church for settlement (18:17).

That Matthew reworded what he read in Mark so as to reflect theological and ecclesiastical interests of a later period is admitted

even by relatively conservative commentators. Mitton, for instance
(1975, pp. 42ff) gives the following examples:

1. Mk. 6:5–6. Jesus could perform few miracles in his own
   country, and was surprised at the people's unbelief. By the
   time Matthew wrote, reverence for his divine nature made it
   appear inappropriate that he should be represented as limited either in power or knowledge; so Matthew (13:58) deletes
   the 'could not', and also the reference to Jesus's surprise.

2. Mk. 10:18. "Jesus said . . . Why callest thou me good?" Any
   suggestion that he was not good is eliminated by Matthew,
   who has "Why askest thou me concerning that which is
   good?" (19:17).

3. Mk. 4:38. The disciples rebuke Jesus for apparently not caring
   whether they perish in a storm at sea. Mt. 8:25 deletes any
   suggestion of indifference on Jesus's part.

4. Matthew (and Luke too) tend to modify harsh references in
   Mark to the disciples; for these two later evangelists, these
   men were reverenced and entitled to the utmost respect.
   Mitton gives three examples of such changes, illustrating
   "how the later faith of the church" intruded upon what he
   calls "historical accuracy" (p. 44).

5. "The influence of later times . . . can also be seen in the way
   some of the severe elements in the moral teaching of Jesus
   were softened by Matthew to bring them more within the
   reach of church members" (p. 45), as when the absolute
   prohibition of divorce (Mk. 10:11) is reworded so as to allow
   the husband the right in the case of the wife's adultery (Mt.
   19:9 and 5:32).

Head does not consider the above material, consisting as it does
mainly of Matthew's deletions, sufficient to *prove* that Matthew is
secondary to Mark (although it can surely illustrate this dependence
once the latter has been established on other grounds). He finds
much more persuasive proof to lie in the way certain titles for Jesus
are used in the two gospels. He shows, for instance, that in Matthew
persons inside the faith address Jesus as *kurie* (vocative of the noun
meaning 'Lord'), while those outside it address him as *didaskale*

(vocative of 'teacher'). These two nouns are used so consistently in this way that Matthew can be held to have imposed a system here on his Markan material—particularly as in the non-vocative uses of the noun 'Lord' he follows Mark very closely. Here, then, we are not working with mere deletions from Mark, but with what can be held to be positive amendments. Head obtains similar results from study of the use of other Christological titles ('Messiah', 'Son of God', 'Son of man') in the two gospels. In all these cases, he says, we have "coherent, plausible, pervasive and positive redactional alterations made by Matthew in his representation of the Markan traditions" (1997, pp. 258–59).

Matthew's gospel ends with the risen one's directive to "go . . . and make disciples of all the nations, baptizing them into the name of the Father and of the Son and of the Holy Ghost" (28:19). This formula is not paralleled in other first-century Christian literature, and is a step towards post-NT trinitarian thinking. When the synoptic pre-crucifixion Jesus tells the twelve what they are to do, he specifies preaching and casting out demons (Mk. 3:14–15; 6:7–13), healing the sick and raising the dead (Mt. 10:8; cf. Lk. 9:1–5), but says nothing about baptizing. To have baptism enjoined by the risen one is intelligible as a consequence of the significance ascribed to it in the early church, where it sealed admission to the faith. For Paul, it signified dying and rising with Christ—going into the water symbolized burial, coming out of it meant resurrection, a new beginning. In thus dying with Christ, the believer became one with him and so died to the power of sin (Rom. 6:2–11).

Notwithstanding the acceptance of the gentile mission at 28:19, Matthew's overall orientation is strongly Jewish: not "a jot or tittle" of the Jewish law is to pass away (5:18); the disciples are to missionize only "the lost sheep of the house of Israel" (10:6, cf. 15:24). Wrongdoers within the Matthean community who refuse to be corrected by their church are to be treated as tax-collectors and as (unconverted) gentiles, i.e. expelled (18:15–17). This Jewish orientation involves knowledge of Jewish customs, and also 'Semitisms' (grammar, syntax or vocabulary in the Greek that seem to be influenced by Hebrew or Aramaic). These do not, as has sometimes been claimed, necessarily imply either an early or a Palestinian provenance; for, as Sanders observes, "certain segments of the

Church, up to about the year 135, were in as close contact with Jewish communities as other segments were with Hellenistic communities". He notes too that Christianity moved north (into Syria) and east, as well as into the Hellenized west, and that many second- and third-generation Christians were Semites (1969, pp. 195–96, 231). He also gives some interesting examples of the way Matthew introduced Jewish elements lacking in the equivalent narratives in Mark—a feature also documented by Head (1997, p. 186). In his more recent work, Sanders reiterates his earlier view that "sayings in general do not tend to become either more or less 'Semitic'" as the tradition develops, and that Semitisms "do not help establish authenticity" (1985, pp. 15, 358 n47).

If, then, Matthew's gospel was written for a community which consisted mainly of Jews, they were nevertheless in serious conflict with non-Christian Jews. It is probably because these latter had accused Matthew's community of not keeping the Jewish law that his Jesus is made to say (in a verse unique to this gospel) that he has not come to destroy the law, but to fulfil it (5:17): the law is still valid, but only as interpreted by Matthew's community. The behaviour of non-Christian Jewish groups is roundly, even ferociously condemned, most strikingly in chapter 23, where the scribes and Pharisees whom Jesus there indicts surely stand for Jewish contemporaries of the late first-century author with whom he and his community are in conflict. Such unconverted Jews are unequivocally stamped as outsiders: "The kingdom of God shall be taken away from you and shall be given to a nation bringing forth the fruits thereof" (21:43)—the 'nation' being not an ethnic group, but Matthew's church, which accepted the gentile mission.

As we saw, Matthew's attitude to unconverted gentiles is equally negative; and his Sermon on the Mount—the code of conduct of his church, put into Jesus's mouth—includes anti-gentile statements (5:46–47; 6:7–8, 31–32). Sim, who has recently published a thoroughly frank and lucid account of Matthew, comments (1996, p. 203ff) that his community clearly avoided contact with the gentile world as far as possible, yet suffered some persecution at its hands (see Mt. 10:18; 24:9). Sim understands this as having taken place during and after the Jewish War with Rome, when Jews in Syria and elsewhere in the eastern regions of the empire were persecuted by their gentile neighbours, who would not have distinguished between mainstream Jews and Jews of Matthew's predominantly Jewish Christian community. For Matthew both Jews and gentiles could become acceptable only by becoming Matthaean-type Christians—that is, keepers of the (reinterpreted) Jewish law. Hence this community will have had no sympathy with the law-free Christianity of the Pauline (and other similar) churches which—after the elimination of the Jerusalem church in A.D. 70—formed the majority. Indeed, Matthew's polemic (7:21–23; 24:11–12) against those who, although they acknowledge Jesus as Lord and prophesy and work miracles in his name, are nevertheless "workers of lawlessness" (*anomia*), is surely directed against the law-free Christianity then predominant. (Most English translations obscure this by rendering *anomia* as 'wickedness', thus blurring its antithesis to *nomos*, the law.) Those Christians who "work lawlessness" are to be "cast into the furnace of fire" (13:41–42). The Matthaean church was thus completely isolated—alike from Pharisaic Judaism, from pagan groups and from most Christian communities—"hated" in fact "by all nations" (24:9). Sim argues persuasively that it was this isolation in an alien world that prompted the strong apocalyptic elements in Matthew's gospel which modern readers find so distasteful: Matthaean Christians are to be vindicated, all other groups, Christian or not, will be consigned to hell, where they will burn for eternity. The theme of everlasting torment is much more heavily emphasized in this gospel than in most other early Christian documents.

Albert Schweitzer and others have held fast to a pre-A.D. 70 date for Matthew by pointing to a number of logia there in which Jesus suggests that his second coming will occur within the lifetime of the audiences he was addressing, Schweitzer relied heavily on Mt. 10:23 (unique to Matthew) where the disciples are told that they will not have missionized all the towns of Israel before Jesus comes again; and he argued that this constitutes a delusion to which the evangelist would have been careful not to commit Jesus, had he been writing some fifty or sixty years after his death. However, many commentators now agree that this verse does not record what had been said by the historical Jesus, since it occurs in a passage which conflates Markan and Q material. He is here being made to speak not to the historical disciples, but to Matthew's church, giving instructions about the founding of Christian communities over a considerable period, and declaring that the mission to Israel will not have been completed before the end comes. Davies and Allison accordingly note that Schweitzer's conclusions "have been contradicted on all sides" (1991, p. 196). They stress that, while Matthew records the sending out of the missionaries (10:5–6), he is careful—in contrast to Luke—not to include Mark's statement that they returned. (Mk. 6:30 is included by Luke at 9:10, but not by Matthew.) Thus "the mission to Israel has never concluded. It continues, which is why the command to go to 'all nations' (28:19) includes Israel" (p. 190). Mt. 10:23 reflects the evangelist's concern that the mission to Jews not be abandoned in favour of an exclusively gentile one (p. 192). These two commentators note that, although Matthew's text here goes beyond the historical situation of the twelve to include that of missionaries in his own day, such passing from the past to the present without explicitly noting the fact need not occasion surprise, as "the phenomenon . . . occurs elsewhere in early Christian literature" (pp. 179–180). The wording given to Jesus's speech in Matthew does at least suggest this transition. He begins by addressing the twelve, warning them that individual private houses may not accept their message (10:5 and 13). But he goes on to foretell what is better understood as persecution of Christian missionaries generally, who will incur universal hatred (verses 21–22), presumably in their attempts to missionize the whole world; and from verse 26 his repeated injunction "fear not" is accompanied by consolatory assurances, such as "he that loseth his life for my sake shall find it" (verse 39).

Strong evidence for a post–A.D. 70 date for Matthew's gospel is the way in which the author inserts an allusion to the destruction of Jerusalem in that year into a parable which reached him with no such allusion, namely Jesus's parable of the great supper (22:2–14), which is paralleled, without the insertion, both in Luke (14:15–24) and in the Gospel of Thomas. Here is Matthew's version, with his insertion italicized:

> (2) The kingdom of heaven is likened unto a certain king, which made a marriage feast for his son, (3) and sent forth his servants to call them

that were bidden to the marriage feast: and they would not come. (4) Again he sent forth other servants, saying, Tell them that are bidden, Behold, I have made ready my dinner: my oxen and my fatlings are killed, and all things are ready: come to the marriage feast. (5) But they made light of it, and went their ways, one to his own farm, another to his merchandise: (6) *and the rest laid hold on his servants, and entreated them shamefully, and killed them. (7) But the king was wroth; and he sent his armies, and destroyed those murderers, and burned their city.* (8) Then saith he to his servants, The wedding is ready, but they that were bidden were not worthy. (9) Go ye therefore unto the partings of the highways, and as many as ye shall find, bid to the marriage feast. (10) And those servants went out into the highways, and gathered together all as many as they found, both bad and good: and the wedding was filled with guests . . .

In this allegory the marriage feast represents the joyous and plentiful Messianic age, and the slaves sent out to urge the guests (the Jews, the chosen people) to come are the OT prophets. When the invitation is refused, "other servants" (Christian missionaries) are sent to renew it, but these the invitees even kill; whereupon the king (God) sends armies to burn their city, after which the Christian mission addresses Jews and gentiles indiscriminately, "both bad and good". The italicized passage, where the evangelist makes his point that the city was destroyed, and as a punishment, is absent from the versions given in Luke and in the Gospel of Thomas. Matthew's text runs on naturally if it is deleted; for after the military expedition, the preparations for the supper remain exactly as they had been, and "the rest" with which the italicized passage begins connects only clumsily with the preceding statement that "they went their ways".

Verses 6 and 7 are, then, quite obviously an insertion, with the armies sent by the king figuring the Roman armies which besieged and captured Jerusalem, killing and enslaving many and burning much of the city. J.A.T. Robinson admits that verse 7 has almost universally been taken as a retrospective prophecy of these events of A.D. 70 (1976, p. 20). Attempts to deny this amount to arguing that a post–A.D. 70 writer would have given much more detail about the sack of Jerusalem. This overlooks the fact that an insertion into a pre-existing parable must necessarily be brief; and brief though it is, it effectively brings up to date the history of God's dealings with the

Jews. The statement that the Christian mission brought in "both bad and good" (verse 10) introduces a distinction not made in the Lukan parallel, and reflects Matthew's conviction that both types are present in the Christian churches—a point made in other passages which are unique to Matthew, for example 13:36–43, and 47–50, where the kingdom is said to include both good and bad fish. This seems to be directed against Christian groups which did not follow the Matthaean code of how the law should be kept. 24:11–12 (also unique to Matthew) suggests that such "lawless" Christians were missionizing and demoralizing Matthew's own community. They figure here as "false prophets", leading "many astray", with the consequence that "the love of the many shall wax cold".

The only real alternative to the above interpretation would be to admit that Mt. 22:6–7 is an insertion referring to Jerusalem's destruction, but to regard it as interpolated into Matthew's gospel by a later hand, so that a pre-A.D. 70 date might still be possible for the gospel itself. However, the judgement on the Jews enunciated in these two verses accords very well with Matthew's own theology. He has already made Jesus say at 21:43 (quoted above) and at 8:10–12 that the kingdom is to be taken from them; and in his passion narrative "all" the people demand Jesus's crucifixion and—in a verse unique to this gospel—answer Pilate's plea for clemency by shouting: "His blood be on us and on our children" (27:25). The evangelist surely wrote this looking back on the destruction of Jerusalem, and thinking that the children of the speakers in this verse paid in this way for their parents' guilt over Jesus's death. (That the destruction of the city was God's punishment of the Jews for their rejection of Jesus had become a Christian commonplace.) Paul, writing by A.D. 60, could still believe that all Israel would eventually be saved (Rom. 11:2–12), but by Matthew's time Christian hostility to Judaism had hardened.

γ Luke-Acts

Luke begins his gospel by stating that "many" before him had undertaken to compile a narrative about Jesus. He not only knew but used the one of these documents (Mark) which is extant. That he had "many" predecessors (not said to have been eyewitnesses) does not suggest an early date for his own gospel. He claims in this context that the traditions he records *originated* from "eyewitnesses and ministers of the word", but does not place himself among them or their associates, and says they delivered their reports to "us", meaning the Christian community (cf. L. Alexander 1993, p. 112)—to 'us Christians', not to him personally. (The 'us' is expressly distinguished from the 'me' in this sentence.) Subsequently the "many" wrote of Jesus, and he himself is improving on what they wrote (. . . "it seemed good also to me to write").

Luke's gospel has an even clearer allusion to the events of A.D. 70 than what we found in Matthew—an allusion that is the more significant as it occurs in a verse where the author has deliberately rewritten what he read in Mark in order to introduce it. We saw that Mk. 13:14 reads: "But when ye see the abomination of desolation standing where he ought not (let him that readeth understand), then let them that are in Judaea flee unto the mountains". I said above that this is not an allusion to anything that happened in the Jewish War with Rome, but to a later situation. Luke, however, turns it into such an allusion. He has retained the final clause about flight to the mountains, but has reworded the rest to give: "But when ye see Jerusalem compassed with armies, then know that her desolation is at hand" (Lk. 21:20). It is hard to believe that this conscious and deliberate emendation was not based on knowledge of the sack of the city after Roman armies had surrounded it. There are other small touches (both deletions and additions) in Luke's rewriting of this apocalyptic speech by Jesus in Mk. 13 which point to such knowledge (I have given the details in *HEJ*, pp. 113–17)—as does also the speech at Lk. 19:41–44, unique to Luke, where Jesus foretells that the days shall come upon Jerusalem "when thine enemies shall cast up a bank about thee and compass thee round, and keep thee in on every side, and shall dash thee to the ground". The Greek word here translated as *bank* means 'stake', 'palisade' or 'rampart'. Josephus, who wrote as an eyewitness of the events of 70, tells that the Romans under Titus erected siegeworks round Jerusalem after failing initially to capture the city by direct assault.

This evidence is enough to convince most scholars that Luke wrote after 70. Conservative apologists, however, still object that neither Luke nor Matthew would have been so brief in alluding to the sack of Jerusalem had they been writing after the event, but would have mentioned not merely the burning of the city (specified by Matthew), and the palisade or bank (the 'barricading' recorded in Luke), but more of the siege's distinctive features. Guelich, in a very conservative handbook, observes in this connection that the barricade comprised a four-mile wall, and that dissensions among the Jews helped the besiegers, as did famine within the city.[11] But to expect mention of such details fails to take cognizance of the fact that both evangelists were restricted, in that Matthew was making what could only be a brief insertion in an existing parable, and Luke was rewriting part of a single Markan verse. Luke was in fact anxious not to dwell on the importance of A.D. 70, as he wanted to stress that its events did not presage the end (as some of his Christian predecessors had obviously supposed); for he follows his references to Jerusalem's "desolation" with an assurance that the gentile occupation of it will continue indefinitely, "until the times of the gentiles be fulfilled" (21:24; this verse is, again significantly, unique to Luke). Only then will there follow signs of the end, such as earthquakes, terrifying celestial phenomena, and the appearance of the Son of man on the clouds (verses 25–27). Clearly, then, Luke does not regard the destruction of Jerusalem as itself an apocalyptic event. As Esler has noted, "it is difficult to credit a Christian living before 70 C.E. with such an attitude" (1987, p. 28).

I am not disputing that an observer of the strained relations between Jews and Romans in Palestine might have guessed, before the outbreak of the war in A.D. 66, that Jerusalem and its temple would be destroyed as a result of Roman action against an insurgent people, just as later major upheavals, such as the severance of the American colonies from the motherland and the French Revolution, were repeatedly predicted. Thus the logion "there shall not be left here one stone upon another" (Mk. 13:2 and parallels in Mt. and Lk.) could have been said by a first-century Jesus (or put into his mouth) before the A.D. 60s, and is not nearly as suggestive of a post–A.D. 70 date as is Matthew's insertion into an earlier version of a parable, or as Luke's specific references introduced into his rewriting of Mark's apocalyptic discourse. Nevertheless, it is surely significant that Paul, who believed Jesus's second coming to be near, knew nothing of a forthcoming destruction of the temple—whether or not as an event of eschatological importance—nor of any prophecy by Jesus on this matter.

J.A.T. Robinson supports the argument that an *ex eventu* prophecy about Jerusalem's destruction may be expected to specify considerable detail by pointing to the book of Baruch, from the OT apocrypha, and to 2 Baruch, the Syriac apocalypse of Baruch (1976, pp. 20–21, 316). The former is not a book of prophecy at all, but purports to have been written by Baruch in exile in Babylon in 583 B.C., "in the fifth year *after* the Chaldeans had captured and burnt Jerusalem" (1:1–2). Jerusalem and its destruction are central themes to the whole book (which is certainly not the case with the NT), so it is not surprising that they are mentioned at every turn. The exiles are said to recognize that the terrible fate which has come upon the Holy City is the righteous judgement of God on their sins, that "nowhere under heaven have such deeds been done as were done"—note the past tense—in Jerusalem, because God was venting his wrath upon the Jews (2:2, 19–20). The author was obviously writing much later than he pretends, and it suits Robinson to suppose that he wrote even later than A.D. 70, and that his account of the capture of the city in the sixth century B.C. is tinged with memories of its capture in 70. This is by no means generally accepted,[12] and in any case we are not here faced with what purports to be prophecy. Far from giving unequivocal references to A.D. 70, the book, as Nickelsburg notes, has "no unambiguous historical allusions" which betray when it was written, and is "a prime example of a book whose time of composition is difficult to date" (1981, p. 113).

2 Baruch (the Syriac apocalypse of Baruch) might seem more to the point, as it is at least a book of prophecy, and is unanimously dated post–A.D. 70. It purports to be Baruch's report of what he experienced and the revelations he received immediately before and after the destruction of Jerusalem in the sixth century B.C., but at 32:2–4 two destructions are foretold. There is also some parallel with Josephus's account of the fall of the city in A.D. 70 (*The Jewish War*, 6:293–301), in that in chapter 8 a voice is heard from the

temple bidding the invaders enter the city because God has abandoned it. The author is also updating the book of Daniel. There, the
fourth and last of the empires which were to oppress the Jews had
been Greek, whereas here it is inferably Roman—"far more tyran-
nical and savage than any of those that went before it", and "it will
extend its rule like the forests on the plain" (39:5). However, none of
these allusions are particularly blatant, even though Jerusalem and
its fall are central themes of the whole. Much better examples of
detailed *ex eventu* prophecies are works which outline a whole
sequence of historical events in a given empire, such as the history
of Alexander's Greek (Macedonian) empire, recognizable in the
book of Daniel from histories of the period (such as the first and
second books of the Maccabees in the OT apocrypha). Here the
author was not restricted to brief allusions and could pretend to be
foretelling in detail what had happened up to his own time of
writing.[13]

Luke's gospel, like the others, was originally anonymous. The
earliest extant statements purporting to establish the author's
apostolic credentials are "from the last decades of the second
century, some eighty years, perhaps, after the date of writing"
(Evans 1990, pp. 5–6). As Matthew does, he 'edits' his Markan
material—he adapts it to his own purposes. An instance is his
concern to give additional weight to Peter, reflecting the importance ascribed to him in the early church. In Mark (1:16–20) Simon
(Peter) is called to discipleship at the same time as others and in the
briefest of narratives. Luke expands this by making Peter follow
Jesus as a result of witnessing an otherwise unrecorded demonstration of his miraculous powers (Lk. 5:1–11). That others were
present and similarly affected is relegated in this account to an
afterthought. Clearly, for Luke, "as Paul is to be given a special call
(Acts 9:1ff), so must Peter be" (Evans 1990, p. 287). Luke's gospel
outdoes the other two synoptics most notably in its coverage of the
resurrection in its final chapter, without which their testimony to
this decisive article in the faith "would be jejune indeed" (*Ibid.*, p.
79).

Luke edits Q as well as Mark, and one factor which guided him
was his sympathy with the poor and the deprived. His Jesus blesses

not "the poor in spirit" (Mt. 5:3), but "ye poor" (Lk. 6:20), and adds a curse on "you that are rich"—a clumsy addition in an address to disciples who have left everything in order to follow their master. Other material unique to Luke includes the parable of Lazarus and Dives, likewise prompted by the author's intense dislike of wealth (see below, p. 227). Other parables represented only in Luke are less clear in their teaching and have bewildered commentators. The story of the prodigal son (Lk. 15:11–32) has "often been hailed as 'the gospel within the gospel' ", yet "what it is intended to teach is by no means easy to establish"; and interpretation of the tale of the unrighteous steward (Lk. 16:1–13) has "long proved very difficult" (Evans 1990, pp. 589, 596). Obscurity in these and other parables is commonly attributed to the loss of their original context and intention in the course of their transmission, during which attempts were made to rework them and make them relevant to later states of affairs. If this is so, it constitutes further evidence that the text we now have is at some considerable remove from the early relevant traditions.

If Luke wrote his gospel after A.D. 70, he wrote Acts, which he himself calls a sequel, even later. Conservative scholars still argue that he must have written it before the trial and death of Paul, which he would otherwise have mentioned, and before Nero's persecution of Christians in Rome of A.D. 64, on which he is similarly silent. But Luke knew that Paul had stood before Nero's court in Rome, for at Acts 27:24 he is made to tell his shipmates that they will all survive the voyage, an angel having informed him that he "must stand before Caesar" and so will reach Rome safely. Acts concludes by stating that, once there, he lived in relative freedom, in lodgings at his own expense "for two whole years". Haenchen is surely right to say that whoever wrote this knew that, after these two years a change occurred, and what it was that happened, namely that Paul was condemned and executed (1968b, p. 647). The author of Acts has already earlier gone out of his way to make him tell Christian clergy in Asia not only that imprisonment and affliction await him, but that he will never subsequently return to the areas he has missionized (20:25). This sorrowful pronouncement is repeated at 20:38, and surely implies that the author knew that Paul was never released but died a martyr. But he could hardly say so outright because, for him, Paul was the bearer of the triumphant and invincible word of God, and in Acts is given a career which reflects this triumph. The author therefore goes no further than to "introduce the shadows of martyrdom as they fall, not too darkly, across his hero's path" and to "indicate that Paul was aware of what was to happen" (Barrett 1974, p. 240).

As for Nero's persecution of Christians, the author of 1 Clement seems to have alluded to it—not surprisingly, as he wrote from Rome, and his letter is normally dated in the 90s; but no other Christian writer mentions it before Melito, Bishop of Sardis, about 170. This long silence suggests that it had been local—confined to Rome and not extending to the provinces—and was quickly terminated. Nero committed suicide in 68, the Senate then voided his legislative acts, and Christianity seems to have co-existed with the authorities in the empire until a deterioration began around A.D. 90.

Luke's attitude in Acts to Rome is decidedly friendly. He may well have been concerned to counter the kind of anti-Roman sentiment evidenced in the book of Revelation (which most scholars date in the 90s), and have recognized such provocation as a danger to Christianity. Commentators have repeatedly observed that one purpose of Acts is to represent Christianity as entirely innocuous politically, as contravening no Roman laws. Hence Acts repeatedly makes Roman officials behave with tolerance towards Christians—and this means, in effect, towards Paul, for it is he who carries Christianity westward from Jerusalem into the Roman empire. An author who supplies so many examples of tolerance on the part of the Roman authorities would have been glad indeed to report Paul's acquittal, and the evidence suggests that he fails to do so not because he wrote before the case had been decided, but because he knew that it did not lead to an acquittal. It would have spoiled his pro-Roman stance to have ended his book with a Roman execution of his hero.

Some find it strange that, if Luke knew of the events of A.D. 66–70, he failed to allude to them in Acts. C.F. Evans, however, justly finds this objection "singularly unconvincing". He notes in his commentary on Luke (1990, p. 14) that "it is difficult to imagine how or where such a reference would have been germane to the narrative in Acts, or could have been made with any semblance of verisimilitude". The article on Luke's gospel in the 1992 handbook edited by Green finds (p. 499) Stephen's speech in Acts 7 the necessary suitable context for such an allusion. Before considering this argument, we shall do well to note that this speech is altogether strange, both because of its inordinate length and because so much of it is irrelevant to the situation in which it was supposedly spoken. Its first forty-five verses do not attempt any answer to the question that has just been put to Stephen by the High Priest, namely: is it true that he had alleged that Jesus would destroy the temple and alter the customs that Moses had handed down? Instead of answering this charge, Stephen launches into an edifying account of God's dealings over the centuries with the people of Israel, reviewing the life of Abraham in seven verses, of Joseph in eight, and of Moses in twenty-five. Numerous critics have recognized all this as the sort of sermon that would have been preached at a synagogue festival—adapted, however, by polemical insertions to show that the Jews had repeatedly failed to do God's will. The Sanhedrists are represented as listening both to the long and irrelevant account of their nation's sacred history, and to the anti-Jewish material, even though the latter includes gross misrepresentation of a passage from Amos. He, protesting against the hollow splendour of the sacrifices of his day, had argued: God does not want sacrifice because, in the ideal wilderness period, Israel did not offer up sacrifices: "Did you bring me sacrifices and gifts, you people of Israel, those forty years in the wilderness? No!" (5:25–26, *NEB*). Stephen, following the Greek (Septuagint) version, takes this to mean: Israel in the wilderness did offer sacrifices, but to idols, to "the tents of Moloch", instead of to Yahweh. This is not in the Hebrew original at all, but allows him to imply that Amos was accusing the Israelites of idolatry even during their early wilderness period. Finally, Amos alludes to the threat of Assyrian conquest—"captivity beyond Damascus". Stephen updates this to read "beyond Babylon", thus making it refer to a much later captivity (7:42–43). Surely no one can suppose that he really undertook to convince the Sanhedrin with a Septuagint passage that deviates substantially from the Hebrew text, and which he even distorted. It looks as if what we have here is the voice of Luke's own late first- or early second-century gentile Christianity that has written off the Jews.

As, then, Stephen's speech is a Lukan composition, a post–A.D. 70 Luke could have included a reference to the events of the Jewish War with Rome, had he thought it appropriate to do so. It is, however, important to be clear what, from the premisses of apologists, would be required as evidence of post–A.D. 70 writing. It would have to be something more substantial than the prophecies which Luke had already put into Jesus's mouth in his own gospel—namely that Jerusalem would be surrounded by armies and by a siege wall, that not one stone of the temple would be left upon another, and that the city would be trodden down by gentiles (19:43; 21:6 and 24)—if these statements are to be taken as not sufficiently specific to have been written from knowledge of the actual later events. Thus when Stephen calls the Sanhedrists stubborn, stiff-necked sinners whose fathers killed the prophets just as they themselves killed Jesus (7:51–53), it would not betray a post–A.D. 70 hand if Luke had made him add something like: 'but within a generation or so you will all pay for your wickedness'; for this would be no more specific than what has been accepted in the gospel as genuine prophecy. What the argument requires is that a post–A.D. 70 Luke may reasonably be expected to have given quite detailed references to future events in a speech which in fact—quite unlike the speeches of Jesus to which I have referred in Luke's gospel—is nowhere represented as prophetic at all. The whole is concerned only with Israel's past and present. In so far as it is relevant at all to Stephen's appearance before the Sanhedrin, and to his martyrdom which immediately follows, it brings out that what will lead to his own death will be the same perversity that has already—in Luke's view—characterized Jewish behaviour for a very long time.

Stephen's speech is but one of those in Acts where Greek distortions of the Jewish scriptures are used in the course of an attempt to win over Aramaic-speaking Jews (see below, p. 143 and note). This alone shows that such appeals are not authentic records of earliest Christian Palestinian preaching, but concoctions of a Hellenistic community which had inadequate information about the early Jerusalem church. They repeat again and again in various wording the early Christian kerygma or credo, and support it with the scriptural proofs which were adduced by Hellenistic Christianity.

Speeches comprise nearly one third of the whole of Acts, and Wilckens (1974) has shown that the missionary addresses of Peter and Paul are primarily summaries of Luke's own theology of the late first century. Kümmel's handbook, appraising Wilckens's work, finds it "incontestable" that these speeches are "the decisive literary means by which the author of Acts stamps his own theological meaning on the narrative tradition that he has employed" (1975, p. 169).

Prominent in this narrative tradition are miracle stories which show how the growth of the early church was furthered by direct supernatural guidance. A particularly crass example is the story of Philip the Evangelist converting a high Ethiopian official (8:26–40). First, an angel instructs Philip to take a certain route, without indicating for what purpose. He obeys, comes across the Ethiopian, and is then told by "the Spirit" to join him. It is hardly mere coincidence that at that very moment the man is reading, of all scriptural passages, "He was led as a sheep to the slaughter" (from Isaiah 53), so that Philip now has opportunity to "preach Jesus unto him" from this text. It then happens that water is available with which he can baptize the man; whereupon he is snatched away by the Spirit to another place, leaving the Ethiopian to go, undisconcerted, happily on his way. This is surely no more than an edifying little tale of the progress of the Christian mission which the author was glad to take up into his book.

Acts indicates the advance of Christianity not only with such individual stories, but also by means of summaries which generalize the actual incidents recorded. Thus we learn at 2:42–45 that the newly-won converts

> continued steadfastly in the apostles' teaching and fellowship, in the breaking of bread and the prayers. And fear came upon every soul: and many wonders and signs were done by the apostles. And all that believed were together, and had all things in common; and they sold their possessions and goods, and parted them to all, according as any man had need.

Similar summaries occur at 4:32–35 ("And the multitude of them that believed were of one heart and soul . . .") and at 5:12–16 (". . . And there also came together the multitude from the cities round about Jerusalem, bringing sick folk, . . . and they were healed every one"). Commentators have observed that in fact there were no 'cities' round about Jerusalem (Haenchen 1968b, p. 199) and that it is altogether clear, both from Luke's gospel and from Acts, that he "obviously had no accurate conception of Palestinian geography" (Kümmel 1975, p. 141). In this third summary, the sick are confident that Peter will not even need to touch them, that their cure will be effected if his shadow falls upon them—just as, later, contact with Paul's handkerchief suffices to heal sufferers (19:12). Protestant theologians tend to be embarrassed by this portrayal of the apostles as super-magicians, and so there is minimal resistance to Kümmel's conclusion that all these summaries, just as much as the speeches, express theological ideas of the author: they attest his "representation of the primitive church as the ideal community which, in complete harmony and with common possessions, leads its life of prayer- and table-fellowship, respected by everyone and guarded by its miraculous deeds" (p. 167). This was not conscious idealization, but was how the author and Christians generally of the late first century will have viewed the original period.

This picture is poles apart from that which emerges from the epistles of Paul and of others who were actually involved in the acrimonious factional strife which truly characterized those early days. The discrepancy is one reason for rejecting the claim of Irenaeus and later Fathers that Acts was written by someone who had accompanied Paul on the missionary journeys it records, and who can even be identified as the 'Luke' mentioned in epistles. ("Luke the beloved physician" is named at Coloss. 4:14; and at 2 Tim.4:11, Paul, represented in this pseudonymous letter as awaiting execution in Rome, calls 'Luke' his sole remaining companion.) But the author of Acts knows nothing of the central tenets of Paul's theology (of, for instance, his critical view of the Jewish law). He makes the—in reality—fiercely independent Paul into Peter's subordinate. He even makes Peter, not Paul, initiate the mission to gentiles; and he turns the Pharisees into sympathizers of the

Christians on the ground that they shared belief in resurrection. I have argued this whole matter in detail elsewhere (particularly in chapter 7 of *HEJ*) and here will merely refer readers to the evidence summarized by Kümmel, from which he concludes that the author of Acts was unacquainted with "the most pregnant features of the historical Paul" and was "so misinformed about his activity" that he can scarcely have been his travelling companion (p. 181).

Finally with reference to Acts, it is of note that its text is unique in the NT in that it exists in two substantially different ancient forms, 'Western' and 'Neutral' manuscripts. The Western manuscripts have a text some ten percent longer than that in what are now accepted as the superior ones. The 'Western' witnesses are characterized by a number of obviously secondary features due to conscious editing of an earlier document. The following are among the many examples noted by Haenchen in his commentary:

1. Liturgical expansions. To "Stephen wrought signs and wonders" (6:8) are added the words "through the name of the Lord Jesus Christ".

2. Additions of concrete details which give stories a more authentically life-like appearance. Thus Peter and the angel did not merely walk through the gate leading into the town, but also "descended the seven steps" to reach the street (12:10). Again, the people addressed by the silversmith, presumably indoors, are said to "run out onto the street" before shouting out in rage and filling the city with confusion (19:28).

3. Attempts to remove unevenness. 15:34 (a verse represented only in Western manuscripts) tells that Silas remained in Antioch. This tries to explain why his presence there is presupposed in verse 40, in spite of his having (according to verse 33) gone elsewhere.

Some of the scholars who wish to believe that all or nearly all manuscripts of the NT give us what was originally written have accounted for the embarrassing discrepancies between the two textual types of Acts by supposing that the author later revised it and that both editions have survived. But this hardly does justice to the frequent contradictions between the two types. Haenchen mentions, as a signal example, the conversion of the cultic stipulations of the Jerusalem 'apostolic council' into moral ones in some Western witnesses of 15:20 and 29 (1968b, p. 390n). R.P.C. Hanson (1985, p. 36) finds that, in this variant, the ritual prescriptions have been "entirely misunderstood", taken out of their "original intensely Jewish context", and fashioned into a list of moral prohibitions, with the addition of the 'Golden Rule' (Do as you would be done by) as a general guide for conduct. Purposeful editing rather than misunderstanding is likely to underlie these changes, for they effectively remove the contradiction with Paul's account of the same council, according to which no ritual stipulations were imposed (Gal. 2:6).

δ John

The fourth gospel may have been known by the end of the first century, but was not accepted as reliable until considerably later. Christians of around A.D. 100–150 of whom writings are extant (namely the author of 1 Clement, Ignatius of Antioch, Polycarp of Smyrna and Justin Martyr) made no discernible use of it; and Papias, around A.D. 130, knew of the apostle John as a link in Christian tradition about Jesus, but not as the author of a gospel (See Haenchen 1980, pp. 5–15, for a review of the evidence). Then, towards the end of the second century, the picture quite suddenly changes, and from the beginning of the third century almost everyone agrees that the fourth gospel is acceptable and was written in old age by the apostle John, son of Zebedee, one of the twelve.

If this ascription is true, it is surprising that the twelve play hardly any part as a group in this gospel—they appear only at 6:67–70—whereas disciples such as Nicodemus, Nathaniel, and Lazarus (all unknown to the synoptics) appear at decisive points. Furthermore, why was John not named earlier than ca. A.D. 180 as the author? Part of the answer is that, in the second century, Valentinian gnostics used and valued this gospel as support for their own aberrant views, with the result that some Christians even rejected it altogether as a heretical work (Details in Lindars 1972, pp. 28–29). Moody Smith, summarizing, says:

> If the Gospel had been known or acknowledged in the second-century church as the work of John, or of any apostle, its relative disuse among the orthodox in the second century and the outright opposition to it in some circles would be difficult to explain. Probably the almost simultaneous ascription of the Gospel to John and the wide acceptance and citation of it in the church were not unrelated. (1986, pp. 73–74)

Quite so. 'Apostles' were regarded as guarantors of the true and pure tradition, with the result that, from the early second century, there arose what has been called a "vast array" of literature ascribed to them, some of which survives, often only as fragments, in collections of NT Apocrypha (such as that by Hennecke, 1963 and 1965). Any custom, rite or tradition not documented in the Bible and thought to be older than living memory was readily regarded as apostolic. Thus in the late second-century dispute about the appropriate day on which to celebrate Easter, both sides in this 'Quartodeciman' controversy claimed to be following the tradition handed down to them from the apostles; and by the fourth century the church regarded in this way practically everything of importance in its origin, worship, and teaching, so that there was an apostolic creed, an apostolic church hierarchy, and so on. Unfortunately, says Evans, this image of the apostle by which the church came to think of itself is "for us almost if not entirely pure fantasy, and the literature which promoted it is the literature of the imagination" (1971, p. 26).

Obviously enough, the readers of the fourth gospel were not eyewitnesses of Jesus's ministry, for the author frequently finds it necessary to explain Jewish items to them (1:41; 4:9, and many others). Hence the statement that "the Word became flesh and dwelt among us and we beheld his glory" (1:14) cannot mean that the writer himself was an eyewitness: the 'we' refers to all Christians who have rightly perceived the word of God in Jesus and have thereby beheld his glory. The 'we' at 21:24—the whole of this chapter 21 is almost universally regarded as a later appendix to the gospel by another hand—states that "we know" that the witness of the disciple who wrote "these things" is true. This represents the endorsement of the community in which this gospel originated, and was added probably from fear that it would not easily win wide acceptance beyond this community, as indeed proved to be the case, for as we saw it was initially elsewhere appreciated primarily in heretical circles.

There are various indications that the Johannine community formed a somewhat isolated group. Apart from the gross discrepancies between the mainstream tradition of the synoptics and the account of Jesus's ministry given in the fourth gospel, the Johannine version of Jesus's love command is instructive in this regard. In Matthew and Luke the disciples are told to love their neighbours, even their enemies; in John, however, they are to love one another (13:34–35), i.e. those who share the same beliefs concerning Jesus. This restriction characterizes the dualism pervading this gospel; those who accept its message are saved, but all others are evil. Jesus here prays not for his disciples alone, but "for them also that believe on me through their word, that they may all be one" (17:20–21). Thus love between members of the community serves to unify it.

I have already mentioned that there are major differences between John and the synoptics (above, p. 13). In John, Jesus's ministry (his adult life prior to the Passion) is sited principally in Jerusalem, whereas in the synoptics there is no visit to Jerusalem until the final week of his life. A substantial number of incidents in John's account of this ministry are without any synoptic parallel. They include—in addition to the very considerable discourses—the wedding feast at Cana, where the miracle Jesus works is designated the first of the "signs" which manifested his glory and confirmed his disciples' belief in him (2:11); the meeting with Nicodemus (chapter 3); the encounter with the Samaritan woman, told at length in chapter 4; the healing of the sick man at the pool of Bethesda (5:2–16); the cure of the Jerusalem man born blind (9:1–12); and the raising of Lazarus at Bethany (chapter 11). The story of the woman taken in adultery is also unique to John, but manuscript evidence shows it to be but a late addition. Overlap with the synoptics occurs most strikingly apropos of the cleansing of the temple (2:13–21), the healing of the nobleman's son (4:46–54), the feeding of the 5,000, together with the story that follows of Jesus's walking on the water (6:1–21), and the anointing (12:1–8). However, "in every case the time or location is changed and the whole scene is differently imagined" (Lindars, 1972, p. 27). After the Prologue, the stories of the Baptist's preaching and the call of the first disciples (all in the opening chapter), the first half of the fourth gospel consists mainly of a series of "signs"—miracles, mostly different from those of the synoptics, and including no exorcisms—punctuated by Jesus's explanations, in discourses quite different from his synoptic speeches, of their true significance. Since it was not feasible to interrupt the passion narrative in this way, the farewell discourses (again quite un-synoptic) are placed as a preface to it (chapters 14–17). None of the synoptic parables are included in any of the discourses. The passion narrative itself deviates significantly from the synoptic versions.

From all this, it looks as though the author of John used sources which differed extensively from the synoptics, even when they recorded what purported to be the same incidents. Moody Smith's conclusion is that "probably John's Gospel is the distillation of the theological perspective of a Christian community which had access to a body of tradition about Jesus [that] had been much more freely shaped to conform it to the community's beliefs than in the case of the synoptic Gospels" (1986, p. 14). Lk. 1:1 may serve to remind us that there were "many" gospels, not now extant, on which later evangelists could draw. The ecclesiastical tradition that John wrote with full knowledge of the synoptics is clearly a defensive strategy to make it seem plausible that his purpose was to complement them.

An important doctrinal difference pertains to eschatology, the doctrine of 'the last things'. In the synoptics Jesus refers repeatedly to the kingdom of God, and to its imminent appearance. In John the kingdom is mentioned only at 3:3 and 5, and is not represented as an imminent and drastic re-ordering of the world. Instead, the stress is on a new quality of life, gained here and now by being 'born from above', regenerated through faith in Jesus. "I give my own sheep eternal life" (10:27–28)—a life which can be enjoyed at once through coming to belief in him, and of a quality quite different from that of the everyday life we all know. "He that heareth my word and believeth him that sent me hath eternal life . . . and hath passed out of death into life" (5:24). At 17:3 Jesus expressly equates knowledge of himself and of God with eternal life. He speaks not, as in the synoptics, of coming on the clouds of heaven to effect a final judgement, but of manifesting himself to the church of his disciples after his resurrection (14:21–24).

It is, however, difficult to make unqualified statements about the doctrines of the fourth gospel, as it is full of unevennesses and inconsistencies. These are so striking and so puzzling that very many commentators attribute them to multiple reworking of earlier material by several later hands. In his Anchor Bible Commentary, Fr. R.E. Brown posited five compositional stages, and dated the first edition of the gospel around A.D. 75–80 and its final redaction at ca. A.D. 100. Haenchen favoured a less complicated scheme of three stages: (1) a 'Vorlage' (source document), used and supplemented by (2) the 'evangelist' himself, whose version was finally edited by (3) a "conservative redactor" (1980, pp. 36–37, 44). The author of the 'Vorlage' kept to the (by then) traditional view of Jesus as a worker of miracles which authenticated him as Messiah; the 'evangelist', often through the medium of the theologically sophisticated discourses, reinterpreted the miracles as pointers to the revelation, through Jesus, of the invisible God. Thus the feeding of the 5,000—the only miracle to be narrated in all four gospels—serves in one such discourse to indicate that the true bread is Jesus himself (6:35), although the people who have been fed have failed to reach this understanding (6:26). As for the final redactor, his changes include distancing himself from the 'here and now' eschatology of the evangelist, and reintroducing the older view (for instance at 5:28–29) that the dead will rise from their graves for judgement at the end. The whole of chapter 21—following the solemn conclusion of chapter 20—is very widely regarded as an appendix, possibly from this later hand. It is incidentally the only chapter in which there is any mention of the two sons of Zebedee, and this does not suggest authorship of the whole gospel by one of them—particularly when we find that the very incidents in which Zebedee's son John appears in the synoptics are missing from the fourth gospel.

In the Johannine discourses Jesus debates with Pharisees and "the Jews" generally not, as in the synoptics, over interpretation of the Jewish law, but about his own supernatural status. He styles himself the Father's ambassador and the phrase 'the Father who sent me' recurs repeatedly. He thus existed before being sent to Earth: "Before Abraham was, I am" (8:58). The Father is greater than he (14:28), yet "my Father and I are one" (10:30; see 17:11 and 21), and "anyone who has seen me has seen the Father" (14:9). Believers are in a highly privileged position:

> He that believeth on me, the works that I do shall he do also; . . . And whatsoever ye shall ask in my name, that will I do, that the Father may be glorified in the Son. (14:12–13)

The 'high' Christology of this gospel, making Jesus a supernatural personage who existed before he came to Earth, is comparable to what Paul had believed of him as early as the 50s. But to have Jesus himself stating it in elaborate discourses, supposedly spoken in the 20s, goes far beyond anything in the Pauline or other early epistles, or even in the synoptic gospels. Jesus, as Paul conceived him, "emptied himself" of all that was divine about him in order to come to Earth as a man, and certainly did not go about proclaiming his divinity (see below, pp. 50f).

Jesus's Jewish audiences in John naturally find his claims incompatible with Jewish monotheism (5:18; 10:33), and there is mention of expulsion of Christians from the synagogue. This is prophesied at 16:2, but other references betray that it had already occurred when this gospel was written (9:22; 12:42). Another indication of a relatively late date of composition is that there is no mention in this gospel of Sadducees (the high priestly party), nor of Herodians nor "the scribes", all of whom figure in the synoptics. They are groups which are likely to have disappeared from the scene after the destruction of Jerusalem and its temple in A.D. 70. Moody Smith notes (1995, p. 50) that "scribes are seldom if ever mentioned in Jewish sources after the New Testament period". John's characteristic designation of those who oppose Jesus is either "the Jews" or "the Pharisees"; and after A.D. 70 the main Jewish opponents of Christianity will have been Pharisees.

How different the fourth gospel is from the synoptics is apparent from its farewell discourses. They form the Johannine equivalent of the synoptic apocalyptic speeches (Mark 13 and parallels), in that in both cases Jesus reveals to disciples what is to come. In John, it is not cosmic catastrophe and final judgement that are coming, but a "paraclete", a counsellor, comforter or advocate, who will replace Jesus in the form of the Holy Spirit. He assures his disciples that he will not, in dying, leave them to be "orphans"; at his request, the Father will give them "another Comforter" (*paraklēton*), who will be with them for ever as "the Spirit of truth" (14:16–18). All believers in him will have this Spirit after he has been "glorified" (7:39), i.e. crucified and raised from the dead. He himself actually imparts it to the disciples by breathing on them when he appears to them after his resurrection (20:22). In the farewell discourses before his death he had told them that this Spirit "will teach you all things" and also "bring to your remembrance all that I said unto you" (14:26). There are "many things" which at this stage he cannot say because they "could not bear them"; but "when the Spirit of truth is come, he shall guide you into all the truth . . . and declare unto you all the things that are to come" (16:12–13). His guidance will consist of new words of Jesus, presumably for new times and new problems. In this sense, the Spirit "will bear witness of me" (15:26). None of this is represented in the other gospels. Jesus's imparting of the Spirit by breathing on the disciples on Easter morning is a sophisticated—commentators say a 'profound'—exploitation of the story of the creation of man, made into "a living soul" when "the Lord God breathed into his nostrils the breath of life" (Genesis 2:7). The evangelist's idea is that, in a similar way, Jesus's disciples had their whole being transformed; and this has become one basis for claims of many modern 'charismatic' believers to be speaking infallible words of the Spirit-paraclete.

The contradiction between the fourth gospel and Acts here is striking. In Acts the Spirit comes to the disciples (by now 120 in number) like a mighty wind from heaven, and only at Pentecost, fifty days after Easter, whereas the fourth gospel combines Easter and Whitsun into a single incident. That the OT is used in a sophisticated way for this purpose is not the mark of early tradition.

Acts is likewise not an early work, and the relevant narrative in both shows that, although there was no uniform tradition concerning this matter, on which they could draw, the conviction had nevertheless arisen that there was a clear division between the time of Jesus's earthly life and the time when the Spirit was available to his disciples. That the divide is portrayed in two such different ways does not suggest that there was a real, underlying historical occurrence.

In the next section of this chapter, we shall see that the earliest Christianity of which we have evidence is that represented in certain epistles, written in some cases before and in others independently of the gospels and unacquainted with any Palestinian ministry of Jesus in the A.D. 20s. These earliest Christians worshipped a vaguely conceived and distant Jesus who had been crucified in unspecified circumstances, had risen from the dead, and whose 'Spirit' subsequently spoke to them and instructed them. By the time the fourth gospel was written it had come to be supposed that Jesus had himself, during his incarnate life, promised this instruction and had himself, in his risen state, imparted his Spirit—initially to disciples who had been with him before his death. Similarly, there was an earliest Christian belief that Jesus had existed with God as a supernatural personage before coming to Earth in human form. In the fourth gospel this doctrine has, as we saw, been developed so as to make Jesus himself, while on Earth, expatiate on his relationship with the Father, and even commune with him about their time together prior to the incarnation (17:5). In sum, whereas in the earliest (pre-gospel) documents, certain beliefs about Jesus are stated, in the fourth gospel Jesus is represented as enunciating or enacting them himself—and not only in his risen state. These are relatively late developments.

Nevertheless, apologists continue to repeat the well-known argument which C.S. Lewis put in several of his publications (for instance 1940, pp. 11–12), namely: either we must accept Jesus as what "the records" represent him as claiming to be—Lewis obviously had the fourth gospel in mind and assumed the others to be in line with it—or we must take him for "a raving lunatic of an unusually abominable type" who made such claims unjustifiably. It is a common apologetic strategem to represent in this way a quite unreal alternative as the only defensible one to the view being advocated. In the present case, this involves scorning the option that 'the records' might include legends: the gospels, Lewis elsewhere tells us, "are not artistic enough" for that, for their stories are characterized by little irrelevant but realistic details alien, so he says, to ancient purposeful imaginative writing which betray the hand of an eyewitness of a real scene. What he gives as an example of this could not have been worse chosen, namely Jesus bending down and writing with his finger on the ground when the Pharisees bring him a woman taken in adultery and ask him whether she should be stoned in accordance with "the law of Moses" (Jn. 8:3ff). Of this "scribbling in the dust", says Lewis,

> Nothing comes . . . No one has ever based any doctrine on it. And the art of *inventing* little irrelevant details to make an imaginary scene more convincing is a purely modern art. Surely the only explanation of this passage is that the thing really happened? The author put it in simply because he had *seen* it. (1979, p. 82)

As we saw, the whole incident is mentioned only in the fourth gospel, and is absent from the best manuscripts even of that. It was obviously added by a late editor who thought it too good to miss. That the detail of the scribbling has no function in the story is not true: it shows that, by in this way initially ignoring the Pharisees' question, Jesus is well aware that, as the text states, they intend it as a trap and hope to lure him into contradicting the law. Even in the case of more plausible examples of details which do no more than give life to a gospel story, clerical exegesis is well aware that they may have been contrived for this very purpose (as when the miracle story of Mk. 4:37ff represents Jesus not merely as asleep in the boat, but as "asleep in the stern on the cushion"). Lewis would have condemned such exegetes as "extreme modernists, infidel in all but name" (*Ibid.*, p. 44). It is still not uncommon to hear that it is merely a series of ephemeral fashions that has put in question much of what the NT alleges, and hence that 'modernist' critical views of the Bible are based on this deplorable tendency to be 'up to date', and not a trustee of tradition. Those who take this view can of course appeal to the NT itself, where the faithful minister is told to "guard that which is committed unto thee", to turn away from "knowledge which is falsely so called", and to contend earnestly for "the faith which was once for all delivered unto the saints" (1 Tim. 6:20; Jude 3).

As for the addition of details for verisimilitude being "a purely modern art", Lewis could surely not have been unaware of the way in which ancient apocryphal gospels add more and more secondary details to the canonical accounts. One obvious example is the second-century infancy narrative known as the Protevangelium of James, where the journey of the holy family to Bethlehem for the birth of the child is elaborated. Joseph "saddled his she-ass" and sat Mary on it. "And they drew near to the third milestone. And Joseph turned round and saw her sad, and said within himself: 'Perhaps that [i.e. the child] which is within her is paining her' . . ." etc. etc. (Hennecke 1963, p. 383). Nativity plays, mediaeval and modern, have drawn heavily on such apocryphal accounts precisely because they are so rich in their details.

J.A.T. Robinson's recent attempts to assign an early date and a basic reliability to the fourth gospel have not met with acclaim. I see no reason to dissent from the following comment by Robinson's clerical reviewer, the late Professor Anthony Hanson:

> Does Robinson believe that John's picture of Jesus is true to history? He would probably answer: 'Not entirely, but at least as much as that of the other gospels is.' Here I simply cannot agree: a figure who claims 'before Abraham was I am' seems to me to be very far indeed from historical reality. . . . When I compare the Jesus of the Fourth gospel with the Jesus of the Synoptic Gospels, after making every allowance for the extent to which the Synoptic writers have 'divinized' and theologized their subject, I must certainly conclude that John's Jesus has undergone a more thorough and more conscious modification than has the Jesus of the Synoptics. . . . The supposition that an eye-witness composed the gospel is simply inadmissible. I would still put the completion of the Fourth Gospel in the last decade of the first century A.D. (*Times Literary Supplement*, 8 October 1976, reviewing Robinson 1976)

It would be difficult for any unbiased scholar who had assessed the evidence to dissent from this. Defence of the fourth gospel is today largely doublethink, as when C.J. den Heyer declares that although "we know" it to be "considerably less reliable" than the synoptics, it may yet "provide more information about the real Jesus than a modern historian who has constructed a historically reliable picture" (1996, p. 164).

It is of course those who cling to the traditional doctrine of the incarnation—that Jesus was both truly God and truly man, and not merely an obscure human being who did nobody is quite sure what—who find the claims made in the fourth gospel particularly impressive. Meynell, who holds that even "the most stringent historical criticism" of the NT has not impaired this doctrine (1994, p. 80), tries to silence those who doubt it by imputing to them an unacceptable position as the only possible alternative to faith: the author, or at any rate the "main authority" behind John's gospel, was "either a credible witness to the matters that he seems to report, or the most influential liar in history" (p. 95). This authentication comes the more readily to Meynell, since he finds the Johannine discourses not so very different from Jesus's sayings in the synoptic gospels; for "material closely related to the synoptic tradition" is so closely embedded in the discourses as to be "apparently inseparable" from their argument (p. 74). This really means no more than that the author took brief phrases from synoptic-type sources and spun such material out into elaborate speeches which are his own compositions (see Lindars's 1972 commentary for examples). This does not make him a 'liar', but shows that he believed—as did Paul and many early Christian preachers—that he "had the mind of Christ" (1 Cor. 2:16), and that what he wrote was a legitimate extension of Jesus's teaching (Lindars 1972, p. 53). To suppose that, either stories in a sacred text are true or else they must have been maliciously invented by liars, is to betray total lack of understanding of the processes by which myths are formed.

We may note that Meynell speaks of John's use not of the synoptic gospels, but of "the synoptic tradition"—the term commonly used, and which I shall also use, to designate not these three gospels themselves, but earlier material from which they drew. All four gospels are of course to some extent based on earlier traditions not extant in documentary form—traditions about Jesus's teaching and miracle-working, and about how and when his death occurred. Even if the gospels are unreliable, this earlier material, or some of it, might be credible; and so we have next to ask: to what extent do extant Christian writings that are earlier than the gospels confirm either these gospels or the traditions underlying them?

C. DO EARLIER CHRISTIAN WRITINGS SUBSTANTIATE THE GOSPELS OR THEIR UNDERLYING TRADITIONS?

α Paul's Supernatural Jesus Become Human

The earliest extant Christian documents are those among the letters ascribed to Paul which are genuinely his (and not written later in his name). They include the four major epistles (Romans, 1 and 2 Corinthians and Galatians) and several others, all written by A.D. 60, at any rate before Jerusalem began to suffer during the war with Rome which began in A.D. 66; for Paul mentions current dealings he is having with a Christian community in Jerusalem which was obviously still untroubled by any such upheavals.

For Paul, Jesus was fundamentally a supernatural personage who sojourned only briefly on Earth as a man. This idea that he had previously existed in heaven is, as we saw (above, p. 43), emphasized in the (late) fourth gospel, but is not discernible—or at any rate not explicit—in the synoptics, and smacks too much of mythology for many Christians of today, who also feel that a personage who was a man only for a brief interim between incarnation and exaltation to heaven could not have been the truly human Jesus in whom they would fain believe. From this standpoint it would be disconcerting to find his pre-existence asserted in the very earliest Christian documents, and attempts are made to interpret Paul as after all not alleging it, even though his language on the matter is fairly explicit:

> When the fulness of the time came, God sent forth his Son, born of a woman, born under the law, that he might redeem them which were under the law . . . (Gal. 4:4–5).

According to James Dunn, this need not necessarily mean: sent forth from heaven to be born on Earth; for 'sent forth' could mean

God's commissioning or 'sending out' of the man Jesus on his
Palestinian mission; and 'born' could refer to him as "one who had
been born, not to his birth as such". Furthermore, 'born of a
woman' was a familiar Jewish phrase to denote simply 'man', so
that the reference could be to Jesus' humanness, not to his birth. In
sum, Dunn's suggestion is: the passage could mean that God
commissioned his son, a typical human being, a Jew, to redeem
Jews. But if Paul is in fact simply referring not to a heavenly figure
sent to Earth to be born as a man, but to the man Jesus and his
ministry in Palestine, why did he bother to say that he was a man?
Dunn admits that this is an objection "of some weight" to his
proposed interpretation (1989, p. 40). And the next verse states that,
after his Son had redeemed us, God sent "the Spirit of his Son into
our hearts". This is surely a sending from heaven; if so, the sending
of the Son is likely to have been the same.

At Rom. 8:3 Paul writes of "God sending his own Son in the
likeness of sinful flesh as a sacrifice for sin". This again seems to
mean that Jesus was sent from heaven in human form; but Dunn
proposes that the point here is not that the Son became human, but
that he was identified with sinful humanity (p. xviii). He develops
this idea further in his interpretation of the Christological hymn
Phil. 2:6–11, according to which Christ Jesus (I quote Dunn's own
rendering)

> being in the form of God
> did not count equality with God as something to be grasped,
> but emptied himself,
> taking the form of a slave
> becoming in the likeness of men.
> And being found in form as man,
> he humbled himself
> becoming obedient to death. . . .
> Wherefore God has exalted him to the heights . . .

This is normally taken to mean that the heavenly redeemer conde-
scended to assume the enslaved condition of humanity, and was
then enthroned by God. The 'but' which introduces the third line
shows that the contrast is between 'the form of God' (line 1) and 'the
form of a slave' (line 4), the latter state being achieved by Jesus's

'emptying himself' of the former (line 3), and thereby becoming 'in the likeness of men' (line 5). This 'emptying' can only mean that he surrendered all in himself that was divine so as to become human. (The doctrine of later Christian orthodoxy that Jesus, while on Earth, combined both divine and human nature in his one person was quite unknown to Paul.) The next sentence (beginning with line 6) states that, having become human, Jesus humbled himself even further, in that he became obedient (to God) unto death. This obedience is clearly distinguished from his assumption of human form (which was the subject of the previous sentence) and represented as an additional act of humility. But Dunn—surely arbitrarily—takes the 'emptied himself' in line 3 as already a reference not to Jesus's transformation of himself into a human being, but to his death on the cross, and sees in the whole passage a contrast between the life and work of the man Jesus and the life of Adam (who, unlike Jesus, did, by eating the fruit, 'grasp at equality with God': see Genesis 3:5 and 22). Dunn says:
Jesus "freely chose to embrace the death that Adam experienced as punishment." He was thus "the man who undid Adam's wrong", and to do so he did not need to be any more pre-existent than Adam had been. So interpreted, "Phil. 2:6–11 is simply a way of describing the character of Christ's ministry and sacrifice" (pp. 118–120), and refers solely to the behaviour of the human historical Jesus who 'emptied himself' by offering everything, even his own life, to further God's purpose.

Dunn notes that some regard his exegesis of this hymn (and of the comparable one at Coloss. 1:15–20 which we shall study in the conclusion to this chapter) as "insubstantial and wholly implausible, if not absurd, if not perverse" (p. xviii). It is important to his interpretation that Jesus's ministry in Palestine was well known to Paul and to his readers, and we shall see below how he tries to justify this view in the face of Paul's silence about all the details of this ministry. But first I need to make clear the extent of this silence. I have covered this ground more than once before, much of it recently in chapter 2 of *The Jesus Legend*, where I respond in detail to the gross misrepresentation of my position on these matters that is offered in John Redford's Catholic Truth Society pamphlet *Did*

Jesus Exist? (1986), which purports to answer my book of the same title, the first edition of which had been published eleven years earlier. Nevertheless, as this whole matter is of crucial importance, I need to give a fresh account of it here, especially in view of the many attempts that have been made to show either that Paul is not really silent about Jesus's life, or that his silence (and that of other early Christian writers) does not impair the view that Christianity began with Jesus as he is depicted in the synoptic gospels.

β Paul's Remarkable Silence

There are certainly statements in Paul's letters which, if read from prior knowledge of the gospels, seem to imply that he must have known of Jesus's ministry as depicted there. Mark, followed by Matthew (but not by Luke, neither in his gospel nor in Acts) states that Jesus had a brother named James. Acts represents as leader of the Jerusalem church a certain James, with whom Paul had dealings, but never suggests that this person was Jesus's brother. Now Paul mentions "James the brother of the Lord" (Gal. 1:19) and also a group named "the brethren of the Lord" (1 Cor. 9:5). This James was personally known to Paul, and if he were a blood brother of Jesus, then Paul and Jesus were contemporaries.

It is, however, quite possible to take Paul's words as references to members of a 'brotherhood', to a group of Messianists, led by James and not related to Jesus but zealous in the service of the risen Lord. I have gone into this important matter in considerable detail in chapter 8 of *HEJ*, and so I can be brief here. In Acts, Jerusalem Christians are called "the brethren" (1:15; 9:30) and are addressed as *"andres adelphoi"* ("men who are brethren"). This, says Evans (1990, p. 91) had its origin in the Jewish use, frequent in the OT, of 'brother' for a fellow Israelite, a co-religionist who is also a compatriot. In other religions too, 'brother' often denotes a member of the same religious community (*Ibid.*, p. 620). Moreover, in two gospels that are independent of each other (Matthew and John), the risen Jesus is made to call followers who are not his blood relatives "brethren" in circumstances that are sufficiently similar to warrant the supposition that both evangelists are here drawing on a common source, a resurrection story in which Jesus made some statement about his 'brethren' in the sense of a group of followers.[14]

This would then be evidence for an early (pre-gospel) use of the word as meaning a Christian group serving the Lord.

For Paul, Jesus was "the power of God and the wisdom of God" (1 Cor. 1:24), who assisted God in the creation of all things (1 Cor. 8:6). I find it hard to believe that, with such terms, he was speaking of a contemporary Jew who had a family of brothers. A further difficulty in supposing Jesus and James to have been brothers will occupy us below (p. 69).

As well as to James, Paul refers also to Cephas. The Aramaic *Kepha* and its Greek equivalent *Petros* (Peter) both existed as names in pre-Christian times (Caragounis 1990, pp. 24, 116). 'Cephas' is mentioned in four chapters of 1 Corinthians and in the first two chapters of Galatians. 'Peter'—along with the name 'Cephas'—occurs only at Gal. 2:7-9 (although some manuscripts have replaced 'Cephas' with 'Peter' in some of the other passages). Cullmann dismisses, as "completely unfounded", doubts as to whether the two names designate one and the same person (1962, p. 20n). But it does seem strange to call the same man by two different names within a single sentence. O'Neill (1972, p. 37) conjectures that 'Peter' has been introduced into Paul's original text here in order to incorporate the view, familiar to us from the usual interpretation of Mt. 16:18, that Peter (not James) was the leader of the Jewish church. O'Neill thus regards the words italicized in the following literal rendering of the relevant part of the sentence as glosses:

> They, seeing that I have been entrusted with the gospel of the uncircumcision, *as Peter [that] of the circumcision*, for the [one] operating *in Peter* to an apostleship of the circumcision operated also in me to the gentiles. . . . (Gal. 2:7-8)

If the italicized words are excised—they are there in the extant manuscripts, but these are considerably later than the original—then Paul never mentions 'Peter', but only 'Cephas'. Elsewhere in the NT, 'Cephas' is mentioned only at Jn. 1:42, where Jesus tells Simon: "You shall be called Cephas"; and the evangelist adds: "which means Peter".

The disciple Simon is named 'Peter' by Jesus in the synoptics (where 'Cephas' is never mentioned), and in different circum-

stances in each of these three gospels. The variety in the nomencla-
ture is striking. In Matthew, for instance, the name occurs as
'Simon' (twice), as 'Peter' (twenty times), and as 'Simon Peter'
(three times).

To judge from Paul's references, Cephas must have been an
important figure in the Jerusalem church. Even if he did occasionally call him 'Peter', there is nothing in Paul's writings to support
the view that he had the career and the connection with Jesus
alleged of Simon Peter in the gospels. In the situation described in
Galatians, Cephas is threatening what matters most to Paul, who
condemns this behaviour in the strongest terms. Anxious as he is to
resist these pretensions, he would surely have alluded here to one or
other of the discreditable incidents in the career of the Simon Peter
of the gospels if he had had in mind this person, who was rebuked
by Jesus as "Satan", fell asleep in Gethsemane and went on to deny
his master in cowardly fashion—to mention only some of the
material that would have supported Paul's condemnation of him.[15]

Tyler infers from what is said of Cephas at 1 Cor. 9:5 that Paul
knew that "Jesus's disciple Peter was married" (p. 70). But Paul
never speaks of Jesus's 'disciples', but only, as in this passage, of
those who like himself were 'apostles'; and he does not say that they,
any more than he, had known the pre-crucifixion Jesus. For Paul, an
apostle needed to have experienced his own vision of the risen Lord
(1 Cor. 9:1). The idea that an apostle had been a disciple of Jesus
during his ministry came later, and the author of Luke-Acts was the
first to use the term fairly consistently in this sense.[16] That this was
not its early meaning is clear from Rev. 2:2, where the church at
Ephesus is congratulated for having "tested those who call themselves apostles but are not". If this meant (twelve) companions of
Jesus, they could have been identified without being put to the test
and "found false". What is meant here is the testing of persons who
claimed to speak and to prophesy under the influence of the Holy
Spirit.

A very relevant point is Paul's own insistence that the gospel he
preached did not reach him "from man, nor was I taught it, but it
came to me through revelation of Jesus Christ" (Gal. 1:11–12). He
reiterates this independence from what his fellow apostles had been

teaching: "I conferred not with flesh and blood, neither went I up to Jerusalem to them which were apostles before me" (verses 16–17)—not, at any rate for the first three years of his Christian life, and later only for the purpose of justifying his circumcision-free mission to gentiles. It is customary to dispose of these statements by noting, first and correctly, that Paul "nowhere claims that his gospel differed essentially from the faith of those who were Christians before him" (Thompson 1991, p. 67). It is then argued, by adducing the gospels, that these pre-Pauline Christians, including James and Cephas, had been personally acquainted with a recently executed Jesus and witnesses of his teachings and actions. If, however, we construe their faith purely from what Paul says about it and about them, without introducing gospels which did not exist when he wrote, we have no compelling reason for supposing that the faith of James and Cephas owed any more to personal acquaintance with a recently active Jesus in the flesh than did Paul's own faith. To argue, as has often been done, from 2 Cor. 5:16 that he was simply uninterested in the 'historical' Jesus, while other apostles were not, is—as is now widely acknowledged—to misinterpret this passage.[17]

If we now turn from Paul's statements about fellow Christians to what he says about Jesus as a man, we find firstly that he regards Jesus's human existence as of the greatest importance: without it there could have been no redeeming crucifixion. But he does not give this crucifixion even a setting in time or place, nor mention any of its attendant circumstances. The most that is said on this head in his epistles is that "the Jews" killed Jesus, for which crime "the wrath is come upon them to the uttermost" (1 Thess. 2:14–16). As this totally uncompromising hostility to the Jews is uncharacteristic of Paul—Rom. 11:25–26 has the very opposite doctrine that "all Israel shall be saved"—this Thessalonian passage may be a post-Pauline interpolation alluding to the devastation of Judea and the ensuing destruction of Jerusalem by the Romans in A.D. 70;[18] or it may be genuinely Pauline and mean that, because of the "filling up of the measure of their sins" (verse 16), God has cancelled the privileged position of the Jews, has hardened their hearts against Christian truth and deprived them of his grace (Cf. Paul's aggressive attitude to the 'old covenant' in Gal. 3:19–25 and 4:21–31). Even if genuine, the Thessalonian passage shows merely that, in Paul's view, Jesus as a Jew, "a minister to the circumcision" (Rom. 15:8)—he does not credit him with any mission to gentiles—was killed, as one might expect, by Jews.

As for what occasioned this death, most English translations misleadingly represent Paul as saying that Jesus was "betrayed" (1 Cor. 11:23), thus imputing to him knowledge of the gospels' Judas story. But the Greek verb here in 1 Corinthians is *paradidōmi*, which means not 'betrayed', but 'delivered up', or 'handed over', as is said of the servant of Yahweh in Isaiah 53. (Paul characteristically derives some of his obviously minimal knowledge of the human Jesus from the OT.) The NEB, aware that 'betrayed' would go beyond what the Greek says, understands the verb as a reference to Jesus's "arrest". Paul's idea is that Jesus was 'given over' to the martyr's fate—by God, not by some third party.[19] Paul seems ignorant of all that in the gospels is stated as having led up to this fate. Furnish summarizes the relevant silence with a quite formidable catalogue: "No cleansing of the Temple, no conflict with the authorities, no Gethsemane scene, no trial, no thieves crucified with Jesus, no weeping women, no word about the place or time of the crucifixion, no mention of . . . Judas or Pilate" (1989, p. 42)—only of the supernatural forces supposedly involved.

Theissen and Merz, in their "Comprehensive Guide" to the historical Jesus, think to discredit my assessment of the Pauline evidence by noting that Paul was aware that "some 'rulers of the world' were involved in Jesus's death" (1998, pp. 582–83). This invites the supposition that, when Paul wrote of "the rulers of this age", he had in mind Pilate, and perhaps also Herod Antipas and the Jewish high priest Caiaphas, and their behaviour as depicted in the gospel passion narratives. Theissen and Merz must know that most scholars allow that the contexts in which Paul uses the term "rulers of this age" and similar terms show quite clearly that he means them as designations of supernatural forces which have long harrassed humanity, but have now been subjugated by Christ's saving act. Paul says that these rulers are "coming to naught", and that none of them had any inkling of

God's "wisdom that hath been hidden, which God foreordained before the worlds for our glory" (1 Cor. 2:6–8). This wisdom is Christ (Coloss. 2:2–3), hidden as a "mystery" for long ages with God in heaven, but now manifest to believers (Rom. 16:25–27; Coloss. 1:26). He tricked the evil spirits who rule the world by appearing on Earth divested of all his heavenly splendour (see above, p. 50), so that, failing to recognize him, they caused him to be crucified, thereby ensuring their own demise, heralded when he manifested his true status and powers at his resurrection (See below, pp. 156f for relevant quotations from the epistles, and also Wells 1991, pp. 96–106, for fuller discussion of them). The article *archōn (ruler)* in Kittel's standard *Theological Dictionary of the New Testament* observes (I, 489), that Paul is "not referring to earthly rulers" and that arguments to the contrary "are not convincing". This article also gives OT and other parallels to the use of the term 'rulers' to denote celestial beings. See also Earl Doherty's assessment (1997, p. 71) in an article which brings out quite remorselessly the incompatibility of the Jesus of the gospels with the Jesus of the epistles.

Paul's silence about the time, place, and circumstances of Jesus's death is sometimes explained by supposing that, since Jesus was 'the risen Lord', such historical data were of very subordinate interest. But from Paul's premiss of the supreme importance of knowing "Christ crucified" (1 Cor. 1:23 and 2:2) one would expect him to be explicit about the Passion and at least to specify the when and the where. He is so imprecise about it that he may well have thought that it occurred one or two centuries before his time of writing. We know from Josephus that at these earlier dates holy men had been crucified alive in Palestine and not, as was the usual Jewish custom, only after they had been executed by other means.[20]

Other early Christian writers share Paul's silence about the circumstances of the Passion. Not until we come to letters written once the gospels (or at any rate once many of their underlying traditions) had become available do we meet the statement that Jesus stood before Pilate. This is affirmed in the epistles of Ignatius of Antioch and, within the NT, in the

Pastoral epistle 1 Timothy. The Ignatian letters I accept, with most scholars, as written ca. A.D. 110, and not as later forgeries;[21] and the Pastoral epistles, although ascribed to Paul are, as we shall see (below, pp. 78ff) really early second-century works. The many scholars who concede that they are post-Pauline are certainly not motivated by any desire to convict Paul of ignorance of what is said of Jesus's life in the gospels, and would repudiate any suggestion that he was thus ignorant. It is, then, surely significant that a historical setting to this life, so noticeably absent from what are generally accepted as genuine Paulines, is to be found in one of the Pastorals, which are so widely admitted on quite other grounds to be of later date.

If we now ask what can be learned from Paul of Jesus's pre-crucifixion life, the answer is: nothing except that he was descended from David (Rom. 1:3) and born of a woman under the Jewish law (Gal. 4:4). Paul never mentions Mary or Joseph (nor does any other NT epistle writer) and says nothing to suggest that the birth was from a virgin mother. For him, Jesus was "declared to be the Son of God with power" by dint of his resurrection (Rom. 1:4), not by a supernatural birth, nor by manifestations of power such as miracle-working or exorcisms during his lifetime. He never even suggests that Jesus had been active in Jerusalem or Galilee. Tom Wright, Dean of Lichfield, says again and again in his 1997 book that Paul preached "Jesus of Nazareth", whereas in fact Paul never mentions Nazareth and says nothing to link Jesus with the place. Within the NT, the title 'Jesus of Nazareth' is used only in Acts.

The position is no better in respect of Paul's knowledge of Jesus's teaching. He never suggests that Jesus taught in parables, although these are quite central to the synoptic teaching. He also never suggests that Jesus was involved in doctrinal conflicts with Pharisees. At no point in his letters where he is expounding the central content of his gospel does he cite or clearly allude to any saying of Jesus. No question was more central to Paul than whether it was necessary for Christians to keep the Jewish law, yet the controversies on this matter recorded in his letters, and even in Acts, show no knowledge of the various teachings on the law that are ascribed to Jesus in the gospels. In these, the parts of the law most prominent are the regulations about sabbath and about food; and if Jesus's attitudes on these matters had been as lax as some gospel passages suggest, this would surely have surfaced in other documents where these issues are to the fore. According to Mk. 7:19, for instance, he declared all foods clean. Paul can have known nothing of this, for he records a furious quarrel with Peter as to whether it was permissible for Christian Jews and Christian gentiles to eat together (Gal. 2:11–16), and it took a thrice-repeated post-resurrection revelation even to half convince Peter to permissiveness on the matter (Acts 10:9–17).[22] Again, at Gal. 4:10 Paul reproves Christian opponents on the ground that they observe special "days", and this must include sabbath observance. But he does not support his case with any suggestion that Jesus had transgressed the sabbath, had allowed his disciples to do the same, and had justified such action publicly in debate—all of which is alleged in the gospels. As to the all-important matter as to whether Christians needed to be circumcised, Paul obviously knew of nothing in Jesus's teaching or behaviour to which he could appeal, and has to resort to a quite desperate argument in order to controvert the clear doctrine of Genesis 17:10 ("every male among you shall be circumcised"). How arbitrary Paul's argument is has been well brought out by E.P. Sanders's summary of it (1991, pp. 55ff).

The conflicts over the law in the Pauline churches would be equally incomprehensible if Jesus had expressly endorsed it in its entirety, as other gospel passages have him do (see above, p. 21); for then Paul's critics could have silenced him by appealing to such logia, and he would certainly have been quite unable to persuade James and Cephas, as he did at a Jerusalem conference (Gal. 2: 6–10), to sanction his mission of a law-free Christianity for gentiles. It seems, then, that the pro-law statements in the gospels are as questionable as any anti-law ones, and for this reason Sanders is inclined to reject as inauthentic the entire section of the Sermon on the Mount which runs from Mt. 5:17 to

6:18—except the Lord's Prayer (6:9–13)—particularly as so much of it is out of line with other synoptic passages.[23] Synoptic statements about a mission to gentiles or their eventual inclusion in the kingdom could well come from after the time that the gentile mission was started, while the restriction of the disciples' mission to Israel (Mt. 10:5–6, 23) is equally suspect, as it could derive from a section of the Palestinian church which itself opposed the gentile mission. Sanders concludes that the controversies over the matter in the early church are understood best "if we attribute to Jesus no explicit viewpoint at all" (1985, pp. 219–221). In this connection it is surely significant that, according to the deutero-Pauline epistle to the Ephesians, the fact that "the gentiles are fellow heirs, members of the same body and partakers of the promise in Christ Jesus", has been revealed "by the Spirit"—not by any teaching of the historical Jesus!—to his holy apostles and prophets" (3:5–6).

All that one can extract from Paul by way of knowledge of Jesus's teachings is some half-dozen mentions of "words" or "commands" of "the Lord", mostly on relatively peripheral matters. Some of these were certainly not spoken by the pre-crucifixion Jesus. 2 Cor. 12:9, for instance, is expressly said to be what the Lord said personally to Paul, in answer to a prayer, and so the speaker must have been the risen Lord, as Paul did not know Jesus before his resurrection and, as a persecutor of Christians, certainly did not then pray to him. 1 Thess. 4:15–17 gives the Lord's assurance that even those Christians who have died before his (imminent) second coming will share its benefits. Nothing in the gospels corresponds to this ruling—not surprisingly, as the problem of the fate of the Christian dead (as distinct from the question of whether there will be any resurrection for anyone) could hardly have been a pressing one at the time of Jesus's supposed ministry. When Paul here introduces the assurance with "This we say to you by a word of the Lord", he is probably making known by whose authority he speaks and affirming his insight as a Christian, rather than appealing to a particular Jesuine saying.

The question of the raising of the dead is prominent in

1 Corinthians, where Paul, most anxious to dispel doubts on the matter, adduces no 'word of the Lord' for this purpose, even though in all three synoptic gospels Jesus repudiates the Sadducees' denial of the doctrine (Mk. 12:18ff and parallels). Instead of referring to this, Paul tries to carry conviction by asking: Why is baptism undertaken on behalf of the dead? (It would be pointless if they are not to be raised.) Why are apostles ready to endanger their lives for their convictions? (They will gain nothing from it if there is no resurrection.) We may as well live as libertines, he adds, if death—soon to befall us all—is the end (1 Cor. 15:29–32). He then, quoting a line from Menander that had survived as a proverb, advises discretion in the choice of associates: "Evil company doth corrupt good manners." (But had not Jesus characteristically kept company with "publicans and sinners" and told the Jewish authorities that "the publicans and the harlots go into the kingdom of God before you"? Mt. 9:10; 21:31) Finally, he responds to the question "with what manner of body" the dead will be raised, and answers: as "spiritual", not as "natural" bodies: "We shall bear the image of the heavenly" (verses 44–49. But he does not appeal to Jesus's authoritative ruling: "When they shall rise from the dead, they . . . are as angels in heaven" (Mk. 12:25). Instead he, characteristically, quotes the OT in support, and relies also on a few spurious analogies, saying, for instance: a perishable human body is duly buried like a seed, and just as the seed will be "raised" as a plant, so the body will be raised as imperishable.

Some of Paul's 'words of the Lord' are regarded even by numerous Christian commentators as words of the risen Jesus, given to early Christian prophets speaking in his name. It is perhaps significant that we are here dealing with words of "the Lord", not of 'Jesus'. This in itself suggests that the appeal is not to an earthly teacher, but "to the risen, reigning *Christ*, the church's *Lord*" (Furnish 1968, p. 56; author's italics). Although Paul uses the name 'Jesus' 142 times, "no saying is ever presented as a saying of Jesus" (Boring 1991, p. 114). Such words of the Lord may be called 'prophetic' because they represent, not what a historical Jesus had once said, but what he now says in his

resurrected state. Drawing critically on earlier work by Bultmann, Käsemann, and others, M.E. Boring shows that, in this
sense, early Christianity was a prophetic movement: "The early
Christian prophet was an immediately inspired spokesperson for
the risen Jesus who received intelligible messages that he or she
felt inspired to deliver to the Christian community or, as a
representative of the community, to the general public" (1991, p.
38). Paul preferred this type of intelligible utterance to glosso-
lalia, to ecstatic speech "in tongues" which could not be immediately understood and required an interpreter (see below, p. 86),
and which was more likely to have unsettling effects at communal worship. Hence he concludes what is regarded as his earliest
extant letter with the exhortations: "Quench not the spirit,
despise not prophesyings" (1 Thess. 5:19–20). Thus, at the
earliest point at which we see the Hellenistic church, prophecy is
already present. It is associated with "knowing mysteries" (1 Cor.
13:2) and is one of the gifts of God's grace (Rom. 12:6). These
texts from three different letters show that it was a constituent
part of church life (Boring, pp. 59, 61). Mark is the first writer to
put all the sayings he collected from different sources—however
they may have originated, whether as sayings of an earthly or of a
risen Jesus—firmly into a pre-Easter framework, "as an element
in his creation of the Gospel form", and, Boring complains,
scholars still tend to see the material too much through post-
Markan eyes" (p. 28).

That four of Paul's half-dozen 'words of the Lord' occur in 1
Corinthians, his only letter which includes detailed discussion of
Christian prophesying (chapters 12–14), in itself suggests some
relationship between such prophecy and the tradition of these
words. Paul here states at length in what manner spiritual gifts
such as speaking in tongues or prophesying may be indulged by
the congregation at worship in church. The "prophets" present
should, he says, speak in orderly succession, not all at once, "for
ye can all prophesy, one by one, that all may learn" (14:31).
Women he excludes from the exercise of these gifts. "Let them
keep silence in the churches" and ask their husbands in due
subjection at home "if they would learn anything" (verses 34–35,

hard to reconcile with the earlier statement, at 11:5, that they may "prophesy"—presumably at communal worship—provided they keep their heads veiled). He then adds:

> If any man thinketh himself to be a prophet or spiritual, let him take knowledge of the things which I write to you, that they are the commandment of the Lord (14:37).

But there are no extant words of Christ which correspond to any of these prescriptions. The historical Jesus, speaking by hypothesis at a time when there were no churches, is not on record as having given instructions about how to prophesy or speak in tongues in church, nor about whether women might participate. Paul can only mean that the things he has written should be considered as orders from the Lord not because they are words of Jesus handed down to him by historical tradition, but because the Lord has guided him by his Spirit. "Paul thus refers [here] to his *own* apostolic authority" (Räisänen, 1987b, p. 80. Author's italics).

The statement at 1 Cor. 9:14—that "the Lord ordained that they which proclaim the gospel should live of the gospel"—can also be regarded as a disclosure made by the risen Lord. This claim for financial support of Christian preachers from the communities they served is likely to have been a community regulation which was secured by anchoring it in this way to divine authority. Priests of most religions and at all times have claimed such support and represented the claim as the will of God. That Paul alludes to this question repeatedly (Evans 1990, p. 448 lists the relevant passages) shows its importance for Christian missionary practice.

The only appreciable overlap between words of Jesus in the gospels and words of the Lord in Paul are the references, in two remaining passages, to rulings on divorce and to Jesus's so-called eucharistic words (both in 1 Corinthians). The statement on divorce again represents a community regulation, made firm by being put into Christ's mouth. In time, Christian prophets and their audiences would naturally suppose that he must have spoken during his lifetime in the manner they thought his Spirit spoke to them. I would claim that this accounts for what correspondence there is (and it is far from complete) between the logia on divorce in Paul and in the gospels. Sanders and Davies, anxious as they are in their valuable 1989 book to make the most of Paul's citations from "the Lord", nevertheless admit that there are "very substantial disagreements" between Paul and the synoptics here. Although they hold fast to the position that "there can be no reasonable doubt that Jesus said something on divorce", they allow that we do not know exactly what, but merely that "he was against it". His "teaching was revised as it was applied to different situations" (pp. 131, 327–28).[24] In other words, what the NT teaches on matters of social importance is likely to depend on which of its books (or which portion of one of its books) one consults. Finally, the "tradition" embodied in 11:23–25, which Paul says he "received from the Lord", and which includes eucharistic words of Jesus, is what Neirynck, with numerous other commentators, has called "a quotation of a liturgical tradition" (1986, p. 277). This pericope represents Jesus as instituting a cultic act which existed as a regular part of Christian worship in Paul's time. Once such a practice had been established, it would be natural to suppose that Jesus had ordained it. The Dead Sea Scrolls have shown that a cultic act of this kind already existed in the Jewish background to Christianity (see below, p. 00).

Apologists like to give the impression that, against my position, there is considerable Pauline evidence, of which they mention only a fraction. It is, of course, the sparsity of any direct reference to Jesus's gospel teachings that has prompted interpreters to seek what they call 'resonances' of them, and, as Furnish has said, "with patience and imagination the possibilities can be multiplied like loaves and fishes" (1968, p. 59). Paul does indeed give teachings that in the gospels are attributed to Jesus, but he does so without any suggestion that they derive from him. Far from 'echoing' what Jesus had already said, they surely represent ethical doctrines only later put into his mouth. For instance, Paul gives it as his own view (Rom. 13:8–10) that the law can be summed up in the OT injunction "Thou shalt love thy neighbour as thyself." According to Mt. 22:37–39 (cf. Lk. 10:25–28) Jesus taught that the whole law depends on two commandments: first "love the Lord thy God" and second "love thy neighbour as thyself". One could, however, never gather from Paul that Jesus had expressed himself on this matter, and the fact that the double command of the gospel Jesus—love of God, love of neighbour—is reduced in Romans 13 to the single one of love of neighbour (which the gospel Jesus puts very firmly second) presents "a grave difficulty to those who . . . wish to see Paul reverently dependent upon Jesus's words" (Furnish 1968, p. 57). Moreover, at 1 Thess. 4:9 it is not Jesus but God who is said to have taught Christians to love one another, and the injunction not to repay evil for evil is given in this same epistle (5:15) without any suggestion that Jesus had taught it (as according to Matthew he did in the Sermon on the Mount). In Romans Paul repeats the same injunction (12:17) and also says "bless those that persecute you" (12:14) and "judge not" (14:13). One would surely expect him in such instances to have invoked the authority of Jesus had he known that Jesus had taught the very same doctrines (as was so, according to Mt. 5:44 and 7:1 and Lk. 6:28 and 37). In the same epistle he urges Christians to "pay taxes" (13:6), but does not suggest that Jesus had given such a ruling (Mk. 12:17). I noted in Wells 1982 (p. 33): it is much more likely that certain precepts concerning forgiveness and civil obedience were originally urged independently of Jesus, and only later stamped with supreme authority by being attributed to him, than that he gave such rulings and was not credited with having done so by Paul.

Allison (1982, p. 11) makes much of the fact that Paul's "bless those that persecute you" is clustered, within eight verses, with two kindred sayings ("Render no man evil for evil" and "Be not overcome of evil but overcome evil with good"). Allison finds this significant, since there is a cluster of similar sayings at Lk. 6:27–36 (here, of course, as words of Jesus). He holds that the one cluster must have borrowed from the other, and that as the Lukan one has "high claim to be genuinely dominical" (it is present in Q and therefore earlier than Luke) the direction of borrowing must have been from Jesus to Paul, making Paul in touch not only with traditions underlying the synoptics, but with "the Jesus of history". But since the overall theme of Jesus' sermon at this point in Luke is—as Allison himself says—"love of neighbour and of enemy", resemblance between the two clusters is hardly surprising; and he of course recognizes that the Pauline one does not purport to reproduce 'words of the Lord'.

I find Allison's other examples of Pauline "echoes" of synoptic material equally unconvincing, although his criticisms of attempts by earlier scholars to impute knowledge of Jesus's synoptic sayings to Paul are effective. But he goes on, quoting L. Goppelt, to claim (p. 22) that early Christian writers who obviously knew the gospels cite the gospel traditions ("die Evangelienüberlieferung") as little as does Paul, so that his failure to do so need not, any more than theirs, imply ignorance. Goppelt's example is the failure of Acts to cite pre-resurrection words of Jesus from the gospels. But Acts, far from being silent about 'gospel traditions', shows the kind of knowledge of them that is totally absent from the Pauline writings. It links Jesus with Nazareth, alludes to his baptism, states that he taught, performed many miracles and healings (including exorcisms, 10:38), was betrayed by Judas, indicted by the Jews in Jerusalem (who wanted a murderer to be released in his stead, 3:14) and tried by Pilate. The author even points us to his own gospel, Luke, for he follows it where it diverges from the others (for example in stating that Jesus was tried by Herod Antipas, as well as by Pilate). Acts also agrees with the gospels in recognizing Jesus as "the Son of man" (7:55–56)—a title never given to him in the epistles.

This information is given mainly in Acts' missionary speeches, and these follow a strikingly regular pattern, irrespective of whether Peter or Paul is the speaker, or whether Jews or gentiles form the audience: first, Jesus's life, Passion and resurrection is outlined, often with emphasis that the disciples had witnessed these events; then proofs of his status are adduced from the OT, and finally there is a call for repentance. (Only Paul's words in Lystra and Athens deviate from this pattern, eliminating in the manner of second-century apologists Christology likely to alienate gentiles.) As Acts begins with a reminder that "all that Jesus began both to do and to teach" has been already covered in the author's gospel, it is not surprising that these speeches give the Christian message in a condensed form, nor that narrative statements about what was preached are couched in quite general terms: Philip preached to Samaritans "good tidings concerning the kingdom of God and the name of Jesus Christ" (8:12); Paul spoke for three months in the synagogue at Ephesus, "reasoning and persuading as to the things concerning the kingdom of God" (19:8); and in Rome he persuaded the Jews "concerning Jesus, both from the law of Moses and from fhe prophets" (28:23).

Acts is not a very early work, and it is only the *earliest* Christian literature, not early Christian literature as a whole, as Goppelt and Allison suppose, that is uninformative about the gospel traditions. This earliest literature—I indicate its extent on p. xvi above—comprises considerably more than just the Pauline letters. The letter to the Hebrews, which Lindars (1991, pp. 19–21) gives reasons for dating around A.D. 65–70, supplies an instructive example. At 2:6 the phrase 'Son of man' is quoted from Psalm 8, where it means simply 'a human being'. In the following verses the author of Hebrews quotes the very next words in the Psalm to establish the exalted status of Jesus, yet he values the phrase 'Son of man' solely as indicating solidarity with the human race. There is no awareness that the phrase could be used—as repeatedly in the gospels (for instance at Mk. 14:62)—to indicate precisely the exalted status for which the epistle is here pleading. Lindars draws the obvious conclusion: there was no 'Son of man' title in the Christology of early Christianity, and the use of the phrase in this way is "a development within the sayings tradition of the Gospels" (1991, p. 40n).

For a detailed account of the failure of early non-Pauline epistles to corroborate what the gospels say of Jesus, see chapter 2 of my *HEJ*.

These overall silences by different authors are significant. If Paul alone had written as he did of Jesus, one might just possibly be able to attribute this to some personal idiosyncrasy, but a consistent silence by numerous independent early writers about matters which, had they known of them, they could not but have regarded as relevant to their purposes, cannot be so explained. This very important point has been ignored by most of my critics, who write as though I base my whole case on the silences of Paul. Characteristic is Ian Wilson, who calls them the "linchpin" of my arguments, and gives no indication that I show such silence to be pervasive throughout all the earliest Christian documents. Wilson admits to "pro-Christian bias" (1996, p. 7), and it is amply reflected in the tone of his comments ("Professor Wells and like detractors", who writes "scholarly-looking" books and, with his "likes", seizes on a "ready excuse" to discount significant evidence; pp. 41–43). Having narrowed the issue down to the silences of Paul, Wilson thinks them quite easy to explain: Paul never met the pre-crucifixion Jesus, and "it is therefore hardly to be expected that he would be full of chapter and verse on Jesus's biography" (p. 42). To suggest that Paul is merely 'not full' of such biographical allusions is a gross understatement and a facile way of discounting the significance of his silences.

Equally significant is that the silence of the earliest documents is not maintained in epistles written sufficiently late for their authors to have been cognizant of at any rate some elements of the synoptic tradition. We saw this apropos of the way they refer to the Passion (above, pp. 57f); and when we come to 2 Peter, we find "for the first time clear [epistolary] reference to a pre-Passion event in Jesus' life", namely the transfiguration (Thompson 1991, p. 43). Thompson adds that this letter is arguably the very latest NT epistle: scholars are now nearly unanimous that it is pseudepigraphical, and many of them date it in the second century. France allows that today, even among evangelical Christians, few would try to defend its Petrine authorship with any enthusiasm (1993, p. 51). Outside the canon, 1 Clement, probably as late as the turn of the century, did not know the gospels (see note 6 on p. 258 below), yet specifies mercy, forgiveness, and reciprocity as teachings of Jesus, and says that he warned against causing the elect to stumble; and Ignatius of Antioch tells his fellow Christians that Jesus was born of the virgin Mary, baptized by John, crucified under Pilate and that after resurrection he ate and drank with his followers as a real body. One would look in vain for such specific information in the early epistles as listed on p. xvi above. They appear to be unaware not only of the gospels but also of the basic traditions underlying them. The reasonable inference, then, is: either these traditions are entirely legendary, or they refer to a Jesus figure (probably historical) quite different from the Jesus of the earliest documents. As we shall see (pp. 101ff below), evidence favours the latter hypothesis.

Finally, I revert to the question as to what links there were between Jesus and the leaders of the Jerusalem Christian community (James and Cephas), with whom Paul had dealings. It is almost universally supposed that James was the brother of Jesus, and thus that Paul, James, and Cephas alike worshipped a Jesus recently executed at the behest of the Jerusalem authorities as a Messianic pretender, as "king of the Jews" according to the gospels. But if the Jerusalem authorities had found Jesus sufficiently dangerous to have eliminated him, is it plausible that they would then have left unmolested, for a generation or more, his close followers in that same city who were implicating themselves in all that he had stood for by proclaiming that his resurrection had vindicated him as God's Messiah, and that he would shortly return and inaugurate his kingdom? Followers who thus proclaimed his persisting power would surely have been recognized as defiant of the authorities who had so recently killed him, and as much a threat to public order as he himself had been. It seems, then, that we must abandon the premiss that James and Cephas (any more than Paul) were closely linked—by blood relationship or by personal acquaintance—with a recently active Jesus who had been found worse than merely troublesome. If, however, they and the community they led in Jerusalem constituted no more than an obscure Jewish sect, worshipping, as Paul did, a distant figure who was probably quite unknown to the authorities of the time, then it is understandable that they were allowed to survive untroubled.[25] M.P. Miller has justly noted that this problem of reconciling the gospels' view of Jesus's Passion and execution with "the establishment and survival for more than a generation of a Jerusalem church as a Messianic movement in that same city has hardly ever surfaced, let alone been adequately addressed" (1995, p. 7). It is, he adds, a problem which should "make one far less inclined to suppose that the Gospel Passion narratives constitute sources from which one can extract and reconstruct the historical circumstances and reasons for the death of Jesus" (p. 20).

A further significant factor is that Paul accepted from James and Cephas "the right hand of fellowship" (Gal. 2:9). He would not have done so, had their Christology conflicted with his own. For him, the only valid ideas about Jesus were those which he himself preached (2 Cor. 11:4), the only valid gospel what he himself taught, and anyone deviating from it was to be roundly cursed (Gal. 1:8). If I have shown that Paul did not believe that Jesus died and rose as, when, and where the gospel narratives suppose (see further below, p. 125), it surely follows that James and Cephas did not believe this either. The 'Jesus event', understood on the basis of these gospel narratives, has all too long been uncritically accepted as what has been called "a kind of theological Big Bang whose initial moments"—particularly as they pertain to the resurrection—are "quite resistant to precise description, but which nevertheless is thought to account for almost everything that followed" (Kloppenborg 1996, p. 247).

γ Attempts to Explain Paul's Silence

Few apologists find it necessary to offer any account of why early Christian writers other than Paul write as uninformatively as they do. But his prominence in the canon makes his silence too conspicuous to be ignored, and there are two standard ways of accounting for it: either to deny that it is really substantial, or to admit its considerable extent while offering reasons for stamping it as innocuous. Sometimes both these tactics are to some extent combined, but the former of the two predominates with De Jonge, Mitton, and Wenham, whose arguments I will now consider.

De Jonge has persuaded himself that Paul did in fact use "the Jesus tradition" where his arguments needed it, and that, as they did not often require it, he will have known more of it than is revealed in his letters. Paul, he implies, *must* have known the substance of what the gospels tell us: "He speaks about the pre-existent Lord, but cannot possibly have bypassed his earthly ministry" (1988, pp. 87–88). Of course he must have known about this ministry if it had taken place only very few years before his own conversion to Jesus worship, and if it had run the course outlined in the synoptics. But this is precisely what I am putting in question.

Mitton finds specific Pauline references to the Jesus tradition by giving his own interpretations of epistolary passages which he does not even specify. Admittedly, we all have to interpret Paul to make sense of him, but we should not present our interpretations as if they were his actual statements. Paul, he says, knew that Jesus "died at the time of the Jewish Passover" (p. 35). This presumably interprets 1 Cor. 5:7, where his death is compared with the killing of the passover lamb: "Our passover also hath been sacrificed, even Christ". Paul means by this that the old dispensation has been superseded: "Purge out the old leaven", he says at the beginning of the same verse. Many commentators (for instance Ruef 1971, p. 42 ad loc.) agree that all this has nothing to do with the date of the crucifixion or the Last Supper: the identification of the death with the Passover is "first and foremost theological and is not dependent on chronology".

Mitton further argues that Paul knew that Jesus's "earthly life was lived in poverty". This obviously interprets 2 Cor. 8:9: "Ye know the grace of our Lord Jesus Christ, that though he was rich, yet for your sakes he became poor, that ye through his poverty might become rich". We cannot take this to mean that Jesus was initially a rich man, but disposed of his assets so as to live as a pauper, for this is not alleged even in the gospels. The verse as a whole shows that the reference is not to a life lived in poverty, but to Christ's condescending to forego the richness of his supernatural status so as to assume lowly human form, as outlined in the hymn in Philippians quoted above. This was the 'poverty' which enabled him to die for our salvation, 'so that we might become rich'. Paul puts this doctrine of the incarnation in financial terms because in this context he is urging the Corinthians to give more generously to the fund he is raising for the Jerusalem church. Mitton probably had Buchanan's 1965 article in mind, which unconvincingly suggests that, because Paul is here pleading for money, his allusion to Jesus's example may not refer to the incarnation at all.

Mitton goes on to claim "meekness and gentleness" as among the "aspects of the character" of Jesus known to Paul. The reference is surely to 2 Cor. 10:1: "I entreat you by the meekness and gentleness (NEB 'magnanimity') of Christ"; but Paul here probably means no more than that Jesus displayed these qualities in that he allowed himself to be "sent" by the Father to Earth in human form as a sacrifice (Gal. 4:4–5), as is implied by 2 Cor. 8:9, already quoted. In any case, Paul is not saying that Jesus displayed these moral qualities in a *recent* historical existence; and when he mentions Jesus's ethical qualities, he is always referring, as in these passages, either to his incarnation or to his death (for instance "obedient unto death", Phil. 2:8), to neither of which he gives a specific historical context. Of the incarnate life between the birth and the death he has nothing to say. All this was perfectly clear to some of the older commentators.[26]

Sceptical attitudes towards the kind of views on Christian origins that most scholars accept must, says Mitton, "be fully proved and not just stated as fact, as if they had been already proved" (p. 60). Had he applied this standard to his own account of Paul's knowledge of Jesus, he would have had to deal with the subject far less superficially. Surprisingly, he makes the damaging concession that, if Paul's letters were not prefaced in our printed Bible with "the predominantly factual material of the gospels", then "their theology and Christology would have sounded like empty and irrelevant dogma without the personal content provided for the word 'Christ' in the Gospels. Without the Gospels, the Christian faith becomes merely a beautiful idea, not a fact of history" (p. 62). Quite so (unless, perhaps, the 'beauty' of some elements of the 'idea' might be queried). Christians would see how very true this is if they would try, by way of experiment, to banish from their minds all they know of Jesus from the gospels (which did not exist when Paul wrote) and then read through one of the major epistles, such as Romans.

A much more elaborate attempt to show that Paul knew what later came to be recorded in the gospels is mounted in David Wenham's 1995 book, which the Dean of Lichfield has hailed as "the fullest, best, and most recent study of the relationship between Jesus and Paul" (Wright 1997, p. 190). Wenham finds that there is "massive evidence of Pauline knowledge of Jesus-traditions" (p. 381). I can illustrate the manner in which he reaches this conclusion with his example of the use of the word 'Abba'—Aramaic for 'father'—in Paul and in the gospels. Paul uses it twice and the gospels do so once, and I will first indicate its context in them.

At Mk. 14:35 Jesus in Gethsemane "fell on the ground and prayed that, if it were possible, the hour might pass away from him". No one could have heard his prayer—he was ahead of his companions as he spoke—but the next verse repeats its substance in direct speech, in words which are surely no more than the early church's reverend and conjectural elaboration of this tradition that he prayed here:

> Abba, Father, all things are possible unto thee; remove this cup from me; howbeit not what I will, but what thou wilt.

Although this is the only occasion in the four gospels when Jesus addresses God in this way, it has nevertheless been frequently supposed (for example in Charlesworth 1989, pp. 132–34) that he probably used 'Abba' in all the passages where the texts make him address God as 'Father' or 'the Father' or 'my Father', or even 'our Father'. It has been further supposed that this is a very familiar form of address, equivalent to the English 'dad' or 'daddy', and so expresses his especially close relationship with God. This interpretation—popularized by the conservative NT scholar Joachim Jeremias, and hence seized upon by innumerable preachers—has become difficult to defend. Vermes noted what he charmingly called its "incongruousness" (1983, p. 42). It would surely be not merely incongruous but downright ridiculous to suppose that 'Father' (*patēr* in the Greek, with no mention of 'Abba') could be replaced with 'dad' or 'daddy' in passages such as the solemn 'Consecration Prayer' of Jn. 17, even if rendered in more modern English than that of the RV:

> These things spake Jesus; and lifting up his eyes to heaven, he said, Father, the hour is come; glorify thy Son so that the Son may glorify thee. . . . And now, O Father, glorify thou me with thine own self with the glory which I had with thee before the world was . . .

Moreover James Barr has noted that the Aramaic Targums (translations or paraphrases of the Hebrew Bible) use 'Abba' in solemn utterances made by adult or even elderly men, so that when children used it, they were using an adult word. He also noted that in the Greek of the NT the adult word *patēr* is repeatedly used, but never a diminutive or a word that particularly belongs to the speech of children, even though such alternatives were available in the Greek of the period.[27]

Paul uses 'Abba' in two passages. At Rom. 8:15 he tells that "ye received the spirit of adoption" (as sons of God), "whereby we cry, Abba, Father". Because we have been thus adopted (as a result of Jesus having redeemed us), God "sent forth the Spirit of his Son into our hearts, crying Abba, Father" (Gal. 4:4–6). The Spirit was, then, sent to us from heaven (see above, p. 50) and makes us cry out with the Aramaic word and its Greek translation. It has often been observed that this 'crying out' of the Aramaic and Greek forms of the same word suggests some kind of liturgical usage in the Pauline communities. Even Wenham allows that this is "quite likely" (p. 125); and Vermes has shown that 'Abba' was used in the prayer language of the Judaism of the day (1973, pp. 210–11). The reasonable inference is that Mark, on one single occasion, has put a liturgical prayer formula into Jesus's mouth. For Wenham, however, Paul's use of 'Abba' is "the most important evidence" pointing to his "direct contact with the Jesus tradition" (p. 125). If this is the most impressive piece of evidence that he can muster, it is hardly necessary to come to terms with the rest.

The usual alternative way of claiming knowledge of the synoptic tradition for Paul is, as I have indicated, to admit that he mentions very little of it, but to see no significance in this. Tyler even points to speeches by Winston Churchill and Margaret Thatcher as supplying meaningful analogies in that they too were silent about helpful predecessors who were yet well known to them: "One might have expected so well-read and history-oriented a figure as Winston Churchill to have quoted from outstanding defenders of civilised behaviour and of the virtues of democracy and liberty—ancient and modern—in his famous and uplifting war-time broadcasts, not least in those specifically beamed into occupied Europe, as this would have furthered his case" (pp. 71f). The obvious answer is that Paul was addressing people who accepted the supreme importance of Jesus, but were nevertheless in danger of falling victim to what he regarded as an erroneous Christology—"another Jesus" (2 Cor. 11:4), and not what he preached (Gal. 1:6–9). Hence any appeal to a clear Jesuine ruling on the issues in question would have sufficed to settle them. Churchill, on the other hand, was not confronting audiences who disagreed with his views on democracy and liberty. Occupied Europe did not need allusions to Thomas Jefferson and others to be persuaded that liberation was desirable, and anything of this kind would have been seen as pedantry and totally unappreciated. As for Mrs Thatcher, she, says Tyler, might be expected "to have quoted the many arguments and examples put forward by Professor Milton Friedman, the high priest of Monetarism, to justify her own radical . . . policies . . . It is quite extraordinary that she did not follow this approach in her orations". She would in fact have given her opponents leverage by appealing to protagonists of one school of economic thought which was controversial and opposed by others. Most of her audience had never heard of Friedman and would not—as Paul's audiences did Jesus—have accepted him as an undisputed authority.

Most of those who find Paul's silences innocuous do so on the ground that he had no need to mention the Jesus tradition as he could assume that his readers already knew it well. James Dunn gives a version of this argument. He sees that to follow the considerable scholarly "consensus" that Paul knew or cared little of Jesus apart from his death and resurrection would really mean accepting damaging implications for the view that Christianity originated from a Jesus who was a near-contemporary of the earliest extant references to him. Dunn argues against the 'consensus' that Paul did not mention Jesus when he "echoed" his teaching because to have done so would have spoiled the effectiveness of allusions to it to which his readers were ready to respond on the basis of knowledge of it which they shared with him:

> In communities bonded by such common experience and language, there is a whole level of discourse which consists of allusion and echo. It is the very fact that allusions are sufficient for much effective communication which provides and strengthens the bond; recognition of the allusion/echo is what attests effective membership of the group. Who has never belonged to a community where 'in-jokes' and code allusions or abbreviations both facilitated communication between members of the group and left outsiders at best able to function only on the surface of the exchange, without recognizing implications and ramifications obvious to the insiders?

Dunn's argument amounts to this: I might have occasion, while addressing a literary society conversant with the novels of Charles

Dickens, to say 'I'm waiting for something to turn up'. But it would spoil the 'in-joke' if I were sufficiently ill-advised to add, before such an audience, 'As Mr. Micawber used to say'. By the same reasoning, for Paul to have cited Jesus explicitly would have been to "force, as it were, the web of allusion and echo into the open" and so to "weaken the bonding effect of the web of shared discourse". "In other words, what we find in the Pauline paraenesis in terms of echoes/allusions to the Jesus tradition is just what we would expect" (1994, pp. 177–78).

This argument assumes very substantial Christological agreement between Paul and his addressees, whereas in fact, as we have seen, he was here very much at loggerheads with them and failed to invoke Jesus's authority on what were obviously controversial issues, such as keeping or not keeping the Jewish law. Even in Romans, addressed to Christians whom Paul had not himself missionized, there is no single direct citation of Jesus's teaching. Nor does Dunn explain why allusion and echo later cease to be relied upon, and the very opposite behaviour becomes standard. Why is it that epistles, written like Paul's to Christian communities but a generation or more later—when the traditions underlying the synoptics (if not they themselves) were widely available—do explicitly appeal to Jesus's authority on ethical matters in a way that is totally foreign to all earlier epistles (not only to the Paulines)?

It is instructive to compare Paul's extensive use of the OT with his quite minimal use of Jesus tradition. When he directs each one of us to "please his neighbour", since "Christ pleased not himself" (Rom. 15:2–3), he admits that he learned this from the OT quotation he gives here: "The reproaches of them that reproached thee fell upon me"—a verse from Psalm 69 which tells what treatment the faithful devotee of Yahweh must expect. The early church soon came to regard it as summing up Jesus's experiences during his ministry; but for Paul it probably indicated no more than the spirit of self-sacrifice in which Jesus went to his death, so that the reference would once again be as in so many other instances to this final sacrifice, not to supposed earlier incidents. Dunn regards this pericope of Rom. 15:1–5 as perhaps "the most striking" instance of Paul actually alluding to Jesus's life-style, yet has to allow that his appeal here is "primarily to Christ's denying himself by submission to the cross" (1994, pp. 168–69).

Any reader of Paul can see that all his important doctrines are buttressed by an appeal to the OT. But he very strikingly does not do what Matthew repeatedly does, namely cite it as foreshadowing incidents in Jesus's incarnate life, such as his virgin birth, his settling at Capernaum, his teaching in parables, his triumphal entry into Jerusalem, and his disciples' desertion of him at his arrest.[28] Paul shows no knowledge of such incidents, nor of John the Baptist, whose preaching was, according to all three synoptics, foretold in the OT, and whom both Matthew (11:11) and Luke represent as Jesus's forerunner and hence as greater than any ordinary mortal. Paul makes no mention of him because John the Baptists's preaching had in fact nothing to do with Jesus or Christianity (as is clear from what Josephus says of him: see below, p. 211). This is still discernible in Mark, where he preaches about the baptism of repentance which he himself administered (1:4); but Matthew has more strongly Christianized him, making him, for instance, voice the same message as does Jesus about the coming kingdom (Mt. 3:2=4:17). Paul uses the OT apropos of what really did concern him: namely to demonstrate that every Jew and every gentile is under the power of sin, that justification comes from faith in Jesus, not from keeping the Jewish law; that salvation is not for the Jews as a nation, but only for those who accept Christianity; and to support his views on predestination, and on the nature a Christian's body will have at his resurrection. He also appeals to these scriptures for guidance on problems of church order—to show, for instance, that women should cover their heads in church, and that unintelligible ecstatic utterance has an unsettling effect on the congregation. Most significantly of all, it is to the OT that he appeals when he gives ethical precepts: love your neighbour, leave retribution to God, give generously in a good cause, and so forth.[29] Thus in addressing Galatian Christians, who are inclined to "bite and devour" one another, he quotes "the law" (notwithstanding his own often fiercely critical attitude to it), i.e. Leviticus 19:18: "You shall love your neighbour as yourself" (Gal. 5:14–15). There is a degree of explicitness here that is totally lacking in any supposed echoes of the synoptic Jesus tradition. Yet the Christians addressed in these epistles were, on Dunn's hypothesis, "steeped in the language and thought forms" of the Jewish scriptures, and as familiar with them as with "the message of Jesus" (p. 177).

Dunn has certainly taken cognizance both of the problem posed by the earliest Christian references to Jesus, and of the inadequacy of the customary way of resolving it. But his own solution is not a viable alternative. One could strengthen it a little by questioning whether Paul's addressees knew the OT as well as Dunn, and many others, suppose, since many Christians in the Pauline congregations were former idolaters (1 Thess. 1:9; 1 Cor. 12:2; Gal. 4:8, etc.) and therefore gentiles, not Jews; and although they were obviously prepared to accept the OT as authoritative, they will nevertheless have needed to have it spelled out to them. One might also note that Paul uses the OT so much in Galatians because he is there opposing Judaizers who were trying to persuade gentile Christians to accept circumcision. The Judaizers will surely have quoted the OT for their purpose, and Paul will have needed to respond in the like manner. Nevertheless, not all the churches he addressed were primarily gentile ones: the Roman church clearly included many Jews; and it remains striking that his letters to churches which he himself had founded use the OT in a quite different way from the evangelists, and with so little regard to the Jesus tradition as represented in their gospels. Doubtless, Paul's primary reason for using the OT as much as he did was that, as a strictly orthodox Jew (Phil. 3:5), he had been brought up on it. Yet it remains undeniable that Christian writers obviously familiar with the Jesus tradition use it very differently.

D. THE PASTORAL EPISTLES AND THE PROBLEM OF PSEUDONYMITY

Within the NT, Jesus is said to have been brought before Pilate not only in the gospels and in Acts, but also in one of the three epistles which form a homogeneous group known as the Pastorals, namely 1 and 2 Timothy and Titus. These letters purport to have been written by Paul, but are widely regarded as being from a later hand, writing perhaps as late as the early second century. They share with the genuine Paulines the conception that Jesus existed before he was born on Earth; for they say that he came into the world and was manifested there (1 Tim. 1:15; 3:16), but that his grace had already been given to us "from all eternity" (2 Tim. 1:9). Nothing more is said of his earthly life apart from the fact that he "witnessed the good confession before Pontius Pilate" (1 Tim. 6:13), but this suffices to give his life a historical setting that is totally lacking in the undoubtedly genuine letters of Paul. The Pastorals agree with these latter in focusing on Jesus's death as redeeming sinners (Titus 2:14)—there is no suggestion that he taught or healed disease—and it seems that they do so in order to encourage Christians to face unflinchingly the possibility of persecution from state authorities. Certainly, endurance in the face of it is a major theme of 2 Timothy, whose readers are told that "all that would live godly in Christ Jesus shall suffer persecution" (3:12).

Doubts about the authenticity of the Pastorals began to be raised at the beginning of the nineteenth century, and now even some Catholic commentators are among the many who regard them as pseudonymous.[30] Even the hypothesis that some genuine Pauline fragments are included in them is now seldom entertained.[31] But although the phenomenon of pseudonymity is well attested in the NT apocrypha, and has been cogently argued in the case of numerous canonical epistles, the whole idea that canonical writings could have originated in such a way is naturally repugnant in some quarters, and there are still numerous defenders of the view that the Pastorals are genuinely Pauline. The most recent such defence I have seen is the elaborate 1992 commentary by G.W. Knight.

As it is important to my purpose to argue the case for a late dating of the Pastorals and so for regarding the linking of Jesus with Pilate as a definitely post-Pauline development in Christology, I will set out the relevant evidence under twelve heads.

1. Pauline letters begin to be quoted by later writers from ca. A.D. 95, but there is no certain allusion to the Pastorals until some eighty years later, after which they are quoted regularly.[32] Knight is simply displaying the usual misplaced confidence of defenders of the faith when he declares that the Pastorals "were known and regarded as Pauline in the early church" (1992, p. 13).

2. The oldest extant manuscript of Paul's collected letters (P^{46}, dated ca. A.D. 200) does not include the Pastorals, and there is not sufficient room for them on the few leaves missing from the end of this ancient codex.

3. The Paul of the real Paulines has to battle for recognition, but the Pastorals present him as an unquestioned authority and look back at him "through a haze of hero-worship" (Barrett 1963 p. 30). Defenders of their authenticity explain this discrepancy by saying that Paul wrote them late in his life. (2 Timothy is certainly written as his last will and testament.) If this is so, then Timothy and Titus are strangely portrayed in them. Both men are known from undoubtedly genuine Paulines as co-workers with Paul over years; yet in the Pastorals they are reduced to subordinates who have to be given the most elementary instructions. Timothy is even represented as still young and inexperienced ("let no man despise thy youth", 1 Tim. 4:12) who needs to be warned against "youthful passions" (2 Tim. 2:22) and told how to behave in church (1 Tim. 3:15). He is told to "follow after righteousness, faith, love and peace, with them that call on the Lord out of a pure heart" (2 Tim. 2:22). Titus has to be given equally elementary instructions about selecting clergy. These are not the sort of things the real Paul would have written to old and trusted colleagues. Altogether, it is not clear why Timothy is given so much written guidance, as Paul is only temporarily absent from him, will soon return (1 Tim. 3:14; 4:13), and in any case has already instructed him orally while they were still together (1:3ff). This, together with the elementary and unspecific form in which the exhortations are couched, suggests that these writings were really meant not for him and for Titus, but for the churches in the areas to which they were sent. Their purpose is to show what is required of one who is to occupy a position of leadership in the church, and the two most prominent of Paul's fellow missionaries seemed to the pseudonymous author the most suitable persons to select as addressees for such rulings. The way in which Paul has here become the model authority, authorizing and validating the traditional faith, is paralleled in apocryphal material such as the epistle to the Laodiceans, purporting to come from him, and the Acts of Paul, which includes a letter supposedly written by him, known as 3 Corinthians.

4. The nature of the heresy combatted in the Pastorals does not in itself point to a post-Pauline date. What, however, is revealing is that in some passages 'Paul' is made to foretell that heresy will arise in the future, while other passages betray that it is already very much present in the author's situation. Thus at 2 Tim. 3:1–5 he writes of sinners (within Christianity) who will come "in the last days" and gives a catalogue of their vices. But from the end of verse 5 he slips into the present tense, describing present opponents and apparently equating them with the sinners of the previous verses, so that there results an unpleasant picture of church life:

> (1) In the last days grievous times shall come. (2) For men shall be lovers of self, lovers of money, boastful [etc. etc.] . . . (5) . . . From these also turn away, (6) for of these are they that creep into houses, and take captive silly women laden with sins, led away by divers lusts . . .

We find the same confusion between future and present in 1 Timothy where 4:1 predicts that "in later times some shall fall away from the faith". The usual abuse follows ("the hypocrisy of men that speak lies"); and the false teaching will include a prohibition of marriage and commands "to abstain from meats". But 1:3ff shows that doctrinal error is very much in evidence already: some "have turned away from faith unfeigned" to "vain talking"; and Timothy is to avoid such "godless chatter" (6:20).

The real Paul was not concerned with a future generation, but expected the end to come in his lifetime. The author of the Pastorals poses as Paul so as to invoke his authority to put existing post-Pauline heresy down. He clearly supposed that he himself was living in 'the last days' about which he made Paul prophesy. But for him, these 'last days' are going to last a considerable time, and he uses the phrase as it is used, for instance, in most manuscripts of Acts 2:17, where the overall context of the whole book shows that it must refer to an extended period during which the Spirit is active in the church, and not to an end that is imminent. Acts has abandoned any suggestion of imminence, and some of the traditions on which it drew may well have been known to the author of the Pastorals, who (at 2 Tim. 3:10–12) makes 'Paul' recall his "fortitude and suffering" at (Pisidian) Antioch, Iconium, and Lystra. This corresponds to the narrative of Acts 13:14ff and 14:1ff, where Paul's successive experiences at these three places are recorded.

5. It is also noteworthy that the author of the Pastorals opposes heretics not, as Paul had done, by confronting them with the preaching about Christ, but simply by saying that there is a traditional teaching, from which they have deviated, but which must be maintained: Timothy is to "guard" what has been "committed" to him (1 Tim. 6:20; compare 2 Tim. 1:14); he is in turn to commit what Paul has taught him "to faithful men who shall be able to teach others also" (2 Tim. 2:2). The only passage in the Pastorals which meets the false teachers with argument is 1 Tim. 4:1–5, where their hostility to marriage and their abstinence from certain foods is countered with the doctrine that everything created by God is good. For the rest, the author merely abuses the heretics. In a typical passage they are said to be unruly, vain talkers and deceivers, teaching error "for filthy lucre's sake", liars, evil beasts, idle gluttons, abominable, disobedient and "unto every good work reprobate" (Titus 1:10–16)—another charming picture of church life. It is in this epistle that the word 'heretic' first occurs in the sense of 'misbelievers' (3:10), with all the violent emotional reaction against deviance that was to become such a notable feature of later Christian tradition. Paul himself was certainly capable of abuse. Knight, who at this point (p. 26) says nothing about abuse in the Pastorals, but speaks instead of their "warnings and appeals" concerning false teaching, is glad to point to what he calls the "rather strong language" of the genuine Pauline Philippians 3, where Paul's Christian opponents figure as "dogs", with "their belly" as their God. Nevertheless, for the real Paul, abuse was not a *substitute* for argument.

As, then, the Pastorals appeal to largely unspecified traditional teaching, and do little more than abuse heresy, they make it hard for us to see very clearly in any detail what the author understood by either. Nevertheless, this very vagueness will have facilitated their eventual acceptance into the canon: letters which endorsed 'sound teaching' and condemned 'heresy', without tying themselves down to anything much that is specifically meant, will have been welcome to churches fighting against any kind of deviation from their own teaching.

To give only vague indications of opposing teachers' views, and to denounce such people as greedy deceivers and worse, was apparently a convention among Hellenistic philosophers (Philo, Dio Chrysostom, and others) and served the purpose of strengthening a writer's own claim to impart genuine wisdom. The suggestion has been made that the author of the Pastorals was simply following this practice of stereotyping other teachers, and was not polemicizing against a specific group of opponents (Details in Margaret Davies, 1996b, pp. 89–99). It is obviously true that much of his abuse is no more than rhetorical exaggeration—one really cannot believe that church life was as bad as he paints it—yet his complaint that the false teachers forbid marriage, enjoin abstinence from certain foods, and also that they have wrong ideas about resurrection (2 Tim. 2:18), does indicate that for all his vagueness, he was targeting specific opponents and was not just employing a literary convention.

6. The banality of the Pastorals is quite un-Pauline. Most of their moral teaching, says Houlden, is "the commonplace ethics of the Hellenistic world of the period", and it is hard to believe that Paul would "drop so many of his central ideas" and "take on so many of the more flatly conventional concepts of the period" (1976, pp. 31, 32). I know that even Shakespeare wrote passages of which numerous of his contemporaries would have been capable, and which critics have distinguished from passages on which his reputation genuinely rests. But the banality of the Pastorals is consistent and sustained. Their author purveys other men's theology and tries (not altogether successfully) to make a consistent whole of what he took from disparate sources. His greatest objection to the teachers he condemns is that they were original, and nearly all his own doctrinal statements have been held to be quotations.[33] Unlike Paul—who, as we saw, believed Jesus's second coming, his parousia, to be imminent—he is propounding an ethic by which Christians can live decently and properly in a continuing world. The Pastorals so strongly emphasize the civil virtues that editors have called these letters 'bourgeois'.

One aspect of this Christianity of good citizenship is advocacy of marriage, of running an orderly household and of bringing up children in the faith. Margaret Davies, in her two very thorough studies of the Pastorals and of recent discussion of them, has contrasted this teaching with that of the genuine Paulines, noting that 1 Corinthians 7 recommends that people who have received a charisma from God should remain unmarried and so be free to devote themselves to the affairs of the Lord, whereas the Pastorals imply that church leaders should be family men and celibacy is advocated only for elderly widows (1996b, pp. 27, 95, 102).

7. The Pastorals do use words that were important to the real Paul, but when they do so, the Pauline doctrine is "nearly always lost—transposed into a new key, deprived of its cutting edge" (Houlden, p. 28). A good example is what is said of 'the law', which in 1 Timothy is no more than something that guarantees order in society by holding sinners and criminals in check. There is no suggestion of Paul's view that, in spite of the salvific role that had been reserved for it in God's plan, the law cannot be fulfilled, leads to sin and convicts humanity of sin. The author of the Pastorals seems to be trying to strike a balance between contradictory statements that Paul had made. He knew Paul's declaration that the law was "good" (Rom. 7:12 and 16), but knew too that Paul had spoken very critically of it—"Christ is the end of the law" (Rom. 10:4)—and so he combined these two positions by saying that the law is good if used "lawfully" (1 Tim. 1:8), that is, for putting down criminals (a list of vices follows), and that it is not laid down for the just and righteous at all. He obviously did not need to wrestle, as the real Paul had done, with the question of whether gentile Christians needed to keep the Jewish law. This in itself suggests that he was writing in a situation where Judaizers were no longer threatening the peace of the church, and where the place of gentiles in it had become comfortably assured.

8. Paul's argument at Rom. 9:6–29 implies the predestinarian view that God selected some persons for salvation and others for damnation even before they were born, and that his decision stands irrespective of how well or badly they behave in their lifetime. Such thinking tends to arise in a minority group unsuccessfully preaching to and in conflict with a majority. It consoles this minority with the assurance that God himself has precluded any success to their efforts and gives them the idea of an elect predestined to salvation

to explain why they alone can see the light. At the same time potential converts need to be assured that every individual can be saved by harbouring correct religious beliefs and behaving morally; hence this doctrine is also represented in the same epistle (Rom. 9:30–10:21). The contradiction between these two standpoints is seldom sensed, and hence occurs in the OT, in the Qumran scrolls, and in the Koran, as well as in numerous Christian writings.[34] What is very noticeable, however, is that the predestinarian element in Paul's teaching is eliminated in the Pastorals, where the author uses Pauline language—the very language which the real Paul had used in advocating predestination—in order to state the contrary, more optimistic doctrine (Compare Rom. 9:19–24 with 2 Tim. 2:20–21). For the Pastorals, "God willeth that all men should be saved" (1 Tim. 2:4).

9. Although the Pastorals insist that the faithful Christian must expect to reproduce in his own life the sufferings of Jesus (2 Tim. 2:10–12), they never mention that he died by crucifixion—not even when stating his witness before Pilate—whereas this forms the basis of much of what the real Paul says, and is central in 1 Corinthians, Galatians, Philippians, and Colossians. Hanson finds the total absence of any reference to the cross of Christ in the Pastorals "really astonishing" and in itself enough to show that Paul did not write them: "One cannot help suspecting that Paul's profound doctrine of the cross was simply too deep for [this] author" (1982, p. 42). Knight (p. 33) weakly defends its absence by noting that the word 'cross' is absent from some genuine Paulines, such as Romans and 2 Corinthians. But the theology of the cross is still present there: "Knowing this, that our old man was crucified with him, that the body of sin might be done away . . ." (Rom. 6:6); "for he was crucified through weakness, yet he liveth through the power of God"; hence "we also are weak in him, but we shall live with him . . ." (2 Cor. 13:4).

10. A marked difference between the genuine Paulines and the Pastorals is the ordered structuring of the church in the latter. Beare's very informative 1955 article gives the details. Paul's genuine letters (apart from the brief Philemon) are addressed to whole communities: "To the churches in Galatia"; "To the church

of God which is at Corinth, with all the saints who are in the whole of Achaia". He does not, within the body of these epistles, turn to any group of leaders, as is done, for instance, in the post-Pauline 1 Peter 5:1: "The elders among you I exhort". Philippians, however, is abnormal in that it is addressed "to all the saints in Jesus Christ who are at Philippi, with the overseers (*episkopoi*) and deacons". *Episkopoi* has come to be rendered as 'bishops', but the Greek means no more than persons with authority to oversee or inspect. They are here certainly persons of some prominence in the congregation, but whether they acquired their prominence by appointment to an office is questionable. (It is interesting that, here in Philippians, *episkopoi* is used in the plural, not, as in the Pastorals, in the singular, where it occurs with detailed itemization of the duties and qualities which the person so designated must possess.) The only ministry of office to which the real Paul clearly and repeatedly refers is that of the apostle—a title he gives to himself and to some few others. He does not apply any other title to any particular individual. Titus he calls "my brother", "my partner and fellow worker in your service" (2 Cor. 2:13; 8:23); Timothy is "our brother and God's minister in the gospel" (1 Thess. 3:2). Paul seldom mentions officers of the congregation at all, and when he does so he usually speaks of their functions—"he who teaches" (Gal. 6:6; cf. Rom. 12:7), and "those labouring among you and leading you in the Lord" (1 Thess. 5:12). This does not suggest that they had established titles. At 1 Cor. 16:15–16 he mentions the initial converts in Achaia, says they have dedicated themselves to "the service of the saints", and urges the churches he is addressing "to be in subjection to such [persons], and to everyone that helpeth in the work and laboureth"; i.e. they are worthy of the respect and loyalty of those whom they are serving.

1 Corinthians 12 details the different "spiritual gifts" possessed by different members of the congregation. In the wording of the Revised Standard Version (RSV), some are prophets, others miracle workers, healers, helpers or administrators; others speak in tongues, and yet others interpret such speech. All these capacities are exercised not in virtue of appointment to an office, but as a result of the prompting of the Spirit. 1 Cor. 14:26–33 shows that in

these Pauline congregations anyone can take the floor with a psalm, a teaching, a revelation, or a prophecy with which to edify the company. There are no officers to prevent a disorderly scramble at the common meal; for the only advice Paul gives to obviate such a thing is "wait for one another" (1 Cor. 11:33). Such informal arrangements were feasible in these Pauline churches, as they seem to have consisted of groups small enough to meet in the house of one of the richer members: Rom. 16:3–5 mentions the church that is in the house of Prisca and Aquila (cf. 1 Cor. 16:19); at Rom. 16:23 Gaius is said to have hosted a whole church; and Coloss. 4:15 mentions another house church. One gets the impression that the influential persons at such gatherings were not appointed to an office, but acquired what leadership they had because of their zeal and ability.

By the time the Pastorals were written, the freedom which the variously spiritually endowed persons had enjoyed in the Pauline churches to perform their various works had led some to preach a wisdom or *gnōsis* of their own, stigmatized in these letters as "godless chatter". We saw how fiercely such persons are here reviled, and that, to countervail them, the author stresses the need to "guard" the apostolic doctrine and keep it free from innovations. This is to be done by a "presbyterion", a body of elders who ordain ministers "with the laying on of . . . hands" (1 Tim. 4:14). Knight allows (p. 31) that the "laying of hands on those set apart to serve" is not mentioned in any letters ascribed to Paul other than the Pastorals; but he thinks to vindicate the practice as early by appealing to Acts 13:2–4: "The Holy Ghost said, Separate me Barnabas and Saul for the work whereunto I have called them. Then, when they had . . . laid their hands on them, they sent them away". This is a good example of the need to adduce this late work if the Pastorals are to be accepted as Pauline. The term elder (presbyter), used of Christian ministers in Acts, in the Pastorals and in other post-Pauline epistles (James, 1 Peter), is not used at all in the genuine Paulines. Acts 14:23 goes so far as to represent Paul as appointing elders in his churches—an example of the way Acts retrojects later developments into this early period.

The Pastorals sometimes equate the (un-Pauline) term

'elder' with *episkopos,* as at Titus 1:5ff, where—in the rendering of the NEB—Titus is to appoint *"elders* in each town", and in doing so is to "observe the tests" which Paul prescribed, since, "as God's steward, a *bishop* must be a man of unimpeachable character" (italics added). Commentators believe that the two terms originated independently ('elders' probably in the Judaean and 'overseers' (bishops) in the Pauline churches) but that, by the time of the Pastorals, they were both accepted as designating the same office. They are equated in other Christian documents of the late first or early second century, such as the later chapters of 1 Clement, and Acts 20:17–18 and 28, where Paul is represented as summoning the presbyters of the church of Ephesus and addressing them as "bishops".

Timothy and Titus themselves are represented as having very considerable authority. Timothy can ensure that elders who rule well receive double pay (1 Tim. 5:17). He can ordain whom he wishes, but with due care in selecting suitable persons ("lay hands hastily on no man", 1 Tim. 5:22; cf. 2 Tim. 2:2). The author spells out in detail the qualities required:

> The bishop must be without reproach, the husband of one wife, temperate, soberminded, orderly, given to hospitality, apt to teach, no brawler, no striker, but gentle, not contentious, no lover of money, one that ruleth well his own house, having his children in subjection with all gravity . . . , not a novice. (1 Tim. 3:2–6. Titus 1:7–11 gives a similar specification.)

The admonition here to gentleness and avoidance of contention fits ill with the savage abuse that the author heaps upon dissidents. What is, however, clear from all this is that "we have reached a time when the Church is setting a high value on stable and peaceful congregational life, and therefore values highly the leadership which will perpetuate it" (Houlden, p. 74). The very fact that these letters are addressed to individuals, not (as are the genuine Paulines) to congregations, shows the importance which 'bishops' had achieved. Margaret Davies points to numerous passages in the undoubtedly genuine Paulines which require the whole community to take responsibility for matters of law and order, whereas the Pastorals never do this (1996b, p. 69). They are concerned that there should be a supply of reliable and authoritative teachers to guard and communicate a fixed deposit of credal truth and to exemplify proper behaviour.

The Pastorals, then, testify to the existence in their time of a regular ordained ministry, whereas the real Paulines, instead of stressing authority, are concerned to allow the whole congregation direct contact with the Spirit. Against this, Tyler, for example, claims that the structure and organization of the early church cannot be readily ascertained from the NT: "there is considerable flexibility regarding the ministry" and "considerable uncertainty about the 'hierarchy'", so that "clear-cut distinctions are not easily maintained" (pp. 77–78). But the distinction between Paulines and Pastorals in the matter of elders is perfectly clear, and can be blurred only by introducing the evidence of Acts. It is also noteworthy that the non-Pauline but early epistle to the Hebrews, like the genuine Paulines, shows no development of an institutional ministry, but refers the community it addresses only to "your leaders" (13:17).

A further feature of church organization in the Pastorals that is unknown to the genuine Paulines, but documented in early second-century writings (epistles of Ignatius and of Polycarp) is the existence of an order of widows (1 Tim. 5:3–16). They must fulfil certain conditions to be "enrolled" and perform certain duties in return for the church's care.

It is because so much in these letters consists of instructions about ordering the beliefs and life of the church that they have come to be known as 'Pastoral'; and their emphasis on these matters makes them comparable to such later compositions as the Didache and the Apostolic Constitutions, which supposedly originated from apostles, but really developed over time as community manuals.

11. The chronology the Pastorals require cannot be fitted into what we know of Paul's life from the other letters ascribed to him, nor even from Acts. A preferred apologetic way of resolving this problem is by supposing that he wrote the Pastorals after his Roman captivity mentioned at the end of Acts. Certainly, unless recourse is made to what Hanson (p. 16) calls "some desperate expedients", it has to be argued that, if Paul did write them, his

imprisonment recorded at the end of Acts was not terminated by his execution, but by release, after which he missionized (for the first time) in Crete, as presupposed in the letter to Titus, and (anew) at Ephesus, as implied by 1 Timothy. In 2 Timothy he is again in prison (1:8; 2:9), in Rome (1:16–17), and is conscious that his end is very near (4:6ff).

That Paul wrote this second letter to Timothy during a Roman imprisonment subsequent to the one recorded in Acts was first cited—in the fourth century, and as "tradition"—by Eusebius (*Ecclesiastical History*, ii, 22). Knight nevertheless speaks (p. 22) of "strong evidence" for this second captivity, which Kümmel more appropriately calls "an ungrounded construct" (1975, p. 378). Certainly, in the understanding of the author of Acts, Paul did not return to his churches in the east after the imprisonment with which the work concludes; for he makes Paul, on his way to Jerusalem (and thence as a prisoner to Rome) tell the elders of Ephesus that they will never see his face again (Acts 20:25. I have already noted the anachronism of confronting Paul with 'elders'). This statement is underlined by stressing (verse 38) the grief it caused them (see above, p. 31). What little evidence there is for further missionizing after the situation at the end of Acts has Paul going not eastwards but westwards from Rome.[35]

12. Finally, there is the language of the Pastorals. Margaret Davies has noted that, although these letters are short, they "exhibit a remarkably large number of words which are found nowhere else in the New Testament, and even more which are found nowhere else in the Paulines". She adds that their style and vocabulary "represent a higher form of koine Greek", evidenced in both pagan and Jewish writers of the first and second centuries, but certainly not in the undoubtedly genuine Paulines. If Paul nevertheless wrote them, he must, after writing his other letters, have made a concentrated study of Hellenistic literature which would have required both strong motive and considerable leisure. Similarities in language and style between Acts and the Pastorals suggest that the two authors shared the same kind of Hellenistic education—not that the author of Acts was with Paul in Rome;[36] for Acts shows no knowledge of Paul's letters, never suggests that he wrote any,

and—in spite of detailing his missionary journeys—knows nothing of a mission in Crete. Titus, whom according to the Pastorals he left behind to consolidate his mission there, is never mentioned in Acts.[37]

Kenny's 1986 study of quantifiable features of style of the letters ascribed to Paul in the canon concentrates not on vocabulary (apart from the use of adjectives), but on the various types of particles, conjunctions, favoured prepositions, and favoured grammatical cases governed by them. He finds that, from these tests, Titus, but not the other two Pastorals, comes out "under suspicion" of being non-Pauline. This does not make all three of these letters genuinely Pauline; for, he adds, "style, like a signature, can be voluntarily varied by an author and impressively copied by a forger" (pp. 98, 120–21).

Now that I have reviewed the considerable evidence for regarding the Pastorals as post-Pauline, it is worth noting that the confrontation between Jesus and Pilate mentioned in 1 Timothy is correlated with an attitude to governing authorities that is decidedly less positive than that advocated in early Christian documents which do not bring the two men into contact with each other. Paul had declared that the authorities punish only wrongdoers (Rom. 13:1–7). 1 Peter 2:13–14 takes the same view: governors are sent by the emperor "to punish those who do wrong and to praise those who do right". Neither writer links Jesus with Pilate, and, writing what I have just quoted of them, they surely cannot have believed that their Jesus had been condemned—and that recently—by a Roman governor. When, however, we reach 1 Timothy, where Pilate is introduced and where persecution is threatening, we find enthusiasm for governors correspondingly muted. Timothy is to see that intercession be made "for all that are in high places, that we may lead a tranquil and quiet life" (2:1–2).

The Pastorals are important for my overall view of Christian origins; for if it could be shown that Paul wrote them, my thesis that he had no knowledge that Jesus appeared in court before Pontius Pilate could not be sustained. But I do not find that what is urged in support of Pauline authorship puts me here seriously at risk. Traditionalists all too often do not find it necessary to argue the matter at all. R.H. Fuller, himself an Anglican priest, justly complained that "conservative evangelical" scholars (he instanced G.E. Ladd) can treat the Pastorals as Pauline "without argument" (1994, p. 149). And what conservative theological handbooks have to say on the subject does not command respect. For instance, Hawthorne's 1993 *Dictionary of Paul and His Letters*, includes an article by E.E. Ellis which stamps regarding the Pastorals as pseudepigraphic as nothing better than nineteenth-century beholdenness to what is now obsolete philosophy. F.C. Baur, it is said, denied that they were by Paul because of "his Hegelian reconstruction of early Christian history"—as if he had not relied on the empirical evidence of the relevant historical documents, but had deduced supposedly historical 'facts' from arbitrary philosophical principles! His followers, we are told, likewise held that "the earliest congregations had no structured ministries"; and it is implied that they took this view not because their study of the undoubtedly genuine Pauline letters led them to it, but because "deep in their consciousness" were embedded "theories of egalitarianism, of historical and social progress, and of biological evolution" (pp. 659–660). It is regularly implied in such writing that only scholars who support traditional Christian views are free from absurd bias. Knight's commentary is truly scholarly compared with this, but, as I have indicated, is arbitrary in some of its defensive judgements, and has to rely heavily on Acts. We saw that even Catholic scholars have now begun to impugn the authenticity of the Pastorals. This is significant, as Catholics have been especially attached to these letters as being among those NT books which insist on the importance of "guarding" the traditional faith—something which is not pressed in the genuine Paulines favoured by the Reformation churches. Catholic scholarship has valued the Pastorals as by Paul also because they would then indicate that an ordained ministry was a feature of the primitive church.

There is admittedly no unanimous verdict concerning the Pauline authorship of the Pastorals, but there is certainly a negative majority one. At any rate, Knight allows that, since the late nineteenth century, "repudiation of the Pauline authority of the Pastorals has become a mark of critical orthodoxy" (p. 21).

Characteristically for conservative NT scholarship, this statement, while conceding that there is a majority against some traditional view, manages to taint the critical view with an opprobrium of blind conformity to a trend.

The Pastorals also confront us with the wider issue of pseudonymity in NT epistles such as other pseudo-Paulines, and also the epistles 1 and 2 Peter, James, and Jude. In an article that has become classic, Aland accounted for the origin of the earlier among these by pointing to the spirit-inspired 'prophets' who came forward with revelations. We saw how, in the Pauline communities, they spoke in the name of the risen Lord. Ignatius of Antioch, writing a full fifty years later to Philadelphian Christians, could still call (in his chapter 7) disclosures he himself had made to them the preaching of the Spirit itself, "the very voice of God". The Spirit could also move such preachers to speak in the name of Paul or Peter or some other apostle deemed important by their congregation. But instead of just speaking in an apostle's name, they might read out a letter from him in the service of worship. There was no deception: the congregation knew that the address had been written by the person reading it out, but they supposed, as he himself did, that he had received its substance through the Spirit from the apostle. What they were hearing was simply a written version of the kind of thing they were accustomed to hearing in any congregational meeting. What had happened, says Aland, was "nothing but the shift of the message from the spoken to the written word". In this change, it would have been irrelevant, even misleading, to name the instrument, the person through whom the message was delivered to the community, for he was not the real author. Hence when early pseudonymous writings of the NT claimed the authorship of the most prominent apostles, this "was not a skilful trick of the so-called fakers in order to guarantee the highest possible reputation and the widest possible circulation for their work, but the logical conclusion of the presupposition that the Spirit himself was the author" (1961, pp. 44–45).

Aland goes on to say that, by the time the Pastorals and 2 Peter were written, the situation had, however, changed. Manifestations of the Spirit were gradually losing impetus, except within gnostic forms of Christianity. This change may have been partly due to the dampening of the excitement that had gone with earlier expectations of Jesus's imminent return to Earth. With the abating of the prophetic impulse there arose what Aland calls "the awareness of history". The church was beginning "carefully to distinguish between the apostolic past and the present. . . . It was no longer possible by means of Spirit-possession to throw a bridge across the generations and to speak as the mouth of an apostle" (p. 47). Writings which nevertheless continued to be published under the name of an apostle were at this stage conscious fictions: the author put himself "back into the time of the apostles in order to use them and claim their authority for the demands of the present by a more or less successful imitation of their way of thinking and writing" (p. 48). The Pastorals even attempt to represent the circumstances in which the historical Paul supposedly lived: "The information about the sojourn of the various co-workers in the fourth chapter of 2 Timothy, the first trial of Paul, the instructions for the addressees, as well as the end of the epistle to Titus evince such a thorough knowledge, such a simulated perspective, and such a reconstruction of Paul's personal affairs, that we can hardly avoid assuming an intended forgery" (p. 46).

In sum, early Christian literature includes real letters (such as those by Paul, Ignatius, and Polycarp); spirit-inspired epistles such as 1 Peter; and deliberate forgeries. Much of the remaining material is anonymous, including the synoptic gospels and Acts, but it was not long before their authority came to be based on the supposed fact that their authors were 'apostles' (or their close associates), understood as named persons who had been directly or indirectly closely associated with the historical Jesus.

iii. Conclusion: The Origins and Development of Christology

It really beggars belief that Paul, anxious as he was to inculcate numerous ethical principles (such as 'judge not' and 'practise forgiveness'), knew that Jesus had taught them, yet did not appeal to his authority on such matters. Nor is it believable that both Paul and the Christians who strongly opposed him in an ill-tempered quarrel on the question of obeying or ignoring the Jewish food laws knew yet ignored rulings which, according to the gospels, Jesus had given on this matter. Nor is it plausible that Paul's convictions on the second coming left him indifferent to eschatological statements supposedly made by Jesus which eventually came to be recorded in the gospels. Nor can I accept that what Jesus had supposedly said on all such fundamental issues was of no interest to all other early epistle writers either, or simply presupposed by them as known to their readers. It will not do to say that allusions to these matters cannot be expected in epistles; for those written late enough to have known traditions which in due course found their way into the gospels do allude to them. I have instanced the way in which the Pastoral letter 1 Timothy and the letters of Ignatius of Antioch give the Passion the historical setting which the gospels accord it. Ignatius also mentions the virgin birth and the baptism by John; 2 Peter alludes to the transfiguration, and Ignatius and the author of 1 Clement record a significant portion of the teaching. Stanton, in his latest book, frankly calls it "baffling" that Paul fails to "refer more frequently and at greater length to the actions and teaching of Jesus", particularly at points where "he might well have clinched his argument by doing so". Stanton is aware that other epistles present us with "similar problems" (1995, p. 131). But many writers fail to recognize these problems, and go straight to the gospels for their portraits of Jesus. Typical is Markus Bockmuehl, Cambridge lecturer in Divinity, who mentions the epistles as supplying "a small and somewhat uncontrolled sampling of the ways in which tradi- tions about Jesus were used in first-century Christian discourse", and who then turns immediately "to the four canonical gospels for the fullest picture" (1994, p. 17).

The silences of these early epistles are 'baffling' only if it is assumed that their Jesus is the same person as the Jesus of the gospels. The ministry of the latter is, as we shall see, arguably traceable to the career of an itinerant Galilean preacher of the opening decades of the first century; but the Pauline Jesus seems to have a different origin. He may have been to some extent modelled on gods of pagan mystery religions who died and were resurrected, but he clearly owes much more to a particular early Christian interpretation of Jewish Wisdom traditions, as I will now try to explain (with some unavoidable overlap with what I have said on this subject in *The Jesus Legend*).

It is not in dispute that many religious ideas among Jews and early Christians originated as a result of musing on and extracting hidden meanings from existing sacred and semi-sacred texts. Paul says that "whatever was written in former days"—he has sacred writings in mind—"was written for our instruction" (Rom. 15:4). Now there was an ancient Wisdom myth which explained the underlying goodness of creation and also the undeniable evil in it by combining two ideas: that a Wisdom figure stood at God's side and participated as he created the world (Proverbs 8:22–31), and that when Wisdom sought an abode on Earth, mankind refused to accept her, forcing her to wander from one place to another, until finally in despair she returned to heaven:

> Wisdom found no place where she might dwell. Then a dwelling-place was assigned to her in the heavens. Wisdom went forth to make her dwelling among the children of men, and found no dwelling-place. Wisdom returned to her place and took her seat among the angels. (1 Enoch 42:1–2)

An alternative and less pessimistic version of the myth is given in Ecclesiasticus. Wisdom is still personified and represented as God's agent in creation. She says: "I am the word which was spoken by the Most High" (24:3), alluding to the opening chapters of Genesis where God creates the universe by speaking words of command ("Let there be light", etc.). And she still traverses the whole Earth, seeking an abode. But in this version the creator finally gives her a home in Israel, where she lives as the Torah, "the covenant-book of God Most High, the law which Moses enacted to be the heritage of the assemblies of Jacob" (24:23).

For Philo, the Jewish sage of Alexandria who died around A.D. 50, Wisdom was almost identical with the 'word', the 'Logos', the highest of God's 'powers' which functioned now independently of him, now as aspects of him. Wisdom is, in Greek, feminine, while Logos is masculine. How, then, can the two be equated? Philo gave what R.M. Grant calls a "vigorously sexist" explanation: although Wisdom's name is feminine, her nature is masculine; "she is subordinate to the male Father as 'the feminine always comes short of the male and is less than it'" (Grant 1990, p. 32, quoting Philo).

Christian theologians took up this idea. Origen said: "We should not imagine that, because of the feminine name, wisdom and righteousness are feminine in their being". Grant quotes this (p. 33) and comments: the existence of this gender question may help to explain why the masculine word 'Logos' came to be preferred as a designation of the Wisdom figure who is so close to God. Already in the fourth gospel Jesus figures as the Logos.

Admittedly, although Philo could speak of the Logos in personal terms (for example as Son, Man, High Priest), he nevertheless regarded it not as a person but as some kind of expression of the mind of God. But, as Talbert has shown, he was allegorizing a myth, already current in Alexandrian Judaism, in which a heavenly redeemer figure, described as Logos or Wisdom among other terms, certainly did figure as a person. From Talbert's evidence (1976, pp. 421ff), there can be no doubt that a myth of such a "figure who descended and ascended in the course of his/her saving work existed in pre-Christian Judaism alongside first- and second-century Christianity" (p. 430).

The influence of Jewish Wisdom literature on Paul is undeniable: statements made about Wisdom in this literature are made of Jesus in the Pauline letters. At 1 Cor. 1:24 Paul actually calls Christ "the power of God and the Wisdom of God"; and Paul's Jesus, like the Jewish Wisdom figure, sought acceptance on Earth, but was rejected, and then returned to heaven. At Coloss. 2:3 we read of "Christ in whom are hid all the treasures of wisdom and knowledge". Like Wisdom, he assisted God in the creation of all things (1 Cor. 8:6). This idea is spelled out in the Christological hymn of Coloss. 1:15–20 (I quote Dunn's rendering):

> He is the image of the invisible God, the first born of all creation;
> For in him were created all things in heaven and on earth. . . .
> All things were created through him and to him.
> He is before all things,
> and in him all things hold together.

To take these Jewish and Christian statements as meant literally would be to commit both religions to a good deal of mythology, and so is understandably resisted. Dunn, who as we saw (above p. 49) denies that Paul thought of Jesus as pre-existing in heaven before his birth on Earth, interprets the Colossian verse "in him were created all things" as possibly "simply the writer's way of saying that Christ now reveals the character of the power behind the world" (1989, p. 190). For Dunn, Paul thought of Christ as God's Wisdom in the sense of the man who fulfilled God's predetermined plan of salvation (p. 178, with reference to 1 Cor. 2:7). Jesus's pre-existence is thus attenuated to an existence before his birth as an idea in God's mind. Likewise, Dunn thinks it unlikely that the Jewish statements represent Wisdom as a divine agent, distinct from God himself. They must, he says, be interpreted within the context of Jewish monotheism, and when they are set within this context, there is no clear indication that they have "gone beyond vivid personification"; "The Wisdom passages are simply ways of describing Yahweh's wise creation and purpose" (pp. 170, 174). Dunn recognizes, as we saw, that his views on these issues have met with severe criticism from colleagues, although some are understandably "grateful" to him—the word is John Macquarrie's (1990, p. 58)—for his attempts to free the sources from obviously mythological ideas. Here it is sufficient to observe that Jewish statements which may have been originally merely "some form of poetic hyperbole" (Dunn, p. 167) can readily have been taken more literally in the course of time. When Ecclesiasticus (24:8) speaks of Wisdom "setting up its tent" on Earth, this could easily have been taken to mean that Wisdom had been incarnated, since 'house of the tent' or simply 'tent' is used (even in the NT at 2 Cor. 5:1 and 4) in the sense of man's earthly existence. Jewish monotheism did not stop Jews from speculating about semi-divine figures any more than Christian monotheism has prevented Christians from seeing Jesus as God.

Another aspect of pre-Christian Jewish Wisdom literature was the genre known as the 'wisdom tale' according to which the righteous man—no particular person is meant—will be persecuted but vindicated post mortem. In the Wisdom of Solomon his enemies have him condemned to "a shameful death" (2:20), but he then confronts them as their judge in heaven, where he is "counted among the sons of God". Cognate is the martyrological book 2 Maccabees, with its belief in the resurrection of the faithful; and 4 Maccabees adds to this the idea that someone steadfast in the faith unto martyrdom can benefit others because God will regard his death as a "ransom" for their lives, as an expiation for their sins (6:28–29; 17:21–22). That a martyr's death could function as an atoning sacrifice, to be followed by his immortality, was, then, a not unfamiliar idea in Paul's Hellenistic environment. Furthermore, Paul must have known of historical crucifixions of holy Jews in the second and first centuries B.C. which made a strong enough impression on the Jewish world to be repeatedly alluded to (see above, p. 57); and such knowledge could well have seemed to him to confirm what the Wisdom literature was telling him, namely that a pre-existent personage had come to Earth as a man to suffer a shameful death there.

Paul's are not the only early epistles which describe Jesus in terms familiar from the Jewish Wisdom literature. The letter to the Hebrews likewise declares that the Son existed before the world, which God "created through him", and that he "reflects the glory of God" (1:2–3). Talbert notes that this term 'reflection' is used only here in the Bible, but is used of Wisdom in the Wisdom of Solomon, and of Logos in Philo. Hebrews 1:3 also speaks of the Son as "upholding the universe by the word of his power"—a concept and language found in Philo's discussion of the Logos (1976, p. 437). Talbert concludes that there can be little doubt that "the early Christian myth of a descending-ascending redeemer was taken over from Hellenistic Judaism" (p. 440).

It is, then, not surprising that the figure of Wisdom in the Jewish literature has occasioned some consternation among commentators. In John Day's 1995 symposium, Roland E. Murphy notes (p. 232) that "attitudes have ranged from embarrassment to condemnation". As examples he mentions G.E. Wright, who confessed in 1952 that "he did not know what to do with the wisdom literature in Old Testament theology", and H.D. Preuss, who in 1970 "found it dangerous to preach from these books".

The pagan environment of earliest Christianity also cannot have been unimportant. The classical scholar Dihle allows that many of the features of the pagan mystery cults found their way into Christianity (1971, p. 13). Some of these cults worshipped a saviour god who died a violent death and was then revived or resurrected. Osiris, for instance, is said in very ancient records to have been dismembered, reassembled by Isis and "rejuvenated", i.e. restored to life. Of course there are differences both between the various mystery religions and between them and Pauline Christianity. Yet the Osiris cult and the Eleusinian mysteries were part of Paul's background, and one does not expect a new religion to be absolutely identical with its antecedents. The parallels between some of the relevant Christian and pagan rites and doctrines were certainly close enough to have embarrassed second-century Christians. Justin Martyr, for instance, after describing the institution of the Lord's Supper, as narrated in the gospels, goes on to say: "Which the wicked devils have imitated in the mysteries of Mithra, commanding the same thing to be done. For bread and a cup of water are placed with certain incantation in the mystic rites of one who is being initiated." (*Apology*, I, 66. The Christian cultic meal sometimes consisted of bread and water: see *JEC*, p. 264.) He is not accusing the Mithraists of simply copying, but supposed that evil spirits anticipated Christian truths, as when he noted (in his *Dialogue with Trypho*, 70): "When I hear that Perseus was begotten of a virgin, I understand that the deceiving serpent counterfeited also this." Justin's theory is that the demons knew from the prophets that Christ was to come and what he would be like, and therefore devised such gods as Bacchus, Hercules, Asclepias, and Mithras to resemble him before his time, so that he would seem unimpressive when he did come. That the demons likewise anticipated Christian sacraments (baptism as well as eucharist) is a simple extension of this theory which, as Ramsey notes (1993, p. 200), was reiterated by later Christian writers. That the Lord's Supper existed before Christianity is clear from 1 Cor. 10:21, where Paul tells the Corinthian flock that they "cannot drink the cup of the Lord and the cup of devils", nor "partake of the table of the Lord and of the table of devils". Pagan cults, then, had their own ritual of 'holy communion', prior to and independent of Christianity. The same is true of the pre-Christian Jews whose views are evidenced in the Dead Sea Scrolls.[38]

J.Z. Smith's recent detailed comparison of early forms of Christianity with the pagan religions of late antiquity has shown how hard scholars have tried to insulate the former from the latter: "The central task has been the protection of the uniqueness of early Christianity, its *sui generis*, or non-derivative nature" (1990, p. 79).

Explaining the 'mystery' elements in Paul exclusively by appeal to the religious history of Judaism was, he says, felt to be acceptable; for Judaism "served a double (or a duplicitous) function. On the one hand it has provided apologetic scholars with an insulation for early Christianity, guarding it against 'influence' from its [Hellenistic] 'environment'. On the other hand, it has been presented by the very same scholars as an object to be transcended by early Christianity" (pp. 65, 83). First, then, Judaism is used to minimize Christian similarities with the pagan mystery religions; then Judaism is itself belittled so as to minimize its similarities with Christianity.

Surprisingly, Smith himself is reluctant to admit any dependence of Christianity on the mystery religions, particularly apropos of the death and resurrection of the gods worshipped in these cults. R.M. Price, reviewing his book, challenges this reluctance, and also rejects as improbable the suggestion, commonly made, that the mysteries borrowed the death and resurrection motif from Christians; for, "as Reitzenstein pointed out long ago: which direction of borrowing is more likely when one religion is newer and converts from the older faith are streaming into it bringing cherished elements of their familiar creeds with them?"[39]

Throughout Christian history there have been two opposite assessments of the similarities between Christianity and pagan religions, these latter being regarded either as diabolical impostures or as sincere gropings towards the truth that God finally revealed in Christ. Both views can be found in the NT (the second is adumbrated by Paul at Acts 17:22ff), but in ante-Nicene theology Tertullian well represents the first and Origen the second.

If we now turn from the Jesus of the Pauline and other early Christian letters and inquire into the origins of the Jesus figure of the gospels, it is relevant to consider the non-Markan material underlying and common to Matthew and Luke. As we saw, it is widely agreed that neither of these two evangelists took this material from the other, but that both drew it from a common source, a Greek document known now as Q (= Quelle, German for 'source'), not extant but reconstructable from this non-Markan overlap between the two extant gospels. Christopher Tuckett's 1996 survey gives a full account of recent work on Q, and also his own very considered assessment of the beliefs and nature of the early Christian group responsible for it. Many attempts have been made to divide Q into chronological layers with a developing Christology, but, without rejecting these theories, I find it less controversial to follow Tuckett in trying to assess the theology of the work as a whole.

Tuckett accepts the majority view that Q originated some time between A.D. 40 and 70, in northern Galilee or thereabouts: for the places it assigns to Jesus's activities are Galilean, and it links him with John the Baptist, known from Josephus to have been executed some time before A.D. 39. Moreover, Q is thoroughly Jewish in its theological orientation (for example towards the Jewish law) and so—unlike, for instance, Mark—was not written at any great ideological distance from the situations it purports to describe.

Wisdom traditions underlie Q, but not in the same way as they do the Pauline letters. In Q Jesus is not identified with Wisdom, but both he and John the Baptist are represented as messengers sent by Wisdom to preach the need for repentance before an imminent and final judgement; but they were ignored or rejected by their Jewish audience. Jesus, designated 'Son of man' in many of the relevant passages, experienced hostility, suffering and rejection in his life on Earth, but will shortly return and exercise a key role in this coming judgement. Tuckett shows that this idea of a figure of the past being kept in heaven to reappear at the end-time in some capacity was a widespread one; and in Q Jesus's role in the final judgement is not dissimilar to that ascribed to the Son of man figure in 1 Enoch (on which see below, pp. 181ff). Thus the 'Son of man' sayings in Q show a pattern of suffering for Jesus on Earth followed by "a vindication and retribution in the divine court"—all this being "remarkably similar" to the story-line of chapters 2 to 5 of the Wisdom of Solomon and to chapter 62 of 1 Enoch: in all three cases, "the one presently experiencing hostility and rejection will play a key role in deciding the fate of his erstwhile 'opponents'" (p. 275).

In sum, the religious community responsible for Q cultivated the memory of a Jesus as their founder figure, an authoritative teacher who should be obeyed. They urged their fellow Jews who had earlier rejected his message to change their ways and accept it as a last chance to avoid the doom that would otherwise overtake them. Although there is a good deal of Wisdom-inspired legend in this portrait of Jesus, the specific references to the places and to the relatively recent time of his activities, and the theological orientation which fits the scene of Judaism, make it seem reasonable to accept that the whole is based on the life of an actual itinerant Galilean preacher of the 20s or 30s, although it is surely hazardous to try and decide which details are really authentic.[40] What is so very striking is the difference between this Jesus and the Pauline one, in spite of the influence of Wisdom traditions in both cases. Q does not mention Jesus's death, and does no more than hint that the hostility extended to him may have been what led to it; he is represented as the last in a long line of Jewish prophets sent out by Wisdom whose messages met with apathy, rejection, even persecution. Q certainly does not regard his death as redemptive and does not explicitly mention his resurrection. It never calls him 'Christ' (Messiah) and has no allusion to eucharist, nor indeed to any social or cultic practices which would separate its group from mainstream Judaism. In all these respects the Jesus of Q differs from the Jesus of Paul, who was "delivered up for our trespasses", "put forward" by God "as an expiation by his blood", and "raised for our justification" (Rom. 3:25; 4:25).

Something like the Jesus of Q, rather than the Pauline Jesus, seems to have been what minority groups of Jewish Christians—branded as heretical by the Fathers—persisted in worshipping. Eusebius mentions Jewish Christian "Ebionites" who regarded Jesus as a highly moral, simple man. Earlier, Irenaeus tells that they denied the virgin birth, kept the Jewish law and rejected Paul as a lawbreaker. Even earlier (ca. A.D. 150) Justin Martyr alludes to an unnamed group of Jewish Christians who regarded Jesus as purely human (Details in S.G. Wilson's survey of Jewish Christianity, 1995, pp. 148ff). These 'heretics' were surely closer to a truly historical Jesus than were the Pauline communities.

Tuckett does not suggest that the two Jesus portraits refer to different persons, but to my mind it is not feasible to identify them, and the suggestion that there was more than one Jesus figure (real or legendary) underlying earliest Christianity is not altogether outrageous in the light of Paul's own complaint that there are people who "preach another Jesus whom we did not preach" (2

Cor. 11:4). By the time we reach Mark's gospel, the two have been
fused into one: the Galilean preacher of Q has been given a salvific
death and resurrection, and these have been set not in an unspecified past (as in the Pauline letters) but in a historical context
consonant with the date of the Galilean preaching. Movement
towards dating the earthly life of the Pauline Jesus in a relatively
recent past is intelligible even without the influence on later
Christians of Q: for Paul's Jesus came to Earth "when the time had
fully come" (Gal. 4:4), and this soon developed in Pauline-type
communities into the more specific statement that he had lived "at
the end of the times" (Hebrews 9:26; 1 Peter 1:20). Even if this
originally meant no more than that his first coming had inaugurated
the final epoch (however long) of history (the epoch that would
culminate in his return as judge), it would in time be taken to mean
that he had lived in the recent past. And to post-Pauline and post-Q
Christians of the late first century, familiar as they were with
crucifixion as a Roman punishment, his death by crucifixion—already attested by Paul, but not given any historical context in his nor
in other early epistles—would have suggested death at Roman
hands, and hence during the Roman occupation of Judea from A.D.
6. From such a premiss, coupled with the Q datum of Jesus as a
contemporary of John the Baptist, Pilate would naturally come to
mind as his murderer, for he was particularly detested by the Jews,
and is indeed the only one of the prefects who governed Judea
between A.D. 6 and 41 to be discussed in any detail by the two
principal Jewish writers of the first century, Philo and Josephus.

Another significant factor is pointed out by Alvar Ellegård in a
carefully argued article (1993), where he reiterates his earlier
published reasons for regarding the Jesus of the gospels as essentially a myth, and replies (with exemplary urbanity) to scholars who
have criticized him for this. The evangelists, he says (pp. 170, 200),
will have known that Paul and his fellow apostles experienced their
visions of the risen Jesus about the year 30, and naturally assumed
that the crucifixion and resurrection had occurred shortly before.
This is not what Paul had alleged (cf. below, p. 125), but it would
seem plausible enough half a century later, when they were writing
outside Palestine, in the Diaspora, after earlier events in Palestine

had been obscured from their view by the disruptive war with Rome from A.D. 66.

The importance of Q for Christian origins has been recognized for some considerable time. The Marburg theologian Walter Schmithals argued (1972) that Q helps us to answer the crucial questions: why is it, if Christianity was inaugurated by Jesus's own preaching, that not only Paul, but early Christians generally, although they believed that he had lived and died on Earth, did not seem to care what he had taught, believed or done, or what sort of man he had been; and how can we explain, given such antecedents, the interest in his doctrines and biography which the gospels seem suddenly to bring into Christian tradition late in the first century and which established itself as an essential part of Christian thinking and teaching only with Justin and Irenaeus from the mid-second century? Schmithals answers that this interest, documented in Q, represents the view of Jesus's original followers that he was a prophet whose message was rejected—a view which persisted in an isolated Galilean community at a time when most other Christians accepted "the Easter events" which deflected interest away from his pre-crucifixion life. Mark, says Schmithals, wrote in order to win the Galilean community over to the majority view. It has long been recognized as one of the peculiarities of Mark's gospel that, although its Jesus appears as the Messiah and works many miracles, he repeatedly enjoins people to keep silence about his exalted powers and status, even in circumstances where the injunction could scarcely be obeyed because the miracle was so public (see below, p. 149, and, more fully, *The Jesus Legend*, chapter 5). Mark's purpose, says Schmithals, was to explain, by means of the device of this 'Messianic secret', why he was not recognized for what he was by his Galilean audiences.

I have given a fuller account of Schmithals' book in *HEJ* (pp. 212–16). Like Tuckett, he makes what I consider to be the mistake of supposing the Pauline and the Q traditions to refer to the same person. His suggestion that the 'Easter events' extinguished interest in Jesus's pre-crucifixion preaching could explain why the earliest extant documents do not record this preaching, but not why they fail to mention the when and where of his earthly existence, and even the historical setting of the crucifixion of this person who (they nevertheless insist) did live on Earth and die on the cross. Nevertheless, Schmithals shows clearly enough that early Christian communities were of two types, with radically different views of Jesus.

Since much of the NT depicts Jesus as the Messiah, some of what we find in it is adapted from the wide range of Jewish Messianic ideas of the time. Apologists have often wrongly supposed these ideas to have been sufficiently uniform to warrant the claim that Jesus's career—his ministry, Passion, death and resurrection—is so out of line with them that the gospel accounts of these events could not have been devised as stories to fit what the Jews expected. However, even Ladd, who makes this claim (1979, pp. 37, 93), agrees that "there was no uniformity of eschatological beliefs" on which Christians could draw (p. 58); and Vermes allows that, if we take account not only of "the general Messianic *expectation* of Palestinian Jewry", but also of "the peculiar Messianic *speculations* characteristic of certain learned and/or esoterical minorities", then it is correct to say (as he quotes other scholars as saying) that "the word Messiah has no fixed content", and that, "even if there may have been . . . a tendency to connect the word especially with the expected Son of David . . . there still remained a wide range of variety in details" (1973, p. 130; Vermes's italics).

The variety can go beyond ideas about a son of David. The Dead Sea Scrolls predict the coming of two Messiahs, only one of whom will be a royal personage descended from David; and in one passage what is said of him is remarkably paralleled at Lk. 1:32–35 where the angel Gabriel tells Mary that her child

> shall be great and shall be called the Son of the Most High, and the Lord God shall give unto him the throne of his father David. And he shall reign over the house of Jacob for ever; and of his kingdom there shall be no end . . . [He] shall be called holy, the Son of God.

The Qumran passage reads:

> Son of God he will be called and Son of the Most High they will name him . . . His kingdom will be an everlasting kingdom . . . He will judge the earth in truth. . . . The Great God . . . will give peoples into his hand and all of them he will cast down before him. His sovereignty is everlasting sovereignty.

Collins argues that this prediction refers to the royal Messiah, and that although the use of some of the titles he is here given has some warrant in 2 Samuel 7 and Psalm 2, the parallel with the Lukan text is so close that it is "overwhelmingly probable" that Luke borrowed the titles either from this Qumran writer or from a source tradition common to both of them (1997, pp. 82ff, 158).

However, Luke took only the titles; he did not make his Messiah, Jesus, into a war leader, as the royal Messiah of Qumran was expected to be. One of the texts there was even interpreted in the 1950s as implying that he would be killed in battle; but subsequent study made it clear that he is the one whom this text represents as doing the killing. Vermes (1973, pp. 139–140) shows that the few sporadic references in rabbinic literature to a slain Messiah are all later than the second Jewish War with Rome, and may have been prompted by the tragic fate of Simeon bar Kosiba, hailed as Messiah but killed in that war in A.D. 135. As we saw above (p. 99), some pre-Christian Jews did indeed believe that the death of a just martyr would be followed by his immortality and could also function as an atoning sacrifice. Nevertheless, as is noted in the second volume of the revised English edition of Schürer's standard work, "however much the idea of a suffering Messiah is, from these premises, conceivable within Judaism, it did not become a dominant notion" (p. 549).

The NT does of course claim the OT as replete with prophecies about the suffering and death of the Messiah; but whether it is justified in understanding this OT material in this way is another matter. Isaiah 53 tells of a "servant of Yahweh" who was "wounded for our transgressions" and led "like a lamb to the slaughter"; and at Zechariah 12:10 there is an enigmatic reference to someone "whom they have pierced". The contexts in which these and other comparable passages occur seldom if ever suggest that any reference to the Messiah was intended, even though in Justin Martyr's *Dialogue with Trypho* the Jew is represented as allowing (in chapters 89 and 90) that "it is clear that the scriptures declare that the Christ is to suffer" and "to be led away like a sheep". Ladd, with others, supposes that the apostles found, "in the light of the Christ event", a "deeper meaning" in the relevant OT material than appears in its original contexts (1979, pp. 67, 107), and that this is why Peter and

Paul can in Acts preach that "God forshewed by the mouth of all the prophets that his Christ should suffer" (3:18; 17:3). Acts would have us believe that the Jerusalem Jews were greatly impressed by Peter's sermon and, far from regarding what he said as going beyond their scriptures, accepted it in their thousands (4:4). But the suggestion that suffering for the Messiah was foretold by "all the prophets" is ridiculous.

The other Messiah of the Qumran texts was to come with the Davidic one, but would take precedence over him. He was to be a priest of Aaron's line, and would atone for the sin of the people—presumably not by dying but by offering the prescribed sacrifices. He was also to be a teacher, patterned on the historical Teacher of Righteousness who had been prominent in earlier days of the community represented in the relevant scrolls. To this historical teacher, the scrolls tell us, God had "disclosed all the mysteries of the words of his servants the prophets" and had put into his heart the source of wisdom for all those who understand. When the scrolls were first studied, some scholars thought that the priestly Messiah was to be this same Teacher of Righteousness, resurrected and returning at the end of days—a view which Collins now dismisses as "wild speculation" (p. 86).

Luke was not alone in refusing to regard the royal Davidic Messiah as a militarist king. Sanders points to Psalms of Solomon 17:33f—a passage in "a hymn written approximately in 63 B.C.E., the time of Pompey's conquest of Jerusalem". It "looks forward to the time when a son of David will purge Jerusalem of evil people. This future son of David, however, 'will not rely on horse and rider and bow, nor will he collect gold and silver for war. Nor will he build up hope in a multitude for a day of war' " (1993a, p. 89). Here, then, we have a son of David who acts in some respects like David, although "the conception has changed: there will not be any real fighting" (pp. 240–41). This is quite typical of the way names and titles from the salvation history of the past can be used, even though substantive changes are made.

In sum, the idea of the Messiah was repeatedly redefined in changing circumstances over the centuries. There was no coherent picture, "no paradigm or checklist by which to discern whether a man was the Messiah" (Charlesworth 1992, p. 14). No rigid distinction can be sustained between a 'politico-national' and a 'spiritual' conception of the Messiah (De Jonge 1966, p. 132). Hence, says Sanders, we cannot read the Psalms of Solomon and the Qumran texts "and then say that we know what 'Messiah' meant and consequently what the early Christians thought when they called Jesus 'Messiah' or 'Christ.'" All we can really know is that the person of whom this word was used "was considered to be the 'anointed' of God, anointed for *some* special task" (p. 241). Christians kept the title but redefined it in accordance with their own experience, so that Jesus became "a new kind of Messiah, one who had acted as a miracle-worker and prophet during his lifetime, but who was also the heavenly Lord who would return at the end" (p. 243).

Despite the very great difference between the Jesus of the early epistles and the Jesus of the synoptics, and despite that between the latter and the Jesus of the fourth gospel, most scholars persist in representing the NT as a unity. Neill and Wright declare that all the traditions gathered together in it "relate to one event, which must have been staggeringly great, and to one Person, who must have been unlike any other person who has ever lived". All "bear witness with singular unanimity to one single historical figure, unlike any other that has ever walked among the sons of men", etc. etc. (1988, pp. 204, 312). It is always possible to make these traditions into a 'unity' if this is described in sufficiently general terms. The texts of course agree in presenting him as a figure of supreme importance: "a greater than Solomon is here"; "blessed are the eyes which see what you see" (Lk. 10:23–24; 11:31). Hence Reumann is able to say that the whole NT is unified by the theme of faith in Jesus Christ (1991, p. 290). It would surely be extraordinary if there were not this amount of agreement between its parts. One would not expect a book in the church's own canon to be telling us that he is unimportant and that faith in him is a rotten idea. Reumann notes other generalities, such as stress on the importance of "love" in many passages (p. 30). But even between the NT and non-Christian religious documents one could find a good deal of uniformity apropos of abstractions such as love, mercy, charity, justice, and so

on. He also finds that "eschatology of one type or other" can be
expected in every NT book (p. 32). The general term disguises very
real differences. Will Christ return almost immediately and end the
present world-order, as Paul and the book of Revelation supposed;
or will he come only when "the times of the gentiles be fulfilled"
(Lk. 21:24)? Or are we to accept the fourth gospel's suggestion that
he will send the Spirit, the Comforter, instead of returning himself?
I can sympathize with Evans's despairing statement that "there is
no greater conceptual or doctrinal mess than eschatology" (1971, p.
71).

The situation is no better with regard to the significance of
Jesus's work; his death may be either the essential condition for
man's salvation, or the typical fate of a prophet and without
soteriological significance (see note 2 to this chapter 1 on p. 255
below). We saw that even his person is not the same throughout.
James Dunn, who unconvincingly denies that Paul represents him
as a pre-existent supernatural personage, is aware that he is undeni-
ably so portrayed in the fourth gospel. Dunn knows equally well that
elsewhere (notably in the speeches attributed to Peter and Paul in
Acts)[41] he nevertheless figures as a man elevated to high status only
when God raised him from the dead. Dunn regards these two
assessments of him as ultimately one and the same; but this, as the
Finnish theologian Heikki Räisänen observes, is to "stretch the
reader's imagination to breaking point" (1997, p. 192).

In an earlier book, Räisänen has shown that it is not only in
conservative scholarship that one meets enthusiastic overall assessments of the NT. It is only what is written on particular, limited
issues that often shows scientific detachment; there, "value-laden
theological categories such as 'revelation' or 'inspiration' are seldom used . . . Considerable theological diversity within the New
Testament is taken for granted, and no attempt is made at harmoniz-
ing the differences". But all this changes abruptly when one turns to
synthesizing accounts. Now "we hear a good deal of God revealing
himself definitively in Christ". Diversity in the texts is often only
reluctantly admitted, and the existence of an underlying unity is
"postulated rather than argued . . . Divine revelation is often spoken of as if its existence were self-evident". All in all, "an acute

analyst turns into a pious preacher when faced with the task of synthesis" (1990, pp. xii–xiii). Such a preacher assumes that these writings, forming as they do a holy book, must reflect the unity of God himself and of the truth. Without this dogma, why, asks Evans, should it be supposed that they "should exhibit a unity other than that which they possess through emerging from communities which had a good deal of belief and practice in common?" (1971, p. 34).

The Fathers had to explain away not only the inconsistencies in scripture, but also those between it and church doctrine; and the mediaeval theologians who followed them were committed to patristic authority as well: all had to be represented as a unity. The result provides what a recent commentator has called "the spectacle of some of the greatest minds in European history devoting their lives to the systematic misrepresentation of ancient texts—truly one of the wonders of intellectual history" (Hood 1995, p. 3).

iv. Review of the Main Arguments of Chapter 1

The arguments and supporting details given particularly in the second half of this first chapter will be largely unfamiliar to the general reader who is not a NT specialist, and so a brief resumé, tabulating what is said and where in that second half, will perhaps be of help. Numbers of pages which give summarizing or general statements are underlined.

p. 49
The question at issue is: does Christian writing earlier than the gospels (shown in the first half of this chapter to be works of the late first century) confirm either the gospel accounts of Jesus or the traditions underlying these accounts?

pp. 49–51
The earliest extant Christian documents (not later than A.D. 60) are Paul's letters. His Jesus pre-existed as a supernatural personage in heaven before his brief sojourn on Earth as a man. Attempts to deny that Paul ascribed such pre-existence to him do not hold up.

p. 52
It will be shown that Pauline (and other early Christian) letters are silent about all details of Jesus's ministry familiar from the gospels. This is of crucial importance for

deciding whether Christianity began with Jesus as depicted in the gospels.

pp. 52–57   The few Pauline passages which seem nevertheless to suggest that Paul did know details of Jesus's ministry and death give this impression only because they are today read and interpreted from knowledge of the gospels, which did not exist when Paul wrote.

p. 57   Even the circumstances of the Passion are mentioned neither by Paul nor by other early Christian writers. Only later epistles (canonical and others) place Jesus in the first century and link him with Pilate.

pp. 58–60   As for Paul's silence about what for the gospels are very important aspects of Jesus's *pre*-crucifixion life, he makes no mention of a virgin birth, nor of miracles, nor of activity in Galilee or Jerusalem, nor of teachings. Paul's failure to appeal to rulings by Jesus about keeping or transgressing the Jewish law is particularly significant.

pp. 60–63   His appeal to some half-dozen 'words of the Lord' does not break these silences, as the 'words' derive from the *risen* Lord, not from the historical Jesus.

pp. 64–65   Paul taught certain ethical doctrines independently of Jesuine authority—doctrines which only later came to be ascribed to Jesus.

pp. 67–68   Paul's silences are shared by other early epistles. Only later ones show familiarity with the synoptic tradition. The significance of this discrepancy cannot be overestimated (see p. 57 above).

pp. 70–78   Attempts by apologists to deny this discrepancy or to discount its significance.

pp. 78–91   The Pastoral epistles—one of which links Jesus with Pilate and hence was acquainted with at any rate some features of the synoptic tradition—are shown to be late and pseudonymous.

p. 91   Importance of this for my view of Christian origins.

pp. 93–94   Why these and some other epistles are pseudonymous.

pp. 94–95   Summary of inferences to be drawn from this protracted study of epistles and their relation to the gospels: the Jesus of the early epistles is not the Jesus of the gospels. The ministry of the latter may well be modelled on the career of an itinerant Galilean preacher of the early first century; the former derives largely from early Christian interpretation of Jewish Wisdom figures, with some

2

Miracles in the New Testament and Beyond

Although I have allowed that some features of Jesus as he is portrayed in the synoptic gospels may well derive from the biography of an actual itinerant Galilean preacher, there are many narratives in all four gospels that must unhesitatingly be set aside as unhistorical. Among these I include all references to miracles, and it is the purpose of the present chapter to justify this exclusion, which results not from any *a priori* assumption that miracles are impossible, but from demonstration that the evidence offered in the NT in support of them is insufficient to warrant their acceptance. They were nevertheless treasured in patristic discussions of the two natures of Christ as evidence of his divinity, just as the reality of his sufferings was held to establish his humanity. A Christ who walked on water could otherwise readily be held 'not to have come in the flesh' and to have only *seemed* to have experienced pain, as the 'docetists' or 'seemers' attacked in 1 Jn. 4:1–3 did in fact suppose. How difficult it was for doctrine to do full justice to both of the two natures is illustrated by Clement of Alexandria's Christ, who, as Maurice Wiles tells us (in Moule's 1965 symposium on miracles, pp. 230–32), did not really need food and drink, but took them only in order to confound such docetists. For Paul this whole problem had not arisen, for his Jesus had not, while on Earth, possessed two natures, but in coming to Earth had 'emptied himself' of all that was supernatural about him (see above, p. 50) and had worked no miracles.

i. The Virgin Birth

The two great miracles framing Jesus's life are his virgin birth and his resurrection. The evidence for the former is now very widely admitted to be inadequate, and that for the latter has become increasingly regarded as suspect.

Nothing in the NT justifies the traditional date of Jesus's birth, and the celebration of Christmas on 25th December began only in the fourth century. The Roman emperor Aurelian had in A.D. 274 made this day the birthday of the Unconquered Sun, and now the victory of Christ, the true sun, over this heathen cult was to be made manifest in this way.

The circumstances of the saviour's birth and infancy are narrated, within the NT, only in Matthew and Luke, and are not mentioned or alluded to in its other twenty-five books, where only wishful thinking has been able to discern anything of the sort.[1] Also, the relevant accounts in these gospels are mutually exclusive. I have set out the details at some length elsewhere (WWJ, chapter 3) and here I restrict myself to a brief summary. Both Matthew and Luke assert that Jesus was born without a human father, yet both represent him as belonging in the unbroken male line of descent from David. Each evangelist supplies a genealogy in order to prove this, and the two genealogies are incompatible. In both gospels, the accounts of Jesus's ministry which follow their birth and infancy narratives are clearly based on material which knew nothing of these narratives. Finally, Matthew represents the nativity as fulfillment of prophecy by means of fantastically arbitrary interpretation of numerous OT passages.

The consequence of all this is that defence of the birth and infancy narratives is now widely agreed to be quite a hopeless task. As the Catholic scholar Küng acknowledges, "today even Catholic exegetes concede that these stories are historically largely uncertain, mutually contradictory, strongly legendary and in the last analysis theologically motivated" (1976, p. 441). They serve to certificate Jesus as truly Son of God from the very beginning of his earthly life, and so to correct any suggestion that he may have achieved this status only at his resurrection (Rom. 1:4) or at his baptism at the beginning of his adult ministry (Mk. 1:11; see *The Jesus Legend*, pp. 11–12). On the Protestant side, the case against accepting that Jesus was virgin born is set out with some fullness in Geoffrey Parrinder's 1993 book.

Nevertheless, the doctrine of the virgin birth still has defenders, who include not only fundamentalists but scholars such as C.E.B. Cranfield who, while allowing that it is "beset by many problems and difficulties", mounts a tentative vindication of it (1988, pp. 177ff). Hence it is appropriate here to scrutinize some of the many statements in the relevant narratives that have been rejected as unbelievable and to see how they are still defended. I select two such: the imperial census, unique to Luke's account, and the star of the magi, unique to Matthew's.

Doctrine required that Jesus be born in 'David's city' of Bethlehem. For Matthew, who makes the holy family reside there, this presented no problem. Luke, however, has them reside in Nazareth and to get them to Bethlehem for the birth he maintains that, in the days of Herod the Great, "there went out a decree from Caesar Augustus, that all the world"—the whole Roman empire—"should be enrolled", i.e. registered for taxation. And so "all went to enrol themselves, every one to his own city. And Joseph also went up from Galilee, out of the city of Nazareth, into Judaea, to the city of David, which is called Bethlehem, because he was of the house and family of David; to enrol himself with Mary, who was betrothed to him, being great with child" (2:1-5). Sanders's expostulation at what he calls this "fantastic device" for moving the family eighty miles to the place necessary for the story is worth recording:

> According to Luke's own genealogy (3:23–38), David had lived forty-two generations before Joseph. Why should Joseph have had to register in the town of one of his ancestors forty-two generations earlier? What was Augustus—the most rational of the Caesars—thinking of? The entirety of the Roman empire would have been uprooted by such a decree. Besides, how would any given man know where to go? No one could trace his genealogy for forty-two generations, but if he could, he would

find that he had *millions* of ancestors (one million is passed at the twentieth generation). Further, David doubtless had tens of thousands of descendants who were alive at the time. Could they all identify themselves? If so, how would they all register in a little village? (1993a, p. 86)

Some have defended the journey to Bethlehem by appealing to the Egyptian papyrus which records the edict of Vibius Maximus (A.D. 104) that those who for any reason are away from their own *idia* should return home to enrol themselves. Someone's *idia* can mean either his private property or his 'peculiar district'. In *JEC* (p. 39) I quoted papyrologists to the effect that the former meaning seems required by the context here, since the census returns that have been preserved show that the owners of houses had to give their names and the names of those living with them and the address of the house as well; and the correctness of the entries was everywhere assured by official inspection by the local authorities. Obviously, such inspection would have been difficult unless the returns were made where the property was situated.

Even if Joseph had to go to Bethlehem, Mary would not have been required to accompany him, for Luke makes him register there because he was descended from David. Mary, however, was not: she was kindred to Elisabeth (mother of John the Baptist) who was "of the daughters of Aaron" (Lk. 1:5), and so a Levite of the priestly tribe.

Further historical difficulties with Luke's census (and unconvincing attempts to dispose of them) are set out in the revised English edition of Schürer's standard work (1973, pp. 399–427), where it is noted that history does not otherwise record a general imperial census in the time of Augustus. Moreover, Matthew has it that "Jesus was born in Bethlehem of Judaea in the days of Herod the king" (2:1)—late in Herod's reign, as he died while Jesus was still a baby (2:19–20). Chronological data in Luke likewise strongly suggest that the birth occurred near the end of Herod's reign.[2] But a Roman census could not have been carried out in Palestine in the time of King Herod, for his territory was not part of the empire. A client ruler such as he may have paid a lump sum as tribute to Rome, although it is "improbable" that he did so: such exactions were more likely in the later period of the empire, when the political power of the *reges socii* was more restricted, and in any case payment of a tribute has no bearing on the possibility of a Roman census on his territory.[3]

A further problem is Luke's statement that the census he alleges was "the first enrolment made when Quirinius was governor of Syria" (2:2). A census under Quirinius could not have taken place in the time of Herod, for he died in 4 B.C., and Quirinius did not become governor of Syria until A.D. 6.[4] Josephus mentions a census which Quirinius organized at that time in Judea, which had just been incorporated into the province of Syria, as Augustus had deposed Herod's son Archelaus (*Antiquities of the Jews*, 17:344; 18:2). Josephus makes it clear here that it was altogether novel for the Romans to raise a tax in Judea, and that it caused the Jews to revolt. It is quite obvious that Luke had this census of A.D. 6 in mind, but antedated it and supposed it to have occurred in Herod's lifetime. Attempts by Christian apologists to escape this conclusion may fairly be described as pathetic.[5] Even the Judean census of A.D. 6 would not have affected Galilee (and Joseph and Mary in Nazareth in Galilee) as Luke supposes. On Herod's death, his kingdom was divided between his sons: Archelaus was given Judea, Antipas Galilee. It was only Archelaus who was deposed in A.D. 6 and his territory made part of the empire. Antipas continued as ruler of Galilee until A.D. 39, and a Roman census was no more possible on his territory than it had been on Herod's. Only the most conservative apologists still cope with this difficulty by speculating that Joseph and/or Mary may have had property in Bethlehem and so had to participate in a Judean census. There is no hint of this in Luke. On the contrary, Lk. 2:7 states that the couple tried to put up at an inn in Bethlehem, but had to be content with a manger. This does not suggest that they had property of their own there. Moehring was quite justified in saying in 1972 (p. 146) that Schürer (the fourth edition of whose book was published 1901–09) had dealt adequately with those who had defended what Luke says about the census, and that "most of the more recent attempts to rescue the historical reliability of Luke . . . rest more on the hope that the reader may not have access to the material in Schürer than on new evidence or fresh ideas". This remains true of the situation today.

If we now turn to discussion of the star in Matthew's birth narrative which guided the magi to Bethlehem, we find the distinguished American Roman Catholic scholar Fr. R.E. Brown stating that "those who wish to maintain the historicity of the Matthean magi story are faced with nigh insuperable obstacles" (1979, p. 188). The magi already know from what they have been told in Jerusalem (2:8) that the child they are seeking is in Bethlehem, so if they need a guiding star, it is to identify not the village, but the actual house (cf. 2:9 and 11). A star that came to rest over one particular house is quite unheard of. Apologists who give evidence of possibly striking celestial phenomena about the time in question do not realize that this is as much a reason for admitting that the story could easily have been invented as for allowing that it actually happened. Brown is well aware of this, and says:

> Christians, sharing the general belief that celestial phenomena marked the birth of great men, may have reflected on astronomical peculiarities at the time of Jesus's birth, e.g. a supernova, or Halley's comet, or a conjunction of Jupiter, Saturn, and Mars, and, in retrospect, may have fastened on one or the other as a sign from God that His Son was going to be born. (p. 190)

Another factor is that the prophecy of Balaam at Numbers 24:17 ("There shall come forth a star out of Jacob, and a sceptre shall rise out of Israel") was interpreted, already before Christian times, as a reference to the coming Messiah, and so may well have helped to prompt Matthew's story, even though he does not actually cite this passage. Davies and Allison (1988, pp. 234–35) point out that in this section of his narrative (chapter 2 in our printed texts) he confines his citations of prophecies to passages which supply him with place names (Bethlehem, Egypt, Ramah, Nazareth) and which can in this way be made to serve the geographical orientation of his story. While these two commentators think that the tale should "probably" be assigned to "haggadic imagination" rather than to history, Luz (1990, p. 132) can see nought but "legend" in it; for, apart from the description of the star being not "astronomically plausible", the behaviour of the actors is also unconvincing: Why did Herod not at least send a spy along with the Magi to ensure that he would learn of their findings even if they themselves defaulted? And why should "all Jerusalem" be "troubled" (2:3), as he was, at the news of the Messiah's birth?

Subsequent elaborations of this story illustrate the well-known fact that the latest version of a legend is often the most detailed and specific. The recently published *Oxford Companion to the Bible* notes:

> In Western Christianity the Magi are assumed to have been three in number since three gifts are mentioned; eastern tradition gives their number as twelve. They traveled by camel, as is normal practice in the desert regions even today. Their names (Balthasar, Melchior, and Caspar, in the west) are supplied [even] later. The fact that they are wealthy and converse with King Herod leads to their identification as three kings (art. 'Magi', in Metzger and Coogan 1993).

The articles 'Immanuel' and 'Virgin Birth of Christ' in the same handbook include the following brief but telling comments on the two birth and infancy narratives as a whole:

1. Only the Greek translation of Isaiah 7:14, not the Hebrew original, reads "a virgin shall conceive and bear a son" (the Hebrew has 'young woman', not 'virgin'), and so Matthew can quote this (at 1:23–24) as foretelling Jesus's birth only because he used a Greek Bible. Moreover, Isaiah's prophecy posits no miraculous conception and referred to the military and political situation facing him and the King of Judah whom he was addressing; it "required fulfillment in the eighth century B.C.E."

2. Any alleged references in the NT to the virgin birth outside these two narratives are "at best vague allusions" (see note 1 on p. 273 below).

3. The whole idea is quite intelligible as a creation of the early church (cf. p. 116 above. Cranfield [p. 186] emphatically denied this, and thought it very difficult to explain how the church came to believe in Jesus's virgin birth if it is unhistorical).

4. "Miraculous human birth stories are common in biblical tradition, going back to Abraham and Sarah . . . , and numerous references to deities impregnating women are found

within the Greco-Roman tradition". (Cranfield had objected [p. 181] that "none of these alleged parallels is a real parallel". But how close would they have to be to count as significant? R.M. Price [in the context given on p. 101 above] has asked, appositely: Would the mother have to be named Mary, or the child Jesus? A new religion must be expected to be a rehash, not a replica, of earlier ideas.)

However, the handbook does not wish to be totally iconoclastic, and allows that "ultimately, the issue will be decided by a person's faith stance and view of scripture".

Some have shrugged off the birth and infancy narratives by asking: why make a fuss about where Jesus was born? Nazareth will do as well as Bethlehem, and it would not even matter if it was Tunbridge Wells, as his 'message' is what counts. The obvious answers are, first, that, as we shall see, only some of what is ascribed to him as his 'message' is lovable, and considerable ingenuity has been required to make the 'hard sayings' acceptable; and second, the two birth and infancy narratives state quite clearly that he was born in Bethlehem; and if this can be shown not to be true—by this I mean if it is beyond reasonable doubt that the relevant stories are legends—then the overall reliability of the NT can no longer be assumed, and it will have to be admitted that evangelists shaped their accounts (at any rate in some instances) in accordance with Messianic expectations, or in accordance with *some* considerations which had nothing to do with historical accuracy. It is awareness of the importance of this issue that leads some apologists to make such desperate efforts to defend the two narratives. Others, seeing that they are indefensible as history, suppose, with for instance Bishop Spong, that their "mythological language . . . in no way minimizes their importance": from Jesus's life "there emanated power, love, and life such as the world has never known", and in claiming that he had no human father these narratives are "profound interpretative accounts . . . designed to assert that the power present in [his] life was beyond the capacity of human life alone to produce" (Spong 1993, pp. 166, 168, 183).

The doctrine of the virgin birth initiated the mariology that has subsequently grown to such great proportions—not because evidence supports it, but as a result of believers' emotional needs. Wiles is able to quote both a Protestant and a Catholic authority who admit as much. The Protestant tells that, although "the weighty theologians" tried to contain the growth, "the pious monks and the simple devotion of the people kept pushing along the glorification uncontrollably until today we have, even officially, the doctrine of the Bodily Assumption". The Catholic says in effect the same, but without any implied negative judgement on the whole development, which he calls "one of the most touching cases of piety being in advance of science, stimulating science to ratify the intuitions of love" (Quoted by Wiles 1967, pp. 89–90). It is a most instructive example of the forces from which creeds are made—and sustained. Apropos of this latter, an observation by Fr. R.E. Brown in the 1993 updated edition of his *The Birth of the Messiah* is of interest. The book is a reprint of the original 1979 edition, with a lengthy 'Supplement' covering subsequent discussion of the birth and infancy narratives in Matthew and Luke. It is in this supplement that he tells how an article by a Spanish Jesuit, published in the 1970s and suggesting that the virginal conception could be treated as a legend, "brought indignant petitions by over 10,000 Spaniards, a restatement of belief by the Spanish bishops' commission on faith, . . . and a warning from the Jesuit general" (p. 701).

With their strong emotional appeal, such articles of faith can long survive, even when, for many people, they have ceased to carry complete conviction. As the charming stories of events surrounding the birth of the god-man some 2,000 years ago are recited and re-enacted every Christmas, few celebrants will be troubled by thoughts as to whether such a birth ever occurred, or whether the accompanying miracles ever took place. Hundreds of years before Christianity, the birth, life, and exploits of Herakles were celebrated by the Greeks, and few worshippers will have questioned the belief that their hero, still in his cradle, actually strangled the serpents sent by the goddess Hera to destroy him. Philosophers who asked: 'But are these stories true?' would have been dismissed as spoil-sports.

ii. The Resurrection

Ideas about the resurrection of the dead entered the OT only in one of its latest books—Daniel (Collins 1993, pp. 60, 392, 395, observes that the resurrection language of Isaiah 26:19 is regarded by the majority of commentators as metaphorical, as that of Ezekiel 37 quite obviously is). Paul cannot quote any OT passage to substantiate his claim that Jesus rose "on the third day according to the scriptures" (1 Cor. 15:4). There is no such passage as Ladd allows when he comments, feebly, that "we cannot be certain as to what specific texts, if any [!], Paul had in mind. He may have had in mind the frequency with which 'three' appears in the Old Testament" (1979, p. 108). However, the intertestamental literature expresses a great variety of views about an after-life: these include resurrection of the body (perhaps for the righteous only), or immortality of the soul (for all or only for those who gain it by proper conduct), or no resurrection at all (Barr 1992, pp. 23, 106, 113). I have noted above (p. 99) that the Jewish Wisdom literature does seem to have influenced Christian views of Jesus's resurrection, and that Paul's Hellenistic environment was familiar with the idea that a martyr's death could function as an atoning sacrifice, followed by his immortality. Apologists suppose that the resurrection of Jesus is more believable if there had been no earlier ideas that might have prompted belief in it. But they cannot establish that such ideas were lacking. On the contrary, it has been justly said that "the disciples' understanding of the aftermath of the death of Jesus in terms of resurrection was dependent on the emergence of that concept within the Judaism of the immediately preceding centuries" (Wiles 1974, p. 131), and that the NT concept of resurrection is only one of several NT ideas derived not directly from the OT, but from "the types of Judaism which had developed in the intertestamental period". Others include "the kingdom of God, the Son of man, parables, thaumaturgy and belief in demons" (Evans 1970, p. 31).

The first thing to take cognizance of in evaluating the data concerning Jesus's resurrection is that it consists of earlier and later layers of tradition. The earliest is the simple series of statements at 1 Cor. 15:3–5 that Christ "died" (in unspecified circumstances) "for

our sins according to the scriptures", was buried, was "raised on
the third day according to the scriptures" and appeared (in unspecified circumstances and after an unspecified interval) to Cephas and
to "the twelve". Paul introduces these statements by saying that they
comprise the substance of what he had preached to the Corinthians,
the fundamental tenets, belief in which ensures their salvation
(verses 1–2). He designates this "gospel" as what he himself
"received" and what he has in turn "handed on". If he means that
he had learned his "gospel" as tradition from human predecessors,
then he is contradicting what he had written to the Galatians,
namely that there is only one "gospel" and that it did not reach him
from human sources (see above, p. 54). Paul is quite capable of
saying different things to different people (or even to the same
people) for different apologetic purposes, and some commentators,
instead of trying to harmonize the data, admit that there is a real
contradiction here that can be explained with reference to the two
different situations in which he was arguing his case. In 1 Corinthians he was addressing Christians who were confident that they
possessed the Holy Spirit, and who in consequence over-indulged
spirit-inspired behaviour, such as making unintelligible utterances
("speaking with tongues"), perhaps to the neglect or even rejection
of what was prescribed by tradition. In Galatians, however, he was
addressing a community that was unduly inclined to accept traditional ideas and practices, particularly circumcision; and so there
he declares that his gospel is independent of tradition and came
directly to him in a supernatural disclosure from the Lord.[6]

One reason for taking the series of statements in 1 Cor. 15:3–5 as
a traditional creed which Paul is here quoting is that each one of
them is introduced with the word *hoti* (stating 'that' something is
the case), as would be appropriate in introducing the propositions
of a credal formula. There follows, surely as a supplement to any
pre-existing formula, for there is now no *hoti*: "Then he appeared to
above five hundred brethren at once", some of whom have since
died, then to James, then to "all the apostles". Finally Paul adds,
quite obviously as supplementary to any traditional formula: "Last
of all . . . he appeared to me also". The mention of the 500 seems
out of place in a list which otherwise names only notable personages of Christian communities. As we saw (above, p. 54), in the

earliest Christianity an apostle's authority depended on his having seen the risen Lord; and so the list, without the 500, may have been originally compiled as evidence of the credentials of the persons named in it, and the reference to the 500 added later when the list came to be understood not as stating who had apostolic credentials, but as evidence for the resurrection. (This view is argued in Price 1995, pp. 82–83.) This addition could even be post-Pauline, for an appearance to 500 was surely too good a piece of evidence to be ignored, and had it been early tradition it would presumably have surfaced in some form in the gospels, even though they, as later documents embodying later traditions, present a quite different account of the appearances from Paul's. The appearance to James is admittedly also not in them, but it did not disappear from the tradition completely, for it is represented in the apocryphal Gospel According to the Hebrews (Hennecke 1963, p. 159).

I must stress that, although Paul clearly implies that all these appearances were quite recent occurrences which went back no more than a few years, he does not say that they followed the resurrection immediately, or even soon. Even Archbishop Carnley, whose book on the resurrection is the most valuable study of the NT evidence that I have seen, says that Paul's "message involved the startling claim that Jesus had been seen alive three days after his death and burial" (1987, p. 140). It is the resurrection, not the appearances, that Paul puts three days after the burial. He does not say that the burial was recent, nor that the appearances followed soon after the resurrection. People who claim to see a ghost do not necessarily suppose it to be the wraith of someone recently deceased.

The Pauline letters, then, do not make the death, burial, and resurrection into recent occurrences experienced by men who had known Jesus in his lifetime. We recall that Paul does not suggest that Cephas, with whom he quarrelled in Antioch over observance of the food laws, had known Jesus personally (cf. above, pp. 54f). It is the gospels which make, not only the resurrection appearances, but also Jesus's life and death into events experienced by contemporaries of Paul; and once this feature of the gospel accounts is accepted, it is possible to argue that Jesus's crucifixion will have destroyed all the hopes of those who had known him, and that only his resurrection—or at any rate belief that he was risen—could have restored their shattered confidence and enabled them to continue preaching as they did. However, Geoffrey Parrinder, who did not wish to question the reality of the resurrection, pointed out from his extensive knowledge of other religions that this is a decidedly "shaky" argument, since other religious leaders died and were not resurrected, yet their religions spread rapidly: "Success of the religion and glorification of the founder, without doctrines of resurrection, are phenomena seen in many religions, for example those of the Buddhists, Jains, Zoroastrians, Confucians and Sikhs". He mentions Islam as perhaps the most striking example. Muhammad died after only a short illness at the age of sixty-two, and his followers could hardly credit the catastrophe; yet just a hundred years later "his armies were found from China to the heart of France" (1970, pp. 217–18).

Paul's account includes an appearance of the risen one to "the twelve" and this has often been taken as an undeniable reference to the twelve companions of Jesus's ministry who are specified in the gospels. It is, however, noteworthy that Paul mentions this group of twelve only here, in the creed he is quoting. If they had formed an important group, he would surely have mentioned them elsewhere and would not, as he does, have named the leaders of the Jerusalem church as Cephas, James, and John. This "almost complete absence" of any kind of twelve from the Pauline epistles has been called "one of the most disconcerting elements in these letters when they are compared to the Acts of the Apostles" (Bernheim 1997, p. 195) which, not altogether successfully, tries to represent twelve who have been companions of Jesus's ministry—eleven apostles and Matthias—as a body of great importance in the early church (see below, pp. 184f). Moreover, the gospels which, like Acts, give Jesus twelve companions, do not make the risen one appear to them, for Judas has defected. Matthew is quite specific in saying that it was "the eleven disciples" to whom Jesus appeared (28:16); and according to Acts Judas was replaced by Matthias only after the appearances had ended with Jesus's ascension. It seems, then, that the creed quoted by Paul did not understand 'the twelve' as companions of Jesus, one of whom had betrayed him. It is futile to try to harmonize Paul with the gospels here by supposing that 'twelve' in his creed does not mean twelve individuals, but an institution that can be so named whether its complement of members is full or not. Hence numerous scholars have conceded that 'the twelve' in this creed were a body of believers formed only after the appearances had begun, not during Jesus's ministry. There is often some (understandable) hesitation over this, evidenced when Fuller says: "Whether or not the twelve already existed as a body prior to the crucifixion need not . . . concern us" (1972, p. 35). Even Acts can do no better than drop the twelve at the mid point of its narrative and replace them, without explanation, with James and the elders.

We can explain why Paul mentions 'the twelve' in a creed he only once quotes if we suppose—as I did in *DJE*, following Schmithals (1971 pp. 70, 82)—that the community which formulated this creed knew the twelve as a group of enthusiasts who, having heard of an appearance of the risen Jesus to Cephas, thought it presaged a general resurrection of the dead—Christ raised from the dead being regarded in early Christianity as "the first fruits of those who have fallen asleep" (1 Cor. 15:20). In this exalted state of mind the group will have become convinced that Jesus appeared also to them, but, as the hope of a general resurrection that had led to the group's inception was not fulfilled, it will quickly have fallen apart.[7]

It is also noteworthy that Paul does not suggest that the appearances to Cephas, to the twelve, etc., were in any way different from the one he himself experienced; and this latter was a vision of the heavenly Jesus, as is implied even in Acts' version of it (see Acts 26:19). The earliest (pre-gospel) Christian thinking did not make Jesus tarry on Earth after his resurrection, but supposed that he was immediately exalted to heaven, from where his subsequent appearances were made.[8] It is quite consistent with this that Paul understood him to have risen with a "glorious" body of heavenly radiance (see Phil. 3:21), not of flesh and blood, which, he says, cannot inherit the kingdom of God (1 Cor. 15:50). Fuller notes (1972, pp. 20, 115) that, if Paul believed that Jesus's body had been thus transformed, he could not have accepted any tradition (such as we read of in Luke-Acts) that he rose in a physical body and ate and drank.

By the time we reach the gospels, mere visions of the risen Jesus had been felt to be too insubstantial as evidence, and more tangible phenomena were posited: first, an empty tomb. What Fuller says about Paul's apparent ignorance of any tradition about it well illustrates the embarrassment of commentators. He has to admit that what Paul states "cannot be used to imply a knowledge by him or by the pre-Pauline tradition" of the empty tomb story (1972, p. 16), which first appears at Mk. 16:1–8, and the "problematic features" of which "seem to lead to one conclusion", namely that it "is a later legend introduced by Mark for the first time into the narrative" (p. 52). Yet he regards the story as "very early", a "tradition with a long history behind it", and which was welcomed as confirmation of what was already implied by the appearances listed by Paul (pp. 56, 171): that is, if Jesus had been killed and buried, but had subsequently risen, he could no longer be in his tomb. Whether the story was based on fact is "a question to which the historian will never know the answer", and "in the last resort a matter of theological indifference" (p. 179); for "Christian faith is not believing *that* certain things happened", but rather faith in the Christian kerygma or preaching, "a kerygmatic faith" in Jesus Christ "as the saving act of God" (p. 183). As a High Church Anglican priest who knows what problems the documents present, Fuller takes the position: "We know that God raised Christ from the dead only through the preaching of the church and the response of faith" (1994, p. 71).

In the gospels, women visitors discover the tomb to be empty, and it has repeatedly been argued that a legend would have ascribed the discovery to men, as the testimony of women was not then regarded as reliable by Jews. This overlooks the constraints imposed by the story-line of the earliest gospel which represents the disciples as fleeing and deserting Jesus at his arrest (Mk. 14:50), so that only women followers were present at the crucifixion (and they only "watching from a distance", 15:40), and at the burial (15:47). Matthew says the same (26:56; 27:55 and 61), and this contrast between cowardly male disciples who have slunk away and faithful women who watch the crucifixion and burial, and so are then available to tend the tomb, has delighted feminist exegetes (particularly as a corrective to Paul's failure to include any women among the recipients of resurrection appearances). However, Luke very significantly omits the statement that the disciples dispersed at Jesus's arrest, and so is able to say that certain of them (24:24)—it is clear from the context that they were not women—did go to the tomb. John expands this, naming the visitors as Peter and the beloved disciple and reporting on their rivalry. Who the women visitors were depends on which gospel one reads.[9]

These traditions are still adduced in the argument that all parties must have admitted Jesus's tomb to have been empty shortly after his burial in it around A.D. 30, since otherwise orthodox Jews would have simply produced his body and thereby silenced the claim of the early Jerusalem church that he had risen. M.J. Harris (1983, pp. 38f) and S.T. Davis (1993, pp. 79, 183) both hold that the public preaching of the early church would have been challenged, had the tomb not been found empty. Against this, I would note:

1. The Pauline evidence does not support the view that the early Jerusalem Christians worshipped a Jesus who had recently been executed there (see above, pp. 69f).

2. Mark's gospel, where the tomb is first mentioned and said to have been found empty in the 30s, was written outside Palestine, not earlier than ca. A.D. 70, and quite possibly somewhat later. Matthew and Luke are not witnesses independent of Mark, but elaborate and adapt Markan material. Even the fourth gospel, we saw (above, p. 11), used synoptic-like traditions so that what we have in the empty-tomb narratives is "four different redactions for apologetic and kerygmatic reasons of a single story originating from one source" (Carnley, p. 47).

3. The evidence for wholesale Jewish acquiescence in Christian preaching of the resurrection in Jerusalem in the A.D. 30s comes from the early chapters of Acts. We saw (above, pp. 34f) that these speeches, by Peter and others, cannot be historical (cf. also p. 143 below). Nor can the mass conversions which they are represented as occasioning. Davis, taking what is said here in Acts at face value, speaks of "Jerusalem apparently seething with reports of Jesus's resurrection a few weeks after the crucifixion" (p. 80). In fact, however, the Christian community there will have been unobtrusive and as

good as unnoticed (see again, pp. 69f above). Dibelius has made the point, calling these people "a band gathered together in a common belief in Jesus Christ and in the expectation of his coming again . . . , leading a quiet and in the Jewish sense 'pious' existence", a "modest existence", sustained only by "the victorious conviction of the believers" (1956, p. 124). In trying to convince us of the contrary the author of Acts would have us believe that Peter's Pentecostal sermon converted 3,000 Jews (2:41) and his next sermon another 2,000 (4:4), and that altogether early Christianity was no hole-and-corner affair (26:26), but made a great public show and received attention in high places. It is all part of Luke's message that Christianity is essentially God-driven, and is propelled to success after success by the divine power behind it.

If we turn now from the tomb to the appearances, we find the gospel accounts hopelessly contradictory and consisting of stories inspired by different and conflicting motives. Here we no longer, as in Paul, have a mere list, but—except in Mark, the best manuscripts which terminate before recording any appearances—descriptions of appearances in specified circumstances to persons who had known Jesus before his death. As we saw, correlation with the persons listed by Paul is poor; the gospels know nothing of an appearance to over five hundred or to James; and whereas the apostle Cephas (normally equated with Peter) heads Paul's list, the disciple Peter is not vouchsafed any appearance specifically to himself in any canonical gospel except Luke (and even there it is merely said to have occurred and is not among the appearances that are described). Even Ladd finds this "an amazing omission . . . in view of the leading role of Peter in the early church" (1979, p. 91).

Harris, like many conservative apologists, believes that these gospel resurrection narratives can be harmonized, and also finds them "self-authenticating", on the ground that they are sober and straightforward compared with apocryphal parallels which are agreed to be fabrications (1983, p. 62). Ladd's account is likewise a good example of the way he accomplishes what he calls his primary task, namely "to interpret the Gospels as they stand as credible reports of Jesus", "to understand the Bible's perspective of promise and fulfilment in terms of its own view of God and his relation to history" (1966, pp. xiii–xiv). To this end he takes the synoptics as reliable sources and the fourth gospel as complementing them. If they state something as a fact, then it is to be accepted uncritically as such. That the tomb was found empty on Easter Sunday is, then, a "fact", likewise that the grave clothes were undisturbed (1979, p. 132); for evaluating NT claims must not involve calling in question what its books allege as a factual basis for these claims. No secular historian would approach his data in this entirely uncritical way; and this is not—as Ladd supposes—because of Enlightenment prejudices against supernatural phenomena, but because a historian does not rule out in advance the possibility that certain stories in his sources are legendary. Ladd declares that his own approach can best be described as what has been called "Biblical Realism" (1966, p. xiii). Klaus Berger, reviewing his work, prefers to call it "modernized fundamentalism" (1988, p. 363). It is by no means uncommon. R.T. France says his own approach is similar to Ladd's in that he "assumes the essential reliability of the tradition unless there are good reasons for questioning it" (1971, pp. 22–23). When there are, he usually manages to transform them into non-reasons.

Turning now to details, the fourth gospel has it that Jesus's body was anointed before burial by Nicodemus (one of the group of characters known only from this gospel), who used "about a hundred pounds weight" of substance in the process (19:39). Ladd suggests that this may nevertheless have been only an incomplete embalmment, in which case there is no contradiction with Mark, who has it that Jesus was wrapped in a linen sheet, a shroud for burial (with no suggestion of any anointing), and who makes women come to the tomb a day and two nights later with "spices that they might come and anoint him" (15:46 and 16:1). Another problem is that the fourth gospel does not have him buried in a shroud, but in "linen cloths", bandages (Jn. 19:40). The "traditional harmonization" of this with Mark, says Ladd (p. 85), is that the body was initially wrapped in a shroud, which was then either torn into strips, or strips of cloth were wound around it. Then there is the guard of soldiers at the tomb, a feature unique to Matthew. The way he introduces it (27:64) shows that he wants it in order to exclude the possible objection that the disciples could have stolen Jesus's body and then pretended that he had risen. Because of this guard, Matthew has to drop Mark's allegation that the women proposed to enter the tomb (to anoint the body), and represents them as intending only to visit it (28:1). To get them inside, he has to put the guard out of action with a "great earthquake" caused by the descent of an angel whose "appearance was as lightning" and who petrified the guard, rolled away and then sat on the stone sealing the tomb—incidents all unmentioned in the other gospels. As 'selective reporters' they presumably felt free to skip over such minor occurrences. This story of guards who saw the angel, knew that the tomb was empty, and had to be bribed by the chief priests to pretend that the body had been stolen while they were asleep (Mt. 28:11–15), shows that Christian tradition does not, after all, uniformly make only women the initial witnesses concerning the resurrection.

In the fourth gospel Mary Magdalene comes to the tomb alone (in the other three there is more than one woman visitor); she finds the stone already rolled away and two angels inside the tomb (as against Mark's one). In Mark the women fled from the empty tomb "and said nothing to anyone for they were afraid" (16:8). In Matthew, however, they left "with fear and great joy and ran to bring his [Jesus's] disciples word" (28:8). He met them on their way and told them not to be afraid (28:10). This allows Ladd to suppose that this encounter (mentioned only in Matthew) perhaps dispelled their fear and so led them to report their experiences. But it is clear from my quotation of Mt. 28:8 that they intended to do this before the encounter: hence the contradiction with Mark remains, and Ladd has to concede that "this may be one of the unimportant discrepancies which mark the Synoptic Gospels" (p. 85).

Luke's version of the story of the women at the empty tomb does not include a resurrection appearance. Instead, he follows it with an account, unique to his gospel, of an appearance to two disciples (Cleopas and another) on the road to Emmaus, said in the text to be a village near Jerusalem (24:13–32). Ladd believes that this story "possesses historical substance" because the appearance "occurred to two utterly insignificant disciples", only one of whom is even named (p. 86). If it had occurred to named apostles, apologists would be saying that such precise and detailed reporting bore the stamp of authenticity. Stories where the characters are named are still defended in this way, even though it is often the later versions of a tradition which supply the most details. The article 'Names for the Nameless' in *The Oxford Companion to the Bible* shows how irresistible the tendency to provide names for numerous unnamed biblical figures has proved to be. As a result, many traditions identify the second of the two disciples in the Emmaus story as Nathanael, or Nicodemus, or someone called Simon (not Simon Peter), or even as the evangelist Luke himself (*art. cit.* in Metzger and Coogan 1993).

In this Emmaus story, Jesus joins the two men on their journey, and as there seems to be nothing out of the ordinary in his appearance, they take him for some traveller unknown to them. They proceed to tell him that Jesus of Nazareth, "a prophet mighty in deed and word", has just been condemned and crucified, to the disappointment of all their hopes, although his tomb has been reported to be empty and he has been said to be alive. The stranger responds by explaining that all these events happened in accordance with prophecy; and "beginning from Moses and from all the prophets, he interpreted to them in all the scriptures the things concerning himself"—without disclosing his identity. The whole point of this story is clearly to establish in this way that the Passion and resurrection, central to the faith of the church, are firmly grounded in God's overall plan. Jesus does not here actually specify any OT passages, and certainly none that foretold his resurrection (see above p. 123). Nevertheless, as Richard Harries, Bishop of Oxford, concedes: "The story reflects the experience not just of two disciples, but of the church as a whole, in knowing Christ through the [OT] scriptures" (1987, p. 56). The church will have accumulated such passages only over a period of time; but here Jesus is represented as already being able to recite them all.

C.S. Lewis defended the historicity of the gospel resurrection appearances on the ground that the failure of the two disciples in this story to recognize Jesus rules out any theory that the appearances were hallucinations (1947, p. 176). I mention this to show how resolutely apologists reject the possibility that any of the stories in these resurrection narratives are mere legends. For them, if Jesus is said in the gospels to have appeared to persons who had known him during his lifetime, and who yet failed immediately to recognize him, then these are facts on which we can confidently base any interpretation of what actually happened after the death and burial. In reality, the failure to recognize him straight away is an essential element in the effectiveness of the Emmaus story. It alone makes possible the irony of the situation where the 'stranger' is told in detail of events of which he himself has been the victim. Yet although Luke needed this element, he did not find it easy to introduce it into the tale; for how can the two disciples be plausibly represented as failing to recognize a man they have known so recently and so well? To motivate their failure, Luke has to attribute it to some unspecified (but presumably supernatural) power: "Their eyes were holden that they should not know him" (24:16. The verb rendered as 'holden' is *kratein*, 'to secure forcibly'). Not until the very end of the story is this impediment removed: "And their eyes were opened and they knew him" (verse 31), whereupon he vanished.

Luke is certainly very concerned to convince us that the resurrection appearances were not hallucinations, and to this end he stresses the physical reality of the risen one. Although the Emmaus story ends with Jesus "vanishing" into thin air and then reappearing equally independently of physical means to the eleven in a room in Jerusalem (cf. Jn. 20:19 and 26 where he is expressly said to enter through closed doors), he then convinces them that he is nevertheless no insubstantial ghost by inviting them to "handle" his "flesh and bones" and by eating "a piece of broiled fish" in their presence (Lk. 24:31–32, 36–43). Both the Emmaus story of his walking in earthly form, and his subsequent eating fish and inviting physical touch, are unknown to the earlier accounts and are evidently meant to answer the objection that what the disciples had seen was merely a ghost. These corporeal and tangible features are introduced even though they are quite inconsistent not only with the Pauline tradition, but also, as Lampe points out (1966, pp. 50–51), with other elements incorporated into Luke's own narrative, such as the sudden appearance within a room. Wiles has the same inconsistency in mind when he notes, discreetly, that "the differing degrees of physicality" implied in the records of Jesus' resurrection are "puzzling features" (1974, p. 138).

To summarize important differences found so far between the conclusions to the three synoptic gospels, we may say that Mark rests content with making the bare fact of the resurrection clear, and although an appearance to disciples is promised (by the speaker to women at the empty tomb, 16:7), none is recorded in the best manuscripts. The verses which follow 16:8 are, as we saw (above, p. 18), attempts by more than one continuator to introduce (among other material) the kind of appearances known from the two later synoptics. Matthew, for his part, writes what Houlden calls a "free elaboration of Mark" which takes "imaginative steps" to demonstrate the historicity of the resurrection by "squashing the story about the theft of Jesus's body"; while Luke shows "anxiety about his risen Jesus's physicality" and is plainly concerned with "warding off enemies . . . who deny that very fact" (Houlden 1996, pp. 203–04).

A further very significant discrepancy concerns the location of the appearances. In Paul there is of course no location specified at all. In Matthew the eleven are instructed to go to Galilee to see Jesus risen; they do so, he appears to them there on "the mountain where he had appointed them" (28:16), and the gospel ends when he there commissions them to baptize and to teach all nations. In Luke, however, he appears to them only in Jerusalem and its environs, and tells them to "tarry in the city" (24:49). Ladd conveniently ignores this command, given on resurrection day,[10] mentions only its repetition in Acts 1:4 ("He charged them not to depart from Jerusalem"), and interprets the interval between resurrection day and the giving of this command in Acts as allowing time for them to have visited Galilee and returned—even though, according to the previous verse in Acts, Jesus had been with them during this interval, instructing them about the kingdom. Ladd supposes (1979, p. 90) that it "may be of some comfort to many readers" that a scholar of the stature of C.H. Dodd wrote, in his final (1971) book, "as though he considered the appearances both in Galilee and Jerusalem to be true". What Dodd actually did was to list different gospel stories of the appearances and to comment that, while the "dramatic motive" of them all is to elicit the cry "It is the Lord", they differ "in almost all other particulars, and the attempt to harmonize them is not hopeful" (1971, pp. 169f). In this same context he noted that the question whether Jesus had in fact "in some way left his tomb" is one on which the historian "may properly suspend judgment" (p. 167).

Luke does not merely omit any Galilean appearances. He deliberately excludes them, not only by means of the command to stay in Jerusalem, but also by rewording Mk. 16:7, which records what is both a promise and a summons (to be conveyed to the disciples by the women at the empty tomb), namely that "he goeth before you into Galilee; there shall ye see him, as he said unto you". This last clause refers back to 14:27–28, where Jesus foretells that they "will be scattered abroad" (as they are when he is then arrested), but that "after I am raised up I will go before you into Galilee". The purpose of his summoning them is surely that they should establish themselves there as a Christian community. The summons would make little sense if they had to return immediately to the distant Jerusalem, and make their base in that city. Hence these references to Galilee are incompatible with the picture of the Jerusalem-orientated mission which Luke wished to create. And so he omitted Mk. 14:28 altogether, and rewrote Mk. 16:7 so as to change it from a summons to Galilee into a mere reminder that, "while he was still in Galilee", Jesus had predicted his own Passion and resurrection (Lk. 24:6–7). This is not 'selective reporting', but a remodelling of an earlier tradition.

Finally, there is a contradiction, not to be set aside as trivial, between Luke's gospel and Acts (both by the same author) concerning the ascension. In the gospel, Jesus ascends on resurrection day, but in Acts only forty days later, having utilized the interval to give the disciples "many proofs" that he was truly risen and to instruct them "concerning the kingdom of God" (Acts 1:3). It seems, then, that, by the time Luke wrote Acts, he wanted to assure his readers that the disciples were fully instructed and hence reliable guarantors of the teachings which they supposedly passed on. Ladd does not face this inconsistency, but merely comments that "Luke is writing very selectively", and in his gospel "seems to have compressed the account into a single day" (1979, pp. 89, 91). Such compression does not merely select from events of forty days, but telescopes them, and the contradiction remains.

One way of eliminating this contradiction has been to take

Jesus's "parting" from the eleven on resurrection day (Lk. 24:51) as not a final ascension, but only a temporary withdrawal from them. In these closing verses of the gospel, he leads them from Jerusalem to nearby Bethany, raises his hands in solemn blessing, and then "parted from them". Not all manuscripts add the words "and was carried up into heaven", and some commentators take the shorter text as original, not as a scribal attempt to harmonize the narrative with Acts by deleting this reference to the finality of the parting. But a mere temporary parting would destroy the whole solemnity and pathos of the gospel's conclusion—a pathos underlined by the procession from the city and the blessing with uplifted hands. Nor is there any suggestion in the gospel that Jesus returned to the eleven, for its following, final verses record their joyous return to Jerusalem and their continual presence in the temple, blessing God. Even Acts—although it goes on to speak of the forty days and of the ascension as following them—begins by allowing (1:2) that Luke's gospel records all that Jesus did and taught "until the day in which he was received up". Naturally there were sribes who did their best to get rid of this 'received up' (Details in Haenchen, 1968b, p. 107n).

Jesus ascends into heaven and must remain there "until the times of restoration of all things" (Acts 3:21). This idea of a person rapt up to heaven in preservation for the end was a familiar one. Indeed, says Zwiep, "in Jewish thinking rapture (ascension) and parousia (a return from heaven) were seen together as two sides of one coin", with traditions about Elijah forming a particularly striking parallel to those about Jesus: in both cases, a heavenly assumption "inaugurates a period of temporal preservation in heaven with a view to a future eschatological return" (1997, pp. 79, 116). At 2 Kings 2, Elijah is "taken up by a whirlwind into heaven", and at Malachi 4:5 God promises to send him back "before the great and terrible day" of judgement comes; and the NT itself gives ample evidence of popular belief in his return (Mk. 6:15, 8:28, 9:11, and so forth).

Archbishop Carnley is justly scornful of attempts to piece the different resurrection traditions together "in a manner of the pieces of a jigsaw, so as to produce a single harmonious picture" (1987, p. 18). It is surely because the evidence does not lend itself to such treatment that theology today, as he says, offers a spectrum of views, "ranging from belief in the resurrection of Christ as a historical event of the past, to talk of it as little more than a religiously useful story or myth . . . , not to mention a very significant number of theologians who are content to treat the resurrection with a degree of ambivalence or lack of candour which makes it difficult to discern any clear outline of the exact position that they espouse!" The result is a state of theological affairs that is "very bewildering indeed for the contemporary Christian, to say nothing of the large company of bemused spectators outside of the church who must often wonder what this key element of the Christian faith is really all about" (pp. 12, 21). The breadth of the spectrum of opinion about it is evident in a 1994 symposium entitled *The Resurrection*, with nineteen contributors. In the view of one of them (Michael Goulder, a theologian but not a theist), "it would be helpful if Christian scholars would . . . tell their churches that the tale of the resurrection of Jesus has no dependable basis, and is not worthy of serious consideration".[11] The reviewer in *Theology* has hinted that it would be nice if some of the other eighteen were to indicate with equal clarity where on this matter they stand, "for it is not always easy to know".[12]

Carnley's own solution to the perplexities is the not unusual one of dispersing them by introducing the witness of the Holy Spirit: "Our present experience of the Spirit of Christ convinces us that the stories of the empty tomb and appearances are substantially true, i.e. they convince us that Jesus was raised from the dead" (p. 249n). I have criticized this argument elsewhere (*WWJ*, pp. 43–44), and here need note only that to introduce 'the Spirit' as an adequate response to all damaging objections has long been recognized as a weak theological ploy. Strauss, for instance, complained of the way in which Schleiermacher "appeals to the witness of the Christian consciousness as giving us complete certainty in regard to the Saviour" (1997, p. 48).

The most recent book I have seen on the resurrection by a Christian theologian reiterates what has often been said, namely that the appearances were no more than visions, as is clear from the earliest (Pauline) evidence, and that "a consistent modern view must say farewell to the resurrection of Jesus as a historical event"

(Lüdemann, 1995, p. 130). The author here records that, when he first argued this case (in a book in German in 1994), "legal proceedings" against him were called for (p. v). His book is a turgid analysis of the relevant NT evidence, and this English rendering of it includes mistranslations which can confuse the reader.[13] It concludes with the assurance that 'the Easter experience' really tells us no more about Jesus than we already know from his ministry, and is therefore dispensable.[14] This well illustrates how theologians can give up much and yet argue that it is very little.

One can say the same of Uta Ranke-Heinemann's popular paperback *Nein und Amen* (1994). She lost her professorial Chair for Catholic theology at Essen by interpreting the virgin birth "theologically" instead of "biologically", and now holds a Chair for the history of religion there. The 'No' in her title indicates her rejection of the "fantastic ballast of legend and myth" within the NT, while the "Amen" signals acceptance of what she supposes to be the valuable residue—"the life of Jesus and his voice speaking to us" (p. 358). She classes the story of the empty tomb with the legends and quotes, approvingly, the verdict of the Jesuit theologian Karl Rahner that this story does not record a historical event which occasioned the "Easter faith", but itself resulted from a prior conviction that Jesus was risen (p. 162). In her view, his death, resurrection and ascension all occurred simultaneously and have not taken him away from us to another place, but made him "the one who is ultimately near". Resurrection means "the final openness of a future", and we may ourselves still live in hope of it (pp. 166–67, 181–82). This exemplifies the tendency of many liberal theologians to rely on vague, even quasi-mystical interpretations and on forms of words with emotional appeal.

One does not expect a defence of the resurrection from a Jewish scholar, and Pinchas Lapide's book to this effect is such a surprising exception that the publisher of the 1984 English translation has put a triumphant "An orthodox Jew says Yes!" on its front cover. I have criticized Lapide's views in full in *The Jesus Legend* where I note that he allows that the NT remains the only source of information concerning the resurrection, that the relevant narratives contain "much legend", and that nowhere else in the canon are "the contradictions so glaring" (Lapide, pp. 32–34). Surprisingly he tries to illustrate the despair of the disciples immediately after the crucifixion by quoting Jn. 21:3 with the comment: "Peter says in deepest resignation: 'I'll go fishing'. And the others, a pitiful remainder of seven men, . . . said dejectedly 'We'll come along'" (p. 86). There is of course no resignation or dejection here; for this incident in chapter 21 occurs *after* the risen Jesus has already appeared, in chapter 20, to Mary Magdalene and the disciples and given them physical proof that he is alive again. Only the most conservative scholars regard chapter 21 as part of the gospel, and not as a clumsy appendix where the disciples, returning to their old profession (long since abandoned) as fishermen in Galilee, have apparently forgotten that the risen one instructed them in chapter 20 to go out as missionaries and gave them the Holy Ghost so that they can forgive sins or withhold such forgiveness.

In the end Lapide finds that we need faith to accept the resurrection, yet that such faith is "true faith", based on a real occurrence, "for without a fact of history there is no act of true faith" (p. 92). Whether the resurrection is 'a fact of history' is what is in question. If the evidence sufficed to show that it was, 'faith' would not be needed.

In *WWJ* I devoted a chapter to the problems raised by the resurrection narratives, and paid particular attention to the apologetics of Gary Habermas and his supporters in their 1985 debate (published in 1987) with Antony Flew.[15] I have also elsewhere discussed a few obviously ridiculous alternatives to accepting the resurrection as a fact. The most famous of these is the attempt by the eighteenth-century scholar H.S. Reimarus to account for the contradictions in the narratives by supposing that the disciples first stole Jesus's body from the tomb, and then circulated these stories, not consistent with each other, which claimed that he had risen from the dead.[16] The valuable part of Reimarus's account is his clear demonstration—novel at the time—that real contradictions are present. (There are even more of them than he realized.) Morgan and Barton give a sympathetic account of his views, saying that his "fraud hypothesis is less far fetched than it initially appears", in that he was naturally led to explain the discrepancies of the narratives in this way because he retained the traditional view that the gospels were written by eyewitnesses of the events reported in them (1988, p. 54). Nevertheless, as Strauss pointed out in his 1861 essay on Reimarus, it is absurd to suppose that the apostles knew that there was no word of truth in their proclamation of their master's resurrection, and yet spread this story with a fire of conviction that sufficed to change the world.

Other equally unacceptable reconstructions are the 'swoon theory' that Jesus did not die on the cross, but recovered consciousness in the tomb; and H.J. Schonfield's variant of this in his 1965 *The Passover Plot*.[17] The 'swoon' theories interpret the gospel passion stories very selectively and arbitrarily, and all these theories take these passion narratives as their basis, whereas in fact the earliest extant form of the resurrection traditions is the bare Pauline list of appearances. In earliest Christianity, it was, as we saw, by claiming to have seen the risen Jesus that a preacher could establish his authority, so there was a certain disposition towards having such an experience. This does not mean that such a claim was fraudulent. Only those who lack understanding of the processes by which myths are formed will argue that, either a tradition is true, or it must have been invented by cynics who knew the facts to have been otherwise. The earliest Christians were expecting the final judgement, with the resurrection of the dead, and their belief in Jesus's resurrection was surely to some extent prompted by their regarding it as assuring them of the imminence of this general resurrection: it was "the first fruits" of the harvest of the dead (1 Cor. 15:20), a sign that the last days had really arrived (see Acts 4:2). Moreover, it was naturally supposed that, if Jesus was risen, he must surely have given proof that what was seen of him was no mere hallucination or ghost. Other objections, such as the possible theft of the body from the tomb must also, it was surely thought, be refutable by the facts; hence the idea that the tomb must have been guarded. Constructing a situation in the mind in accordance with convictions about what 'must' be (or have been) the case is as frequent today as ever in the past; and so once the belief in Jesus's resurrection was there, it was almost inevitable that, in time, it would come to be defended by the kind of narrative medley that we find in the canonical gospels. The same happened on a less extensive scale in the case of belief in the virgin birth, and in both

cases apocryphal material supplemented the already layered canonical data.

What must surely strike my readers forcibly is the unshakeable
confidence both of those who try to harmonize the data, and of
those who hold that, even if the historicity of the event is surrendered, there is little resulting damage to Christian beliefs. In the
case of the resurrection, this is an attitude which would have
astounded Paul, who insisted: "If Christ hath not been raised, then
is our preaching vain. Your faith also is vain" (1 Cor. 15:14). It all
amounts to a sobering illustration of the way in which an outlook
which has been built up and accepted over many years can survive
evidence or argument of any kind.

Some of the apologetic importance of the virgin birth and the
resurrection—as miracles effected on Jesus—lies in their making
more plausible the miracles of Jesus himself. Christians who accept
the two former as "crowning wonders" cannot, says F.F. Bruce,
"logically deny the possibility of their being accompanied by lesser
'signs'." And so, he adds, we should not reject these latter out of
hand, but consider the evidence for them (1952, p. 17). The context
shows that he is a little disconcerted by the scepticism of some of his
theological colleagues. So let us see how some of the less sceptical
have made out their case.

iii. Harvey's Defence of Miracles Worked by Jesus

A.E. Harvey's chapter on Jesus's miracles has been widely welcomed as a defence of their historicity, although Harvey is slightly
worried by the silence about them in the epistles:

> We know from the epistles that it was possible to speak and write about
> Jesus without any mention of his miraculous power. (1982, p. 98)

He finds this the more surprising since the authors of these letters
had considerable interest in miracles: they themselves were able to
impress their audiences with "the power of signs and wonders"
(Rom. 15:18–19; cf. Hebrews 2:4), with what they call "the signs of
an apostle" (2 Cor. 12:12). I would add that 'signs, wonders, and

powers' was clearly a standing phrase, showing what the missionaries were capable of; yet not until we come to Acts do we find it applied to Jesus, in Peter's description of him as "a man attested to you by God with powers and wonders and signs" (2:22); and there are good reasons for not accepting this and other speeches as early material assimilated into Acts: the proofs from scripture they offer depend on the Greek OT (often where it deviates from the Hebrew) and so were concocted in a Hellenistic community, not spoken persuasively to the Jews in Jerusalem, as Acts would have us believe.[18] Not only the canonical epistles, but also the letters of the earliest Fathers (Clement of Rome, Ignatius of Antioch, and Polycarp of Smyrna) fail to ascribe miracles to Jesus.

Harvey even notes that one would not really expect the Jesus who "emptied himself" of his supernatural status in order to "humble himself" by obediently suffering death on Earth (Phil. 2:5–8) to have been "at the same time capable of performing supernatural feats". But to interpret this early evidence as meaning what it does seem to imply—namely that, for Paul, all of Jesus's life between incarnation and death is summed up in the idea of humiliation[19]—would be to discount the contrary portrait given in the gospels. And so he decides that

> Just as . . . the virtual silence of the epistles with regard to Jesus as a teacher cannot be set against the overwhelming evidence of the gospels that he was one, so we can reasonably accept the impression given by the synoptics of one who was believed to have performed notable miracles as a firm historical datum (p. 99).

In spite of this confident brushing aside of the silence of the earlier documents, a worried note reappears apropos of the exorcisms:

> Apart from the gospels themselves, we have virtually no information whatever about Jesus's exorcisms, and if anyone is to regard the gospels, in this respect as in others, as totally tendentious, there is no ground we can stand on in order to prove him wrong. (p. 109)

Paul represents Christ's death and resurrection as a victory over the evil powers, but does not suggest that he practised exorcism (see below, p. 156).

Generalizing summaries such as "he healed many" (Mk. 3:10)

are taken by Harvey to indicate that "the evangelists seem to have a larger stock of miracles to record than any of them actually makes use of" (p. 101). This hypothesis—that each one offers his own "selection"—enables him to avoid embarrassment over John's miracles being so different from those of the synoptics, as well as to represent each evangelist as not going for the sensational in modestly confining himself to a few examples.

Harvey's reasoning here is based on a naive assessment of the summaries in the gospels which give general statements about Jesus's therapeutic activities. Mk. 3:7–12, for instance, states that a great multitude from many localities followed him, that all who had diseases "pressed upon him to touch him", and that whenever the unclean spirits beheld him, they fell down before him and cried "You are the Son of God". Similar summaries occur at Mk. 1:32–34 and 6:54–56, and they all signal that Jesus continued his work further in the manner already described in particular cases. Such summaries are the obvious way of making detached scenes into a continuous and connected narrative. Hence it is questionable whether they—any more than the summaries in Acts which occupied us above (p. 35)—are really based on knowledge of anything additional to the individual incidents actually reported. From traditions about these latter the evangelists will have built up in their minds a general (and very edifying) picture of Jesus's ministry, and will then have written summaries reflecting this picture in order to link the particular occurrences into a connected whole, and so produce an account which is more than a mere accumulation of details. That this is how they went to work is strongly suggested by the fact that Matthew and Luke make multiple use of Mark's summaries: Matthew, for instance, uses Mk. 3:7–12 twice (at 4:24–25 and 12:15–16), and in this way seeks to achieve an even more connected story than Mark's. The author of the OT book of Chronicles did the same—presumably for the same purpose—with summaries he drew from 1 Kings (Details in Cadbury 1933, p. 394). But commentators are naturally reluctant to regard the editorial summaries in the gospels as no more than imaginative sketches. Cadbury goes no further than to allow that they have been "largely" distilled from the individual stories (p. 393). Dibelius concedes that the evangelists had "hardly any other means of expanding these individual instances into a representation of the whole" (1971, p. 224).

Harvey is aware that many modern readers find the gospel miracles incredible, and counters this scepticism with three observations (pp. 99–101):

i.   Modern knowledge of how mind and body are correlated enables us to regard many of the healing miracles as "natural phenomena", or in other words as not miracles at all.

ii. Jesus never procures rainfall; he goes beyond Jewish (if not pagan) tradition in that he cures lameness and paralysis; and raising the dead is poorly represented even in the pagan stories. There are thus "too many unusual features" in his miracles for us to be able to attribute the stories to "conventional legend-mongering".

iii. They are also unusual in containing "details of precise reporting" which seem to derive from "some historical recollection", and in the "remarkable restraint" of the relevant narratives which show no delight in the miraculous for its own sake.

This is all quite unconvincing. Much of the world's fiction is characterized by 'details of precise reporting', and it is often the latest version of a legend that specifies the most details. Harvey himself allows that "more than any other stories, miracle stories grow in the telling" (p. 110). Some of us see little 'restraint' in the story where Jesus dislodges a "legion" of demons from a man and allows their request to be transferred to a herd of 2,000 pigs which promptly rush into the sea and are drowned (Mk. 5:1–13). 'Restraint' is in any case a very relative term. What is less wild than completely unrestrained fiction is not thereby authenticated—otherwise we should have to accept Origen's argument that Jesus really did raise the dead because what the gospels claim on this head is so modest: only three such cases, and all of persons recently deceased, whereas fiction would have postulated many and have included people who had long been in their tombs (*Contra Celsum*, ii, 48). As for Harvey's "unusual features", R.M. Grant has inferred from his detailed investigation that "a thoroughgoing distinction between Christian and non-Christian miracle stories cannot be made" (1952, p. 173). He mentions, for instance, Greek and Roman stories of control over storms and waters, multiplication of bread, and changing water into wine; and also ascension stories told of Romulus, Empedocles, Augustus, and others (pp. 178–79). E.P. Sanders too finds no "significant difference" between the Christian and the pagan stories, and that Jesus' miracles are "not greatly different from those attributed to other Jews in the same general period" (1993a, p. 163, 1993b, p. 74). The case that this is so has been well made by Vermes, who has pointed, for instance, to the first century B.C. Honi, the rainmaker, and to the first century A.D. Galilean charismatic Hanina ben Dosa. In his autobiography Vermes recalls that it was largely his own studies that made the latter into "a household name among New Testament scholars". He has also examined the titles of 'prophet', 'lord' and 'son of God'—all borne by Jesus in the gospels—in their semitic (Aramaic or Hebrew) contexts, and found them "applied, in biblical and post-biblical Jewish literature, to charismatic holy men" (1998, pp. 210, 213). Sanders wonders why Harvey "did not discuss the Elisha cycle, where there are stories of cures which parallel those attributed to Jesus, such as the cure of a leper (2 Kings 5:1–14; cf. Mk. 1:40–45 and parallels) and the raising of a dead child (2 Kings 4:32–37; cf. Mk. 5:21–43 and parallels)." These, he adds, "may be excluded because they are remote in time, but they nevertheless reduce the uniqueness of the miracles attributed to Jesus" (1985, p. 162).

For Harvey, there are yet further features which make Jesus's miracles unusual for the time and place of his activity:

i. He seldom "procures a cure by means of prayer". Harvey nevertheless allows that "he instructs his followers in both the necessity and the power of prayer for performing miracles" (p. 107). At Mk. 9:29 he tells the disciples that a certain type of demon "can come out by nothing, save by prayer". At Mt. 21:18–22 he makes a fig tree wither away immediately simply by saying "Let there be no fruit from thee henceforth for ever"; and he then tells his disciples that, if they have faith, they can perform miracles in the same way; if they say to a mountain, "Be taken up and cast into the sea", then "it shall be done". He adds: "All things whatsoever ye shall ask in prayer, believing, ye shall receive". All this does not look like an undervaluation of prayer in the context of miracle-working.

ii. "By far the commonest manifestation of allegedly miraculous gifts was the ability to foretell the future from a close observation of present phenomena . . . It is a striking fact about the records of Jesus that they nowhere credit him with gifts of this kind" (pp. 105–06). This is the sheerest special pleading, the aim of which is to insulate the Jesus stories from suspicion of "Hellenistic influence" (p. 106). One can only comment, first that what these stories do credit him with is an ability to make much more marvellous predictions than could have been based on mere inferences from the present. At Mk. 7:29 he tells the Syro-Phoenician woman to go home, where she will find her daughter cured. The second half of Mark is positively characterized by similar predictions: where the colt will be found for his triumphal entry into Jerusalem (it will be male, tied, previously unsat upon); how the room will be found in which he will eat the Passover with his disciples. At Mt. 17:27 he tells Peter that the first fish he catches will have a shekel-coin in its mouth—exactly the sum needed to pay the temple tax due from the two of them. At Lk. 5:4–7 he correctly predicts a miraculous draught of fishes. Second, is it even true that none of his predictions could have been prompted by observation of the present? He predicts his Passion in a situation of growing tension between himself and his opponents. And was there nothing in the demeanour of Judas and Peter to prompt his predictions of betrayal by the one and denial by the other?

iii. "Jesus nowhere appeals to the impressions made by his own miracles as authentication for his personal authority" (p. 112). But he does just this when he says that those who are about to witness his miraculous cure of the man with the palsy will know from this that he possesses the power to forgive sins (Mk. 2:10–11). Harvey himself notes that in the fourth gospel "the evidential value of the miracles as 'signs' authenticating Jesus's authority is strongly emphasised" (p. 101). Again, a Q passage (Mt. 11:2–11; cf. Lk. 7:22) tells that John the Baptist sent his disciples to ask Jesus whether or not he is "he that cometh", the Messiah; and Jesus replies by specifying miracles which authenticate him: "The blind receive their sight and the lame walk, the lepers are cleansed and the deaf hear; and the dead are raised up, and the poor have good tidings preached to them."

These words about the blind, the lame and the deaf clearly allude to Isaiah 35:4–6:

> Behold your God will come. . . . He will come and save you. Then the eyes of the blind shall be opened, and the ears of the deaf unstopped. Then shall the lame man leap as a hart, and the tongue of the dumb shall sing.

Obviously, Jesus is being made to argue that he is indeed the one of whom the prophets have spoken. Harvey himself allows, apropos of the cures of deaf, dumb, blind, and lame in various gospel stories, that "it can hardly be an accident that these four complaints are precisely those which Isaiah names as conditions which will be cured in the coming age". They are, then, "eschatological miracles" (p. 115). For many commentators this means that they are not historical at all, but figure in stories contrived by the evangelists (or their sources) in order to convince readers that, with Jesus, the new age has dawned. Not so, thinks Harvey. His view is that people surely hoped that the new age would be free from congenital ailments, and that Jesus actually cured blindness and other diseases so as to demonstrate to his audiences the possibility of overcoming these apparent barriers to a better world. That musing on Isaiah in the early church is more likely to have been what prompted the Q passage quoted above (and hence indirectly the accounts of the Jesuine miracles which reflect it) is suggested by a remarkable parallel in one of the Qumran scrolls, where it is said that "he will heal the wounded, give life to the dead and preach good news to the poor". Collins believes that God was understood here to work through an agent, specified in the same Qumran text as "the Messiah whom heaven and earth obey" (1997, pp. 88f, 158).

Harvey's account has been welcomed by conservative apologists as showing the superiority of the gospel miracle material to any non-Christian parallels. C.L. Blomberg, for instance, speaks of his "helpful survey of miracle stories" as demonstrating "just how unique the gospel accounts are both in style and in significance" (article 'Healing', in Green 1992). I have gone through Harvey's chapter in some detail in order to show that there is no justification for this claim.

It is worth while to look at two examples of Harvey's "eschatological miracles", namely the pericopes of the healing of a deaf-mute and of a blind man, both recorded only in Mark (7:31–36; 8:22–26), and so similar in their wording that the one has been regarded as a duplicate of the other. They both conclude with Jesus's injunction to the patient not to make the cure known to other people—although this makes no sense in the given situations: those who have brought the patient to him will naturally check on whether the therapy has been effective. Mark is here introducing the doctrine that Jesus's status as Messiah is secret, imposed on much of the data in this gospel, with resulting complications and implausibilities, as I have shown in chapter 5 of *The Jesus Legend*.

In both these pericopes Jesus uses spittle in the process of effecting the cure. All races of antiquity attached magical healing significance to spittle (see the discussion in Hull 1974, pp. 76–78), and this crudity, well-known from pagan parallels and embarrassing to commentators, may explain why Matthew and Luke omitted these two Markan stories. Jesus cures the blind man in two stages, first spitting on his eyes and touching him, then—after asking him whether he can now see at all—touching his eyes. Some commentators (such as Vincent Taylor, 1966, p. 369) have claimed that this shows the whole story to be a true report; for the evangelist would not otherwise have said that two attempts were needed to effect a cure—thus giving opponents of Christianity a chance to denigrate Jesus. One might just as well argue that having the cure effected in two stages was meant to show what a difficult case it was, and to emphasize the great power required in nevertheless mastering it.

In the fourth gospel (Jn. 9:1–12), a blind man—blind from birth (a typical piece of Johannine exaggeration, meant to stress the prodigious nature of his cure)—is likewise cured by means of spittle. Here the purpose is to make manifest the Johannine doctrine that Jesus (far from having a status that is secret) is "the light of the world" (verse 5), and that the Father is manifested in him (14:9). We see from this that entirely different theological conceptions can enlist the same or similar miracle stories in their service.

In the other of the two Markan pericopes—the story of the healing of the deaf-mute—Jesus takes the man aside privately, puts his fingers into his ears, spits, touches his tongue, looks up to heaven and sighs, and utters an Aramaic word of command ("Ephphatha, that is, be opened" 7:34), whereupon the man is immediately healed. The 'sighing' or 'groaning' (the verb is *stenazō*) can be paralleled in the Greek magical papyri, where it supposedly augments the magician's power (Garrett 1989, p. 19). And the Aramaic word "could hardly fail to suggest to a non-Semitic reader of the time the magic word in an unknown tongue, often enough quite meaningless, by which the wandering magician effected his cures" (Beare 1964, p. 135). Beare concludes that both these Markan healing stories "are substantially indistinguishable from other Hellenistic miracle-stories".

The church was—even is—glad to point to miracles still being worked as authenticating its teachings. Gibbon observed, with characteristic irony, that supernatural gifts "ascribed to [!] the Christians above the rest of mankind must have conduced very frequently to the conviction of infidels". As an illustration he instanced the resurrection of the dead which, in the days of Irenaeus, about the end of the second century, "was very far from being esteemed an uncommon event. . . . The miracle was frequently performed on necessary occasions, by great fasting and the joint supplication of the church of the place." If such things were possible, miraculous knowledge of foreign languages presented little difficulty, "though Irenaeus himself was left to struggle with . . . a barbarous dialect whilst he preached the gospel to the natives of Gaul" (1910, I, 458–59, chapter 15). The late Professor Lampe found "one of the most tiresome features of a certain kind of Christian apologetic, common in the church from the second century onwards", to be a "tendency to assume that the truth of Christian doctrine may be proved by the ability of believers to perform apparently impossible feats" (1965a, p. 165). Perhaps this feature would have been less to the fore had Jesus himself not been represented as setting a relevant example. At Mt. 11:20–22 he "began to upbraid the cities wherein most of his mighty works were done, because they repented not. . . . For if the mighty works had been done in Tyre and Sidon which were done in you, they would have repented long ago."

iv. The Gospel Exorcisms

Leslie Weatherhead was minister at London's City Temple for thirty years, and was also a well-known broadcaster. In a book written for persons "immensely attracted by Christ" but who cannot accept some of the traditional dogmas, he says:

> To me it seems a strange mentality by which a man can look up into the starlit sky or even down into a humble flower or listen to a haunting tune or watch a sunset, meditate on some deed of utter self-sacrifice or on the mystery of human love, and say 'I *know* that in this whole universe there cannot possibly be God'. (1967, pp. viii–ix)

Yet I suspect that there have been many astronomers, gardeners, and music-lovers who have not believed in God. The mentality may have seemed strange to Weatherhead, but this is perhaps because he did not realize the strangeness of his own ideas. His notion seems to be that these experiences are so enthralling, so exalted, so intense, that they are best accounted for by 'God'. Would it be equally logical to say that a man must have a strange mentality who can look on the effects of disease and say 'there is no Devil'? Weatherhead seems to think that this is so, for he was "glad to read that so profound a thinker as the late Archbishop Temple" believed in Satan; and he thinks it quite possible that "evil entities" created bacilli and viruses, poisonous snakes "and other organisms which seem the inveterate enemies of human well being" (pp. 187–88). In another book he presses this point, saying that "educated members of all branches of the Christian Church believe in angels", so why jib at "personalities in the universe other than man, opposed to God and working harm in man?" And how about the scriptural warrants for them, such as Ephes. 6:12: "Our wrestling is not against flesh and blood, but against the principalities, against the powers, against the world-rulers of this darkness, against the spiritual hosts of wickedness in the heavenly places"? (1951, p. 101). However, he allows that, from earliest times until today, "much disease has been *wrongly* attributed to demon possession"; and he will go no further than not ruling such a thing out as impossible, "especially in regard to the far-off days of the Biblical narrative and the far-off places of the world"—India, China, and so forth—"where the power of Christ has yet had little chance of overcoming His enemies" (pp. 106, 108).

Weatherhead appeals to an earlier book by W.M. Alexander which claims that Jesus went out of his way to show that he disbelieved in the popular demonology of his day. Hence, it is argued, his own exorcisms cannot be regarded as inventions of the early church. Four examples of his disbelief are given:

i.   He commanded his disciples to gather up the fragments; thus discouraging the idea that demons lurk in crumbs.

ii. He had no faith in the ceremonial washing of hands; so repelling the notion that spirits may rest on unwashed hands.

iii. He asked a draught of water from the woman of Samaria and thereafter entered the city; proving that he had no fear of drinking borrowed water and no belief in local shedim.

iv. He retired repeatedly to desert places and fasted in the wilderness; therein rejecting the popular conception that the waste is the special haunt of evil spirits (Weatherhead 1951, p. 98, quoting W.M. Alexander 1902, p. 54).

Let us look more closely at these four examples.

i. The crumbs were picked up after the feedings of the 5,000 and the 4,000 (Mk. 6:43 and 8:8). No motive is indicated and there is no mention of demons anywhere in these stories. It is in the fourth gospel, where 5,000 are fed, that Jesus commands the fragments to be gathered. This feeding is the only miracle of his Galilean ministry that is recorded in all four gospels, and the only miracle story in the fourth gospel that is identical with those of the other three. He had the fragments gathered "that nothing be lost" (Jn. 6:12). There is no mention of demons, who do not figure at all in the fourth gospel, except for the arch-demon "the devil" (8:44; 13:2), and except for false accusations that Jesus himself is "possessed" (for example 7:20). The notion that a demon can be sent into food so as to enter any one who eats it commonly underlies love charms. If Jesus was trying to discredit such ideas, his command was inappropriate, as crumbs and scraps gathered into baskets are more likely to be eaten than those left scattered in an uninhabited place. How numerous large baskets—twelve in the one case and seven in the other—came to be available in such a place is not something the narrator worried his head about. He surely introduced the collecting not because he wanted it initiated from some recondite (and unstated) motive—we saw that in the synoptics Jesus is not even said to initiate it—but to provide visible and tangible evidence of the reality of the miracle: not only was the multitude sated but the left-overs exceeded the initial supply.

ii. At Mk. 7:1–23 Jesus defends his disciples against criticism that they eat with unwashed hands. Ceremony, not hygiene, is here involved. The story is obviously legendary, drawn up in a Hellenistic community; for Jesus is represented as trying to floor Pharisees, of all people, by presenting them with a mistranslation of their own scriptures: he quotes the Greek OT (the Septuagint) which makes his point just where it deviates from the Hebrew (cf. Nineham 1963, p. 195). The challenge about hand-washing serves merely to intro- duce the wider question as to why the disciples do not live as Pharisees. Jesus responds by saying that moral, not ritual purity is what matters. He is concerned to contrast the important with the trivial, not to discredit superstitious ideas about the trivial. Demons are not even mentioned.

iii. The incident with the Samaritan woman occurs in the fourth gospel (Jn. 4:7ff) where there is no room for the numerous demons so prominent in the synoptics. What is there for Jesus to fear—that she might be contaminating with demons the water she is drawing from the well? In this same context, he is represented as supernat- urally knowing all about her (verses 18, 29), so there can be no question of his fearing she might deceive him. His request for a drink serves merely to introduce the dialogue that follows about the "living water" that he is able to offer. As for the 'shedim', this is the Hebrew word used at Deuteronomy 32:17 to designate heathen gods as mere demons. It is probably a loan word from Assyrian, where it denoted a protective minor deity, represented by the bull-colossus at the entrances of temples. To say that, in entering the woman's city, Jesus proves that he "had no belief in local shedim" is to imply that, had he believed in them, he would have kept away. But why? Are we to suppose that he would have feared their power? He has already told her that he is the Messiah (verses 25–26); he impresses the Samaritans of the city as "the Saviour of the world" (verse 42); and in a later chapter he reminds God of the glory which the two of them had enjoyed together before the world was created (17:5). It would be absurd for such a person to entertain fear of Samaritan shedim. In the synoptics, where he does confront demons, it is always they who fear him.

iv. These same considerations are relevant to the suggestion that because Jesus sojourned in desert places he rejected the popular idea that they are the haunts of evil spirits. Mk. 1:13 tells that "he was tempted by Satan in the wilderness", and so the most powerful of them was very much there.

Weatherhead was doubtless attracted by Alexander's denigration of what he calls the "conceited dogmatism" and "cheap sneers" of the more critical theologians in their discussion of the synoptic exorcism stories, and also by his portrait (p. 60) of Jesus as an extraordinarily sensible and enlightened person who "evinced a deep insight into the processes of health and disease on many occasions." Weatherhead follows this lead, making both Jesus and himself into a proto-psychiatrist, and arguing that the Gerasene demoniac supposed himself possessed by a "legion" of demons (Mk. 5:9) because he had "suffered some shock" at the hands of Roman legionaries, capable of slaughter "as we know from the story of the massacre of the innocents" (Mt. 2:16) which it is even "possible that this patient had witnessed". Jesus "recovered the buried memory of cruelty which had disturbed the patient's mind, brought it to the surface, accompanied by a fierce emotional abreaction". In spite of all this psychologizing, Weatherhead is not going to surrender the miracle: "By no methods known to us can a patient as far advanced in psychosis . . . be brought back to sanity and to a desire to serve the Kingdom of God" (pp. 65–67).

These wild phantasies are surely no more than a printed form of pulpit stuff addressed to silent audiences with no inkling as to what constitutes historical criticism. The 'argument' resembles dreaming, where the slightest resemblance between two things allows the one to evoke the other. Thus 'legion' suggests Roman soldiers, these suggest atrocities, and these in turn Herod's massacre of the innocents—as if Herod, who ruled his own territory, commanded Roman troops or would have needed them to dispose of babies in a village. The story of this massacre is a typical tyrant legend, posthumously blackening the memory of a hated despot. It is not mentioned elsewhere in the NT (not, for instance, in Luke's birth and infancy narrative), nor by any ancient historian—not even by Josephus, who recorded the history of Herod and his family and stressed its horrors. It is also typical of the stories of miraculous escapes from danger with which the infancy of a great man is credited (Oedipus, Moses). Matthew is here modelling Jesus, the second deliverer, on Moses, the first: in both cases, the birth of the child occasions uneasiness in the powers that be, followed by a consultation with wise men, a massacre of children and a miraculous rescue, with Egypt as the land of rescue.

Recent works of reference include some instructive articles on exorcisms. G.H. Twelftree's 'Demon, Devil, Satan' in the ultraconservative handbook edited by Green (1992) concedes that they are absent from the fourth gospel because the relevant traditions were deliberately suppressed. To associate Jesus with such a relatively common method of healing "would have appeared banal" to this evangelist, who chose instead "spectacular miracles" for him, and "miracles which were thought to be the work of God, like the turning of water into wine". More substantial is the section on 'Incantations and Books of Magic', contributed to the 1986 volume of the revised English Schürer by Dr. P.S. Alexander of Manchester University. He calls exorcism the best-attested form of magic among the Jews up to the early second century A.D.; and he notes that magic is "notoriously syncretistic", so that "in many cases it is hard to label a given praxis or text as pagan or Christian or Jewish. It is simply magic, a conglomerate of motifs of diverse origin" (pp. 342, 345–46). David Aune's 'Magic in Early Christianity' calls "the great gulf" which some NT scholars would place between 'the powerful word of the Son' and 'magical incantations' "simply non-existent. The short authoritative commands of Jesus to demons in gospel narratives are formulas of magical adjuration" (1980, p. 1532). C.K. Barrett concedes (after giving the non-Christian parallels) that the only unique feature in the NT exorcisms is their "Christological setting", as special signs of God's power and of his kingdom (1970, p. 57). One does not expect Jewish or pagan exorcisms to have a Christological setting, and this feature may be allowed to be uniquely Christian.

Most substantial are J.M. Hull's articles 'Demons in the NT' and 'Exorcism in the NT' in the Supplementary Volume (Nashville: Abingdon, 1976) of *The Interpreter's Dictionary of the Bible*. He notes that parallels in the pagan magical papyri include the use of the formula 'I know who you are' and of the expression 'I adjure you by God', and also the importance attached to making the demon speak to disclose his name. Jesus is thus represented as sharing the common belief that, to gain control over a demon or god, or even a man, it is necessary (or at any rate helpful) to know his name. Hull also points to the importance of Jewish eschatology as a framework in which Jesus's exorcisms belong; for it is particularly in the intertestamental period that "the final triumph of God is considered to be dispossessing and excluding the evil powers. The advent of the Messiah is accompanied by the overthrow of demons".

Hull's articles also make the very important point that Christian documents which are earlier than or independent of the gospels do not confirm the synoptics' representation of Jesus as an exorcist: not only is there "no specific reference to exorcism in the NT outside of the Synoptic gospels and Acts" (p. 313), but also the Pauline emphasis is upon evil cosmic forces, deprived by Christ of their powers at his crucifixion (Coloss. 2:14–15, 20), rather than on demons causing illness through possession (p. 225). In other words, it is not just that Paul is silent concerning the exorcisms: he envisages Jesus defeating the evil cosmic powers in a totally different way—not by expelling them from possessed persons during a public ministry, but by confronting them at his resurrection, after a life lived in obscurity, during which (contrary to what the gospels say) they had failed to recognize him. Paul insists that he can preach only "Christ crucified", a Christ known as a saviour only in that he died a shameful death to redeem us, not a Christ of signs and wonders of any kind (1 Cor. 1:22–23). For him, Christ was crucified "through weakness" (2 Cor. 13:4); in this same context he details the afflications he has himself suffered because of his Christianity, and implies that weakness and suffering are appropriate to the life of a Christian preacher because they characterized Christ's own life. He refers to the supernatural evil spirits who rule this aeon as "the rulers of this age" (1 Cor. 2:6, 8), or as "the god of this age" who has blinded the minds of unbelievers (2 Cor. 4:4). In the Pauline and deutero-Pauline letters, these spirits are called 'rulers', 'principalities', 'powers', 'dominions', and 'thrones'. Ephes. 2:2 refers to "the ruler of the power of the air", a "spirit now working in the sons of disobedience"; at 6:12 the "principalities", the "powers", the "world-rulers of this darkness", are expressly said *not* to be "flesh and blood" personages, but rather "spiritual hosts of wickedness in the heavenly places". In Paul's thinking, it was these supernatural powers who were ultimately responsible for Jesus's crucifixion: the "rulers of this age", failing to recognize his true identity, incited human authorities to kill him. Had they known God's mysterious wisdom they "would not have crucified the Lord of glory" (1 Cor. 2:7–8). But doing this brought about their own discomfiture; for in dying, Christ "put off from himself the principalities and the powers; he made a show of them openly, triumphing over them in it" (Coloss. 2:15. The NEB renders this as: he "made a public spectacle of the cosmic powers and authorities, and led them as captives in his triumphal procession"). 1 Peter 3:22 likewise declares that "Jesus Christ . . . is gone into heaven, angels, authorities, and powers being subjected to him".

It is clear from all this that the authors of these letters knew nothing of traditions according to which Jesus is recognized already during his ministry by evil spirits who acknowledge him as their most powerful enemy (Mk. 1:24 and 34). It is only by ignoring the evidence of these epistles that Twelftree, in his 1992 article already cited, is able to claim these acknowledgements by the demons in the synoptic gospels as "probably historically reliable", and to comment naively that, although "some ancient exorcists had difficulty in getting demons to speak, . . . Jesus seems to have had no such difficulty". The acknowledgements are better understood as apologetic elements by means of which Mark defends Jesus against the charge that he was in league with Satan and so worked miracles through magic. Mark is in effect saying: if even the demons recognized Jesus as the Holy One of God, he could not have been a mere magician, as would have been suspected of any miracle-worker of the time.

The deutero-Pauline letter to the Ephesians makes the early Christian view of Jesus's relation to the evil powers particularly clear. It insists that it was his resurrection (not any ministry of his) that subordinated them to him (1:20–22). When he ascended on high, he "led a host of captives" (4:8, RSV), and it is natural to regard these as the demonic forces. The enemies conquered at his resurrection are listed as "all rule, authority, power, and dominion", and also "every name that is named" (1:21). The epistle is addressed to gentiles recently converted from a spiritual milieu in western Asia Minor where pagan magical practices were rife, as exemplified in the cult of the Ephesian Artemis (see Acts 19). In elucidating this background, Arnold observes that "the calling of the names of supernatural 'powers' was fundamental to the practice of magic". Magic serves to protect from gods and demons, but it serves also to summon their help for various purposes, such as curing sickness, winning a chariot race, or harming enemies. To speak the name of a god or demon was to summon it, as a preliminary to seeking its assistance.[20] "Every conceivable name of both known and unknown powers is called upon in at least one of the magical papyri". Hence, for the person who has been converted out of a background of magical practices, the statement of 1:21—that the risen Christ sits "far above every name that is named"—would convey the powerful message that "his name *alone*, and not his name in addition to others, is sufficient for a successful confrontation with the 'powers' of evil" (Arnold 1989, pp. 56, 124).

In sum, Ephesians consistently associates Jesus's victory over evil supernatural forces exclusively with his resurrection. If the author had believed that he had acted with supreme authority over them during his lifetime, he would surely have been only too pleased to say so.

Finally, I draw attention to B.L. Blackburn's chapter on 'The Miracles of Jesus' in a 1994 symposium which evaluates the state of current research on the historical Jesus. He discusses the exorcisms with the other gospel miracles, and does not deny that "the gospels testify to the truth of Goethe's description of miracle as 'faith's favorite child'". Hence he faces the question as to whether scholars now regard the relevant stories as based on reliable reminiscence or on "pious imagination and theological creativity", provoked by "the needs of missionary work among gentiles" (Blackburn 1994, pp. 354, 393). He finds that Jesus's revivifications of the dead and his so-called 'nature miracles' are now regularly attributed—"over the protests of some conservative Protestants and Catholics"—to "the early church's capacity for embellishment and/or legend-making" (p. 369). The nature miracles include: from Mark, the calming of the sea storm, the feeding of the 5,000 and of the 4,000, the walking on the sea, and the cursing of the fig tree; from Matthew the coin in the fish's mouth; from Luke the miraculous catch of fishes; and from John the wine miracle at Cana. When these and the raisings of the dead are deleted, there remains "widespread agreement that exorcisms and healings did figure in Jesus's activity" (p. 363). It is pretty obvious that one reason why these are allowed, and the nature miracles not, is that they are regarded as believable incidents, morally motivated, which Jesus or his audiences could have taken for miracles, whether they were truly supernatural or not. The exorcisms are now easier to accept than instantaneous cures of physical illness; for, then as now, there were persons who believed that they were possessed and that an exorcist could release them. Hence numerous commentators have settled for the non-committal proposition that Jesus did the kind of deeds which were miracles to his mind and to the minds of his contemporaries. Yet even this consensus vanishes, says Blackburn, when it comes to deciding which of the relevant gospel stories represent true reminiscences, some scholars even remaining "agnostic toward the historicity of any individual tradition" (p. 393), although perhaps allowing that it could represent a generalized memory of the kind of things that Jesus had actually done (p. 365). Blackburn himself sees that it is hard to discount "the influence of parallel stories from Hellenism and Judaism" (p. 364), although he would clearly like to believe that "at least some of the traditions" preserve genuine reminiscence (p.

393). He stresses that if even only one gospel miracle story is essentially reliable, then Jesus is proved to have worked miracles (p. 362). This invites the retort that the admitted presence of many legendary pericopes does not inspire confidence in the rest. Blackburn's "leading candidate" for authentic reminiscence is "without doubt the Healing of Peter's Mother-in-law" (p. 365):

> And straightway when they were come out of the synagogue, they came into the house of Simon and Andrew, with James and John. Now Simon's wife's mother lay sick of a fever; and straightway they tell him of her; and he came and took her by the hand, and raised her up; and the fever left her, and she ministered unto them. (Mk. 1:29–31)

In the Lukan parallel, Jesus "rebukes" the fever, as if it were a demon. "Andrew, James, and John" are unrepresented in the parallel passages in both Matthew and Luke. Why are they not included in Mark's "they" who came out of the synagogue, when they were clearly among those who went into it with Jesus at 1:21, immediately following his call of them at 1:16–20? If this story is genuine reminiscence, Mark has introduced it in a very clumsy way. Making the patient "minister" to the others, presumably by serving them at table, is likely to be a feature introduced to show how immediate and thorough her cure was, and hence how great Jesus's power. Blackburn is impressed by the story's "precise information concerning both the identity of the sufferer and the geographical locale", and also by its "matter-of-fact tone . . . with no particular christological accent" (p. 366). But I see no reason to dissent from Nineham's conclusion that the story probably reached Mark "like the rest of his material, as part of the general oral tradition of the Church" (1963, p. 81). It "signalises once more", says Anderson, "the authority of Jesus" (1976, p. 92).

v. Wider Questions on Exorcisms

A. EXORCISMS IN THE HISTORY OF THE CHURCH

C.E.M. Joad declared himself unable to believe that evil elements in human behaviour are "adequately to be explained as the by-products of a feeling of inferiority engendered by neglect in school" or as resulting from "suppressed feelings of guilt" (1952, p. 64). It is quite common in popular apologetics—C.S. Lewis exemplified the technique well—to present alternatives to one's own view which are obviously absurd, and to suggest at the same time that they are the only alternatives. Joad is here concerned to show that man is by nature partly evil, and to explain this by invoking the Christian doctrine of "the Fall", which engendered original sin (1952, p. 80). That human beings often behave cruelly is, however, not hard to comprehend without this religious hypothesis. Herbert Spencer said long ago that the human race is not only gregarious but also predatory, and "this has required the nature of its members to continue such that the destructive activities are not painful to them, but on the whole pleasurable: it has been necessary that their sympathies with pain should not prevent the infliction of pain" (1885, p. 570). Expressions of pain or distress in another are the usual signs of defeat and hence pleasurable to the victor. Egoistic instincts are obviously vital to an animal; any species whose members did not stand up for themselves against intruders and rivals would soon become extinct. It is biologically intelligible that some individuals inherit self-assertive tendencies to an excessive degree, just as others are by nature all too ready to sacrifice themselves, having inherited strong social feelings.

The Genesis story of 'the Fall' can be used—with Joad as it was with Augustine—to account for human proclivity to evil only if it is understood as a record of actual historical events. But Canon Maurice Wiles expresses the now prevalent view when he declares unequivocally that we "cannot avoid acknowledging the unhistorical character of the narrative" (1986, pp. 43–44). Furthermore, very serious manifestations of evil are independent of human volition. Joad himself admitted that, for him, this problem was "unresolved" (p. 24), and many other Christians have confessed that it baffles them. Polkinghorne asks, appositely:

> To whose charge is to be laid the severely handicapped child who will never have a normal life? The thirty-year-old dying of cancer with half a life unfulfilled? The elderly person whose life ends in the prolonged indignity of senile dementia? If there is a God, surely these things must be his responsibility. It seems that either he who was thought of as the

ground of the moral law is not himself wholly good, or he is opposed by other equal and conflicting powers in the world. Either way, the Christian understanding of God would lie in ruins.

He adds that, for Christians such as himself, all this "remains a deep and disturbing mystery, nagging within us, of which we can never be unaware" (1983, pp. 20–21).

As we saw from Leslie Weatherhead, a traditional Christian answer has been to attribute evil to demons; and these are held to act with God's permission. Walker notes that Christian writers on magic, witchcraft, or possession "are acutely aware of the danger of Manichaeism, of allowing the devil to become an Antigod, and they mention God's permission, not once only as a general condition and limitation of diabolic activity, but in each specific instance: seducing a witch, entering a human body, successfully tempting a pious man with impure thoughts". The permission is given so that a greater good may result. In the case of possession, this is traditionally held to be "the punishment of sinners and the testing, the refining of the elect" (1981, p. 6). Saul illustrates the former ("the spirit of the Lord had departed from Saul and an evil spirit from the Lord troubled him", 1 Samuel 16:14), and Job the latter (although the Devil did not actually enter his body, but only pestered him).

The early church was positively obsessed with fear of demons. For Jerome, "the entire human population of the world is as nothing compared with the entire population of spirits". The early fifth-century monk Cassian said that "the air between heaven and earth is crammed with spirits, never quiet or finding rest" (Nineham 1993, p. 54). As were the teachers, so were the taught. Literary sources of the fourth century and later reveal that NT manuscripts were sometimes worn around the neck or placed under a pillow to ward off evil spirits. Papyri were used as amulets, inscribed with appropriate texts such as the Lord's Prayer or a healing narrative (Ehrman 1995, pp. 369–370). John Chrysostom alludes (uncritically) to the popular conviction that the Devil will not dare approach a house where a gospel-book is lying (Gamble 1995, p. 238). About the year 1000, the inhabitants of Northern France were haunted by the almost continuous presence of saints, angels, and demons: in an unfamiliar forest one needed to be constantly on the

watch for terrifying beings believed to be lurking in the under-
growth, and one had to be ready with the appropriate defensive
rites, sacred formulas, and invocations of saints (Nineham 1993, p.
230).

The phenomena of possession and exorcism were long mainly a
means of discrediting rivals; first pagan gods—in the early centuries, these were regularly featured as devils (compare 1 Cor.
10:16–21)—and later, in the Reformation period, rival Christian
factions. In the sixteenth century, exorcisms were regularly used by
the French and English Catholics to discredit Huguenots and
Puritans, and by English Puritans to discredit Catholicism. The
basis on which this was done was the belief that demons have a
natural horror of what is really holy—they tremble at the very
thought of God (James 2:19)—and so, from the Catholic standpoint,
if a possessed person is presented with a consecrated wafer or with
holy water or relics, his demon will cry out in pain and convulse
him, thus vindicating Catholic practices. When interrogated by a
priest-exorcist the devil in the demoniac would speak to him of "my
Huguenots" and in general express strong Protestant sympathies.
Some of the patients were doubtless sick with epilepsy or hysteria,
but disease alone would not account for the long-drawn-out, consistent anti-Huguenot propaganda in the French cases; there must
have been some element of fraud on the part of the demoniac, or
the exorcists, or both. That these cases were given so much
publicity—by ensuring large audiences for the exorcisms and
publishing printed accounts afterwards—can only enhance such
suspicions. There are records of similar cases in England at about
the same time, where the anti-Protestant propaganda consisted of
the devils praising Queen Elizabeth and her courtiers and claiming
them as obedient disciples, whereas these same devils could not
endure contact with relics such as the bones of recent English
Catholic martyrs. The same features of publicity and of making the
demons spokesmen of religious rivalry had attended exorcisms in
the early centuries of Christianity in the Roman empire.[21]

Walker explains that, apart from horror and revulsion at sacred
things, the main marks of possession were held to be bodily strength
(something too vague to be decisively tested), knowledge of other

people's secrets (easy to simulate by carefully imprecise guesses) and ability to speak and understand languages not known to the patient. The theological theory here is that "devils, being fallen angels, retain their angelic intelligence; their minds are immeasurably quicker and more experienced than those of men, and their knowledge therefore enormously greater" (1981, p. 13). He did not find any convincing examples of such knowledge in the cases he investigated, and sixteenth-century devils "quite often give feeble excuses for not understanding or speaking Latin or Greek" (pp. 12–13).

Protestant exorcists of the time were more restricted. They could not use Catholic apparatus such as the consecrated host or relics, although they could discomfit the demons by reciting scripture to them. But a greater restriction was the doctrine—contrived in the Anglican church in order to discredit all Catholic miracles at one blow—that the age of miracles had ceased long ago, once Christianity had become securely established and so no longer needed their support. This meant that Protestant clergy could not *command* a spirit to depart, but could resort only to prayer and fasting as entreaties to God to take the demon away, as recommended at Mk. 9:29 ("This kind can come out by nothing, save by prayer", with some manuscripts adding "and fasting"). The eventual expulsion of the demon, while it could not be claimed as miraculous, was represented as vindicating Protestantism on the ground that only the true church could induce God to effect it.

Cases of possession seldom occurred in circles indifferent to religion, and persons who found endless prayer meetings and scripture readings tiresome could escape them by feigning possession. "The boy Thomas Darling in 1596 only felt his fits come on when he was forced to take part in a prayer-meeting". The Throgmorton children had fits from 1589 to 1593 when prayers were said or the Bible read. As a possessed person was not held responsible for his or her actions, supposed possession was a convenient way of expressing forbidden impulses: when the demoniac "burst forth with blasphemies and obscenities, no one subsequently reproached him for doing so". And a child possessed rapidly became the centre of attention and was treated "with affectionate concern" by "otherwise indifferent or repressive superiors" (Thomas 1973, pp.

573–74). As a general scheme to explain the cases he studied, Walker suggests the following:

> A teenager, more often a girl than a boy, starts to have fits, often of an epileptic character, or to have hallucinations, or both, that is, she is genuinely sick. The surrounding group—family, friends, and soon doctors and priests or ministers—respond favourably, that is, treat the patient kindly and pay attention to her symptoms and her wishes. The suggestion of possession may come either from the patient or from some of the group; both will have heard of previous cases, if only from the New Testament, and their knowledge of these will to a considerable extent condition their behaviour. The patient becomes convinced that she really is possessed, that is to say, she is genuinely deluded. Once possession is established, the attention paid to the patient and the compliance with her wishes increase. The first sliding step into fraud probably comes when some utterance of the patient is taken to be that of a possessing devil. The patient soon realizes she has a powerful instrument, and tries out various diabolic speeches or answers to questions. She begins, consciously or unconsciously, to make these conform to the expectations of the surrounding group. She begins to simulate fits, or has perhaps learnt to induce them, when an audience has assembled to witness them. And so the business will go on, day after day, for weeks, months and even years. The patient begins by being sick, and becomes both sick and fraudulent. The surrounding group are usually, but not always, innocent of deliberate fraud; but they do deliberately, though with a clear conscience, exploit the situation in the interests of the true religion. (p. 16)

Possession by a good spirit was always theoretically possible—in Paul's communities the Holy Ghost prompted inspired utterances—but dangerous to a settled orthodoxy, whose doctrines could be compromised by new disclosures. The latest books of the NT already show resistance to spirit-based additions to established doctrines: the faith has been "once for all delivered to the saints" (Jude 3) and the brethren "already have the truth" (2 Peter 1:12).

B. ADVOCATES OF POSSESSION AS A REALITY

The recrudescence of belief in spirit possession in Britain and elsewhere in the last few decades has found some psychological support in the phenomenon known as 'the divided self', where an individual seems to be the vehicle of a personality that is not his own. Sometimes this hypothesis is no more than an excuse for unacceptable behaviour. If I do you a kindness, I will claim that this represents my true self, but if I lose my temper and assault you, I may be tempted to think that some entity 'came over' me or 'possessed' me, and not allow that it was I who misbehaved. Nevertheless, there are genuine pathological cases of divided self, and it is not hard to understand them as extreme instances of something quite normal. As I noted in *Belief and Make-Believe* (p. 65), one's idea of oneself is something only gradually built up, on the basis of experience, and may be fragmented, consisting of ideas of different selves, each one of which is appropriate to a particular setting. In his business environment a man's self is perhaps a hard-headed unscrupulous egoist; at home it may be a benign and sympathetic pater familias; at the club a dissipated rake. Since the materials for each of these models have been gathered from different sets of experiences, they need not interfere with each other. But such immunity from interference involves some degree of mental segregation. In extreme cases there is complete isolation of the two or more selves, but in normal minds this does not occur. William James, in his *Varieties of Religious Experience*, gives many examples: St. Augustine, for instance, enjoying what he called his 'disease of lust' while his other self wanted to live a purely spiritual life. Conflict between the different selves is familiarly experienced as remorse, felt when, having done the wrong thing, we are disappointed because it turns out that we had not, after all, had the kind of self that we supposed, and would have liked to believe we had.

In Britain today, demonic possession is seldom exploited in order to convince rival religionists: the Reformation situation, where people believed that demons shudder before one faction rather than another, no longer obtains—although the motive of opening the eyes of those indifferently or atheistically inclined may still influence exorcists, who can also appeal to the essentially pleasurable emotions of surprise and wonder. A desire to enhance the status of the clergy may also still be important. The Anglican clergy of the sixteenth century certainly jeopardized their prestige by renouncing claims to dispossess by miracle. What can be exploited above all is the perplexity ordinary people feel at the enormity of much that is reported today of human behaviour. Our psychologists are not much help in explaining even acceptable behaviour, so it is perhaps not surprising that they have little that is convincing to say about aberrations.

It remains difficult for those who take the NT and the church Fathers as authoritative to drop belief in demons; and so we find the present Dean of Lincoln convinced that "there is a spiritual warfare going on", that his cathedral is at the centre of a supernatural battle between good and evil, with currents of conflict and hatred swirling round it (Quotation and report in *The Observer*, 23rd July, 1995). The other clergy at Lincoln Cathedral—so this report continues—"regard this as primitive thinking and their Dean as a little potty" (scripture notwithstanding). They are perhaps aware that it is a species of pottiness that has impaired progress in medicine: smallpox used to be attributed to an offended demon, and as long as this belief persisted no progress could be made in finding a cure. But many conservative evangelicals will support the outlook of the Dean and regard possession as a typical manifestation of Satanic resistance to Christian preaching. Hence Blomberg tells us that "exorcisms tend to occur most in conjunction with the preaching of the gospel in lands and areas in which Satan has long held sway and in which Christianity has not flourished"—presumably Leslie Weatherhead's 'far-off places of the world' (see above, p. 152). Nevertheless, Blomberg adds, complacency is inappropriate, for "to the extent that Western societies continue to become more paganized, one may expect a continued revival of healings and exorcisms there as well" (*art. cit.*, on p. 149 above).

In order to counter the objection that many pagan and Jewish miracles are at least as well attested as those of Jesus, Blomberg states in this same article that "God may well use unbelievers to serve his purposes"; and he refers to a book by John Richards for evidence that "the devil certainly employs counterfeit signs to serve his". Richards is an Anglican priest who for nine years was secretary to the Bishop of Exeter's Study Group on Exorcism. He confesses in the Preface to his book that the 'research' underlying it consists mainly of what he has been told by "friends who are actively engaged in the 'ministry of deliverance'". Tyler, however, believes the book to be both "well-balanced and well-researched", and to demonstrate that "at an academic level", the debate about possession by demons "is still open" (p. 122). The reference is to Richards's statement (1974, p. 93) that, in the Royal Anthropological Society's journal *Man*, P.J. Wilson has challenged some of the theories of I.M. Lewis. But in fact neither of these two defends the reality of demonic possession. Lewis studied Somali communities where women, unable because of their inferior status to press their demands explicitly and effectively in secular terms, resort to what he calls "mystical modes of ventilating grievances". They claim to be possessed by spirits, and in this state they "soundly denounce their husbands' shortcomings" (Lewis 1967, p. 627). Once again, we see how alleged spirit possession can serve for expression of otherwise forbidden impulses. Wilson's criticism of Lewis is not a defence of the reality of the possession: he argues that, in these polygamous communities, spirit possession is not so much a means whereby the women come to terms with the men, but rather with each other. Possession, he says, occurs here primarily among women, especially married women, as a means they employ to compete with other wives of their husband. When so possessed, the spirit within a wife will demand luxurious clothing, perfume and delicate foods from him. Wilson interprets this as her reaffirming, through possession, her status and prestige in public. Both Wilson and Lewis give also examples of spirit possession among young Somali men who work away from the community in the dry season and then, on returning to it, meet girls of marriageable age; whereupon some of the men develop symptoms of hysteria which is relieved by the mounting of a dance. This type of possession, say our two authors, is often feigned and used by youths as a means of pointing the direction of their affections towards a particular girl, who is thus drawn into the dance (Wilson 1967, pp. 369–370, 374). Here, then, as in the cases studied by Walker, possession is a means of attracting attention to oneself. In a 1970 article, Lewis refers to his own earlier piece and to Wilson's as arguing on substantially the same lines.[22]

Richards finds that clergy who resist the present-day revival of belief in demons are courting popularity by aligning themselves with a "secular" society which—in view of the current "occult explosion"—is "fast becoming a thing of the past" (1974, pp. 30, 219). He deplores this explosive non-Christian dabbling in Black

Magic, Satanism, witchcraft, astrology, ouija playing, and the like, and attributes it to "the ineffectiveness of the institutional churches" (p. 30), which have turned their backs on true Christian "spirituality" so amply documented in the NT. For him, demons are real: they are "spirit-beings with intelligence and malevolence" (p. 134). They will "chuckle" at priests who fail to take them seriously or who think to deal with them by means of "gentlemanly hints" (pp. 167, 177). They need to be commanded in the name of Jesus Christ (p. 177), to whom, after all, "all authority in heaven and on earth" has been given (Mt. 28:18). To contact them on any other basis—as is done by those who now dabble in the occult outside Christianity—is highly dangerous: "Satanism begins with astrology or ouija playing" (p. 58). The exorcist must be extremely cautious even when commanding the demon in Jesus's name, because of the danger that the spirit may transfer himself from patient to exorcist: a padre who successfully exorcised a boy then himself dropped dead (p. 143). He should not only have ordered the demon out, but also commanded him "to harm no one". One of Richards's colleagues "only learnt this the hard way and now has an injured back" (p. 166). This idea that magic is dangerous is still widespread.[23]

Richards has to allow that there are cases where the 'demon' is no more than a fiction which allows patients to indulge their baser impulses without fear of censure—"a convenient fiction of the lower side" of their nature which "gives them the perfect alibi to behave as they really wish, while at the same time abdicating responsibility for such behaviour." He also allows that alleged possession may be merely "an hysterical device on the part of the patient to attract and keep attention" (p. 107). That these factors are of greater importance than he suggests is pretty obvious from Walker's findings. Another parallel with these is that, although Richards's demons are less overtly sectarian than Walker's, a certain vindication of Catholicism or Anglo-Catholicism can be inferred from their negative behaviour towards Catholic features: they flee at the sign of the cross (pp. 141, 189), curse the Trinity and the Virgin (p. 138) and hate the blood of Jesus (p. 145). A boy possessed by them "fell unconscious to earth as soon as he had to pass a church crucifix" (p. 140).

What Richards regards as present-day realities confirm not only the demonology of the NT, but all its miracle stories. In his own "limited reading" he has "encountered present-day equivalents of so many New Testament phenomena", and would therefore "strongly discourage scholars and preachers from too great an enthusiasm for dismissing as unhistorical what they have not themselves experienced" (pp. 31–32). The relevant 'phenomena' paralleled today include, so he adds, "walking on water, stilling a storm, swallowing poisons unharmed, raising the dead, water into wine, communicating in other languages, the 'rushing mighty wind', etc.". There are also, so he assures us, "a number of contemporary incidents parallel to *everything* in the story of the Gerasene demoniac, including the implied 'possession' of the swine" (p. 216. His italics).

Richards considers himself simply to be stating facts, and declares that it is the theologians' job, not his, to "hammer out" a theology from this raw material. The most imperative task of such a theology would, I suggest, be to explain why an all-powerful and all-benevolent deity permits legions of supernatural entities to practise untold evil. Another task for this theology will be to explain why we should take talk of Satan and Satanism seriously when Satan is an old Hebrew word meaning 'adversary' and was at first a common noun designating an opponent in war or in a lawsuit. It came to be the proper name of one of Yahweh's specialist angels, whose function it was to thwart and punish evil doers; and only gradually did increased powers come to be ascribed to this angel, who eventually was represented as opposed even to Yahweh himself.[24] Even then, the OT nowhere figures him as having hosts of demons as his agents—a view which the Hebrews derived form Iranian religion, possibly at the time of their Babylonian exile.[25]

Although, as I have indicated, Richards avows that his ideas are based more on his pastoral experience than on his reading, he lists (p. 155) a number of "authorities". One of them is Hal Lindsey, who in the work listed stamps the Biblical criticism of German and other theologians as wicked dogmatism inspired by Satan, who "for centuries has delighted in making biblical Christianity appear non-intellectual [i.e. intellectually naive] in the eyes of the world" (Lindsey 1974, pp. 166–68). He is perhaps better known from his earlier *The Late Great Planet Earth*, of which eighteen million copies have been sold. Although it blandly warns us (1971, p. 113) that "we must not indulge in speculation", it claims to infer from the scriptures a scenario for the end of the world, carefully summarized by Steve Bruce as follows:

> An Arab-African confederacy headed by Egypt will invade Israel. Russia and her allies will also attack Israel before turning on the Arab-African forces and destroying them. The Russians will kill millions of Jews before God kills five-sixth of the Russians. With the Russians out of the way, the final all-out war between Western civilization, led by the anti-Christ, and the vast hordes of the Orient led by the Red Chinese will begin. And thus the world ends. Before all this nastiness erupts, born again Christians will be taken up from the world in a 'rapture'. Their role of preaching the gospel will be taken over by the 144,000 Jews who will convert to evangelical Protestantism. At the climax of the final war, Christ will return to earth with the raptured Saints, destroy all the bad guys, and the millennium—the one thousand years of righteousness—will begin. (Bruce 1990a, p. 87)

James Barr has justly noted that Lindsey's "farrago of nonsense" is little different from traditional millenarian thinking (1981, pp. 206–07). To regard such a writer as an 'authority' is utterly grotesque.

On this whole subject of demonic possession, T.H. Huxley's 1889 essay 'The Value of Witness to the Miraculous' is still very much to the point. It discusses the account given by Einhard (a historian of intelligence and character at the court of Charlemagne) of a demon who spoke in Latin through the mouth of a girl to an exorcising priest and declared that he had for a long time been gatekeeper in hell before he set about ravaging the kingdom of the Franks. He also said that his name was 'Wiggo'. And we are to believe, on Einhard's authority, that 'Wiggo' was cast out of the possessed girl. Richards's book might appropriately be entitled 'The Triumph of Wiggo'.

vi. Philosophical Arguments for Miracles

J. Houston, Senior Lecturer in the Glasgow Faculty of Divinity, has recently published a substantial book, the thesis of which is that "putative miracle reports can have apologetic value" (1994, p. 158). They need not, he holds, be dismissed out of hand if accepting them as true "would effectively account for a good deal, including a good deal which is not otherwise easy to account for" (p. 148), and if it is possible to see that "a god could have had some purpose in bringing about an event of the particular sort in question". He then applies all this to the gospel reports of Jesus' resurrection and preceding ministry:

> Take the case of a teacher *whose words sublimely illuminate the human condition* and who has previously been the subject of *well-attested reports* saying he was involved in events contrary to natural law in ways which suggest that he may thereby be divinely approved. Then suppose that this person is further reported, *by reports of some weight*, as having been resurrected, putatively miraculously, after having been put to death by his enemies. In such circumstances reasonable people may perhaps be justified . . . in concluding that God may well have raised him up. (p. 161, Emphases added)

I have emphasized clauses and phrases in this passage which, at various points in this present book I call in question, and on which Houston's argument depends.

I turn now to C.S. Lewis, regarded by conservative Christians as "one of the greatest apologists of the twentieth century" (Chapman, 1988, p. 40). John Beversluis's very telling criticism of him (1985) has been mostly ignored in the voluminous literature on him. Like Houston, Lewis is concerned to defend the possibility of miracles on philosophical grounds. He does indeed claim that the story of "the historical incarnation" has "the master touch—the rough male [sic] taste of reality" (1940, p. 13). But in his book on miracles he defends them primarily by raising human thinking of any kind to a metaphysical plane. "Rational thought", he there insists, "is not part of the system of nature". Against the evolutionist, who holds that reason came on the scene as a late development from natural antecedents, Lewis asks: how could a non-rational system give rise to rationality? Unless, then, each person's reason can be supposed to exist "absolutely on its own", it must be the result of some rational cause, "in fact of some other Reason"; and this leads us to its source in "an eternal self-existent rational Being whom we call God". Each human mind has thus "come into Nature from Super-nature". Having thus established the existence of 'Supernature', Lewis can easily infer the possibility of miracles from his definition of them as "interference with Nature by supernatural power" (1947, pp. 13, 35–37).

Lewis's argument implies that nothing can arise out of anything unless the essential character of the second is already present in the first. Matter, then, cannot be transformed into energy; and with regard to animal capacities, complementary or concomitant characters are not necessary, but any alleged rudimentary form must already contain the essential elements of the form into which it is going to develop. From such a premiss we should have to argue that the bat's wing could not have developed from a hand because the hand does not contain the essential character of a wing; also that the auditory ossicles of the mammal cannot be derived from the bones of fishes' gills and jaws because these do not contain the essential character of the former, namely the conveying of vibrations to the inner ear. And so Romer must have been ignorant of the principles of logic when he wrote, in his standard textbook *The Vertebrate Body*:

> These bones afford a good example of the changes of function which homologous structures can undergo. Breathing aids have become feeding aids and finally hearing aids. (Romer 1949, p. 522)

Lewis of course allows that "what we call rational thought in a man always involves a state of the brain, in the long run a relation of atoms". Yet "Reason is something more than cerebral biochemistry", and "a man's Rational thinking is just so much of his share in eternal Reason as the state of his brain allows to become operative" (Lewis, pp. 49–50). Had he accepted that the essentials of the reasoning process are present in mammals other than man, he would presumably have supposed that they too had assimilated as much of 'eternal Reason' as their limited brains permitted. But when he mentions the possible existence in nature of rational creatures other than man, he has in mind not other mammals, but the possibility of life on "any of the other bodies that float in space" (pp. 63, 147).

Lewis grants that mammals other than man "expect new situations to resemble old ones" (p. 125), i.e. they learn to anticipate certain events from known antecedents. But he denies that this is a process of reasoning. In the revised edition of his book published in

1960 (reissued by Fount Paperbacks in 1974 and still available) he enlarges, in a rewritten chapter 3, on this distinction. An animal's "expectation" that one event will be linked with another results, he says, from mere "conditioning", whereas man links the two by means of a rational "inference" based on "insight" into the real nature of the connection between them. Religious apologists all too often write in this way about 'conditioning' as if it were little more than clockwork. According to Lewis, "the assumption that things which have been conjoined in the past will always be conjoined in the future is the principle not of rational but of animal behaviour" (1974, p. 24). But 'conditioning' is not to be so simply dismissed. Admittedly, when Pavlov's dogs were shown circles immediately before being fed, they soon began to salivate in expectation of food, and did so even when they were shown what resembled circles, namely ellipses of varying eccentricity. If, however, they were given food only after the appearance of a circle, they rapidly ceased to salivate when shown an ellipse. This means that they had learned to distinguish what for their purposes or needs were the essential features of a given situation. Human thinking follows the same sequence and passes from recognizing that two situations are correlated to discerning what elements must be present in the first if the second is to follow. Both the animal and the human being have, in such cases, inferred something, and Lewis himself defines "the mental behaviour we call reason" as "the practice of inference" (1974, p. 23).

Lewis, however, remains convinced that reason is something supernatural, beyond any animal capacity; and he thinks that, if this were not true, we might well find it inconceivable that God, "eternal self-existent Spirit", could—as the central Christian doctrine of the incarnation affirms—become combined with a natural human organism so as to constitute one person. We saw above (p. 114) that envisaging how and with what results the one could have been combined with the other did indeed occasion perplexity. But Lewis claims that any problem is removed once we allow, with him, that in *every* human being reason, as "a wholly supernatural entity", is united so as to form an integrated person with a part of nature; any "difficulty" which we might have with the idea of the supernatural descending into the natural is "overcome in the person of every man" (1947, pp. 133–34; or 1974, p. 114).

If Lewis makes reasoning of any kind partake of the supernatural, others more modestly place only certain types of thinking and experience in a special category. Herbert Dingle distinguishes experiences that are common to all normal people from individual experiences; and on this distinction he bases that between science on the one hand and art and religion on the other. Science, he says, deals with experiences of the former kind; but "each of us has experiences peculiar to himself, or perhaps shared by a limited number of others, which are just as vivid and enduring as those of universal scope". There follows a parable to illustrate the difference:

> If fifty men are gathered together in a room, and one of them has a vivid experience of the presence of snakes of which the remainder are unconscious, we have no hesitation in saying that the snakes do not exist; the criterion of existence is the vote of the majority. Extend that to the whole human race and the whole of their experiences, and you have the field of Science defined. If the vote on a certain type of experience is unanimous except for a few dissentients, the dissentients are classified as 'abnormal', and the unanimity of the 'normal' people admits the experience in question to the category of existence. But now suppose that one, and only one, of our fifty men has a vivid experience of the presence of God in the room. We do not now say that God does not exist; many people, at any rate, would prefer to say that the forty-nine lack a faculty of appreciation which the fiftieth possesses.

Dingle is not the first philosopher to suggest that there are other and no less valid reasons for our religious beliefs than those that can be provided by science. But let us study his argument rather than his all too familiar conclusion. He says:

> Snakes have previously been defined as belonging to the world of common experience; there is no divergence of opinion about the existence of snakes in the Zoo. But there has been no previous admission of God to the world of common experience. The religious experience is *always* an individual matter. (1931, pp. 94–96)

Hence, he adds (p. 121), religion "cannot possibly come into conflict with Science, for Science operates only with common experiences".

The argument appears to be this. If one man sees a snake and a number of others similarly situated do not, then the latter are justified in supposing him to be mistaken, because if there were snakes they would see them too. On the other hand, even if God were present in the room, there is no reason to suppose that everyone would be aware of the fact; hence there is no prima facie reason for rejecting the evidence of an individual just because his experience is not shared by his companions.

In the same way, if one man out of the fifty pronounced that there was stomach-ache in the room, the remaining forty-nine would not be entitled to question it. But is this not because the source of the experience is some untoward occurrence in the private region of the person's intestinal tract, which is less accessible to common observation than a boa-constrictor in the dining-room? And could we not also assume that the man who claims to experience the presence of God does in fact have the experience he so describes, and that it is due to some peculiar event in the private region of his cerebral cortex? We cannot deny the experience of God to persons who claim it; we can deny only the presence of any appropriate and adequate external occasion.

Dingle seems to suppose that we are to exclude from the "legitimate sway" of science all experiences due to accidents in the private economy of an individual's own body; for he claims that "toothache does not exist scientifically" because "it is not a common experience". Yet toothache is real. Similarly, "God does not exist for science", yet he may be real: "If anyone wishes to challenge the statement that God does not exist for Science, he must give instructions which anyone may follow and automatically receive an experience of God" (p. 129). But here the analogy with toothache breaks down. Any dentist surely knows exactly what he can do to make a patient experience toothache.

Dingle also regards "Beauty, Goodness, and Humour" as purely individual experiences. He thinks that there is no meaning in saying that something is beautiful, any more than in asking whether a certain situation is funny, because the question implies a common standard which does not exist. One might just as well say that there is no meaning in asking whether a certain situation is painful or not, or whether a certain load is heavy or not. Science is well acquainted with relative properties, and if the conditions which elicit mirth differed as much as Dingle pretends, our professional humourists would have a very precarious occupation. As to beauty, people of the same race do not differ very much in their ideas of human beauty; and regarding music, poetry, and drama, it is by no means certain that there is no objective criterion that determines what is effective in each of these. The criterion need not be universally applicable. The question is: can we determine, for any race, community or definable group of people, factors in objects or situations capable of evoking a certain emotional response? When Dingle complains of "dividing" aesthetic and humorous experiences into an external cause and a sensitive percipient, he must mean attributing them partly to one and partly to the other. But to what, then, does he object? The reaction of anything, living or not, must be attributed in part to the external conditions and in part to the nature of the thing itself; and there is no plausible objection to analysing animal behaviour in the same way. Mirth is produced by some mirth-provoking circumstance, just as admiration is excited by something admirable. The fact that everybody does not react identically to the same stimulus, especially where his own person or interests are concerned, does not prove that there is no common relation between stimulus and reaction.

Dingle's is but one of innumerable attempts to argue a special status for religious experience (now often called 'numinous experience'), however its relations with more mundane experience are determined. This is often felt to be less vulnerable than directly defending bizarre miracle stories in a sacred text.

3

Teachings and Non-Miraculous Actions of Jesus Ascribable to the Early Church

i. Eschatology and Use of the Old Testament

If in the light of the evidence offered in my previous chapter we discount the gospel miracles, there remain numerous teachings and actions ascribed to Jesus, and we naturally ask whether some of these likewise bear marks of inauthenticity. One matter for investigation is the use he is represented as making of the OT, interpreting it in ways reminiscent of rabbinic debates at the time when the gospels were written. Some examples will illustrate.

At Mk. 12:26–27 and parallels Jesus argues against unbelieving Sadducees that the dead will be raised because God said to Moses (Exodus 3:6) "I am the God of Abraham, and the God of Isaac and the God of Jacob". But they were already dead, and so if God "is not the God of the dead but of the living"—as Jesus avers here in verse 27—it must be true that they will be raised to life again; and so the OT covers the doctrine of resurrection of the dead. Vermes calls this style of reasoning "typically rabbinic" (1993, p. 68). An even clearer example of such learned disputation is the story of the temptation (Mt. 4:1–11/Lk. 4:1–13), which takes the form of a dialogue between Jesus and the Devil where each regales the other with OT quotations which appear relevant only because they are made to bear a meaning alien to their original context. Jesus here shows himself a smarter manipulator of the scriptures than his adversary. Moreover, all the quotations here follow the Greek (Septuagint) translation of the Jewish scriptures, suggesting that this dialogue—to which the gospels in any case supply no witnesses who could have recorded it—was drawn up in a Greek-speaking environment rather than in a Palestinian one.

Some of Jesus's exchanges with the Pharisees are suspect for the same reason. At Mk. 7:6–8 he confronts them with a passage from the Septuagint where the Hebrew original would not have supported his case (see above p. 153): and so the argument surely derives not from him but from the evangelist, forming what Anderson in his commentary calls "part of the polemic of Gentile Christians" (1976, p. 182); they naturally read the OT in the Greek version, and ascribed to Jesus the way it is understood there.

Arbitrary interpretation of the OT is already well established in the early NT epistles. Paul argues—in a manner which William Neil finds "reminiscent of rabbinic disputations" (1967, p. 56)—that since according to scripture God's promises were made "to Abraham and to his issue", we must understand them to have been made to Christ, for if the Jewish people had been meant, scripture would read not 'issue' but 'issues' (Gal. 3:16). 1 Peter and the epistle to the Hebrews recite the attributes of the people of God and assume without argument that the relevant OT texts apply to Christ and his church. Use of the texts in this way could obviously be taken for granted by early Christian writers, but is it plausible that it was Jesus who initiated it in Christian circles? In support of this view, Dodd observed sardonically that the thinking evidenced in such exegesis "is rarely done by committees"—as if individual authorship necessarily points to Jesus as author. Dodd really knew quite well that the pre-Pauline and Pauline churches may well have had "now forgotten geniuses" perfectly capable of what he calls the requisite "creativity" (1952, pp. 109–110).

Of particular interest are Jesus's appeals to the OT apropos of his eschatological teaching. *Eschatos* is Greek for 'last', and eschatology means talk or thought about the last things, the final state of the world. Prominent in this regard is the use made in the synoptics of chapter 7 of the book of Daniel. The vision recorded there is an attempt to reconcile Yahweh's goodness and justice with the fact that many faithful believers were suffering undeserved affliction in their lives. At the time when Daniel was written, they were being persecuted and martyred for their loyalty to their faith by the Syrian Seleucid ruler Antiochus Epiphanes, whose oppression precipitated the Maccabean revolt in the second century B.C. God's goodness and justice is nevertheless vindicated in this book by assuring them that they will receive their due reward in an after-life. In the vision, four huge beasts rise up from the sea; thrones are then set, and seated on one of them is

> one that was ancient of days; his raiment was white as snow, and the hair of his head was like pure wool; . . . A fiery stream issued and came forth from before him: thousand thousands ministered unto him . . .The judgement was set and the books were opened. (7:9–10)

The 'Ancient of Days' is clearly a title of God in his capacity as judge. It is obvious from the sequel that the beasts represent successive empires (verse 23) and/or their rulers (verse 17) as oppressors of the Jews. When the Ancient of Days comes, judgement is given in favour of "the saints of the Most High" who then gain kingly power (verse 22). Many commentators equate them with "the people of the saints of the Most High" (verse 27), to whom kingly power is also given and is said to be everlasting; and they are understood as symbolizing those Jews who remained faithful to Yahweh at the time of the oppression. This is still the majority view, but Collins (1977, p. 144) has argued that 'saints' here means angels—certainly 'saints' or 'holy ones' usually means this in the Hebrew Bible—and that it is only "the people of the saints" who are the faithful Jews, who will join with their heavenly counterparts in the eschatological victory, in that they will enjoy dominion over "everything under heaven" (verse 27).

In verses 13–14, the kingdom is given to a figure in human form ("one like a son of man"):

> I saw in the night visions, and, behold, there came with the clouds of heaven one like unto a son of man, and he came even to the ancient of days . . . And there was given him dominion and glory, and a kingdom,

that all the peoples, nations and languages should serve him; his dominion is an everlasting dominion.

This figure must symbolize either the saints or the people of the saints (if these two are in fact distinct), or both, as all alike are said to receive the kingdom. Collins holds that the figure represents either the saints, which he understands as the angelic host, or possibly its leader, the archangel Michael (prominent in Daniel) who receives the kingdom on behalf of the holy ones. There is of course a correlation between the rule of the saints in heaven and the vindication of the faithful Jews on earth: "It is precisely Michael's rule over the heavenly realm which makes possible the dominion of Israel on the human level" (p. 143).

In Daniel, then, 'one like a son of man' may be taken as representing either a heavenly individual, or a corporate body, the saints. Many later writers, Jewish and Christian, took the reference to be to an individual, whom they termed '*the* Son of man' and equated with the Messiah; and they supposed that he would come not to God, as in Daniel, but to Earth with his angels and with the clouds of heaven at the final judgement. "The Son of man" who comes "with his angels" in numerous NT passages (such as Mk. 8:38; Mt. 13:41 and 16:27) is obviously traceable to an earlier 'Son of man' figure at the head of an angelic host.

The earliest extant Jewish evidence for such interpretation and re-use of these passages in Daniel is found in the 'Parables' or 'Similitudes' of 1 Enoch, which form chapters 37–71 of that composite work. References to the Ancient (Head) of Days at 46:1 and 47:3 indicate that the author used what is said of this person at Daniel 7:9–10, 13–14. 'The Son of man' is introduced at 1 Enoch 46:3–4, and will cast down kings and the mighty from their seats. At 48:10 and 52:4 he seems to be equated with the Messiah (the Lord's 'Anointed'); and he will be seated as judge on his throne of glory (62:5; 69:29). His portrait is filled out with reminiscences of the pre-existent figure of Wisdom, created by God as companion to himself long before the Earth (cf above, p. 96): 48:3 seems to mean that the Son of man was created before the sun and the stars. Collins concludes from this evidence that the 'Similitudes' "take for granted that Daniel's 'one like a son of man' is a heavenly individual of very exalted status", a "heavenly saviour figure" (1992, p. 459). He dates the work at ca. A.D. 50—prior to the fall of Jerusalem in A.D. 70 which passes unmentioned in it, and earlier than Matthew, which is clearly influenced by it (or by some earlier Jewish document with similar ideas) at 19:28 and 25:31. The latter verse introduces an apocalyptic vision of the Last Judgement strikingly similar to that given in 1 Enoch 40ff. Enoch says that "the Lord of Spirits seated the Elect one"—another title for the Son of man, for the two designations are juxtaposed in 62:1, 5—"on the throne of his glory" (61:8). Matthew reads: "When the Son of man shall come in his glory . . . , then shall he sit on the throne of his glory". Both writers go on to describe how the righteous are vindicated and the rest punished. In 1 Enoch angels "cast them into the burning furnace" (54:6), and the righteous enjoy the spectacle of their torment (62:11–12).

Matthew makes more of the doctrine of hell as a place of eternal torment than any other NT book, apart from the book of Revelation; and the speech in chapter 25—in the course of which the "goats" are dispatched to "the eternal fire which is prepared for the devil and his angels" (verse 41)—puts Jesus in such a vindictive light that commentators have been only too pleased to stamp it as Matthew's own elaboration or as drawn from Jewish apocalypses (see below p. 227). It has long been recognized that there is some *literary* connection with 1 Enoch here—or with some Jewish apocalypse with similar ideas that has not survived—and that the one picture is an adaptation of the other. The influence was surely from the Jewish document to Matthew (not in the reverse direction), for it is unlikely that a Jewish author would have made explicit use of the expression 'Son of man' for a Messianic figure after the phrase had been appropriated by the Christians. The other passage in Matthew which has been held to show such influence (19:28) will occupy us below. It too states that "the Son of man shall sit on the throne of his glory". Sim, reviewing the "scholarly debate" on the relationship between the 'Parables' section of 1 Enoch and Matthew, observes that the portrayal of the Son of man as the end-time judge on the throne of glory is found only in these two texts, so that "it is difficult to dispute that there was some contact" between them. He himself thinks that it is not a case of direct dependence of the one on the other, but that both had access to and utilized a Son of man tradition in some Jewish source (1996, pp. 119–121).

Similarly as in 1 Enoch, Daniel 7 is also reflected in 4 Ezra 13, a Jewish apocalypse from the end of the first century A.D. Brown reviews the evidence from both these works and finds that it "suggests that, in apocalyptic Jewish circles of the 1st century A.D., the portrayal in Daniel 7 had given rise to the picture of a messianic human figure of heavenly pre-existent origin who is glorified by God and made a judge" (1994, pp. 511–12). This musing on Daniel 7 in Jewish religious circles well illustrates the process of reflecting on sacred and semi-sacred texts—a process of great importance in the development of religious ideas, as I tried to show in chapter 1 above apropos of the way Paul formed his ideas of Jesus. That the 'Son of man' figure in Daniel 7 appeared "on the clouds of heaven" meant that he could be understood as pre-existent, like Wisdom in Proverbs 8. That "thrones were set" (Daniel 7:9) will have prompted the inference that one of them was for the Son of man; and this in turn suggested that he must have had an active role in the judgement (Collins 1993, p. 81). Collins points to OT passages with Messianic overtones which could also have contributed to his portrait: the account of the Elect one at 1 Enoch 62:2 ("the spirit of righteousness was poured out on him and the word of his mouth kills all the sinners") echoes Isaiah 11:2 and 4; and "the motif of a second figure enthroned beside God has its clearest precedent in Psalm 110, another messianic passage" (p. 82).

The synoptic gospels imply that the 'Son of man' figure is Jesus himself and in some instances the reference is clearly to him in his resurrected and exalted state. Mark represents him as saying that, at the end when the sun and moon are darkened and the stars are falling from heaven, "then shall they see the Son of man coming with clouds with great power and glory" (13:26), "in the glory of his Father with the holy angels" (8:38). Both these passages are paralleled in the two other synoptics. France claims (1971, p. 215) that these and other words of Jesus alluding to chapter 7 of Daniel are authentically Jesuine and also represent an original interpretation of it, in that Jesus did not suppose Daniel to be speaking either of only a corporate body (the saints) or of only an individual (the Messiah), but of both. The authors of the Qumran scrolls—if they commented on this part of Daniel at all—will have plumped, says France (pp. 175, 194), for the former interpretation, and may well have seen their own community as constituting the saints; whereas the Jewish pseudepigraphic and rabbinic literature took the Son of man to be the Messiah. (The collective interpretation is not clearly attested in Jewish circles until the Middle Ages.) But Jesus's interpretation, so France argues, included a corporate element in that he saw his twelve disciples as the nucleus of the new people of God, representing the saints to whom in Daniel kingly power is given (pp. 143–44, 195): the twelve will "sit upon twelve thrones in the regeneration" (when the kingdom of God is established) and will "judge the twelve tribes of Israel" (Mt. 19:27–28). Jesus will, then, sit on a glorious throne as judge, but the twelve will share in his authority.

There are of course difficulties in supposing that Jesus did actually speak these words. First, this is one of the passages dependent on ideas extant in 1 Enoch, which repeatedly refers to the Son of man seated "on the throne of his glory" as judge (for instance 69:27). Second, Paul obviously knew nothing of such a promise to the twelve, as he supposed that the whole body of Christian believers would judge the world (1 Cor. 6:2). Third, the promise has the appearance of a 'floating' saying to which the evangelist has supplied a context; for it is absent from Mark and given in a different context (the Last Supper) and in a different form in Lk. 22:28–30. Even in Matthew, Jesus in the next chapter warns disciples against any desire for pre-eminence and declares that to sit at his side in the kingdom is "not mine to give, but is for them for whom it hath been prepared of my Father" (20:21–23). The promise to the twelve of chapter 19 is best explained as Matthew's assimilation of the thinking of some Palestinian Christian community which entertained vivid apocalyptic expectations and couched them in traditional Jewish imagery. This view of the twelve is quite different from that which was to make eleven of them founders of the 'apostolic tradition' on which the teaching and organization of the universal church was supposedly based (see above, p. 39)—a view already adumbrated elsewhere in the NT, as, for instance, in the words spoken by the risen Jesus at the very end of Matthew, and at

Acts 1:8: "Ye shall be my witnesses . . . unto the uttermost part of the earth". Acts' own subsequent account in fact limits their missionary activity outside Palestine to temporary absences of Peter and Paul in Samaria (chapters 8 and 10), and leaves wider missionary work to Paul. Of nine of the twelve we learn no more than the names and, of the remaining three, James the son of Zebedee was beheaded, according to 12:1–2, by Herod Agrippa I (who died in A.D. 44), and his brother John figures as no more than a shadowy companion to Peter. If the author had known anything of foreign missions by any of them, he would gladly have recorded it as substantiating 1:8. Nevertheless, by the mid-second century Christian writers were claiming that these men had gone out from Jerusalem to convert the whole world (references in Haenchen 1968b, p. 112 n7).

A further instance of use of chapter 7 of Daniel occurs at Jesus's Sanhedrin trial. In Mark's account he is asked by the High Priest "Art thou the Christ?" and replies:

> I am; and ye shall see the Son of man sitting at the right hand of power and coming with the clouds of heaven. (14:62)

If the 'Son of man' and 'the clouds of heaven' derive from Daniel 7, the 'sitting at the right hand of power' (i.e. of God) recalls Psalm 110:1:

> The Lord saith unto my lord, Sit thou at my right hand, until I make thine enemies thy footstool.

This Psalm is generally understood to have been originally a song for the enthronement of some powerful Israelite ruler: the Lord (Yahweh) is inviting 'my Lord' (this king or ruler of the psalmist) to sit in a position of authority where he will be victorious. But for the early Christians it was Jesus who is here prophesied to sit at God's right hand after his resurrection and to overcome his enemies. This is how the Psalm is understood at Hebrews 1:13, which explains that Jesus is superior to all the angels, in that the first verse of this Psalm was spoken by God of him, not of them.

In Daniel the son of man figure comes *to* the Ancient of Days, whereas in Mark's verse the Son of man will be seen first "sitting" at the right hand of God, as in the Psalm, and then "coming with the clouds of heaven", as in Daniel. This sequence demands that the 'coming' be *from* God to Earth and human beings (Brown 1994, p. 497). In Mark's conception Jesus as Son of man sits at God's right hand after his resurrection and comes to Earth with the clouds of heaven as judge at his 'parousia' or second coming. Rev. 1:7 likewise takes his "coming with the clouds" as coming to Earth to effect the final judgement.[1]

The earliest Christian communities believed, as is clear from the Pauline and other epistles, that Jesus would return in their lifetime; and so it is not surprising that words promising this should come to be ascribed to him. Nevertheless the question remains: did he see himself in the role of the Son of man and say what Mk. 14:62 reports at his trial, or is this subtle combination of two independent OT texts a construction of the early church? There is, as one might expect, no agreed answer. We saw, however (above p. 67), that the evidence of the epistle to the Hebrews strongly suggests the latter of these two possibilities.

The early church was painfully aware that most Jews did not believe Jesus to have been the Messiah; so it would be quite natural for Christians to suppose that he had claimed this status to their face and had been condemned by them for doing so. That could be the basis on which not only this logion of Mk. 14:62 but also the whole trial scene in which it figures was constructed. The scene certainly includes numerous features which have led scholars to question its historicity, as the discussion in Nineham (1963, pp. 400ff) shows.

Jesus's apocalyptic sayings do not endear him to modern readers (other than fundamentalists). Vermes regards them, with their stern view of God, either as inauthentic (1993, pp. 159–160), or as describing what God will be like in the new age, when the kingdom comes (p. 200), whereas for the present he is "a loving and solicitous father" (p. 180). The idea is that, although on the Day of Judgement he will be implacably objective and judge those brought before him solely on their merits, for the present he is kindly, caring and clement. This sharp dichotomy between the loving mercy of God and Christ in the present, and their later implacable objectivity, has never been satisfactorily accounted for. Vermes believes that the historical Jesus taught that the kingdom of God was at hand, yet nowhere distinctly spelled out his concept of it, but specified only the conditions for entering it, namely "detachment from possessions, unquestioning trust in God and absolute submission to him" (pp. 146, 148). It seems, then, that had Vermes's Jesus been asked what he meant by saying 'the kingdom is coming soon', he would have replied: 'That I cannot say, but we had all better behave ourselves in the meantime'.

One quite popular way of escape from ascribing to Jesus the view that the kingdom would come with cosmic catastrophe in the near future has been the "realized eschatology" of C.H. Dodd, based on passages which are held to suggest that it has already fully come with his ministry, death, and resurrection. One such passage is the pericope where Pharisees accuse him of casting out devils only by virtue of his alliance with "Beelzebub the prince of the devils". He retorts that his exorcisms no more prove alliance with Satan than does the same activity on the part of Pharisaic exorcists; and he adds: "But if I by the Spirit of God cast out devils, then is the kingdom of God come upon you" (Mt. 12:24–28). Dodd and others take this to mean that, in his view, the kingdom was not merely imminent, but fully present in his own actions. But if this is so, why should not the successes of the Jewish exorcists be good evidence that the kingdom has long been there? Their skills, although admitted in this passage and not condemned as Satanic, are, it seems, to count for nothing, while like skills on his part are to be taken as establishing his exalted status. Moreover, the 'you' upon whom the kingdom is supposedly come are his critics, the Pharisees, not the people he healed, so that the words must be a warning to them; the kingdom is now bearing down upon them, and if they continue to reject him, they will regret it in the immediate future, when God—so he supposed—will intervene to set up his kingdom. Sanders points to the parallel with Mk. 8:38: "For whosoever shall be ashamed of me and of my words in this adulterous and sinful generation, the Son of man shall also be ashamed of him when he cometh in the glory of his Father with the holy angels". Here too, a present positive response to Jesus is of crucial importance, but the kingdom is put in the future; individual commitment now will determine who will enter it when it arrives (1993b, p. 61).

At Lk. 17:21 (unrepresented in other gospels) Jesus tells the Pharisees that the kingdom of God "is in the midst of you" (RSV). He does not mean that it is present in the unbelieving Pharisees, but in himself: hence he will bring it again, and finally, when he returns at his second coming. The verses that follow do in fact say that "the Son of man" will come in the future with destructive cosmic signs, so here again there is no suggestion that Jesus has finally brought the kingdom during his own lifetime.

Dodd's 'realized eschatology' leaves him with the task of disposing of these passages where the kingdom is to come after cosmic catastrophe, and he understandably becomes incoherent when he deals with them. The Great Assize when the Son of man will come in his glory and separate sheep and goats is, he says, not a forthcoming event to which a date might be assigned, but a symbol for "the reality to which the spirit of man awakes when it is done with past, present, and future" (1971, p. 115). Those sympathetic to Dodd's ideas have found these passages equally embarrassing. C.F.D. Moule, commenting on the Markan apocalypse (chapter 13 of the gospel) calls it a way of saying that "there are factors bigger than human" and that God "will have the last word when he has brought history to the end of its course". He adds: "You cannot speak effectively about what is bigger than human without calling in language different from the normal—language about the sun failing, stars falling, and so forth" (1965, p. 102).

The most sustained attempt to free the synoptic Jesus from apocalyptic fanaticism is that of N.T. Wright, who believes that "the great majority of New Testament scholars has misunderstood the nature of apocalyptic" (1996, pp. 56f), that apocalyptic passages in both Jewish and Christian documents about the stars falling from heaven and the Son of man coming with angels on clouds are really merely images expressing the view that God will shortly vindicate his people, and are no more meant literally than when we ourselves speak, as we might, of the fall of the Berlin wall, or the devaluation of sterling in September 1992, as "earth-shattering".[2] But cosmic metaphors apropos of these events occur in contexts where the events are unambiguously what is being spoken of, whereas the references in apocalypses to cosmic catastrophes and to the coming of the Son of man are not similarly set in contexts which show that they are but a figurative way of designating something else. On the contrary, 2 Peter 3:10–12 unambiguously states that at the final judgement "the heavens that now are and the earth" will be destroyed by fire: "The heavens shall pass away with a great noise, the elements shall be dissolved with fervent heat, and the works that are therein shall be burned up"—all this to be followed by "new heavens and a new earth, wherein dwelleth righteousness". Wright can only suppose that we are here dealing with a "misunderstanding of Jewish apocalyptic language" (1992, p. 463n.)—which, however, repeatedly posits the annihilation of the world by fire (References in Russell 1961, p. 275).

What, then, is this "vindication" of God's people to which, in Wright's view, apocalyptic statements refer? In the Jewish documents, he says, it is to consist in military victory of the Jews over their pagan enemies; for Jesus, however, Israel's God was to become Lord of the whole world in a quite different way, in that his own death and resurrection, which he foresaw, would defeat Satan and vanquish evil. He saw the wrath of God bearing down upon the Jews (and leading to the Roman destruction of Jerusalem) because they proposed to fight the Romans instead of accepting his way of peace. So he determined, by means of a voluntary death, to take this wrath upon himself. The Jews believed that the kingdom—God's universal rule—would be preceded by suffering and woe. Jesus believed that, if he took this upon himself, the kingdom would then come; his own resurrection would show that God had vindicated him and that evil was defeated. Wright has taken much of this, as he acknowledges, from Schweitzer. The vague talk about defeating evil does not inspire confidence. In Wright's view, although evil in fact survived Jesus, his resurrection—or at any rate the church's belief in it—did show that "he had in principle [!] succeeded in his task" and had left his followers the "further task of *implementing* what he had achieved", of becoming in their turn "Isaianic heralds, lights to the world" (1996, pp. 659, 660, Author's italics). Wright is merely restating the traditional Christian philosophy of history, according to which love will decisively triumph over evil, and in some unclarified sense has already done so by Christ in his death and resurrection.

These attempts by Dodd, Wright, and others to reinterpret the apocalyptic fanaticism of the texts carry no conviction. It was certainly these very texts which led the church to believe in Christ's absolute uniqueness. They proclaim the imminence of an end which was to include universal resurrection and judgement, and Jesus's own supposed resurrection was understood as indicating that this general resurrection would soon occur: in this sense Paul declares that "Christ raised from the dead" constitutes "the first fruits of them that are asleep", to be followed by others at his (second) coming, and "then cometh the end" (1 Cor. 15:20–24. Cf above, p. 127). It was natural that one whose work was thus so closely linked with final cataclysmic events should be regarded as superior to any predecessor. The end did not come, yet the idea of his centrality and uniqueness was retained by seeing him as the turning point of history, not only of that of God's chosen people, but of the whole world, an image of him powerfully advocated in St. Augustine's *City of God* and later made permanent in the Western system of dating centred on him, B.C. and A.D.[3] This perspective led mainstream Christianity to look not so much to the future—to a second coming that had almost infinitely receded—as to the past, leaving strong and vivid expectations concerning the future to marginal sects.

ii. An Irreducible Minimum of Authentic Information?

Nearly all commentators allow that the gospels include some minimum of accurate historical material. This was true even of Bultmann, and his distinguished pupils (Käsemann, Bornkamm, and others) accepted considerably more than he did. There is nothing surprising in this. Christian theologians want to continue as Christians; Bultmann's way of doing so—compensating for histori- cal scepticism with a faith concocted from existentialist philoso- phy—was obviously not a sustainable position; and so it is not unnatural that his pupils preferred to drop the philosophy and be less sceptical towards the foundation documents. Even so, their scepticism remains considerable, and they are certainly not wit- nesses to be called in support of traditional views.[4]

Favourite texts which have figured among those accepted as supplying authentic information have been a small number which suggest either weakness or inadequacy in Jesus. These at least, it is held, are inconceivable as inventions of his worshippers and are therefore to be accepted as real utterances of his or veridical reports of episodes in his life. Early this century, the Zürich theologian P.W. Schmiedel specified a few such "absolutely credible passages" and called them "foundation-pillars for a truly scientific life of Jesus".[5] They form a base on which a good deal of orthodox Christian doctrine has subsequently been built.

Most of these 'pillars' are from the earliest extant gospel, Mark, and it is supposed that this evangelist was so honest that he was willing to report details which may well have seemed incongruous to him. Some of these passages did embarrass later evangelists, who adapted them so as to render them innocuous. A good example is the logion "Why callest thou me good? None is good save one, even God" (Mk. 10:18). As we saw (above, p. 20), Matthew adapts this so as to eliminate any suggestion that Jesus was not good. Some of the Fathers avoided embarrassment at the Markan wording by taking it to mean: 'By calling me good, you admit my divinity.' If this is what is meant, then the logion could certainly have been created by the early Church! But it is more likely to mean that Jesus, as truly human, did not share God's unique goodness; and such a view could well have been inspired by a feeling for the humility and human kinship of the Son of man.

Commonly adduced is also Mk. 6:1–6 where, coming into his "own country", Jesus "could do there no mighty work, save that he laid his hands upon a few sick folk and cured them. And he marvelled because of their unbelief". We saw that Matthew adapts this passage too. Its purpose in Mark is clearly to stress the importance of faith, often emphasized in the gospel healing miracles. To argue that this logion, or the one previously discussed, could not have been invented is to assume that the sole interest of an evangelist was to exalt Jesus, whereas in fact other motives may well have sometimes interfered with and run counter to that. To record the pernicious consequences of the lack of faith in Galilee is quite in accordance with the doctrine that faith is necessary to salvation.

Jesus's prayer in Gethsemane to be spared suffering and death (Mk. 14:36) is also often regarded as not intelligible except as an authentic utterance, since an evangelist would not ascribe fictive weakness to his hero. Here again, the assumption is that Mark's prime concern must have been exaltation, whereas the point he seems to be making here is the tremendousness of what Jesus is about to do for us—undertaking a burden so heavy as to make even him waver, in spite of his own previous detailed predictions that he must suffer and die, and in spite of his superior moral fibre, brought out here in Gethsemane by contrast with his intimates, incapable even of "watching one hour". Another relevant factor is that the gospels portray him as a model for Christians threatened with persecution and martyrdom; they are "to find in him, either by precept or example the pattern for their own way of facing trial and death. . . . In Gethsemane his behaviour could only be a useful norm if it suggested the tension so common to the Christian confessor and martyr, the tension between the will of God and the natural human shrinking before pain and death" (Cadbury 1951, p. 123)—a tension to be resolved, of course, as in Gethsemane, by submission to the will of God.

The cry of dereliction from the cross, "My God, My God, why hast thou forsaken me" (Mk. 15:34) can also be understood as underlining the greatness of his sacrifice, stressing that in dying alone, deserted by all (by his disciples from the time of his arrest) and mocked by all (even by his two fellow sufferers), he bore his burden with no help from any quarter. The idea that he died a fully human, shameful death, totally removed from the realm of God whence he came, is attested also in the reading of Hebrews 2:9 according to which he died "apart from God". Ehrman regards this reading as original (1993, pp. 146ff) and as expressing the theology that, precisely because Jesus's agony was not attenuated by special dispensation, God could accept his sacrifice as the perfect expiation of sin.

Tyler supplements these examples of 'pillar' texts with Jn. 11:35 where, "unlike ancient and modern heroes, Jesus weeps" (p. 38). That other heroes—divine or otherwise—are never represented as distraught is an astounding statement. Has Tyler never come across Sophocles's Philoctetes or Virgil's Laokoon? There is also the cult of Herakles, as exhibited in plays by Euripides and Seneca. Summarizing the plot of the former, Gilbert Murray tells how, "like a common, weak-hearted man", its hero "speaks of suicide" and has to be deterred by Theseus reminding him of what he is, "the helper of man, the powerful friend of the oppressed, the Heracles who dared all and endured all" (1946, p. 63). In Seneca's play

> the irresistible demigod, victor over all foes, including 'death and hell', is made first to boast of his invincibility, and then, under torture, to shriek and weep. Is it to be argued, then, that those who worshipped him as the mightiest of demigods 'could not have invented' a myth which shows him overthrown by the centaur's fraud and reduced to grovel on the earth in his pain; and that therefore there *must* have been a Herakles who so suffered? (Robertson 1927, p. 149).

It is over the death of his friend Lazarus that Jesus weeps; and when he saw Lazarus's sister Mary and the Jews with her weeping, he "groaned in the spirit and was troubled" (verse 33). The first verb here is *embrimaomai*, and really implies indignation or anger; when used of the behaviour of a prophet, magician or wonder-worker, it signified a frenzy or raving that preceded wonderous deeds (cf. Garrett 1989, p. 19). If, however, Jesus is here expressing grief at Lazarus's death, he nevertheless deliberately delayed his own arrival on the scene (11:6) so as to be able to display his own miraculous powers in restoring him to life and so to engender belief (verses 14–15). The whole story is more trouble to apologists than it is worth. It is unique to the fourth gospel, whose author has decided to make the raising of Lazarus—not the cleansing of the temple, as in the synoptics—the principal reason for hostility to Jesus: the council of Pharisees and chief priests (the Sanhedrin) decides to kill him immediately after this event (Jn. 11:47ff). That the Pharisees are involved in this decisive meeting contrasts with the synoptic accounts, where the Sanhedrin and its groupings are mentioned in the passion narratives, but not the Pharisees. (It has repeatedly struck commentators that throughout the fourth gospel they appear more as an official body than as a party.)

Summarizing, passages which ascribe or appear to ascribe weakness to Jesus can readily be understood not as written without motive, but from motives which differ from the evangelists' supposed unitary purpose of exalting him. The same may be said of Mk. 13:32 which represents him not as weak, but as ignorant—of the precise time when the end will come: "Of that day or that hour knoweth no one, not even the angels in heaven, neither the Son, but the Father. Take ye heed, watch and pray: for ye know not when the time is". The motive here, says R.M. Grant in a context where he discusses also some of the other passages we have been considering, was "to counteract enthusiasm for eschatological timetables" (1963, p. 286). The very wording makes this logion suspect, as a creation of the early church, for Jesus never elsewhere in Mark refers to himself so directly as 'the Son'—that is characteristic of the fourth gospel, not of the synoptics. This and other sayings about his second coming and the end aimed at keeping believers on their toes by affirming that it was all near at hand, yet insisting that its exact date could not be known.

That mixed and even conflicting motives are discernible as underlying different gospel material is the more readily intelligible if we consider the stages through which the traditions about Jesus passed before their inclusion in the gospels. Scholars in the early part of the twentieth century gave reasons for taking Mark's account of the Galilean ministry as a series of separate, short single units (pericopae), each one of which had been transmitted, originally orally, in the preaching and teaching of early Christian communities. Every one of them was designed to represent some point of doctrinal interest, and it is only to be expected that their combination into a unitary gospel resulted in a mixture of interests being evident in that final work. As Cadbury notes, "in a general way the units were consistent. . . . They represent the favourable attitude to Jesus entertained by his followers. But in detail favourable attitudes can vary quite considerably" (1951, p. 118). To say that passages where Jesus appears to be less than on top of it all could not have been invented means that we cannot suggest any plausible motive for inventing them. This is simply not so.

This whole argument—that sayings or incidents can reliably be designated as embarrassing to an evangelist and therefore represent authentic tradition—has recently been pressed by Graham Stanton. He adduces, for instance, Mark's account of Jesus's submission to baptism by John the Baptist who preached "the baptism of repentance unto remission of sins". But Stanton makes no mention of the fact that Justin Martyr betrays that, according to a Jewish notion, the Messiah would be unknown as such to himself and others until Elijah, as his forerunner, should anoint him; and Mark implies that the Baptist is Elijah. Numerous commentators have conceded that

Mark may well have been influenced by the tradition mentioned by Justin (see *WWJ*, p. 98). Stanton also (1995, pp. 152–53) adduces some of the passages I have discussed above, but does not mention the objections to taking them as reliably authentic that have been made by Cadbury, Grant, and others—although on an earlier page and in another context he can complain that scholars "often sound like politicians" in that they "largely ignore the strongest points made by their opponents" (p. 84).

The upshot of this discussion is that uncertainty must pertain even to those elements in the records of Jesus's ministry which have been claimed as most plausibly authentic. Numerous scholars agree that, although many details in these records may well constitute genuine reminiscences, it is very difficult indeed to specify what in them must be accepted as undoubtedly true—particularly as incidents which in themselves are by no means impossible are so interwoven with obviously legendary matter.

4

The Earliest Non-Christian Testimony

i. Roman Notices

If the NT cannot give us indubitable information about a Jesus who lived in the opening decades of the first century, are we any better served by testimony from pagan or Jewish authors?

The early Roman notices of Christ and Christianity have to be admitted as amounting to very little. The historians of the empire, says Mitton, "were interested in extension of territory and struggles for the imperial succession"; and so "it is not surprising" that they did not "specifically record the life and death of Jesus" (1975, p. 31). There is however a letter of the younger Pliny which deals with the practices of Christians and mentions their worship of "Christ". There is also a brief passage in Suetonius that can be understood as mentioning "Christ"; and there is Tacitus's statement that "Christ" was executed under Pilate. All three are from the early second century. Pliny was writing around A.D. 112 to the emperor Trajan; Suetonius was secretary to the emperor Hadrian, who reigned A.D. 117–138; Tacitus wrote his *Annals* about the same time as Pliny wrote his letter.

In a 1985 article M.J. Harris makes a great deal of these notices. He writes lucidly, in a calm, utterly unpolemical tone, but with my work very much in mind; for he knows that, while an absence of pagan references would not tell decisively against Jesus's historicity, pagan notices—if early and independent of Christian testimony—would establish it. He knows too that Christian beliefs require a historical Jesus; and he sees that, now that historical criticism of the gospels as practised by some radical (though Christian) critics has reduced Jesus to "a shadow of a shade", it is no great step to deny all reality to that insubstantial shadow (pp. 359, 368).

Harris begins by claiming Thallus as a possibly early gentile witness, but is rightly tentative about this. I have recently discussed the somewhat complex material elsewhere.[1] He then turns to Pliny the Younger, who wrote asking Trajan whether he was right to leave Christians unmolested provided they were prepared to conform to Roman religious rites and to forswear Christianity. His letter demonstrates no more than that Christians existed in the early second century and worshipped Christ. None of the three major Roman witnesses—Pliny, Suetonius, Tacitus—makes any mention of Jesus, but write only of "Christ"; and Pliny says nothing about his historical existence, nor its possible date. He may well have understood 'Christ' to have been a historical personage, and not a god who had no human existence. Christians (even Pauline ones) had always believed Christ to have lived a human life at some time or other; and the Christians Pliny interrogated were presumably familiar, if not with the gospels (available in written form by then), at any rate with their story, namely that Jesus died under Pilate. Whether he extracted this much from the Christians he encountered we have no means of telling. But even if he did, it represented what, by then, Christians believed, not what was necessarily historically the case.

Suetonius wrote that Claudius (who reigned A.D. 41–54) expelled Jews from Rome because "they constantly made disturbances at the instigation of Chrestus". He probably meant "Christus", which in turn could mean either 'the Messiah' or a particular person, Christ, claiming to be the Messiah; and he was probably referring to disorders resulting from controversy between orthodox Jews and Jewish Christians about the truth or falsehood of Christianity. Francis Watson has noted that Suetonius wrongly concluded—perhaps because of the Christian claim that Jesus, as risen, was still alive—that 'Chrestus' had actually been in Rome in person, stirring up trouble (1986, p. 91). The Christians involved in these disturbances of around A.D. 50 will surely have believed nothing more specific about Jesus's life than what extant Christian writers (Paul and others) were saying on the subject before the gospels became established later in the century; and that, as we saw, does not confirm the gospels' portraits of Jesus.

Harris suggests (p. 356) that Suetonius may have consulted "an earlier historian's version of the riots" which was itself "based on local police records". This is obviously the merest wishful thinking. The whole idea of educated Romans ferreting out, at this time, the historical basis on which a small and despised group believed what was, for these Romans, silly superstitious nonsense, is not sustainable. Historians have noted, from the paucity of references, that most inhabitants of the Roman empire in A.D. 100 were "either unaware of or uninterested in the Christians in their midst" (Barnes 1994, p. 232; see Walsh 1991, pp. 264–65).

More explicit than anything from Pliny or Suetonius is what Tacitus wrote about Christianity apropos of the burning of Rome in Nero's time (A.D. 64). He says that, to scotch the belief that the emperor himself had started the fire, Nero put the blame onto "a class of men loathed for their views, whom the crowd styled Christians". In order to give his educated readers some idea as to who these people were—he evidently did not expect them to know already—Tacitus adds that Christians "derive their name and origin from Christ who, in the reign of Tiberius, had suffered death by the sentence of the procurator Pontius Pilate".

That there had been Christians in Rome under Nero was surely common knowledge when Tacitus wrote this. What he added to it is the reference to an execution under Pilate, and there remains the question as to what source he had for this statement. By the time he wrote, any Christians and any persons who knew anything much of their beliefs could have told him that this was what they believed. He had been governor of Asia (the western third of Asia Minor) ca. A.D. 112, and may well have had the same kind of contact with Christians that his friend Pliny was experiencing as governor of neighbouring Bithynia at that very time. Many Christian scholars have suggested that he looked up official records and found there evidence of Jesus's execution. This, says Harris, is "not impossible" (p. 352), and he would like to believe it to be so, although his own account shows it to be very unlikely. Had Tacitus consulted official documents, he would not have given Pilate an incorrect title—he was 'prefect', and not 'procurator' of Judea—and he was surely not going to be bothered with antiquarian research into what he called a "dire superstition". Nor is there any reason to believe that he consulted Christian writings. Their sheer inelegance did not dispose educated pagans to read them. A.H.M. Jones describes the holy books of Christianity as "uncouth and barbaric, written in a Greek or Latin which grated on the sensibilities of any educated man bred up on Menander and Demosthenes, or Terence and Cicero" (1963, p. 20). Against this, A.W. Mosley claims that ancient historians (he names Tacitus among others) were quick to criticize inaccuracies in their fellow writers, so that, if NT authors had erred in this way, we should expect to find such charges brought against them (1965, p. 26). But a serious writer such as Tacitus would not trouble himself with registering 'inaccuracies' in what he regarded as superstitious stuff which was not even known to the readers he had in mind (otherwise he would not have found it necessary to explain to them who these people who call themselves Christians are). Later, when Christianity had spread and become better known, Celsus and Porphyry did make such criticisms. Porphyry (who died around A.D. 303) called the evangelists "inventors, not narrators of events" (see Hoffmann 1994, pp. 32–36). There may have been more of the same from other critics, but the later church will have made it very difficult for such comments to survive.

I have given three reasons in *HEJ* (pp. 16–17) for holding that Tacitus was merely repeating what he had learnt from Christians or from hearsay: the incorrect title he gives to Pilate ('procurator' was the term for governor current in Tacitus's own day); his failure to name the executed man: he could hardly have found in archives a statement that 'Christ' (the Messiah) was executed on such and such a date; and gladness to accept from Christians their own view that Christianity was of recent origin, since the Roman authorities were prepared to tolerate only ancient cults. R.T. France finds my case "entirely convincing" (1986, p. 23). Sanders says, justly: "Roman sources that mention Jesus are all dependent on Christian reports" (1993a, p. 49). Many Christian commentators, however, continue in complacent acceptance of the Tacitus passage as providing what Markus Bockmuehl, without argument, calls "independent confirmation" that Jesus died under Pontius Pilate—evidence, he says, which is "surprisingly useful" in disposing of my ideas on Christian origins (1994, p. 16 and n).

ii. Josephus

A. THE *TESTIMONIUM* AS INTERPOLATION

In the extant manuscripts of Flavius Josephus's *Antiquities of the Jews*, which was written around A.D. 94, there are two mentions of "Jesus". (He is actually named, not just called "Christ".) These two passages are habitually claimed as the strongest non-Christian evidence in the ancient world to the actual existence of the Jesus of the synoptic gospels—the Jesus who suffered under Pontius Pilate.

The longer of the two passages (*Ant.* 18:63–64) is known as the *Testimonium Flavianum*. It states not only that Pilate had Jesus crucified after he had been indicted by the highest Jewish authorities, but also that he was "a wise man, if indeed one ought to call him a man", that he was the Messiah ("the Christ") who wrought "surprising feats", taught "such people as accept the truth with pleasure", won over many Jews and Greeks, and appeared alive to his followers on the third day after his death. Finally, it is said that "these and countless other marvellous things about him" had been foretold by "the prophets of God", and that "the tribe of Christians named after him has still to this day not disappeared".

Josephus, as an orthodox Jew, would not have written such obviously Christian words, and if he had believed all that they affirm, he would not have restricted his comments to this brief paragraph (and to a single phrase in the other, shorter passage). Hence the most that can be claimed is that he here made *some* reference to Jesus, which has been retouched by a Christian hand. If this is so, then what he as an orthodox Jew said is likely to have been uncomplimentary. But a deprecatory reference would have aroused the indignation of Origen, one of the most influential Christian scholars of the third century; and what he read in Josephus about Jesus—on this see below, p. 220—did not have this effect. He regretted that Josephus "did not believe in Jesus as Christ",[2] but did not complain of the tone of his remarks. As we shall see, Origen probably read some variant of the shorter of the two passages. If there was anything at all where the longer one now stands, it was not in its present form, in which it specifically affirms what Origen categorically denies that Josephus had affirmed, namely that Jesus was the Messiah.

As I noted in *The Jesus Legend*, there is an ancient table of contents of the *Antiquities* which omits all mention of the *Testimonium*. Feldman (in Feldman and Hata, 1987, p. 57) says that this table is already mentioned in the fifth- or sixth-century Latin version of the *Antiquities*, and he finds it "hard to believe that such a remarkable passage would be omitted by anyone, let alone by a Christian summarizing the work". For him, the omission "is further indication that either there was no such notice [of Jesus] or that it was much less remarkable than it reads at present". At least the 'remarkable' elements in it must have been interpolated by a Christian. One of the marks by which an interpolation can be recognized is the failure of later writers to mention it when reference to it can be expected, given the subject they are treating and their point of view. It is, then, significant that, although this paragraph will have suited the purposes of the Church Fathers admirably, particularly in polemics against the Jews, none before Eusebius (in the fourth century) quotes it. We know that Justin Martyr had to defend Christianity, in the debates between Jews and Christians, against the charge that Christians had "invented some sort of Christ for themselves" and had accepted "a futile rumour" (Justin's *Dialogue with Trypho*, 8, a work dated around A.D. 135. The point at issue here was probably not whether Jesus had existed, but whether he was important enough to have been the Messiah). The obvious Christian reply would have been to point triumphantly to the *Testimonium*. That this was not done until the fourth century suggests that the passage did not exist earlier. Feldman names two Fathers from the second century, seven from the third, and two from the early fourth, all of whom knew Josephus and cited his works, but "do not refer to this passage, though one would imagine it would be the first passage that a Christian apologist would cite" (1984a, p. 695). He adds that, even after Eusebius, three fourth-century Fathers and five from the fifth century (up to and including Augustine) often cite Josephus, but not this passage. In the early fifth century only Jerome cites it (and he only once). All this, Feldman says elsewhere (in Feldman and Hata 1987, p. 57), is admittedly an argument from silence, "but as a cumulative argument it has considerable force".

In sum, after Eusebius a century passes before the *Testimonium* is again referred to, and this suggests that some time elapsed before all or most copies of the *Antiquities* came to include it. Defenders of its authenticity point out that it is found in all the Greek manuscripts and in all the manuscripts of the Latin translation of Josephus. But our earliest manuscript containing this part of the *Antiquities* dates from the eleventh century and hence may derive from an interpolated copy. Hence too it is not much of an argument to say, with Tyler (p. 32), that the passage did not come under suspicion for many centuries. In the Middle Ages it was, as Paul Winter tells us (and as we might have expected) "eagerly seized upon as impartial proof of the gospel story"; and it was from the sixteenth century onward that critical voices were raised.[3]

A reason for thinking that the whole of the paragraph has been interpolated is that it breaks the thread of the narrative at the point where it occurs, and its removal leaves a text which runs on in proper sequence. The two preceding paragraphs tell that 1. Pilate, faced with a rebellion by Jews protesting against his behaviour, plans to massacre them, but relents and mollifies them. 2. On a later occasion he does have protestors massacred. Next comes 3., the paragraph which begins with: "And there appeared at this time Jesus", and continues with mention of his wisdom, his miracles, his teaching of the truth, his success in winning over many Jews and Greeks, his indictment by prominent Jews ("men of the highest standing among us"), his crucifixion at Pilate's behest, and his resurrection appearances—all this having been foretold by God's prophets.

There follows paragraph 4., beginning: "Another sad calamity put the Jews into disorder". The Loeb library edition renders this: "Another outrage threw the Jews into uproar". The final word ('disorder', 'uproar') connects this introduction of 4. with the 'uproars' specified in 1. and 2. Thus 3.—the passage about Jesus—occurs in a context which deals with uproar bringing danger or misfortune to the Jews. That 4. should follow immediately after 2. is obvious from the opening words of 4.—*"Another* calamity". There is here no possible reference to 3.

The calamity specified at the beginning of 4. did not result from Pilate's behaviour—as did those of 1. and 2.—but consisted of Tiberius's banishment of 4,000 Jews from Rome because of the wickedness of four. And so Josephus takes the opportunity, before narrating the details, to say something about "shameful practices" at the temple of Isis, also at Rome, under Tiberius. He expressly says that this constitutes a digression from the topic in hand (namely "Jewish affairs") and notes at the end of it that he is returning to this topic: "I now return to relating what happened about this time to the Jews at Rome, as I told you I would". He then, as paragraph 5., gives the details of what led to the expulsion of the 4,000.

R.T. France (1986, p. 28) writes as though the argument that 3. does not fit the context in which it is placed were an outlandish suggestion introduced into the discussion by me. In fact it has been repeatedly urged and sometimes regarded as in itself decisive evidence that 3. is an interpolation (Details in Feldman 1984a, p. 696). France holds that, if 3. has to go, then 4. and 5. would also have to be excised, as Josephus returns to Pilate only at the beginning of the next chapter. I have already replied (*WWJ*, p. 22) saying: my argument is not that all that is said about Pilate must occur in unbroken sequence, but that paragraph 3. occurs in a context which purports to deal with Jewish misfortunes, only some of these being attributable to him. As we saw, when Josephus digresses from this overall context, he confesses, even somewhat apologetically, to doing so.

Feldman noted (in Feldman and Hata 1987, pp. 54, 57), as an

argument for interpolation, that in Josephus's *The Jewish War* there is a statement about the deeds of Pilate which parallels what is said of him in the *Antiquities*, but which has "no mention of Jesus, despite the fact that the length of the account is almost as great". Only in the Slavonic version of *The Jewish War* (known to have plentiful Christian interpolations) is the *Testimonium* inserted into the relevant context and even expanded. He adds that, if Josephus had really made Jesus into a figure of importance, it is remarkable that his great contemporary and rival historian, Justus of Tiberias, apparently made no mention at all of him, even though he wrote a work of Jewish history covering much the same period as that covered in the *Antiquities*, and including the period of the Roman governors of Judea. We know that Justus is thus silent because, although his book has been lost, Photius, Christian Patriarch of Constantinople, read it in the ninth century and was astonished to find that "this Jewish historian does not make the smallest mention of the appearance of Christ, and says nothing whatever of his deeds and miracles" (*Bibliotheca*, 33).

In a second symposium edited by Hata and himself, Feldman reminds readers of how enormous the literature on the *Testimonium* is: for the period 1937–1980 alone, he says, he earlier listed 87 items, "the overwhelming majority of which question its authenticity in whole or in part" (Feldman and Hata 1989, p. 430). He pulls together many of the above arguments for interpolation with the following impressive summary:

> The passage, despite its obvious usefulness in debates with Jews, is not found in any writer before Eusebius in the fourth century. If it had existed in Josephus's original text, we would have expected it to be cited by Justin Martyr in his dialogue with the Jew Trypho, since it would have been an extremely effective answer to Trypho's charge that Christianity is based on a rumor and that if Jesus was born and lived somewhere he is entirely unknown. . . . No fewer than eleven church fathers prior to or contemporary with Eusebius cite various passages from Josephus (including the *Antiquities*) but not the *Testimonium*. Moreover, it is a full century—and five other church fathers, most notably Augustine, who had many an occasion to find it useful—before we have another reference to the *Testimonium* in Jerome . . . and it seems remarkable that Jerome, who knows Josephus so well, cites him ninety times, and admires him so much that he refers to him as a

second Livy, . . . cites the *Testimonium* only once. We may add that the fact that, in the passage in the *War* parallel to the one in the *Antiquities* about Pilate, there is no mention of Jesus, despite the fact that the account of Pilate in the *War* is almost as full as the version in the *Antiquities,* corroborates our suspicion that there was either no passage about Jesus in the original text of the *Antiquities* or that it had a different form. We may also note that Josephus's great contemporary and rival, Justus of Tiberias, apparently made no mention of Jesus. (p. 431)

Against all this, there are features in the wording of the *Testimonium* which have been held to be unlikely to have come from a Christian hand. I list here seven such, with my comments.

i. Numerous scholars regard the statement that Jesus won over not only Jews but also many gentiles as flying in the face of what is said of his ministry in the four gospels. Against this, we may note that, according to Mt. 4:24, "his fame spread throughout all Syria"; and Mk. 3:7–8 tells that a "great multitude" followed him from Galilee, Judea, Jerusalem, and Idumea, and from "beyond Jordan and about Tyre and Sidon." The gospels also represent him as feeding thousands at a time. All these people may not have been 'won over', but anyone familiar with such passages could well suppose that many were. Also, no interpolations could have been made into Josephus's text before his book was available in the 90s, and by then a Christian reader will have known that the risen Jesus had instructed his followers to make disciples of all nations (Mt. 28:19) and that Paul had founded numerous gentile churches. An interpolator will have had the situations of his own day as much in mind as those portrayed in the gospels. The Catholic scholar J.P. Meier supposes that it was Josephus himself who here "simply retrojected the [Christian] situation of his own day . . . into the time of Jesus", since "naive retrojection is a common trait among Greco-Roman historians" (1990, p. 94). One can only comment that there is no reason to suppose that a Christian interpolator would have been immune from such widespread naivety.

Stanton (1995, p. 127) translates the Greek here not as "Jesus won over many Jews and many of the Greeks", but as

"Jesus brought trouble to many Jews", etc. This looks like an attempt to make the whole passage relevant to the theme of its context (misfortunes befalling the Jews).[4]

ii. None of the Fathers before Eusebius used the word 'tribe' in reference to Christians, as it is used in this passage. But neither does it fit Josephus's usage well, for he uses 'tribe' of national groups—such as the Jews, the Taurians, the Parthians. Zeitlin argues that Eusebius himself—the first witness to the *Testimonium*—introduced this word here. He shows that Eusebius had a certain partiality for it, evidenced when he said that Trajan (in his rescript to Pliny concerning how to deal with Christians) and Tertullian (in his report of Trajan's rescript) both wrote of "the tribe of Christians", when in fact neither Trajan nor Tertullian had used the word 'tribe'.[5] 'Tribe' then, was an expression Eusebius was ready to put into the mouth of a non-Christian writer with reference to Christians. Feldman notes that other phrases in the *Testimonium* have been held to be characteristic not of Josephus, but of Eusebius (1984b, p. 827).

iii. The Jewish scholar Joseph Klausner, and others, have found the designation of Jesus as "a wise man" too modest an assessment for a Christian, even though Jesus's supernatural status is suggested by the addition of "if indeed one ought to call him a man" (Details in Scheidweiler, 1954, pp. 241f). But Josephus is very sparing in his use of the term 'wise man', Solomon and Daniel (not David, as Scheidweiler erroneously says) being the only two personages he thus designates (*Ant.* 8:53 and 10:237); so it is questionable whether he would have placed the casually mentioned Jesus in the same category. Scheidweiler (pp. 242ff) believed that this phrase in the *Testimonium* reflects Christian 'Wisdom' Christology: in the third century Paul of Samosata (and presumably the Christian circle around him) equated Wisdom and the 'Logos'; and for advocates of such Christology it would be quite appropriate to call Jesus 'a wise man, if indeed he may be called a man'.

I am not endorsing the views of Scheidweiler—nor

apropos of ii. above, of Zeitlin—but they show how difficult it is to be sure that certain words or phrases in the *Testimonium* are not Christian.

iv. This caveat is relevant also apropos of the characterization of Jesus as a teacher of people who 'accept the truth with pleasure' (*hēdonē*), which some believe to be authentically Josephan, since the same phrase appears eight other times in books 17–19 of the *Antiquities,* but nowhere else in Josephus (Feldman 1984b, p. 826). But Winter (in Schürer 1973, p. 436) points out that it is only 'to accept with pleasure' that occurs in these passages, that *hēdonē* normally denotes sensual pleasure, and that 'to accept *the truth* with *hēdonē*' "sounds extraordinary".

v. Dornseiff regarded the whole of the *Testimonium* as authentic and claimed that, if a Christian had interpolated it, he would probably have written 'This is the Christ', not 'This was the Christ'. But it is surely obvious that a Christian would have hesitated to put such a full-blooded Christian conviction into the mouth of an orthodox Jew. Feldman (1984a, p. 694) is quite unsympathetic towards Dornseiff, particularly towards his suggestion that Josephus could have said someone to have been 'the Christ' and yet have regarded him as no more than a wonder-worker; for the way in which the word is used in the Septuagint means that it will have been understood in the sense of 'anointed', and hence as the King Messiah. In any case, as we shall see below, Josephus, in passages of undisputed authenticity, was careful to avoid calling anybody the Messiah.

vi. Charlesworth asked (1989, p. 93): "What Christian would refer to Jesus's miracles in such a way that a reader could understand them as merely 'surprising works'?". But Charlesworth himself admits in a note (p. 100 n24) both that the Greek here can mean 'wonderful works', and that this is how an early Christian would understand such an expression apropos of Jesus.

vii. Charlesworth asks additionally: would a Christian have written that the Jews who accused Jesus before Pilate were 'first-rate men' or 'men of the highest standing', thus "leaving the impression that he deserved a guilty verdict?" But the impression made by these words may not have been this at all, but rather indignation at the supposed extent of Jewish culpability over his death. In the gospels it is the ruling priests who have him arrested and handed over to Pilate: Luke states expressly that "the principal men (*hoi prōtoi*) of the people were seeking to destroy him" (19:47). The wording in the *Testimonium* is similar: Pilate condemned him "at the indictment of the principal men (*tōn prōtōn andrōn*) among us".

Finally on this question of wording, Feldman mentions a short note (covering less than a full page) by G.C. Richards, who 1. discerns an (unspecified) "flavour of contempt"[!] in the language of the *Testimonium*, 2. claims the phrase 'on the third day' (in the statement about the appearance of the resurrected Jesus) as acceptable from Josephus because he uses the same expression elsewhere (for instance 'on the third day' after a battle, *Ant.* 7:1), and 3. makes the passage non-Christian by himself interpolating 'as they say' after 'he appeared to them', thus supposing that 'as they say' was removed by a Christian censor (Richards 1941, pp. 70–71). That this kind of reasoning can be offered in all seriousness shows to what straits apologists can be reduced.

Tyler has endorsed most of the arguments hitherto mentioned for taking the passage as genuine and has supplied additional ones of his own. He quotes positive comments on Jesus from what he calls four unlikely sources for such remarks, namely H.G. Wells, Einstein, Rousseau, and Napoleon. No one supposes that they are interpolations, and he suggests that Josephus might well have been "equally capable of such remarks as one would not normally expect from a non-Christian" (p. 23). But it is easy to see that these comments from the four modern writers are not aberrations from their overall views,[6] whereas the same is certainly not true in the case of what is ascribed to Josephus in the *Testimonium*. Tyler also claims (p. 33) that an interpolator could reasonably be expected to have made other insertions so as to cover what he inserted here; and as this is not the case, if we do say that the passage is interpolated, we are in effect calling him a "clown" who did not know his job. I find this a strange argument, showing no awareness of the way in which interpolators characteristically fail to deal with, or even be aware of, the problems created by their insertions. A few examples will help to clarify.

1. No one knows when the end will come, "not even the angels in heaven, nor the Son, but (*ei mē*) the Father" (Mk. 13:32). Some scribes could not accept that Jesus was ignorant on the matter, and so omitted 'nor the Son'. Others felt it desirable to be quite explicit that he possessed the relevant knowledge; so they let this verse 32 stand, but expanded the next one with the italicized words: "Look, be wakeful, for ye know not, *but only (ei mē) the Father and the Son,* when the time is" (Details in Head, 1993, pp. 120–121). This introduces a striking enough contradiction between the two verses. One would not, however, call it clowning.

2. "Jesus and his disciples came into the land of Judaea; and there he tarried with them and baptized" (Jn. 3:22). "When therefore the Lord knew how that the Pharisees had heard that Jesus was making and baptizing more disciples than John (although Jesus himself baptized not, but his disciples) he left Judaea" (Jn. 4:1–3). Dodd observed that the parenthesis here "ruins the sentence and perhaps has a better claim to be regarded as an 'editorial note' by a 'redactor' than [almost] anything else in the gospel" (1968, p. 311n.). Lindars suggested that it "may be an editorial addition to bring John into line with the Synoptic tradition" (1972, p. 177), where Jesus is not said to have baptized. The gloss would, he said, have been better inserted at 3:22, "but the habits of glossators are not always logical".

3. There are numerous instances where certain manuscripts of Acts (Codex Bezae and others) expand or adapt the OT quotations in its early chapters so as to make Jewish-Christian missionaries preach that Christ saves all the nations, not only the Jews, when in fact Acts itself represents this idea of a gentile mission as something highly controversial, accepted by the apostles only in later chapters, and then only with

difficulty. Such "unthinking expansions" of the text, as Haenchen called them, reflect notions obtaining at the time when they were made, but conflict with the situation obtaining at that early section of the text (1965, pp. 162, 166). He instanced other rewordings in these manuscripts of Acts which clearly aimed at removing what were felt as inadequacies or contradictions in the earlier text, but which in fact merely introduce implausibilities in their place (pp. 178–79).

4. All attempts to 'improve' an original run such risks. In chapter 6 of Mark, Jesus feeds 5,000 miraculously, and then walks on water, yet his disciples, witnesses of these events, still do not understand that he possesses miraculous powers. Matthew realized that such obtuseness is not to be believed, and so he replaced Mark's "they understood not" by making them acknowledge Jesus as "truly the Son of God" (Mt. 14:33). Matthew did not notice that this emendation makes Peter's later 'confession' that Jesus is "the Son of the living God" no longer the unexpected stroke of divinely inspired genius that Jesus there declares it to be (16:16–18).

These examples show how often adapting a document, in order to dispose of a problem, in fact creates a new problem.

B. DIGRESSIONS AND UNPREDICTABLE OPINIONS

The authenticity of the *Testimonium* has often been defended by claiming that "it is . . . typical of Josephus's style to include short stories as 'digressions' in the course of an ongoing narrative, triggered by some aspect of the main story" (France 1986, p. 28). Tyler (pp. 23–24) supports this claim with the following three examples, the first of which is also given by France:

i. The account of John the Baptist (*Ant.* 18:116) interrupts the narrative of the wars of Herod Antipas with Aretas. But this is in truth no irrelevancy. Josephus first records that Antipas's whole army was destroyed, and then notes that some Jews regarded this as "divine vengeance, and certainly a just vengeance for his treatment of John, surnamed the Baptist", whose maltreatment at Antipas's hands is then related. First, then, we are told of a military defeat, and then of what some people took to be its cause; and stating the latter enables Josephus, as Mason points out, to "weld the episode into his ongoing demonstration that violation of the divine laws brings inevitable punishment" (1992, p. 153. I note here in passing that Josephus does not in any way link the Baptist with Jesus, but presents him as a famous Jewish preacher, with his own message and following, not as a figure in early Christianity).

ii. Antipas rebuilt Sepphoris (to make Galilee safe) and fortified Betharamphtha (to defend Perea). These reports of his building works (*Ant.* 18:27) are not followed immediately with the account of how he built an entirely new city, Tiberias, but are interrupted by a paragraph about the sequence of high priests and governors in Judea. The reason for this, however, is that, while the fortifications earlier mentioned were constructed during the reign of Augustus, Tiberias was built after his death and named after his successor. The intervening paragraph fills in the interval. The whole narrative runs as follows:

1. After Augustus deposed Archelaus and incorporated his territory (Judea) into the province of Syria, he sent Quirinius (A.D. 6) to make a taxation of Syria and Judea, and sent also Coponius, as Quirinius's subordinate, to be the first Roman governor of Judea.

2. Quirinius appointed Ananus I high priest. Antipas, who had not been deposed, saw to construction works in Sepphoris and Betharamphtha.

3. We are then reminded that "Coponius had been dispatched with Quirinius", and are told of his successors up to Pontius Pilate, and of the high priests they appointed or deposed, including Ananus I, deposed by Coponius's third successor. We are also told that, while all this was happening, Augustus died and was succeeded by Tiberius.

4. Antipas, "inasmuch as he had gained a high place among the friends of Tiberius", had a new city built and named after him.

iii. Eutychus, sent in chains to Capri, claimed to have a secret message for Tiberius pertaining to the emperor's personal security, and at this point we are told of Caesar's dilatory nature and the reasons for it. Again, the context shows that this is not an irrelevancy: Tiberius, instead of receiving Eutychus, kept him a prisoner, because this was his usual way. "No king or tyrant was ever more given to procrastination" (*Ant.* 18:169). Then this statement is justified by giving some examples, and Tiberius's reasons for behaving in this way are stated. The whole concludes with: "It was for this reason that Eutychus also failed to obtain a hearing and was held in chains" (18:179).

In none of these passages is there the kind of sheer irrelevancy to context that characterizes the paragraph on Jesus. It is beginning to be clear that some apologists are so anxious to establish the authenticity of the latter that they are prepared to resort to the flimsiest of arguments. Tyler even claims that Josephus may have written the *Testimonium* as his behaviour was "in no small measure unpredictable" (p. 25) for, when captured by the Romans during the Jewish War, he went over to their side and, as Vespasian's prisoner, ingratiated himself with him by predicting that he would one day become emperor. This is surely evidence not of unpredictability, but of a strategy for survival. It is noted (in Feldman and Hata 1987, p. 26) that "Josephus always managed to find a modus vivendi with every ruler, even the ever-suspicious Domitian".

Josephus himself narrates this incident with Vespasian in his *The Jewish War* (3:399–408). Later in this work (6:312–13), he mentions "an ambiguous oracle" in the Jewish scriptures which foretold the emergence of a world-wide ruler from Judea. He is careful not to call this 'oracle' a Messianic prophecy, as he disliked Messianism as the source of many a futile nationalistic uprising. It is quite in accordance with this dislike that he here interprets this oracle so as to deprive it of any element of Jewish nationalism, and says that it pointed not to someone of Jewish stock, but to Vespasian who commanded the Roman armies in Judea at the time when he was proclaimed emperor. It is absurd for Tyler to claim that this interpretation shows not only that he was "no ordinary Pharisee", but also that he was so unpredictable that "it is more than likely that he could have written at least most of what is in the Longer Passage about Jesus".

As further evidence of unpredictability, Tyler mentions (what is quite true) that there are numerous discrepancies between Josephus's *The Jewish War* and his *Antiquities of the Jews*, written some dozen years later, and gives as an example what is said of the High Priest Ananus II—praised in the former work but rebuked in the latter. Two scholars, Steve Mason and Tessa Rajak, have accounted for this discrepancy in different ways, but neither supposes arbitrariness or unpredictability on Josephus's part:

i. Professor Mason (1992, pp. 122, 124–25) finds that the overall treatment of the pre-war high priests, and not only of Ananus, is noticeably more negative in the *Antiquities* because Josephus's aim has changed there. In the *War* they figure as the normal establishment against the wicked rebels, so that this was not the place in which to expatiate on their shortcomings; on the contrary, Ananus is given a speech in which he functions as a mouthpiece for Josephus's own view that Roman power is irresistible, and that to rebel against it is madness. In the *Antiquities*, however, the argument is that Jewish sins, even those of high priests, are invariably punished by God; and so here Ananus exemplifies the lawlessness of many Jewish leaders in the period leading up to the rebellion—a lawlessness punished with the military catastrophe.

ii. Dr. Rajak's explanation is more radical. She suspects "a certain defensiveness" in Josephus's praise of Ananus in the *War* which suggests that his record, like Josephus's own, had a shady area. Both men were denounced by the rebels as traitors to the cause of Jewish independence. Josephus had commanded rebel forces in Galilee (before going over to the Romans), and in his *Life* (189–196) he mentions Jerusalem authorities who wanted him deposed from his position as commander there, and says that Ananus, although he initially opposed them, was bribed to support them. But there is no overall denunciation of his character here, and certainly nothing to correspond with the vicious criticism of him in the *Antiquities* (20:199–203), where he is said to be rash and heartless. This is the context in which the shorter of the two passages about Jesus occurs: Ananus is said to have been responsible for engineering the death of "James the brother of Jesus" through the Sanhedrin. Dr. Rajak discounts it as a Christian interpolation, both because of its "startling divergence" from the very positive assessment of Ananus in the *War*, and because of its harsh criticism of the Sadducees and the Sandhedrin (Rajak 1983, pp. 131 and 151 and n).

As we shall see, there are other and perhaps stronger reasons for regarding the phrase about Jesus in the shorter passage as interpolated. Here, my conclusion concerning the allegation of unpredictability is that it is quite unjust to defend the *Testimonium* by implying that Josephus was so arbitrary and erratic that he was capable of almost any kind of statement. In fact he was a Jewish priest who consistently and passionately advocated Judaism.

C. THE ARABIC VERSION

There is a less obviously Christian version of the *Testimonium* which is quoted in Arabic translation—probably made from the Syriac into which the original Greek had been rendered—by the tenth-century Bishop Agapius of Hierapolis, in his Arabic *World History*. The English equivalent of what he wrote reads:

> Similarly Josephus (Yusifus), the Hebrew. For he says in the treatises that he has written on the governance [sic] of the Jews: "At this time there was a wise man who was called Jesus. His conduct was good and (he) was known to be virtuous. And many people from among the Jews and the other nations became his disciples. Pilate condemned him to be crucified and to die. But those who had become his disciples did not abandon his discipleship. They reported that he had appeared to them three days after his crucifixion and that he was alive; accordingly he was perhaps the Messiah, concerning whom the prophets have recounted wonders". (Quoted in Charlesworth 1989, p. 95)

Obviously, both versions of the *Testimonium*—the Greek in the extant manuscripts, and the Arabic in the (probably multiple) translation—cannot be authentic. Professor Pines of Jerusalem, the scholar who recently rediscovered the Arabic text, believes that it represents Josephus's original, modified by Christian censorship, but less so than is the Greek. But he expresses this view with caution, and allows that other explanations are possible (1971, pp. 68–70).

It is very noticeable that, in the Arabic, the order in which the statements about Jesus are made differs sharply from that in the Greek text—quite apart from the less Christian wording. In the following paraphrases, *both* columns of numbers represent the order of the items in the Greek, and italics indicate words present in only either the Greek or the Arabic:

Greek
1. He was a wise man *and perhaps more than a man.*
2. *He wrought surprising feats.*
3. *He taught people who accept the truth with pleasure.*
4. He won over many Jews and Greeks.
5. He was the Messiah.
6. *When prominent Jews accused him,*
7. Pilate condemned him to be crucified.
8. But his disciples stuck to him.
9. He appeared to them alive on the third day.
10. The prophets had foretold this and much else about him.
11. *The tribe of Christians is still extant.*

Arabic
1. He was a wise man. *He was good and virtuous.*
4. Jews and others became his disciples.
7. Pilate condemned him to be crucified *and to die.*
8. But his disciples stuck to him.
9. *They reported that* he had appeared to them three days later and was alive.
5. He was *perhaps* the Messiah,
10. about whom the prophets have told wonders.

The Arabic does not go beyond calling Jesus a man, makes no mention of his miracles, nor of Jewish involvement in his death, and makes the resurrection merely something alleged by his disciples. Also he is not unequivocally said to have been the Messiah; and the prophets are said to have told wonders about a future Messiah, not specifically about Jesus.

Feldman believes that the additional differences in the order of the items show that the Arabic is not a translation but a paraphrase, based, he thinks, not directly on the Greek text of Josephus as it now stands, but on the quotation of this Greek in Eusebius's *Ecclesiastical History*, "which was the chief source through which Josephus's work was known in the eastern Mediterranean during the Middle Ages" (Feldman and Hata 1987, p. 58). If this is so, then the paraphraser believed that Josephus said these things of Jesus only because Eusebius said that he had said them. Feldman adds that we still have to ask "how a believing Christian could quote Josephus as saying that Jesus 'was perhaps the Messiah' ". He suggests that this may be a modification of the Greek, introduced by Agapius because he realized that, as a Jew, Josephus could hardly have written 'he was the Messiah'. Feldman supports this by noting (p. 57) that Jerome, who knew the passage in the Greek, did the same. On the one occasion when he cites it (in *De Viris Illustribus*, 13, 14), he said that Jesus "was believed" (credebatur) to be the Messiah. That the words 'he was perhaps the Messiah' are Josephan is hard to believe since Origen, as we saw, said that Josephus "did not believe in Jesus as Christ", and so presumably did not have access to a text which allowed that he might have been this. Charlesworth, however, contends that no Christian could have written that Jesus 'was perhaps the Messiah'. Of course not, if he had been speaking as a Christian. But if what we have here is a Christian impersonating an orthodox Jew, he might have thought that the Jew could plausibly be represented as positive about Jesus to this extent, but no further. Charlesworth also thinks that Josephus, opposed to apocalypticism as he was, could very well have written the appreciative words about Jesus in this Arabic version, as Jesus himself "was not an apocalyptic fanatic" (1989, p. 97). To free him from such a charge would involve, as we saw, either setting aside or reinterpreting numerous synoptic passages.

Bammel thinks that Agapius's version may have originated in an Islamic environment, as it states that "Pilate condemned him to be crucified and to die", the last three of these words being unrepresented in the Greek. The Koran denies that Jesus was put to death; hence the contrary assertion became of vital importance to Christians in Islamic times.[7]

The above discussion shows that the Arabic version of the *Testimonium* has by no means been generally accepted as authentic. I have noted Pines' caution, and some of his reviewers have been considerably more cautious.[8] It is surely of importance that the point in Josephus's narrative where the *Testimonium* occurs is exactly where one would expect a Christian interpolation to be made; for, from the time of the traditions represented in the gospels, Pilate was very prominent in Christian thinking about Jesus, and if Josephus had written of Pilate without mentioning Jesus, Christian scribes would have seen this as an omission to be rectified. France concedes that "it is well known that Josephus's works were much used by Christians, and owed their survival to Christian copying; and it is not at all improbable that Christians should have altered the text to suit their own needs—in fact it is generally agreed that they did so" (1986, p. 26. With this latter point, he has in mind the extensive Christian interpolations in the Slavonic version of Josephus). It has been pointed out often enough that, whereas today printed copies of a book are all identical, in the ancient world where books were copied by hand, every individual copy was a newly created scribal artifact which could be as faithful or as deviant as the scribe or his patron chose.

D. THE SHORTER PASSAGE

The shorter of the two Josephan passages about Jesus has been much more widely accepted as a reference genuinely from his hand. The High Priest Ananus II is here described as "a bold man in his temper and very insolent" (in contrast to what is said of him in *The Jewish War*). He

> assembled the Sanhedrin of judges and brought before them the brother of Jesus, him called Christ, whose name was James, and some others. And when he had formed an accusation against them as breakers of the law, he delivered them to be stoned. (*Ant.* 20:200)

I have noted above (p. 213) Dr. Rajak's argument for regarding this passage as interpolated. France (p. 26) not only defends its authenticity, but thinks—as do a number of scholars—that it authenticates the longer one, the *Testimonium*; for it uses the term 'Christ' (Messiah) without explanation, and so, it is argued, presupposes the mention of Jesus as Messiah in the *Testimonium*. In fact, however, in neither passage is any attempt made to explain to the pagan readers to whom Josephus was appealing what the term means; and he never uses it elsewhere, but on the contrary is most careful to avoid it. When he applies a Messianic prophecy to Vespasian, he does not call it such but, as we saw, an "ambiguous oracle" in the scriptures. When he tells that Theudas led a multitude to the Jordan (ca. A.D. 44–46), promising to conduct them over dryshod like Joshua before Jericho, he does not call him a Messianic agitator or pretender, but a "charlatan" who claimed to be a "prophet". This is likewise how he describes the Egyptian who, a decade or so later, led a crowd as far as the Mount of Olives, promising that the walls of Jerusalem would fall down at his word. Feldman has noted that Josephus mentions about ten Messianic figures in the last three books of the *Antiquities* without using the term 'Christ' or Messiah of them. That he avoided it is intelligible, since at the time it "had definite political overtones of revolution and independence", and he was "a lackey of the Roman royal house" (1984a, pp. 689–690). It follows that, even if he did make some mention of Jesus, he would not have called him the Messiah. In sum, that he habitually takes care to avoid the term 'Messiah' makes its sole and unexplained use in the two Jesus passages suspect.

France tries to vindicate the shorter passage also by translating the genitive *tou legomenou Christou* not as (the brother of) 'him called Christ' but as the brother of "the so-called Christ", this being hardly the way a Christian would refer to his Lord. But Justin Martyr, in the mid-second century, uses this very phrase of Jesus in his *Apology* (I, 30): *ton par'hēmin legomenon Christon*—"the one called Christ among us". This use of *legomenos* is certainly not dismissive, but simply indicates what Jesus is 'called', how he is 'named'. The same is true of kindred examples in Matthew. In the passion narrative there it becomes necessary to distinguish the Jesus 'called' Barabbas (27:16) from the Jesus 'called' Christ; and for this purpose the latter is (in Pilate's address to the crowd at verses 17 and 22) once again designated with the phrase used in the shorter Josephan passage. The evangelist himself uses it at 1:16: "Mary, of whom was born Jesus, who is called Christ" (*ho legomenos Christos*); and at Jn. 4:25 the coming Messiah is designated in exactly this way. In none of these instances is there any pejorative implication. Nor are we to translate the same words at Mt. 4:18 as "Simon the so-called Peter". France thinks to counter me here by saying that "Josephus's usage should be determined from Josephus, not from Matthew" (p. 171 n12). Certainly, if we are sure that what we are faced with is Josephan and not Christian; but this is here precisely what is in question. France will have us believe that Josephus uses *legomenos* only with negative intent; for, he says, Rengstorf's *Complete Concordance to Josephus* translates it as 'so-called' or 'alleged'. The use of the verb *legō*, of which *legomenos* is the passive participle, is detailed in volume 3 of this concordance (Leiden: Brill, 1979). An example of Josephus's use of the participle in the sense of 'alleged' is given there, but also many examples of its meaning 'to be named, to be called', and, in the case of persons, 'to have the surname': thus "the third of the Ptolemies was called Euergetes" (*Apion* 2:48). In book 6 alone of the *Antiquities* there are six occasions where we are told the names by which certain places are "called" (6:22, 28, 274, 310, 360, 377); and there is mention of the name by which a certain group of persons is "called" (6:71). In book 8 we learn what certain measures, and what a certain month are called; and there is mention of "wood like that which is called pine" (8:92, 100, 177). In all these cases 'called' translates *legomenos*, with no suggestion that the naming was merely 'alleged'.

Tyler repeats what France says about Josephus's use of *legomenos*. In this instance, as in others, he illustrates the way in which one conservative scholar will triumphantly seize on the argument of another without checking the source material on which the latter's case was based. He is also ready to repeat uncritically even the most implausible defensive arguments, as when he follows (pp. 29–30) scholars—such as the eminent Catholic commentator J.P. Meier—who suggest that a Christian interpolator would have called James not "the brother of Jesus"—too matter-of-fact for a Christian—but 'the brother of the Lord'. I noted against Meier in *The Jesus Legend* (p. 53) that it is not unreasonable to suppose that at any rate some interpolators might be aware that an orthodox Jew could not plausibly be represented as calling Jesus 'the Lord'. We do not have to assume that they all went to work with more piety than sense.

France also refers to Origen apropos of this shorter passage, although he admits (p. 172 n14) that Origen's testimony is not altogether satisfactory. On this somewhat complex matter I have written as follows in *The Jesus Legend*:

> Origen, who refers to Josephus's account of the death of James, claims to have read something rather different on that subject in his text of Josephus from what now stands there. Writing in the third century, he said that, according to Josephus, the fall of Jerusalem and the destruction of the temple were God's punishment of the Jews for their murder of James "the brother of Jesus, him called Christ" (*Contra Celsum*, i, 47). If a text of Josephus had contained any such statement, it could only have been as a result of Christian interpolation. It was the nearest Christians could plausibly get to making Josephus take the Christian view that the fall of Jerusalem was God's punishment for the killing of Jesus. Schürer regarded the passage as an interpolation that has not survived in our manuscripts, but which shows that Josephus was subject to interpolation at this point (where James is introduced), so that the reference to 'Jesus, him called Christ' in our manuscripts falls under suspicion. Moreover, whereas in this extant passage James is said to have been killed on the basis of a sentence of court, Hegesippus and Clement of Alexandria—both Christian writers of the second century—say that he was killed in a tumult instigated by scribes and Pharisees, without prior legal proceedings: he was thrown down from the wing of the temple and finally dispatched with a fuller's club. Those who wrote this can hardly have known of the passage about James as it now stands in Josephus. (pp. 54–55)

In view of all this, it is really quite inappropriate to adduce, as many do, Hegesippus, Clement of Alexandria and Origen as witnesses to the authenticity of this shorter passage.

There remains the question: if the passage is interpolated, how could it have come to be inserted? I argued in *DJE* that Josephus probably wrote of the death of a Jewish Jerusalem personage called James, and a Christian reader thought he must have meant James the "brother of the Lord" who, according to Christian tradition, led the Jerusalem Church about the time in question. This reader accordingly noted in the margin: 'James = the brother of Jesus, him called Christ'; and a later copyist took this as belonging to the text and incorporated it. Other interpolations are known to have originated in precisely this way.

Apart from the two questionable passages in Josephus, Jewish literature is totally unhelpful concerning Jesus. Even Bockmuehl, who stoutly defends many traditional positions favourable to Christian beliefs, finds it "safe to conclude that Jewish literature outside Josephus contains no demonstrably early information about Jesus of Nazareth which is independent of Christian sources" (1994, p. 14). We cannot, then, be surprised at the desperate efforts that have been made both to salvage some mention of Jesus from the hand of Josephus, and to insist that he was not uncritically repeating what Christians were at that time claiming, but had independent information.

iii. The Absence of Independent Testimony

Some Christians find in the Roman and Jewish notices welcome assurance that their faith has a solid historical foundation. Leslie Weatherhead speaks for them when he says that, from what is "vouched for by pagan historians who had no axe to grind and no interest in what Jesus said or did, . . . we can be quite sure of his historicity". He finds it "good to feel that the Christian religion is based on the objective reality of the historical Christ whose real existence in time and space is as well vouched for as that of Plato" (1967, p. 69). Such a solid basis is obviously required if this religion is to give him "the comfortable thought" that in all life's perplexities he is "in the hands of a loving, wise and finally undefeatable Power" (p. 167). And so thanks to Pliny et al., he does not need to worry that this might be a delusion. I am not, of course, saying that Pliny and the others show that it is, but merely giving one reason why the significance of what they say has been so often exaggerated.

Mitton holds that "these secular historians" not only confirm that Jesus lived, but also that he was "executed under Pontius Pilate—enough to counter the extreme claim of some skeptics" (1975, p. 32). We have seen, however, that it is only Tacitus and Josephus (the latter in a disputed text) who mention Pilate in connection with the founder's crucifixion; and they were both writing late enough to be doing no more than repeating—directly or from hearsay—what Christians were by then saying, so that their testimony cannot be taken as assured independent confirmation of these Christian beliefs. Tacitus, we saw, was too contemptuous of

Christianity to have made any serious inquiry into its origins; and Josephus—if he really did write anything at all on the subject—was unlikely to have gone further than hearsay, for in the *Antiquities of the Jews* he employed his sources "not only negligently, but also—at least where it is possible to check them—with great freedom and arbitrariness", with only "occasional" evidence of any critical attitude towards them (Schürer, 1973, p. 58). In the course of an extended discussion of his reliability as a historian, it has been noted that, when he and Philo cover the same events, the latter "has greater historical credibility despite the fact that he is a philosopher and a theologian rather than a historian" (Feldman and Hata 1987, p. 29).

To assume that Roman records included anything about Jesus for inquirers who wanted more than hearsay is gratuitous. The Fathers, embarrassed by the lack of pagan documentation, tried to make it good by accepting, as genuine, documents forged under pagan names,[9] and by simply alleging that relevant pagan documents did exist. Thus Justin, addressing the emperor in his first Apology ca. A.D. 155, summarizes the story of the crucifixion and then says (chapter 35): "That all these things were so you may learn from acts which were recorded under Pontius Pilate". Tertullian then elaborated this suggestion. Writing in Carthage in A.D. 197, he alleged that Pilate wrote a report to Tiberius telling him of all the miracles and prodigies at the crucifixion and resurrection, and that it can still be consulted in the Roman archives (*Apology*, chapter 21). In chapter 5 he tells us that Tiberius reacted by bringing the matter before the senate and proposing to set Christ among the gods, which, however, the senate declined to do. Later Christian writers (Eusebius and others) repeat this story, but no apologist before Tertullian mentions it, and "no modern historian believes it" (Bettenson 1956, p. 229n). We are asked to believe, said Gibbon:

> *that* Pontius Pilate informed the emperor of the unjust sentence of death which he had pronounced against an innocent, and, as it appeared, a divine personage; and that, without acquiring the merit, he exposed himself to the danger, of martyrdom; *that* Tiberius, who avowed his contempt for all religion, immediately conceived the design of placing the Jewish Messiah among the gods of Rome; *that* his servile senate ventured to disobey the commands of their master; *that* Tiberius,

instead of resenting their refusal, contented himself with protecting the Christians from the severity of the laws, many years before such laws were enacted or before the church had assumed any distinct name or existence; and lastly *that* the memory of this extraordinary transaction was preserved in the most public and authentic records, which escaped the knowledge of the historians of Greece and Rome, and were only visible to the eyes of an African Christian, who composed his Apology one hundred and sixty years after the death of Tiberius. (1910, II, 39, chapter 16)

5

Ethics in the New Testament and in the History of Christianity

i. Jesus and Belief in Him as a Guide to Personal Behaviour

If, as the previous chapters of this book have argued, one cannot with any confidence specify what in the gospels is likely to be historically true, do gospels or epistles perhaps nevertheless contain ethical doctrines of value?

The Sermon on the Mount includes the maxims: "Do not resist evil", turn the other cheek to anyone who strikes, let him who would take your coat have your cloak as well, and be perfectly confident that God will provide food and clothing (Mt. 5:39–40; 6:25–26). All this presents considerable difficulties to apologists. If it is wrong to resist evil, why did Jesus himself cast out devils, heal the sick and abusively denounce what he took for Pharisaic hypocrisy (Mt. 23:13ff)? Doctrines in the Sermon are commonly made acceptable by denying their plain meaning. Mayhew, for instance, sees that not resisting evil would mean not only suffering injustice oneself, but also standing passively by while one's family and associates are ill-treated; so he pretends that Jesus intended only "to challenge Christians to think before reacting to wrong-doing in a forceful way", to "consider whether on certain occasions the

224

wrong-doer ought not to be allowed to get away with it" (1989, pp. 2,4). Individual maxims, he adds, are to be subordinated to the whole: "God has been revealing his will for us in scripture and through the Spirit and we have to work hard to get the message" (p. 100)—as if uniformity could be extracted from the totality. We certainly will have to 'work hard' if God formulates his 'message' in what, on Mayhew's hypothesis, will have to be admitted to be thoroughly misleading language.

The pretence that there is uniformity is sometimes dropped in the face of obvious contradictions within the NT. Gal. 3:28 makes both male and female "all one in Christ Jesus", whereas 1 Cor. 14:34–35 puts women in a decidedly subordinate position; 1 Tim. 2:12 goes even further, and permits "no woman to teach or to have authority over men". If it is allowed that a choice must be made between these two standpoints, how can we know which cancels the other? France, facing this problem, admits that "there is no basic rule of thumb" that can be applied in such cases, and that our "instinctive preferences" for certain parts of scripture to others "are normally derived from the tradition within which we have been brought up" (1995, p. 94). He is aware (p. 16) that one situation in which this became very apparent was the discovery by Christians in the early nineteenth century that slavery was not after all an essential feature of the way God has ordained human society. To this I shall return.

Whether unbelievers might be saved is another issue on which the NT equivocates. There are passages which represent God as predestining a majority to sin and damnation (see above, p. 84), yet 1 Tim. 2:4 has it that "God desires all men to be saved". Even in this epistle there is some qualification of this, in that God is said to be the saviour "especially of believers" (4:10). Paul himself, as someone who earlier blasphemed and insulted Christ, figures here as an outstanding example of those "who were in future to have faith in him" and (presumably thereby) "gain eternal life" (1:13–16); and at 2 Tim. 3:15 salvation is "through faith in Christ Jesus".

The doctrine of punishment for those who themselves consciously reject Jesus's message[1] is no more than sectarian fanaticism from which civilized apologists of today distance themselves as best they can. A passage of relevance here is the vision of the Last Judgement in the final section of Jesus's final discourse (before his arrest) at Mt. 25:31–46, and clearly, in this position, carrying heavy emphasis. It states that the Son of man—earlier passages show that this is Jesus himself—will confront "all the nations" (every human being) in his glory, and divide them, with the blessing of his Father, into "sheep" and "goats". The former are promised "the kingdom prepared for you from the foundation of the world" because of their acts of kindness towards any one of "these my brethren"; for, he adds, any such act, done towards even the humblest of these, was done towards himself (verse 40). The "goats", however, are told that, as they had failed to act charitably towards "one of these least", they are to be consigned to "the eternal fire which is prepared for the devil and his angels". Commentators would like at least to feel assured that the 'brethren', the woeful neglect of whom is to be so drastically punished, are any needy and deprived persons anywhere. But 'brethren' indicates a setting in a particular community. It is in Matthew's community that Jesus still lives, and the text states clearly enough that things done (or left undone) to one of the brethren were done (or failed to be done) to Jesus himself. Hence damnation is to come to those who have distanced themselves from this community, or even to those inside it who have failed to respond to him properly. An earlier passage specifies that the angels of the Son of man "shall gather out of his kingdom all things that cause stumbling, and them that do iniquity" (*anomia*, see above, p. 23), "and shall cast them into the furnace of fire; there shall be the weeping and gnashing of teeth" (13:41–42). Matthew took one reference to such weeping and gnashing of teeth from Q, but developed a particular liking for the phrase and for what it conjures up, and so used it additionally not only here but also on a further four occasions.

The acts of charity to needy brethren that are specified in the vision of the Last Judgement in chapter 25 comprise: giving them food, clothing, or shelter, or visiting them when they were sick or imprisoned. Some exegetes have seen here a reference to missionaries sent out by Matthew's community: persons who have failed to befriend them are to be damned. Sim argues that the purpose of the whole passage is to meet the need of these missionaries for vengeance and consolation: "They can be satisfied and consoled that the many who have rejected and mistreated them in the past and will do so in the future will receive their just punishment at the hands of the Son of man" (1996, p. 234).

This whole scene is clearly indebted to Jewish apocalyptic literature, and present-day Catholic teaching is glad to set this and similar passages aside by attributing them to this baneful influence.[2] A 1995 Church of England report calls them mere "imagery" which clothes the doctrine that "the final and irrevocable choosing of that which is opposed to God" leads to "total non-being".[3] Linfield (1994, p. 65) points out that numerous recent apologists have likewise understood 'eternal punishment' not as punishment 'ever-lastingly in progress' but as 'of everlasting effect', in that it consists in completely annihilating the offender, not in tormenting him. At the same time it is still felt desirable to regard the 'eternal life' promised to the 'sheep' in the same context in Matthew as of endless duration; and this is believed not in virtue of the word 'eternal', but because of "other dimensions" to eternal life, "indi-cated by different phraseology" (p. 66).

Centuries ago, Christians themselves were the first to protest when pagans defended stories of sordid behaviour by the gods with the argument that these accounts are not to be taken literally. The Christian Arnobius (d. ca. A.D. 330) called this "the sort of thing that is used to bolster up bad cases in the courts".[4] It is presumably awareness that special pleading is involved in taking hell and its fires non-literally that prompts some, with Tyler, to allow that consciousness of pain for ever may be implied. But this does not unduly worry him, since wherein "consciousness" consists even in this life is not yet understood by scientists (p. 63).

Luke's sympathy with the deprived caused him to make his Jesus threaten penalties even to those who have lived comfortably: "Woe unto you that are rich! for ye have received your consolation. Woe unto you, ye that are full now! for ye shall hunger. Woe unto you, ye that laugh now! for ye shall mourn and weep" (Lk. 6:24–25). In the parable of Lazarus and the rich man (also unique to Luke), the latter goes to hell and is "in anguish in this flame". It is not said that he had been a man of bad character, only that in his lifetime he had "received good things" (16:24–25). In these passages heaven and hell have the function not of rewarding virtue and punishing wickedness, but the very different function of redressing the misery or, as the case may be, the happiness of this life. The same doctrine appears in the epistle of James, where the rich are told to "weep and howl" for the "miseries" that are coming to them (5:1). The threat is not restricted to the godless rich; to be rich is in itself a sin leading to condemnation. No wonder that fears have been generated even in upright and conscientious Christians if they were neither unhappy nor impoverished. Strauss recalled, as a typical case, how his pious and thoughtful grandfather brooded over future punishment, and was throughout his life tormented by the thought that, for every one soul saved, thousands are doomed to the flames (1997, p. 38).

The 1995 Church of England report concedes that talk of hell fire "has been used to frighten men and women into believing", and has to allow that "moral protest from both within and without the Christian faith" has done much to discredit such a "religion of fear". Protests from Jewish scholars have been vehement, particularly in view of the Christian proclivity to represent Judaism as a religion of hate and vengeance and Christianity as an advocacy of love;[5] whereas in fact both the Jewish and the Christian scriptures and traditions include barbarous separatist and tribalist doctrines together with their opposites. The attitude to enemies of Psalm 137:9 ("Happy shall he be who takes your little ones and dashes them against the rock") must be set against such passages as:

> If thou meet thine enemy's ox or his ass going astray, thou shalt surely bring it back to him again. If thou see the ass of him that hateth thee lying under his burden, and wouldest forbear to help him, thou shalt surely help with him (Exodus 23:4–5). If thine enemy be hungry, give him bread to eat; and if he be thirsty, give him water to drink; for thou shalt heap coals of fire upon his head, and the Lord shall reward thee. (Proverbs 25:21–22, where the ethical sentiment is spoiled by the motive prescribed for the behaviour)

If apologists take the sting from passages which consign unbelievers to eternal damnation, they risk committing themselves to the opposite extreme—that belief is entirely optional and irrelevant to salvation. Here the Church of England report already quoted on the one hand takes pains not actually to exclude non-Christians; it appeals to Galatians 5, which teaches that the fruit of the Spirit is "love, joy, peace, patience, kindness, goodness, trustfulness, gentleness, and self-control". Hence "those of other faiths and indeed of none who display such fruit" are responding to the Spirit of God, who is "savingly at work in them" and "will bring his work to fulfilment" (p. 173). Yet on the other hand "fullness of relationship to God is possible only in Jesus Christ" (p. 182), who "can in no way be seen biblically as one among many examples" (p. 166). So atheists will be saved if they behave themselves, while Christianity is nevertheless more than just a folk-religion for Europe and for areas of missionary activity. This, the authors of the report say, is a position "that could be labelled 'an open and generous exclusivism' or 'a Christocentric inclusivism'" (p. 171).

The harshness of the ethical teaching of the synoptic Jesus is well documented in Richard Robinson's *An Atheist's Values* (1964, pp. 140–155), which John Bowden calls "one of the great books of modern British philosophical humanism" (1988, p. 107), and where it is noted that Jesus not only condemns unbelievers, but also neglects his family relations for his gospel (Mt. 12:46ff), which he expects to result in parricide and in the betrayal of brothers and children to death (Mt. 10, especially verse 21). He recommends improvidence and taking no thought for the morrow (Mt. 6:34). We are not to lay up treasures on earth (6:19), but should give to everyone who asks (Lk. 6:30) and imitate birds who "sow not, neither do they reap or gather into barns" (Mt. 6:26). Robinson comments that as a complete substitute for thrift and prudence, Jesus recommends prayer and faith: "Ask, and it shall be given to you." Here again it is sometimes pretended that such injunctions do not mean what they say: that for instance the passage about the ravens which neither sow nor reap, and so forth (Lk. 12:22ff) is merely a warning against over-reliance on dividends or against allowing thrift to degenerate into greed.

The obvious comment on some of the unappealing precepts in the NT is one which the premisses of many Christians—that Jesus was morally and 'spiritually' perfect—do not permit them to make, namely that some of these doctrines cease to appear so repulsive if they are understood as intelligible responses to situations facing the early church. It is because this is true of so much of the synoptic ethical teaching that it is, as Robinson notes, unsystematic and occasional, consisting of many separate and independent sayings, and so giving little or no judicious guidance in cases where rules of conduct conflict. Many early Christians were poor and could find consolation in supposing that poverty was not only virtuous but also religiously enjoined. Hence the logia where Jesus is made to praise it and to repudiate wealth. Even prudence was dispensable to people who believed that God's kingdom was imminent, so that seeking it was all that mattered (Lk. 12:29–31). Again, families will have been split over whether to accept the new faith, particularly from the time when the rupture with Judaism had gone beyond healing. In such circumstances a Christian may well have found himself hating other members of his family as the cost of his discipleship. Hence the logion of Lk. 14:26–27. Embarrassment arises when such logia are presented to the modern reader, ignorant of the circumstances in which they originated, as timeless principles calling for his unqualified assent. It is then that there arises the temptation to argue that they do not really mean what they say.

Another defect of the synoptic teaching is, for Robinson, that "the ideal of truth and knowledge is wholly absent" from it; and as Jesus "never recommends knowledge, so he never recommends the virtue that seeks and leads to knowledge, namely reason." What he demands is faith, by which he means both faith in himself and also "believing certain very improbable things without considering evidence or estimating probabilities" (pp. 145, 148–49). Tyler seems to think that the complaint here is not (or not only) that Jesus undervalued knowledge, but that he was himself ignorant; for he counters by saying that, because Jesus was truly human (as well as truly divine), his knowledge was naturally limited, and that the Christian estimate of him does not imply that he knew more than Einstein (p. 60). "It was not part of Jesus's mission to be an Aristotle or an A.J. Ayer" (p. 65)—as if Robinson's argument implied that it was! In actual fact, although the gospels do not specifically ascribe knowledge of science or philosophy to Jesus, his ability to divine the thoughts of friends and enemies alike, and to predict down to the finest details what will befall him and others (see above, pp. 147f), stamps him as omniscient.

Fathers of the Church went so far as positively to disparage all knowledge that was not useful to salvation. A well-known example is Tertullian's insistence that Athens (Greek philosophical thought) and Jerusalem (Christian faith) are totally disparate and that "after possessing Christ Jesus there is no need for us to be curious, nor, after the gospel, for us to be inquisitive. Believing as we do, we desire no further belief. For this is our first belief, that we ought not to believe anything else".[6] On this basis apologists continue to argue that salvation depends upon revealed truth to which unaided reason cannot attain.[7] I allow that reason, in the sense of inferences from evidence, does not solve a problem when the evidence is insufficient or the inferences too complex for even the best minds. Yet insights which claim to transcend reason have repeatedly turned out to be nugatory.

Disparagement of reason and knowledge often proceeds from an awareness that knowledgeable people are capable of unacceptable moral judgements, since character often has a greater influence than knowledge on behaviour. One can foretell with some assurance the actions of someone whose character is known, but merely to know the extent of his knowledge will indicate only what methods he is likely to adopt, not the objects for which he is likely to strive. Christian apologists, however, stress the limitations of reason and knowledge primarily in order to safeguard doctrines, such as that of the incarnation, which are not rationally defensible. The relation between the Father and the Son had to be defined in such a way as to avoid polytheism on the one hand, and a monotheism which reduced Jesus to mere manhood on the other. These incompatible requirements were met by affirming that Father and Son were (and are) two and yet one. Harnack noted that "from this time onward Dogmatics were for ever separated from clear thinking and defensible conceptions. . . . The anti-rational . . . came to be considered as the characteristic of the sacred" (Harnack 1961, p. 49n).

As God incarnate Jesus was, then, divine, and so when Robinson complains that, while he preached humility, "he weakened his effect by insisting with considerable asperity on his own divinity or semi-divinity, and demanding that everyone should believe in him" (pp. 151–52), Tyler answers that, as he was in fact divine, he was justified in drawing attention to his status, and that he nevertheless "did show real humility when He washed the apostles' feet" (p. 61). Robinson has not overlooked this incident, as it occurs only in the fourth gospel (Jn. 13:1ff), and he is criticizing the Jesus of the synoptics, leaving it to apologists to explain why the Johannine Christ is so very different. Tyler himself allows that "there is no moral doctrine in John, except for general recommendations to keep the commandments" (p. 115). The foot-washing is not only, unlike the moral teaching, absent from the synoptics; it introduces five substantial chapters of farewell discourses unknown in substance and in manner to their version of this final communal meal, and lacking the eucharistic words so prominent in their version of this farewell. To accept this as the authentic account of that occasion is tantamount to abandoning all confidence in the synoptics.

ii. Social Ethics

Robinson also complains that Jesus did not give any ruling about war. Here I must myself demur and point to Mt. 5:9 ("blessed are the peacemakers") and 26:52 ("all that take the sword shall perish by the sword"). Admittedly, both logia occur only in Matthew. They are not compromised by Mt. 10:34 ("I came not to send peace but a sword"), for the reference here is not to war but to religious divisions within families, as both the context and the Lukan parallel (where 'the sword' is replaced by 'division', 12:51) show. It is also Matthew alone who specifies complete non-resistance ("resist not him that is evil", 5:39). Yet both Matthew and Luke include 'turn the other cheek' and 'let him who would take your coat have your cloak also'; so there is much material for the pacifist here, and G.H.C. Macgregor's 1936 book is a signal example of how a pacifist can exploit it. "A nation following the way of Christ might", he says, "feel called upon to adopt a policy of total disarmament" and so "incur the risk of national martyrdom". But even if it paid this price, it would thereby "set free such a flood of spiritual life as would save the world" (pp. 103–04). This is absurdly optimistic. A nation yielding to bullying and to threats may indeed in the short term, by thus showing itself pacific, win the approval of all who are uncommitted, but in the long term it may equally well encourage the same kind of bullying in the case of future events that are similar. Both submission and the threat of retaliation are found, as instinctive reactions, in many animals. The former serves well in some cases, especially between rivals, but will be of no avail where one animal aims at destroying the other. Macgregor holds (p. 134) that some nation must begin the total refusal to go to war—an argument recently revived apropos of nuclear disarmament. But what reason is there to believe that hostile forces will be so impressed and constrained by such a self-renunciatory attitude that they will follow suit? The ambition of their leaders is often an insuperable obstacle to reconciliation and co-operation. Some third-world leaders of today are perfectly capable of suggesting to their subjects that the annihilation of Europe and America would be a humanitarian enterprise. History has examples enough of what happens when power is confronted with weakness. The Athenian democracy was ruthless to its own allies. The Romans were ruthless towards Carthage and themselves received little mercy when they in turn were overrun. The Israelites under divine leadership set a grim example, and Muhammad was fairly thorough. Macgregor was writing at a time when many were impressed by the gentle methods adopted by Gandhi. It is too often forgotten that such methods are effective only against a government with a tender conscience, or against one that cannot afford to ignore the tender consciences of its subjects. British acts of violent suppression in India gave rise to protests in Britain which were embarrassing to the government. Gandhi had many articulate supporters in Britain, where his books were published and his speeches fully reported. He even visited England himself and could be interviewed by reporters. A ruthless regime, of which there are now plenty, would allow nothing of this kind, and will not be shamed by displays of magnanimity.

Hays, whose 1997 study of NT ethics has been greeted with considerable clerical acclaim, is well aware that, in calculable terms, total non-violence in resisting evil is "sheer folly" (p. 343). He nevertheless thinks it should be binding on a Christian community which accepts, as he does (p. 10), the pre-eminent authority of the NT, for such, he says, is the unambiguous witness of these scriptures. This means that we must not resort to violent resistance if our spouse, our child, or our neighbour is attacked: "There is no foundation whatever in the Gospel of Matthew for the notion that violence in defense of a third party is justifiable". And Matthew's standpoint is shared by the rest of the NT: "Armed defense is not the way of Jesus" (p. 324). Hays is not concerned with the historian's problem of whether Jesus did actually propound the doctrines ascribed to him in the NT. It is these scriptures as they stand which, for him, represent ultimate authority (pp. x, 159–160). Reason and experience, he says, may tell us that non-violent submission can prove fatal; but reason and experience are not to be pitted against the witness of the NT; they may come into play only in enabling us to interpret it, not to overrule it (p. 341). And so we are to choose total non-violence "in the hope and anticipation that God's love will finally prevail through the way of the cross, despite our inability to see how this is possible" (p. 343).

Hays allows that none of this "makes any sense unless the nonviolent enemy-loving community is to be vindicated by the resurrection of the dead". It makes sense "only if the God and Father of Jesus Christ actually is the ultimate judge of the world", "only if all authority in heaven and on earth has been given to Jesus" (p. 338). It presumably follows that a cut-throat need not be violently hindered, because we are confident that his victims will rise from the dead and be vindicated. This seems to be the price that we must pay for accepting the whole "eschatological perspective" of the documents.

It would follow that going to war against Hitler was wrong. Hays counters the question "What if Christians had refused to fight Hitler?" with the counterquestion: "What if the Christians in Germany had emphatically refused to fight *for* Hitler, refused to carry out the murders in concentration camps?" (p. 342). The obvious answer is: if Hitler had met with widespread disobedience in his own country, war would have been unnecessary. But this was not the real situation with which the rest of Europe was faced in the 1930s, and to substitute for the reality a hypothetical situation which did not obtain is mere evasion of the issue.

For Hays, "the place of the soldier within the church can only be seen as anomalous" (p. 337); "*Christians* have no place in the military" (p. 400, Author's emphasis). He does not seek the excommunication of those who believe that war may, in certain circumstances, be justified, but he does believe that Christians who do not accept renunciation of violence are "living as 'enemies of the cross of Christ'" (p. 463, quoting Phil. 3:18), even though, as he is well aware, "the historic majority of Christians" have lived in this way.

The record of the churches has indeed been anything but pacifist. It includes the Crusades and the Spanish and Portugese conquests of America. In the Middle Ages and in the 150 years following the Reformation, when belief in Christianity was almost universal in Europe and was held much more strongly than today, religion was the chief instigator of hatred and bloodshed. Even quite recently, 'ethnic cleansing' of Bosnian Muslims by Christian Serbs has been sanctioned by the church[8]. In the Protestant New World of the late seventeenth century, the influential preacher Cotton Mather regarded the terrain as the undisturbed realm of Satan prior to Christian settlement there, and urged his church to attack the native inhabitants, whom he equated with the ancient adversaries of Israel and who like them were to be disinherited by divine decree, and so make way for the new Israel. Such a way of reading the OT was by no means uncommon, and has prompted Räisänen's comment that "holy books can be . . . a curse as well as a blessing" (1997, pp. 78–79). The curse is very apparent when a church is powerful enough to try to enforce its own interpretation of them, believing as it does in its duty to save souls from the eternal perdition consequent upon heresy. On this basis, as late as 1832, Pope Gregory XVI could denounce liberty of conscience as "madness"; and Pius IXth's 1864 'Syllabus of Errors' condemned the view "that every man is free to embrace and profess the religion he shall believe to be true, guided by the light of reason". Those who protested against such rulings were, for centuries, systematically put down by the church whenever it had the power. High-minded Catholics in democratic countries of course deplore all this, and do not regard such features as intrinsic to Catholicism. But (as Hanson and Fuller observe in their still valuable 1948 critique of the Roman church) we may appropriately judge the church by what it did for centuries in circumstances where it could enforce its will, rather than by statements from civilized adherents in countries where it has largely lost the power to do so.

I am not suggesting that the Catholic record is uniformly bad, or that Protestant churches have always, or even characteristically, behaved better. Criticism of unsavoury military regimes in Central and South America by local Catholic clergy and church workers in defence of human rights has recently cost many of them their lives. In some cases the regimes were led by evangelical or religiously indifferent generals who found conservative Protestantism "much more congenial than the socially activist Catholicism promoted by liberation theology" (Bruce, 1990b, pp. 217–18). Reinhold Bernhardt notes that

> 8,000 fundamentalist missionaries are active in Guatemala alone, supported by North American parent organizations. . . . Not a few of the missionaries collaborate with the secret police and the military. The extremists among them even take part in the persecution of Catholic and Protestant priests who do not join them. But it is above all the Indios who are brutally persecuted by being billeted in 'defensive villages', tortured, and murdered. A preacher from the fundamentalist group El Verbo declared: 'The army does not massacre Indians. It massacres demons, and the Indians are possessed by demons; they are Communists'. (1994, p.9)

The response of the central Catholic authorities to priests who, against all this, support liberation theology has been, quite predictably, less than enthusiastic (details in McBrien 1994, p. 143). Nevertheless, it is undeniable that many Christians have made and are making notable contributions to the improvement of social conditions. To what extent this has been due to their Christian beliefs is not easy to assess; for people who believe that religion is a great force for betterment may readily believe that what they consider the better parts in their conduct are religiously based, even though the non-religious arguments for such actions are in themselves cogent. I am saddened when apologists make the kindliness and selfless philanthropic work of many Christian persons and organizations into a scoring point by asking, with a sneer: 'Where are the humanist hospitals?' Thousands of clergy and persons in religious orders have a livelihood (and hence time and energy for charitable work) merely from professing their religion, and many charitable foundations have been endowed on a religious basis when bequests to non-religious organizations were illegal, or when such organizations were not even tolerated. Furthermore, 'atheism' still has, for many, strongly negative emotional associations. People will give to 'Christian Aid' whether they are believers or not (provided, in the latter case, they do not fear that the 'aid' is simply missionary propaganda). I wonder how much money an appeal for 'atheist aid' would bring in. Nevertheless, such charities as Oxfam and War On Want were entirely secular foundations. It has also to be said that the ethical stance of the world's major religions is, even today, far from entirely laudable. With the best will one can muster, one cannot but find the attitude of some of them to one of our most pressing problems, namely the urgent need to limit population, totally unhelpful.

As Jesus says so little on social questions, we cannot be surprised at finding basic disagreements, even between clergy of the same Christian denomination, not only on population limitation, but also on the justice of capital punishment, homosexuality, and other significant ethical issues. Between denominations the differences can be crass: the edicts of the Dutch Reformed Church in apartheid South Africa did not command wide Christian assent. With such examples in mind, Grünbaum justly concludes that "even if a person is minded to defer completely to theological authority on moral matters, he or she cannot avoid deciding which one of the conflicting authorities is to be the ethical guide", so that in the end such deference means choosing a preferred set of clergymen "who become the moral touchstone of everything by claiming revealed truth for particular ethical directives" (1994, pp. 110–11). One can only hope that, in such cases, the choice does not fall on the kind of clergy—Christian and other—whose views are detailed in this 1994 article, which Grünbaum's reviewer in *Ethics* (July, 1995) has called "a brilliantly biting attack on the view that theism is logically and/or motivationally necessary for underwriting morals".

How variegated Christian motives can be is well illustrated in the instances of capital punishment and slavery. Although Quakers had long been totally abolitionist, it was not a Christian but a deist, the Italian Beccaria, who with his 1764 book on 'Crimes and Punishments' initiated more widespread acceptance of humane ideas on capital punishment. When in 1810 the deist Sir Samuel Romilly tried to introduce Beccaria's views, and those of Jeremy Bentham, to the British political scene, his bill to abolish the penalty of death for three minor property offences, including the theft of five shillings from a shop, was defeated in the Lords, where seven bishops, including the Archbishop of Canterbury, voted

against it. Their theology persuaded them that humanity is fundamentally unregenerate and depraved, and would resort to all
manner of criminality if not restrained by fear of hanging (Potter
1993, pp. 36–37). Potter's book shows that the Anglican Church
embraced total abolition "only at the eleventh hour", in the 1960s
(p. 204). As for slavery, Klingberg's study informs us that Christians
were probably responsible for carrying millions of negroes out of
Africa and that "in the process they caused an equal number to be
sacrificed" (1926, p. 18). One reason why there was considerable
resistance within Christianity to the emancipation movement was
that slavery is endorsed in both Old and New Testaments.[9] Wilber-
force "confessed with chagrin that the 'high-and-dry' conservative
party then prevailing among the Church clergy obstructed the anti-
Slavery cause or were at best indifferent, while Nonconformists and
godless reformers proved his staunchest allies".[10] The abolition of
slavery was not, then, a direct result of Christianity, but some
Christians, at a certain stage in its history, exerted an influence in
that direction. Other, more potent factors would have sufficed
without this aid, and Christianity itself, in its most humane form,
was the consequence of some of these factors, indebted—as in the
case of capital punishment—to the thinking of deists and others
who did not accept any revelation. "It can hardly be denied", says
France, "that it was the changing nature and values of secular
society which were the catalyst that led Christians to re-examine
their understanding of the Bible on this issue" of slavery. He is here
comparing appeals to Biblical texts which endorse slavery with
appeals to texts about the position of women by those who do not
want them as priests—two issues where "at some points the
similarity is a little too close for comfort". "It would have been
easy", he adds, "for an eighteenth-century Christian to argue that
the emancipation of slaves was a product of the secular liberal
agenda which it was the duty of all faithful Christians to resist in the
name of the biblical world-view" (1995, pp. 16–17). Evidence that
Christians with an economic interest in the slave trade did argue on
precisely such lines is surely not hard to find.[11]

C.E.M. Joad, in a book written after his conversion to Christianity, allowed that "man's inhumanity to man has never risen to

greater heights than among Christians, and no sin in the whole calendar has been committed more flagrantly and more continuously than by the professed servants and ministers of the Church". He nevertheless tried (in the manner of Boccaccio's second story in the *Decameron*) to turn this to account by adducing it as a reason for allowing the Church a supernatural origin: how otherwise, he asks, could it have survived "the excesses of its ministers and members?" (1952, p. 244). The obvious answer is that it has been able to enforce its beliefs, often by savage means, until relatively recent times. As late as 1697, a young man (Thomas Aikenhead) was hanged at Edinburgh for denying that three can be one, that Moses wrote the Pentateuch, and for a few other criticisms of orthodoxy. The savagery of the prosecution and of the attendant circumstances of this case are described by Macaulay in chapter 22 of his *History of England*. Even in the nineteenth century 'unbelief' frequently resulted in ostracism, for it was still axiomatic that only religion could impress moral notions on the mind—particularly on the minds of the industrial working classes, feared as sources of radical political opinions. Susan Budd's study of the English scene showed her that "until the 1890s or so, the worthy infidel was a contradiction in terms" (1977, p. 89). The subsequent growth of openly admitted agnosticism and atheism among the eminent, and the decline of organized religion among nevertheless respectable people, meant that religion began to be defended in a different way, as "the source of wonder, joy, and emotional warmth in life" (p. 175).

The Christianity one is likely to meet in England today is largely free from intolerance. Once the Reformation had created a plurality of Christian organizations, the price of enforcing conformity to the national church turned out, in the long run, to be unacceptably high for a democratic society. As a result, socially similar people—people who are not outcasts but equally respectable—attend different religious guilds, and so find it hard to believe that only one particular creed has the truth. In such a situation, says Steve Bruce, "one ends up with the . . . position of supposing that all these organizations, in their different ways, are doing God's work" (1995, pp. 4–5, 10). These divisions have also promoted scepticism about any form of Christianity among those not already committed to one or other of its forms (just as divisions within a political party discredit it with outsiders), so that toleration can result from indifference. Even among believers, only the most conservative take the old religious sanctions seriously. Many suppose that one may still be a Christian without having to believe or do anything in particular, so that one does not have to go to church if one has something else to do. Who, then, wants to make himself unpopular by protesting against an institution which does not inconvenience him?

Christianity comprises a multiplicity of beliefs—beliefs about historical facts, about right conduct, and about the constitution of the universe. To those of us who view these beliefs as outsiders, the first and last of these three sets seem to be mostly false, except where they have been adopted from non-religious sources. As for the beliefs about right conduct, these include encouragement, if not obligation to participate in what appears to us as meaningless ritual, beginning with baptism, which only the Zwinglian churches have made into an entirely non-supernatural rite, a mere sign of admitting someone to the Christian community. It is true that most parents see in baptism no more than the giving of a name and thus an identity to their child, but clergy still maintain the reality of 'baptismal regeneration' (in accord with Titus 3:5). Christianity's purely ethical requirements are derived from moral conventions of various origin and value. Even the most acceptable of the principles preached by Christians tend to be undermined by being associated with many indefensible beliefs. In teaching social and wholesome behaviour to young people, we should have some more valid sanctions or reasons as a basis. Why, asks the young man or woman, must I act thus or thus? The reply is made: because it is the will of God. What then if they read the history of the Christian church and discover what barbarities were committed century after century for this very reason? Admittedly, the religious sanction on behaviour has the advantage that, if God can see through brick walls, we shall have to be more careful than if we only have Mrs Jones downstairs to worry about. But this is no ethical advantage unless the behaviour of which God is believed to approve is what a humane ethical consciousness would endorse.

iii. Orthodoxy, Heresy, and Ecumenism

The history of Christendom well illustrates the ease with which different Christians have created a Jesus in their own image, so that there have been many and varied portraits over the centuries, with stark contradictions between some of them. Catholic orthodoxy attributes this to over-emphasis of certain aspects of his teaching or behaviour. In any heterodox tendency, says Ramsey, there can be observed "the willingness to push a single aspect of a given mystery to its logical extreme, with the result that other aspects lose their rightful place or disappear entirely" (1993, p. 75). Catholic orthodoxy, then, has the truth and other people are wrong.

This view is based on the theory that orthodoxy resulted from uniform teachings going back to Jesus himself and continuing through the apostles. It has come under increasing challenge from studies of the NT and of the early Fathers which show how diverse early Christian beliefs in fact were; and there is now very wide acceptance of the main contention argued (originally in 1934) by Walter Bauer (1972), summarized by Maurice Wiles (who himself accepts it) as:

> Heresy is not deviation from an already implicitly known truth, which orthodoxy preserves by the process of rendering it explicit at the points under challenge from heresy. Orthodoxy and heresy are rather alternative possible developments of an initially inchoate and variegated movement. Conflicting views can both expect to find support at differing points in the Christian past; and both will necessarily be innovative in developing the inchoate views of their predecessors in the face of changing circumstance and new experience. (Wiles 1991, p. 201)

Bauer's standpoint is represented most recently in Lüdemann's book on *Heretics*, which traces how, from an early plurality of groups, an 'orthodox' church developed with fixed doctrines and institutions, from which 'heresy' was finally excluded by "the victorious party, which, following a well-tried recipe, . . . suppressed the documents of the groups that it had overcome, and finally also exterminated their defenders" (1996, p. xiv). Reviewing Lüdemann's book, Houlden (1997) notes that, even in the late first century, some Christian communities had begun to demonize dissidents, the Johannine epistles constituting "early, chilling evidence of readiness to adopt this behaviour". After Constantine, bishops could call upon governmental authority to enforce their decisions. Hence "we can see that in religious settings, as in others, it is political power that creates history's winners" (Pearson 1997, p. 185).

The Reformation break with Catholic orthodoxy resulted in a new multiplicity of sects, all with entrenched doctrines of their own; and against this situation the modern Ecumenical movement has been able to make little headway. John Kent describes it as "the great ecclesiastical failure of our time" (1987, p. 203. The whole chapter which these words introduce gives the evidence for them). The movement was a natural response to a situation where religious interests were felt to be threatened by the impact of a secular society. Graham Shaw, himself a Christian minister, notes that "ecumenical politeness and denominational weakness grow together. Faced by an irreligious culture and a secularized society, there is a strong temptation for Christians to look with favour on any sign of faith or reverence". Hence Christianity's "recent conversion to being nice, while in itself commendable, is also an aspect of its defensiveness, the anxious smile of insecurity" (1987, p. 146). The secular threat promotes religious cohesion, just as a threat to territorial or to class interests promotes territorial or class cohesion. At the same time, the tendency to disintegration in all these areas is chronic, and is decisive whenever the requisite spurs to cohesion disappear or are weakened. One can see this in the case of confederations of states where dissolution is prevented only by continuance of a common danger, or by the compulsion of a powerful member, or by the complete loss over a long period of the original sense of separateness. Inertia may be important here and in the acceptance of traditional creeds, and is strengthened by time. People commonly submit to dated religious articles of faith, even to suffering and injustice from a regime if these are not intolerable, rather than undertake the effort and danger involved in revolt. This is especially the case when the wrongs are of long standing and when habit has rendered them less painful. Small wrongs, if new, may produce a stronger reaction than great wrongs which are old.

In the case of Christian bodies, the differences between most of them are far too radical to surmount even the common danger of secularism. Liberal Christians can have little in common with the 1960 Chicago Congress of World Mission, which gave the message that "in the days since the war, more than one billion souls have passed into eternity and more than half of these went to the torment of hell fire without even hearing of Jesus Christ, who he was, or why he died on the cross of Calvary" (Quoted in Bowden 1988, p. 166). A significant number of American churches adhere to such traditional ideas, and this has helped to keep them relatively full (with some 40 percent of the total population) although, as Bruce has shown, this is not the only relevant factor.[12] In England, recruitment to such traditionally-minded religious bodies is quite insufficient to compensate for defections from the mainstream ones, which have quietly dropped hell, and so can no longer appeal to the potent motive of fear. This liberalisation of the faith was intended to make it relevant to the modern world, but "had instead the effect of making the churches irrelevant to the needs of twentieth-century men and women" (Watts 1995, p. 11). Liberal theologians are hard put to stabilize some residue to the faith, as when Räisänen allows that, although " 'Kingdom of God', 'resurrection', 'redemption', 'Christ', even 'God' may be thoroughly problematic as concepts or ideas, . . . they may still serve as evocative symbols", with the advantage that symbols "can be freely moulded" (1997, p. 202). He goes on to quote John Hick's reflection, concerning the doctrine of incarnation, that Christians might more readily accept variety of belief between them if what held them together were "seen as the use of the same myths rather than the holding of the same beliefs". This is an enormous step away from the centuries of debate as to which doctrinal propositions are to bring death to their proponents, and indicates a readiness to regard even central tenets as provisional.

Conclusion: Reason and Tolerance

My demonstration that the four canonical gospels contain much legend, that the fourth is in serious conflict with the other three, and that these themselves are not uniform, will not be new to those conversant with critical theology, although I can claim to have set out the facts in a conveniently readable form. What is not generally known—indeed seldom even admitted—is the extent to which the gospel portraits of Jesus are not only unconfirmed but actually at variance with what is said of him in earlier Christian writings. The Jesus of the Pauline and other early epistles is a basically supernatural personage about whose historical existence as a man—presumably in a somewhat distant past—very little indeed was known. The Jesus of the gospel passion and resurrection stories is based on this earlier Jesus, but has been set in a historical context relatively recent to the evangelists, but unknown to the earlier Christian writers. The pre-passion Galilean ministry, as depicted in the synoptic gospels, is based on an entirely different figure. Some elements in the life there ascribed to him may derive ultimately from the life of a first-century itinerant Galilean preacher; but to separate out such authentic material from the mass of unhistorical narrative is a well-nigh hopeless task. There is little agreement among critical scholars as to what of it is authentic—only that much of it is not. They then either, in the manner of Geza Vermes, nevertheless confidently proceed to construct what they take for "the real message of the real Jesus" (1993, p. 146), as if this could be identified without difficulty; or they play down the importance of a historical basis to Christian faith and suppose, with Marcus Borg, that "the core validity of Christianity has to do with its ability to mediate the sacred, not with the historical accuracy of any particular claim" (1994, pp. 193, 199 n30).

The inadequacy of both these positions is to some extent realized, even within the church. It is of course the former of the two which is sufficiently concrete, factual and unemotional to be the more susceptible to attack from countervailing evidence, and this has now become overwhelming. Hence John Bowden, Anglican priest and Managing Director of SCM Press, feels forced to the conclusion that "the Bible can no longer be used as a history book" and that it is time to start abandoning the OT narrative, the gospel narrative, Acts, and the *Church History* of Eusebius as a basic framework for our understanding of Christianity, since it is all "ideology, party history, which does not fall within the canons of what is acceptable history for us". He sees, however, that to implement this revision would result in "almost unthinkable" upheavals in both Christian and Jewish communities.[1] One really cannot envisage mainstream churches, let alone conservative sects, giving up the claims made in the creeds and in the sacred books.

Practically all commentators retain belief in Jesus's crucifixion under Pilate and hence accept the historical framework given to his life in the gospels. (Bowden is no exception to this.) Much is made of the fact that his existence—and by this is meant his ministry and his subsequent crucifixion in the opening decades of the first century—was not impugned even in antiquity. "No ancient opponent of early Christianity ever denied that Jesus existed. This is the Achilles's heel of attempts by a few modern scholars such as G.A. Wells to deny that Jesus existed." Thus writes Graham Stanton in a dismissive footnote.[2] If such denials were made at all in the earliest days of Christianity, one would expect them from Jews rather than from pagans, as Jews encountered Christians and their ideas from Christianity's inception. It is clear from 2 Cor. 11:24 ("Of the Jews five times received I forty stripes save one") that both Paul and the

Jews who punished him regarded the Christian movement as falling within Judaism.[3] And some Jews may well have found the Jesus portrayed by early missionaries—the Jesus figured in the early epistles—not credible as a historical personage: for this Jesus, in his human aspect, is a shadowy figure, not said in these documents to have taught or worked miracles, nor to have lived and died recently in specified circumstances. But what non-Christian Jews of the mid-first century thought of him, if anything, is not extant. Rabbinic traditions make their first extant appearance only a good century later, and moreover have been censored in the course of their transmission—"by Christians out of hostility . . . and by Jews as a means of self-protection" (Wilson 1995, p. 170). Pagans, for their part, will have had little by way of open conflict with earliest Christianity, and surely not enough exposure to it for their writers to take note of it before the gospels had become available. Subsequent opponents, Jewish and pagan alike, will have gathered from these gospels that Jesus was a teacher and wonder-worker of a kind perfectly familiar in both the Jewish and the pagan world. As he could thus be assigned to a familiar category, there was no reason to query his historicity. References to him as a teacher and 'magician' are prominent in the rabbinic notices (Details in Wilson 1995, pp. 186ff).

R.P.C. Hanson (1985, pp. 176ff) has copiously illustrated the fact that questioning the historicity of any gods was not common in antiquity, when even some Christian writers allowed that pagan saviour gods had existed, although only as "mere men". As to Jesus's existence in the early first century, any even half-way plausible questioning of it must have depended, from the early second century, on awareness 1. that the gospels are not the earliest of the relevant extant documents, and 2. that what they say is not confirmed by earlier Christian writings. Even today the vast majority of Christians are unaware that the first of these propositions is the case: they naturally suppose that canonical gospels which outline Jesus's ministry were composed earlier than epistles written to post-crucifixion churches. Or, if they are aware that the gospels are later, they will suppose them to contain authentic and reliable traditions which do antedate the epistles and correlate well with what is said of Jesus in them. From either of these premises, the second of the two propositions listed above will not even occur to them. Can one expect more from commentators in antiquity? The church has allowed practically none of the pagan criticisms to survive except as quotations in Christian refutations of their views. Nevertheless it is clear from what, for instance, Arnobius recorded of them in the early fourth century that, like most people today, they assessed Jesus from what is said of him in the gospels, from which they gathered that Christians were foolish enough to worship a being who was born a man, behaved as an ordinary magician, and died a death which would have shamed the lowest of mankind.[4] Here was substance enough for their rejection of him, and it is unrealistic to expect them to have pursued their investigations into what for them was obvious rubbish to the extent of discriminating the documents and recognizing the problems which arise from such discrimination—something which has been only slowly and painfully achieved in modern times. Kümmel shows in his account of the history of NT criticism that it was not until the beginning of the twentieth century that some theologians both recognized a gulf between the Jesus of the gospels and the Pauline Christ and were aware of its importance for any theory of Christian origins.[5]

Stanton is well aware that "Christianity as it has been understood by most Christians down through the centuries would be holed beneath its waterline if historians were to conclude that Jesus did not exist" (1995, p. 192). What I have questioned is the historicity of a Jesus who lived and died in the manner portrayed in the gospels; and the matter is not settled by appeal to Jewish and pagan acquiescence from the time these gospels were available which can readily be otherwise accounted for. Nor are this and other questions of supposed historical fact on which Christian beliefs are based to be settled by introducing the witness of 'the Spirit' to make good deficiencies in the evidence. Morgan and Barton see clearly enough that "tradition is only tradition" and hence must be subject to critical scrutiny; and their book gives a good account of how this has been done by generations of NT scholars. But then they add: "Tradition is not to be confused with the event of revelation or the guidance of the Spirit in the present" (1988, p. 291). This introduces a quite arbitrary criterion which can be used to authenticate anything.

Today more serious questions than ever before are being asked about the reliability of the Old as well as of the New Testament. While much in the books of Genesis to Judges has long been regarded as mythical, the books of Samuel and Kings have been accepted as basically historiographical (apart from such elements as the exploits of Elijah and Elisha). Now, however, a group of scholars is claiming that very little in the OT gives reliable testimony even of this monarchical period (from around 1,000 B.C. to the collapse of the state and the deportation to Babylon of 586 B.C.), and that the OT as a whole dates from the reconstitution of the state, after the exile, in the Persian empire and later, from the fifth century B.C. It is not denied that the documents as we have them are to some extent based on earlier material; but it is contended that such relics have been adapted to the social and ideological settings of later situations to such an extent that what the earlier situations were really like cannot be inferred from them: David and Solomon, for instance, if they existed at all, did not have anything like the importance and power the Bible attributes to them.[6] Professor R.N. Whybray (1996, p. 71n) names and specifies publications of five scholars as "notable examples" of those who are propounding such sceptical views. He himself allows that corroborative written material from outside the Bible is limited to a handful of references by name to Israelite kings (mainly on Assyrian and Babylonian inscriptions) from which no continuous history can be inferred, and that archaeological data is likewise inadequate for this purpose, and is also difficult to interpret. He nevertheless believes that, although some of what the OT says of the early Israelite monarchy (Saul, David, Solomon) may well be legendary, the account of the histories of the separate kingdoms of Israel and Judah from 1 Kings 12 onwards is basically reliable, particularly because it treats them with such disfavour: "Far from trumpeting the glorious past, these writers chronicle the ignominious slide of their own ancestors into a fully merited disaster". Professor P.R. Davies, one of the group criticized by Whybray, replies (1997, p. 211) that this might well mean no more than that post-exilic writers wanted to contrast a bad past with a reformed present.[7] He is aware that his "respected colleague" has tradition and a majority of opinion on his side, and observes, pertinently, that "we are all attached to sacred stories, even the most secular of us; different sacred stories divide the terrorists of Ireland, the Jews and Palestinians and countless other warring groups. Postmodernists call these 'master narratives', since they organize our social and personal beliefs and actions".

The movement away from hallowed ideas of the past that is deplored in the kind of exhortation recorded even in the later books of the NT itself (quoted above, p. 47), and the contrary tendency to retain such ideas, are alike inevitable. Only part of the external universe has a direct bearing on the life of man, and it is only of that part that his ideas—his inward model of the universe—need to be a fair copy. For the rest, he can build according to his whim. That fire burns and boiling water scalds, that wounded animals attack and offended man retaliates—these things must be accurately represented in the inward model if the individual is to survive. But that the Earth is round or flat, the stars flying sparks or chinks in a canopy, were for long matters that could be settled according to taste. In time, however, parts of the old model that had hitherto without disadvantage been a work of fantasy were found to hamper the construction of the business part of the model. Science and tradition came into conflict. In every society, the model current at a given time will be tested as to some of its features by one mind, and as to other of its features by another, but by no mind as to all its features. In many protected individuals and enclaves the testing will be rare and imperfect, and ample scope left for ancient fantasies. An Oxford Professor of Divinity has called attention to the fact that, "while it may no longer be possible to study theology as if the world came into existence in 4004 B.C., it is still possible in Oxford . . . to do so as if the world went out of existence in A.D. 461" (Wiles 1976, p. 179). Such specialization, while exposing students to the heresies of early Christian times, may well shield them from those of the nineteenth and twentieth centuries. A recent survey claims that "evangelical" theological colleges are training about fifty percent of candidates for ordination as priests in the church of England (Hylson-Smith 1988, p. 352).

In this book I have given a fair amount of space to apologists who, perhaps because of such limitations in their training, are beholden to traditional patristic doctrines. I have paid attention to Roderick Tyler's recent book, both because he represents many such conservative positions, and because he has taken considerable trouble to criticize my views as expressed in some of my previous books. I value his book because it brings together a whole array of apologetic positions. He is also exemplary in his candour, unlike apologists whose fear of exposing the faithful to unsettling opinions leads them to present critical views in merely general and anonymous terms (often with disparaging labels), without enabling readers to identify their source and consult them for themselves—a lack of openness well exemplified in some of what J.A.T. Robinson has written.[8]

Now that mainstream Christianity, instead of threatening with penalties, stresses the serenity and consolations brought by faith, it is commonly supposed—and not only by those within the faith—that all should be left in quiet and undisturbed enjoyment of it, and that it is therefore inappropriate to raise questions as to its truth. There are of course cases where misery can be avoided by ignorance, but it can hardly be claimed that any systematic propagation of error or concealment of truth is on the whole, and not merely in individual cases, beneficial; and so open and candid discussion of theological as of other claims remains the best option. Unfortunately, the defence of any strongly held position, whether favourable or unfavourable to religious beliefs, is apt to involve a good deal of 'forensic' reasoning—the kind used in parliaments and law courts and which Rignano called "intentional reasoning". Science starts with a set of observed facts and tries to devise a theory which connects them; but forensic reasoning starts with a theory to be proved and tries to find facts that will justify it. Settled views on anything deemed to be of supreme importance tend to be linked with powerful emotions, and this creates an indifference to countervailing evidence, so that the critic can hope to appeal only to doubters or waverers. It is not an encouraging prospect for the resolution of important issues.

In the primitive village community, opinions were uniform, inherited through many generations. Nothing like this exists in the present-day West. In modern democratic societies there are many sub-groups, communities within the community, and if someone finds all his friends within one such group, it is the peculiar ethic of that group which moulds his behaviour. Danger arises when the special ethic of such a group is directly opposed to what might be called the common ethic of the whole community. There is no rational reason for either religious people or 'humanists' to form themselves into such a group. Indeed, the term 'humanism' in its most familiar recent use seems to have been assumed by people who could not accept the doctrines of Christianity, but did not wish it to be thought that they were therefore immoral and antisocial. It should be pretty obvious by now that 'humanists' and religious persons, for all their differences, need to work together as far as they can in confronting the very serious problems that face us all. This does not mean that they should blur what divides them. On the contrary, to be clear about these differences should be a step towards realizing that they do not rule out co-operation—something arguably even more important than education; for education may merely render someone's consciousness of his own interests more keen, whereas co-operation promotes sympathy and unselfish interests.

In this connection it is a useful principle to avoid ascribing malice to those who disagree with us, and to try to understand the machinery of human behaviour. There is a natural, if unhelpful, tendency to look for faults in others, particularly if we can thereby blame them for our own difficulties, embarrassments, or misfortunes. When it is impossible to blame anybody, as when a great disaster such as an earthquake occurs, the spirit of mutual help usually shows itself. But when anger can be directed against some kind of person, the emotion tends to find release in that way. Mankind is at present confronted with a whole array of most serious problems, and tackling them is hindered by the nationalism and xenophobia all too much in evidence in the relations between states, and by the militant religious fundamentalism that is rampant. Only a small minority of liberally minded spokesmen of religious communities are moving decisively away from exclusive religious positions of the past and making 'inter-faith dialogue' prominent in their agenda, with sincere efforts to appreciate what is best in each other's traditions without being blind to the worst. The 'humanist' can learn from the urbane tone of these discussions and from the participants' readiness to acknowledge that even cherished convictions can be questioned. Inevitably, however, differences will remain. We all need to embrace the insight which Goethe ascribes to an admirable and very sensible character in his novel *Elective Affinities* (*Die Wahlverwandtschaften*):

> Der Hauptmann . . . den die Erfahrung gelehrt hatte, dass die Ansichten der Menschen viel zu mannigfaltig sind, als dass sie, selbst durch die vernünftigsten Vorstellungen, auf einen Punkt versammelt werden könnten. (Part I, chapter 3)

This man "had learned from experience that people's opinions are much too manifold to be gathered together into a unity, even by the most rational of expositions."

Afterword

Roderick Tyler

I am grateful to Professor Wells for offering me the opportunity to make brief observations on this book. He is particularly concerned that I should not feel that he has been unfair to me.

Rather than go through the text of the book and highlight those areas where I think that what I have to say might have been expressed differently, I suggest that readers of this book might wish to read a copy of my book. I remember a good friend of mine at Oxford in the Fifties saying that he had recently read the lengthy and trenchant criticisms of the ideas of Professor Eugen Dühring by Engels (with a little help from Marx) and adding: "It might have been better if I had read Dühring first". Readers might feel the same in connection with the present book.

Readers of this book who read my book as well will be able to judge for themselves whether some of the strictures uttered by Professor Wells in relation to my book—either in relation to its overall approach or perceived inadequacies or alleged misrepresentations or . . . —are generally valid. There are a few parts of my book where, with the benefit of hindsight, I feel that I might well have phrased things differently; and, if I were writing a reply to Professor Wells's book (relax, I am not!), although as I see it, my central arguments remain sound, there is plenty I would need to reflect upon as a result of the quite astonishing amount of scholarly detail Professor Wells has provided in this book.

Although I am not claiming infallibility (yet!), I think that I can fairly give myself credit for "going behind the scenes" rather more frequently than Professor Wells appears to give me credit for with regard to some of the quotations I give from scholars quoted in my book. Moreover, my book is considerably better balanced (even more open-minded) than might appear from what Professor Wells has to say. I would have liked to provide the more extensive material. Professor Wells would like to have seen me tackle but this would have required the length of my book to be at least twice its actual length.

It is good to see that on p. 103 above Professor Wells, after 25 years (maybe longer) of rejecting any idea that there was even a shadowy Galilaean figure in the early part of the 1st century A.D., now accepts that there may well have been such a figure. Wells still refuses to connect Him with someone who died just outside the walls of Jerusalem in the time of Pontius Pilate; however, in another twenty-five years' time, perhaps Wells will be able to say: "Next year in Jerusalem"!

Notes

1. The Nature of the Evidence

1. Typical is Sir Frederick Kenyon's conviction that "we have in our hands, in substantial integrity, the veritable word of God" (Quoted in McDowell 1990, I, 46). McDowell amasses quotations from ultra-conservative apologists, and his book is correspondingly popular. The blurb on its back cover claims "over a million copies in print worldwide". For a sober assessment of the real situation concerning the NT text, see Elliott and Moir 1995.

2. Luke 22:19b–20 (which includes Jesus's statements that his body is "given for you" and his blood "shed for you") is absent from important ancient manuscripts, and is widely regarded as added by a later hand so as to bring Luke's version of the eucharistic words into line with that of Mark and Matthew. The key elements of the vocabulary of these verses are otherwise foreign to Luke, who elsewhere consistently portrays the death of Jesus not as an atoning sacrifice, but as a miscarriage of justice that God reversed by vindicating him at the resurrection. Luke has even eliminated the notion of atonement from the one source we are virtually certain he had before him, namely the gospel of Mark; for he omits Mk. 10:45 ("the Son of man came . . . to give his life a ransom for many") and so presumably did not find its theology acceptable (see Ehrman 1993, pp. 199–200). Not that the injustice which led to Jesus's death was, in the view of Luke-Acts (both by the same author) fortuitous. On the

contrary, it was "by the determinate counsel and foreknowl-
edge of God" that the Jews "delivered him up" to the
Romans (Acts 2:23 and 3:13). God thus wanted and planned
his death, yet—according to the overall context of these
same verses—the Jews incurred guilt for seeing to it that he
was killed (cf. Acts 13:28). This guilt is mitigated in that they
"acted in ignorance" (3:17), but how could they have been
thus ignorant when Jesus had been attested *to them* (2:22) by
means of stupendous miracles? In all this, Luke is combining a medley of incompatible traditions. As Haenchen wryly
notes (1968b, p. 167), modern Christian communities do the
same.

Chapter 53 of Isaiah includes verses to which early
Christian writers commonly appeal as prophecies of Jesus's
atoning death. The Servant of the Lord is there said to have
been made "an offering for sin", to have been "wounded for
our transgressions and bruised for our iniquities" (verses 5
and 10). Even on the one occasion in Acts (namely 8:32–34)
when Luke quotes from this chapter, and where it plays an
essential part in his statement of the Christian message, he
makes no reference to these or to other verses which imply
atonement.

Some apologists have claimed Acts 20:28 as an exception
to Luke's usual understanding of the death of Jesus. Here
Paul, in his farewell to the "elders" of Ephesus, urges them
to "pastor the church of God which he obtained through the
blood of his Own". It is often held that this, if not Luke's own
view, is at any rate an accommodation to the beliefs of Paul.
But Ehrman observes that, even here, there is no claim that
Jesus died for our sakes—rather that God used his blood to
acquire (not to redeem) the church. Ehrman's study of
Luke's only other reference to Jesus's blood (Acts 5:28), and
of the other mentions of blood in Luke-Acts, shows that in
these books blood most frequently refers to unjust suffering,
especially of prophets and martyrs; and for Luke, Jesus is
above all a prophet and martyr. Blood unjustly shed produces a sense of guilt, followed by repentance, in the
perpetrators. The constant refrain of the speeches in Acts is:

'You killed Jesus', whereupon many of those addressed are cut to the quick and repent (2:23, 37–41). Ehrman concludes that, for Luke, the blood of Jesus produces the church because it brings this cognizance of guilt and so leads to repentance. Paul himself, in the context of Acts 20:28, declares that he is guiltless of the "blood" of the Ephesian elders because he had preached the message of salvation (from the coming judgement) to them: "Only if his hearers repent when confronted with Jesus's blood will they be saved from spilling their own" (Ehrman 1993, p. 203).

3. Thiede complains (1996, p. 110) of "a scholarly straitjacket" which inhibits "open-mindedness and flexibility of approach", and of "factual errors" which "can only be attributed to undue haste", and which make Wachtel's article "an example of inappropriate and palpably wrong statements on palaeographic details" (pp. 171, 177).

4. On p. 1 of this 1996 book, which Thiede co-authored, it is stated that in December 1994 he claimed that the Magdalen papyrus dates "from the mid-first century A.D.", and that he was then "shortly to publish his claims in the specialist journal *Zeitschrift für Papyrologie*". Thiede is aware that Stanton (1995) has pointed out the discrepancy between the December claims and the article in the *Zeitschrift* of the following January. His way with Stanton's comments is to say that, typically of NT scholars, Stanton has made an "effort to exclude early papyrological evidence from Gospel studies" (1996, p. 57). Stanton has of course done nothing of the sort, but has given good reasons for not accepting the evidence adduced by Thiede as early.

5. Conzelmann observes that Papias's remarks about the origin of the gospels "continue to be endlessly discussed, but are one and all historically worthless" (1971, p. 17). Niederwimmer (1967) had already set out the evidence for this negative conclusion, and his work is noticed in positive terms by Telford in the 1995 symposium on Mark which he himself edited (pp. 2, 41). Telford adds that "Mark's Gospel is now widely regarded as the product of a more or less creative

editorial process upon diverse and discreet oral (and possibly written) traditions which had circulated for a generation within the primitive Christian communities that transmitted them."

6. 1 Clement is later than Paul's first letter to the Corinthians, to which it refers; and from its chapters 42–44 we see that the author regarded the age of the apostles—among whom he includes Paul (47:1)—as already so much past that at any rate some of the men they appointed to succeed them had died and been succeeded by their own appointees. Hence this epistle cannot be earlier than ca. A.D. 75–80. Its mention of persons who had lived blamelessly "among us", i.e. in the Roman church, "from youth to old age" (63:3) also implies a post–A.D. 70 date of writing; and most commentators date it in the 90s. Yet, as Lowther Clarke, its 1937 editor, conceded, it shows "no knowledge of the gospels", "no trace of any interest in the Ministry of Christ or in his miracles, not even in the Passion story". What it says of the Passion is based on the portrait of the suffering servant of Yahweh in chapter 53 of Isaiah (pp. 13, 36). These conclusions remain substantially unmodified in Hagner's 1973 study of the use of the OT and of the NT in this epistle. He finds that it "nowhere convincingly alludes to the Johannine literature", neither to the epistles nor to the gospel; and that the sayings of Jesus quoted in its chapters 13 and 46 derive "not from the Synoptic Gospels but from oral tradition" (pp. 273, 287, 332). Hagner does think that it "probably" alludes to Acts, but this is disputed by critical commentators on Acts such as Haenchen.

Although this epistle is known as 1 Clement, it purports to have been written on behalf of the church of Rome and is otherwise anonymous. The name of Clement is not associated with it until ca. A.D. 170, and, as Hagner shows (pp. 1, 3), the Fathers romance about him in their usual way: Irenaeus makes him a disciple of Peter and Paul, and Tertullian has him consecrated Bishop of Rome by Peter himself.

7. At ii, 15 of his *Ecclesiastical History* Eusebius notes (I quote the translation by Lawlor and Oulton (1927), I, 48: "It is said" that Peter "authorized" Mark's gospel "to be read in the churches—Clement has given the story . . . and . . . Papias corroborated his testimony". (The reference is to Clement of Alexandria, who lived half a century later than Papias.) "And [it is said] that Peter mentions Mark in his former epistle, which also it is said he composed at Rome itself". Here our two translators put the first 'it is said' in square brackets, as it is implied, but not stated, in the Greek. But the second 'it is said' is actually stated, and so there is no suggestion that Papias endorsed the hearsay that Mark or Peter were at Rome. Yet this is what many commentators have inferred from the passage.

8. The Swiss historian Jacob Burckhardt (who died in 1897) called Eusebius "the first thoroughly dishonest historian of antiquity" (1989, p. 283). Gibbon specified two passages in which "Eusebius himself indirectly confesses that he has related whatever might redound to the glory, and that he has suppressed all that could tend to the disgrace of religion" (1910, II, 65, chapter 16). Bowden (1988, p. 63) calls his *Ecclesiastical History* propaganda containing a constant series of battles for the truth between the good (bishops, Christian teachers and martyrs) and the bad (Jews, evil emperors, and heretics). He was convinced that what orthodox Christians believed in his time was the true apostolic faith, whereas heretics were dangerous innovators. Lawlor and Oulton (as cited in the previous note, II, 28ff) deny that he was dishonest, but give numerous examples to show that he was biased and uncritical to the point of being naively credulous. In book 1 of his *History* he endorsed the entirely legendary story of the letter of Abgar, king of Edessa, to Jesus and of Jesus's written reply. According to this tradition, the king wrote asking Jesus to visit and heal him, and Jesus then promised to send instead a disciple after his ascension. Eusebius quotes the texts of both letters, "extracted" he says "from the archives at Edessa".

9. At 7:31 Mark puts the Decapolis to the west of the Sea of Galilee when it actually lies to the east, and places Sidon south instead of north of Tyre. Jesus's whole journey to the north, to "the borders of Tyre and Sidon", from which he is here returning southwards to Galilee, is probably a construction of the evangelist, who thought it suitable to place the miracle story of his encounter with the Syro-Phoenician woman (7:24–30) in this Phoenician territory (cf. McCowan 1941, p. 6). Kümmel (1975, p. 97) writes of Mark's "numerous geographical errors", and Nineham lists passages which have relevant "vaguenesses and inaccuracies" (1963, p. 40). But all this is commonly ignored by commentators, and Mitton even assures us that "an indication of Mark's historical reliability is his accurate presentation of the social, historical, and geographical conditions in Palestine in the early part of the first century A.D." (1975, p. 74). For detailed criticism of Mark's "strange geography", see Niederwimmer 1967, pp. 177–183.

10. For detailed discussion of the Markan pre-Passion narrative as community tradition, see *The Jesus Legend*, pp. 133–145. See also Telford's comment in note 5 above.

11. See R.A. Guelich's article 'Destruction of Jerusalem', in Green 1992. He concludes (p. 175) that "nothing in either of the references to the fate of Jerusalem or the Temple corresponds so closely to the events as to necessitate the sayings being created in the light of the events of 66–70."

12. The date of composition of the book of Baruch is discussed undogmatically in Dancy's commentary (1972, pp. 169ff) and in the revised English edition of Schürer (1987, pp. 733ff); also in the article 'Baruchschriften' in volume 1 of Galling (editor), 1957. Dating Baruch after A.D. 70 depends on taking the reference to Nebuchadnezzar and Belshazzar (1:11) as meaning Vespasian and Titus. This has been called unlikely. Robinson (1976, p. 316) claims that the reference to "parents eating their children in the extremities of the siege" can refer only to A.D. 70. Dancy, however, has noted (p. 179) that cannibalism is threatened in Leviticus 26:29

and is said to have happened in the siege of 587 B.C. (Lamentations 4:10). Robinson also claims that Baruch alludes to "the deportation of captives to Rome". In fact, however, Rome is not mentioned, and the deportation is said to have been to Babylon, as occurred in the sixth century B.C.

13. See the article 'Daniel, Book of', in Grant and Rowley's 1963 revision of James Hastings's *Dictionary of the Bible:* "The relations between Syria and Egypt, from the 4th to the 2nd centuries B.C., are described with a fulness of detail which differentiates Daniel 7, 11 from all OT prophecy." The reign of Antiochus Epiphanes "is related with precision in ch. 11; the events from 323–175 B.C. occupy 16 verses; those from 175–164 B.C. take up 25." The traditional interpretation of all this as genuine prophecies made by Daniel in the Babylonian exile in the sixth century B.C. is today maintained only by the most conservative commentators. An excellent critique of their arguments is given by Grabbe (1987). That the 'prophecies' in Daniel were in fact written in the second century B.C. is now established as "overwhelmingly" probable, and even in Roman Catholic commentaries this critical position "has been routinely accepted since World War II" (Collins, 1993, pp. 26, 29, 38, 122).

14. At Mt. 28:9–10, when Jesus appears to the women near the empty tomb, they "took hold of his feet and worshipped him", whereupon he instructed them to "tell my brethren that they depart into Galilee, and there shall they see me." The sequel shows that disciples, not family is meant: "The eleven disciples went into Galilee", saw and worshipped him (verses 16–17). In the fourth gospel Jesus says, in similar circumstances: "Touch me not . . . but go unto my brethren and say to them, I ascend unto my Father". Lindars 1972, pp. 595f, 607 recognizes that it is above all John's exceptional designation of the disciples here as Jesus's "brethren" which requires the supposition that the evangelist was using a source which also lies behind Mt. 28:10. This source will have included some statement about Jesus's 'brethren' in

the sense of a group of his disciples. Each evangelist has reworked the material for his own purposes. Matthew makes the women touch Jesus to show that he is risen in body. John makes him say, in effect: Stop clinging to me and hindering my ascension.

15. Caragounis summarizes the unfavourable elements in Matthew's depiction of Peter as follows: he is presented as "confused, cowardly, without understanding, disliking suffering, giving with a view to future gain, impetuous, impulsive and unstable, stingy in forgiving, overestimating his ability, and denying his master miserably" (1990, p. 99). Caragounis does not query the view that, for Paul, Cephas and the Peter of the gospels are the same person (p. 26). The main thesis of his book is his interpretation of Mt. 16:17–19. Peter has just recognized Jesus as "the Christ"; Jesus calls him "blessed" for his discernment and adds: "Thou art Peter (*Petros*) and on this rock (*petra*) I will build my church". Caragounis argues that *petra* here does not refer to Peter, but to what Peter has just so insightfully said ("Thou art the Christ"). *Petra* here "is employed by Matthew in its usual significance to convey the sense of 'bedrock'" (p. 90). Jesus thus means: 'As truly as you are called Peter, on this rock [i.e. of what you have just said, namely that I am the Christ] I shall build my church' (p. 113). On this view, Peter is not here designated head of the church, which is to be built on acceptance of Christ as its head. Caragounis shows that there is really no evidence elsewhere in the NT, nor in other early Christian literature, to make Peter the foundation of the church. Even in the pseudepigraphic 1 Peter, Christ is the *petra* (2:4–8).

16. See further *DJE*, pp. 126–29; *HEJ*, pp. 63–64; and W. Schneemelcher's 'Apostle and Apostolic' in his edition of Hennecke 1965, pp. 25–31.

17. 2 Cor. 5:16 reads, in literal translation: "From now on we know no man according to flesh; if indeed we have known Christ according to flesh, we no longer know him (thus)". The reference is not to 'Christ in the flesh' (the earthly

Jesus); for 'according to flesh' qualifies the verb 'known', not the noun 'Christ', and Paul's meaning is that he no longer has an 'unspiritual' conception of Christ. Likewise, that he no longer knows any man "according to flesh" means that he no longer judges anybody by worldly standards. It would be absurd to take it as meaning that he has no personal acquaintances or is no longer interested in anyone's biography. Thompson is surely right to say that Paul is here "contrasting two attitudes towards others, the fallen 'this-worldly' way of thinking and the outlook of one who is a new creation" (1991, p. 68). Judged by worldly standards, Jesus who lived obscurely and died shamefully would be of no account. For Paul, this shows the worthlessness of worldly standards.

18. Numerous nineteenth-century scholars argued that 1 Thess. 2:14–16 is a post-Pauline interpolation. Pearson, who agrees with them, gives the details (1997, pp. 58–60). But many recent commentators, reacting against excessive resort to interpolation hypotheses, have accepted the passage as genuinely Pauline, and have supported this judgement with an appeal to 'the unanimous witness of the manuscript evidence'—even though, as Pearson notes (p. 60n), there is no single manuscript of this part of 1 Thessalonians that is datable to before the fourth century, so that we lack textual evidence "for precisely that period in which the text would most likely have been in the greatest stage of flux".

19. For instance, Mack (1991, p. 299) observes that Paul nowhere mentions a third party as involved in the 'delivering' or 'giving' of Jesus—the subjects of these verbs being either Jesus himself (Gal. 1:4 and 2:20, "He gave himself for our sins", "gave himself up for me") or God (Rom. 8:32, "He spared not his own Son, but delivered him up for us all"); or the verb is in the passive voice, implying (as so often in the OT and in early Christian literature) that God was the agent, yet avoiding undesirable mention of his name (Rom. 4:25, "He was delivered up for our trespasses"—obviously alluding to the Greek version of the story of the suffering servant

of Isaiah 53:12: "his soul was delivered up unto death", taken in the early church as a prophecy of Jesus's suffering).

20. Josephus records that Antiochus Epiphanes (king of Syria in the second century B.C..) occupied Jerusalem and had Jews who defied him ("the best men and those of the noblest souls") "crucified while they were still alive"; and that Alexander Jannaeus (a Hasmonean ruler of the first century B.C.) had 800 Jews crucified in Jerusalem, again while they were still living (*Antiquities of the Jews,* 12:255–56; 13:380).

21. Attempts have recently been made to show that the seven letters regarded as genuinely Ignatian—there are additional ones known to be later forgeries—are themselves forgeries, and not written by Ignatius ca. A.D. 110–18. In his 1985 commentary on these letters Schoedel regards only one such attempt as serious, namely that by R. Joly (1979), who argues that the seven were forged ca. A.D. 165. A later date is excluded, as one of them was known to Irenaeus, ca. A.D. 185. But Polycarp, in chapter 13 of his epistle to the Philippians of ca. 135, had already mentioned making a collection of Ignatius's letters; and so Joly has to regard this chapter in Polycarp's letter as interpolated by the forger of the Ignatian letters in order to authenticate his forgery. The principal evidence for this is that Polycarp's mention of "the blessed Ignatius", along with other martyrs, in his chapter 9 assumes that Ignatius is already dead, whereas chapter 13 gives the impression that he had only recently left Philippi and that Polycarp has not yet had news of his fate. One widely accepted solution to this discrepancy—a solution which keeps chapter 13 as authentic—has been to regard this chapter (and the final chapter 14) as a separate and later letter from Polycarp that has been copied so as to become attached to the copy of the letter comprising chapters 1–12. Joly shows convincingly enough that this solution will not do: "If we imagine two letters of Polycarp one after another on the same roll, . . . we must explain how the longer one lost its final salutations after chapter 12 and how the shorter one lost its opening greetings before chapter 13". Caroline

P. Hammond Bammel quotes this from Joly, and agrees
with him that "if we wish to defend the authenticity" of
chapter 13, it "must be seen as an original part of the whole
letter." Contrary to Joly, however, she thinks that such a
defence can be made, and that the discrepancy with chapter
9 is intelligible if Polycarp's "conception of time was sufficiently vague to allow him to speak [there] of Ignatius as a
martyr once out of sight on his journey to martyrdom"
(1982, p. 70). Schoedel decides (p. 7), after reviewing the
evidence, that the cumulative weight of arguments against
the authenticity of the seven Ignatian letters is insufficient to
dislodge them from their place in the history of the early
church. Whether they were written by Ignatius ca. A.D. 110,
or forged in his name some fifty years later, makes no
difference to my argument that they exemplify the kind of
writing about Jesus that is common once the traditions
underlying the gospels had become current, but unknown
earlier.

22. It is sometimes claimed (for instance in Dunn 1994, p. 162),
that Rom. 14:14 ("I know and am persuaded in the Lord
Jesus that nothing is profane in itself") echoes Jesus's
statement given at Mk. 7:15: "There is nothing outside a
person . . . which is able to defile him." Mark understands
this as a declaration that all foods are clean (7:19). Paul is
discussing, at this point in Romans, whether it is permissible
to eat meat and not only vegetables, and he concludes that
neither practice is in itself wrong. It would be strange if he
were alluding to Jesus' teaching in his discussion of such a
peripheral matter, on which he allows both strictness and
permissiveness, when he fails to appeal to anything said by
Jesus when discussing whether Christians must observe
central provisions of the Jewish law. Räisänen has noted that
Paul speaks of Jesus both as one who "came under the law"
(Gal. 4:4f) and as "a servant of the circumcision" (Rom.
15:8), so that "it seems rather unlikely that he would have
attributed a critical attitude to the law to the historical
Jesus" (1987b, p. 248). He also observes (p. 79) that Paul

does not use the statement made in Rom. 14:14 in any of his extended discussions of the law, whereas the 'confidence' he here expresses with the phrase 'persuaded in the Lord Jesus' occurs in other Pauline passages where the same Greek verb is used with the noun 'the Lord', and where no reference to Jesus's teaching can be supposed: "I have confidence in the Lord that you will take no other view than mine" (Gal. 5:10). "I trust in the Lord that I myself also shall come shortly" (Phil. 2:24). "We have confidence in the Lord touching you, that ye both do and will do the things which we command" (2 Thess. 3:4). Paul's feeling "persuaded in the Lord" at Rom. 14:14 seems, then, to represent no more than "a deeply felt personal conviction which he has reached because of his communion with the Lord". He is "drawing on his Christian experience rather than on any saying of the Lord" (pp. 24,247). The NEB interprets the Greek in this way and renders it: "I am absolutely convinced as a Christian that nothing is impure of itself".

23. "The sermon's requirement to fast is curious in view of the complaint against Jesus that his disciples did not fast (Mk. 2:18–22). The ascetic tone is quite different from Jesus's reputation as one who ate and drank, and who associated with toll gatherers and sinners (Mt. 11:19). Toll gatherers, heroes of other passages, are outsiders according to the sermon (Mt. 5:46)" (Sanders 1985, p. 263; 1993b, p. 66); whereas according to Mt. 21:31, they and the harlots "go into the kingdom of God before you."

24. At Mk. 10:2–12 Jesus prohibits divorce and remarriage absolutely, without qualification, for men and women alike. Since in Palestine (where he is addressing Pharisees) only men could obtain divorce, the passage looks like a ruling for the gentile readers of Mark, put into Jesus's mouth so as to give it authority. Matthew, more conversant with Judaism than was Mark, adapts this passage by dropping any mention of the wife divorcing the husband, and also by allowing the husband a divorce in the case of his wife's "fornication" (19:9). In the article 'Divorce' in his *Dictionary of the Bible*

(London and Dublin: Chapman, 1965), J.L. McKenzie mentions a commentator (J. Bonsirven) who avoids admitting
that this is a softening of the unqualified prohibition given in
Mark by claiming that the Greek translated here as 'fornication' really represents an Aramaic word which shows that
Jesus was here speaking of concubinage, not of marriage.
(Positing supposed Aramaic originals is a scholarly game
that has the great advantage of shutting up all except the few
who know Aramaic, who are unlikely to demur.) However,
McKenzie allows that the majority view is that Matthew's
wording represents "a variant tradition", whereas Mark's is
"more original". Since divorce was allowed by Jewish law,
the absolute prohibition of it in Mark is, for McKenzie, "one
of the most revolutionary features of the moral teaching of
Jesus". Yet, as he is aware, Paul allows divorce if a Christian
husband or wife has an unbelieving partner who desires it (1
Cor. 7:12–16). And so, having given an absolute prohibition
as enjoined by "the Lord" (verses 10–11), he departs from
this strictness on his own initiative. He obviously has in
mind the circumstances of his own congregations. In these
newly missionized areas, marriages where only one partner
was a believer will not have been uncommon, and this will
sometimes have led to the breakdown of the marriage.

25. That there was no significant persecution of Christians in
Jerusalem before the War with Rome, which began in A.D.
66, is clear from Paul's letters, which show that he was able
to visit the Jerusalem church at widely scattered intervals
and find a stable continuing organization. Hare adds to this
the fact that "Paul, in summoning his churches to contrib-
ute money for the relief of the saints at Jerusalem, makes no
reference to notable sufferings of that congregation as a
basis for his appeal, as one might expect, had the situation
warranted it" (1967, p. 36). In writing to Christians at Rome,
Paul states, as a general principle, that the governing authorities have been instituted by God, and molest only evil
persons (Rom. 13:1–3). Even Acts, which grossly exagge-
rates the extent and influence of the early Jerusalem church

(cf. above, p. 129), can produce stories of only two martyr-doms—of Stephen and of James the son of Zebedee. Careful analysis of the narrative supports the view that Stephen fell victim to mob violence and was not judicially executed (Hare, pp. 21–22 and references); and in the disturbance following his death, the apostles were left unmolested: "All were scattered except the apostles" (Acts 8:1). James the son of Zebedee was executed at the behest of Herod Agrippa I (Acts 12:2), for reasons not stated. As non-Christian evidence there is only the passage in Josephus (*Ant.* 20:200–03) which tells that another James (said in a probably interpolated phrase to be the brother of Jesus, cf. above, p. 217) was executed ca. A.D. 62 by an intemperate Sadducean High Priest, who was able to effect his purpose only because of the temporary absence of a Roman governor; whereupon those Jews who were equitable and law-abiding were so angered that, with Roman help (!), they had the High Priest deposed.

26. See, for instance, Wrede 1907, pp. 88, 149: "Christ is called [by Paul] obedient because he did not oppose the divine decision to send him for the salvation of the world, although it cost him his divine nature and brought him to the cross. He is called meek because he humbled himself to the lowliness of earth". Saving the world 'cost him his divine nature' because to do so he had to take on human form as a man, and thereby impoverish himself: "The poverty lies in manhood as such, not in any special lowliness" in his life. "He appeared 'in the form of sinful flesh' (Rom. 8:3), whereas he had hitherto been a spiritual being." See further, note 5 to 'Conclusion', p. 292 below.

27. Barr 1988, pp. 175–76. Vermes (1993, pp. 180–83) finds Barr's arguments and conclusions fully justified, although he does not wish to deny that Jesus saw God as "near and approachable".

28. Matthew cites the OT re the virgin birth at 1:23; re Jesus's settling at Capernaum at 4:14; re his teaching in parables at 13:35; re his triumphal entry at 21:4; and re his disciples' desertion at 26:31.

29. At Rom. 3:9–18 Paul quotes four passages from the Psalms and one from Isaiah to show that every single person is under the power of sin. Characteristically he here distorts his sources for the purposes of his argument, as some (if not all) of these passages, in their OT context, quite clearly describe only the impious, not mankind as a whole. See also, for his appeals to the OT: re faith, Rom. 1:17; 4:3; 10:11; re salvation for only Christian Jews, Rom. 9:7ff and 24ff; re predestination, Rom. 9:15; re the resurrection body, 1 Cor. 15:54; re women in church, 1 Cor. 11:8; re ecstatic utterance as unsettling, 1 Cor. 14:21; re retribution as to be left to God, Rom. 12:19; re love of neighbour, Rom. 13:9; Gal. 5:14; re generous giving, 2 Cor. 9:7ff.

30. Hanson (1982, p. 11) lists the following as the most distinguished modern authors of commentaries on the Pastorals who regard them as devoid of any authentically Pauline elements, and composed by a writer subsequent to Paul's day who wished to claim Paul's authority for his material: in Germany, M. Dibelius and H. Conzelmann (3rd edition, 1955); N. Brox (Catholic, 1969); in Switzerland, V. Hasler (1978); in America, B.S. Easton (1944) and F.D.Gealy (1955); in Britain, A.J.B. Higgins (1962), C.K. Barrett (1963) and J.H. Houlden (1976); and, of course, Hanson himself (1982). His list can be supplemented with Frances Young (1994) and Margaret Davies (1996).

31. In my *JEC* of 1971 I accepted that the Pastorals include genuine Pauline fragments, but in my later books I first expressed caution and then made no further mention of this hypothesis. The main reason for taking the relevant short passages as Pauline has been that their references to persons of Paul's acquaintance and to places familiar to him would seem to have no point in these otherwise pseudepigraphic epistles. However, Margaret Davies (in the course of marshalling objections to Pauline authorship of the Pastorals and of countering arguments for taking them as Pauline) has drawn attention to evidence that such personal and geographical references "are found in other clearly pseudony-

mous letters like those of Socrates and the Socratics", and serve an important function in that they "create the impression that the pseudonymous epistle is genuine". In the case of the Pastorals, they "help to depict Paul as the leader of a mutually supportive group of associates who could rely on each other to practise the teaching which the epistle advocates". She adds that a recent study "has also argued that this helps to explain the existence of three Pastoral Epistles rather than one" in that three can better depict a display of friendship among Pauline associates (1996a, pp. 87, 117; 1996b, pp. 111–12). In 2 Timothy alone, twenty persons—most of them otherwise unknown—are named as helpers or opponents of Paul.

Hanson, who in 1966 himself accepted the relevant fragments as Pauline, eventually came to the view that such small fragments of Pauline material could surely not have survived: "Paul presumably did not send picture postcards to his friends during his travels! . . . It looks as if the 'Fragments Hypothesis' was a last desperate attempt to retain some Pauline elements in the Pastorals" (1982, p. 11).

32. Appeal is sometimes made to the letter of Polycarp of ca. A.D 135 which has three phrases similar to those in the Pastorals. They are, however, popular philosophical maxims, and both authors could have derived them from a common source. Kümmel (1975, p. 370) finds that these maxims show only that the Pastorals and Polycarp "stand in the same ecclesiastical and cultural tradition". A few passages from other early second-century authors have also been adduced as supposedly dependent on the Pastorals, but "none is convincing" and "around and immediately after Polycarp, silence prevails" (Barrett 1963, p. 1). It continued until Irenaeus quoted the Pastorals ca. A.D. 185. Marcion, though an ardent Paulinist of ca. A.D. 140, did not include them in his canon and probably did not know of them. Admittedly, Tertullian, writing ca. A.D. 210, said that Marcion "rejected" them. But Tertullian did not for a moment doubt that Paul had written them, and so he will have inferred that Marcion's failure to include them in his collection of Paulines

must have been due to hostility towards them, not to ignorance of them. Tertullian, as shown above (p. 222), was quite ready to assert as fact what his premisses disposed him to believe.

In sum, even if the Pastorals existed when Polycarp wrote, they were not widely known and accepted as Pauline until late in the second century. In the second half of that century, Tatian accepted the letter to Titus but not 1 and 2 Timothy as genuinely Pauline.

33. "One could legitimately claim" of the author of the Pastorals that "his way of teaching doctrine is to quote liturgical and confessional formulae. . . . No attempt is made to work the material into a consistent doctrine" (Hanson, pp. 38–39, who justifies these views in the pages that follow). Furnish agrees that the religious standpoint of the Pastorals is "eclectic" rather than Pauline. Their author has made use of "very diverse concepts and traditions, both Christian and non-Christian" and "has made no effort to harmonize these, even when they are in tension, or to integrate them into some larger theological conception" (1993, p. 114).

34. See Räisänen 1987a for a very helpful account of the contradiction in Paul's thought. See also Räisänen 1997, chapter 2, and, re the Koran, chapter 7.

35. The so-called first epistle of Clement, which most scholars date at ca. A.D. 95, declares that Paul came "to the limit of the west" and, "bearing his testimony before kings and rulers, passed out of this world". Paul himself recorded (Rom. 15:24 and 28) that he intended to travel to Rome and Spain. Clement, who knew Paul's letter to the Romans (he paraphrases a passage from it) obviously inferred from it that he had carried out these travel plans, and that, since nothing more was heard from him, he had died in Spain.

36. In 2 Timothy Paul is represented as in prison at Rome, apparently expecting to be executed. He complains (4:11, 16) that all except "Luke" have abandoned him. Yet he is made to add final greetings from "all the brethren," some of whom he names. The previous reference to his isolation

thus does not ring true, and is more likely part of the author's attempt to portray him as the model apostle, steadfast to the end in the bleakest of circumstances. 'Luke' in this context does not designate the author of what we now call the gospel of Luke, which was still anonymous when the Pastorals were written. The earliest extant statements about its authorship are from the final decades of the second century, a full eighty years after it was written. Nevertheless, as we saw (above p. 36), this reference to 'Luke', together with the mention in Coloss. 4:14 of "Luke the beloved physician", contributed to the patristic theory that Luke-Acts were written by the Luke who was a companion of Paul.

37. Margaret Davies 1996a, pp. 116, 118; 1996b, pp. 20, 107, 109, 112–13.

38. J.C. VanderKam says of the ritual meal described in some of the scrolls that, however one interprets it, "its messianic character, the prominence of bread and wine, the fact that it was repeated regularly and its explicit eschatological associations do recall elements found in the New Testament treatments of the Lord's Supper" (1994, p. 175). He instances other overlaps of organizational and ritual practices, and of some major doctrinal tenets which suggest that "the Qumranites" and the early Christians were "children of a common parent tradition in Judaism" (p. 162). Such overlaps are only to be expected if, as Norman Golb has argued (1995), the scrolls were not written at Qumran but brought there for safe-keeping from libraries in Jerusalem shortly before the Roman attack on the city which culminated in its destruction in A.D. 70. On this basis, they can be understood to represent not the literature of a single and exclusive Qumran-based community, but a great variety of Jewish religious thinking from the first two centuries B.C. and the first half of the first century A.D. Golb shows that even scholars who hold to the view that the scrolls form the library of a Qumran sect have now begun to allow that some—even many—of them were brought from elsewhere

and represent a broader spectrum of religious ideas than can be ascribed to a single sect.

39. R.M. Price, reviewing J.Z. Smith in *The Journal of Higher Criticism* 3 (1996), pp. 140–41, 144.

40. I have argued this case in detail in *The Jesus Legend*, and it represents a departure from my earlier position that the Jesus of the gospels resulted purely from attempts to make the vaguely conceived earthly figure of the Pauline Jesus into something more definitely historical.

41. At Acts 2:22 Peter, addressing the Jews of Jerusalem, speaks of "Jesus of Nazareth" as "a man approved of God unto you by mighty works . . . which God did by him in the midst of you". At 10:38 he speaks of "Jesus of Nazareth" whom "God anointed with the Holy Ghost and with power, who went about doing good, healing all that were oppressed of the devil, for God was with him". Again, "this Jesus did God raise up", and hence "made him both Lord and Christ" (2:32, 36).

2. Miracles in the New Testament and Beyond

1. Cranfield 1988 believes that the following passages may well witness to knowledge of Jesus's virgin birth:

i. The Jews of Jesus's "own country" took offence at his pretensions on the ground that he was a familiar figure, known to them as no more than "the carpenter, the son of Mary", with brothers and sisters whom they knew equally well (Mk. 6: 3). Cranfield takes this failure to mention Jesus's father as a deliberate insult, meant to imply his illegitimacy, and as a hint from Mark that he himself knew quite well that Jesus had no human father. But in the situation envisaged by this narrative, the Jews may simply be represented as being familiar only with the mother, brothers and sisters, because the father was already dead. Mark had no traditions about Joseph, whom he never mentions. There is, however, a

textual variant to Mk. 6: 3 which designates Jesus as "the son
of the carpenter and of Mary". It is well attested, and could
be the original. If so, the change to what is now given in the
printed text could have been effected by a later copyist
familiar with the doctrine of the virgin birth who found it
inappropriate for Jesus to be called 'the carpenter's son' by
people who are represented as knowing him and his family
well.

ii. The Jews tell Jesus "We were not born of fornication" (Jn.
8:41). This again is taken by Cranfield as a charge that Jesus
himself was an illegitimate child, and as an indirect allusion
to what we must understand as the evangelist's own conviction that he was virgin born. In fact, the context shows that
the Jews are here saying: Abraham, even God, is our father,
so that we are God's people. There is no reference to Jesus's
birth.

iii. To those who believe in him, Jesus gave the power to become
children of God, "which were born not of blood, nor of the
will of the flesh, nor of the will of man, but of God" (Jn.
1:13). Cranfield realizes that to see any direct allegation of
virgin birth here would mean ascribing such a birth to all
believers. He nevertheless supposes that John is here "declaring that the birth of Christians, being bloodless and
rooted in God's will alone, followed the pattern of the birth
of Christ himself."

iv. At Rom. 1:3, Gal. 4:4 and Phil. 2:7, Paul uses the verb *ginomai*
(be born, become), not *gennaomai* (be begotten) of Jesus's
birth. But none of these three passages can be made to serve
Cranfield's purpose. In the first of them, Jesus is said to be
"born of the seed of David according to the flesh" (RV),
"descended from David" (RSV), "on the human level born of
David's stock" (NEB). This suggests that he had a human
father, not that his father was the Holy Ghost. (Even in the
gospels, it is not Mary who is descended from David.) In the
second passage, the phrase "born of a woman" echoes—surely deliberately—Job 14:1–2: "Man that is born of

a woman is of few days, and full of trouble. He cometh forth like a flower and is cut down; he fleeth also as a shadow and continueth not". In Galatians as in Job, the emphasis is on man's weakness and wretchedness. There is no suggestion of exalted status, as would be implied by birth from the Holy Ghost. In the third passage Paul, as we saw above (p. 50f), is saying that Jesus forwent his pre-existent supernatural status and "emptied himself, taking the form of a servant [or slave], being born in the likeness of men". Again, extreme humiliation, not exaltation, is implied.

2. Jesus was "about thirty years of age" in the fifteenth year of Tiberius's reign, A.D. 28–29 (Lk. 3:1–2 and 23). This places his birth either near the end of Herod's reign, or within three years of his death, which occurred in 4 B.C. Luke probably envisaged the earlier of these two possibilities, when Herod was still alive, for the whole birth and infancy narrative begins with "in the days of Herod the King" (1:5), and tells first how an angel announced that John the Baptist would be born to the aged Elisabeth. After this announcement—the precise interval is not indicated, but there is no suggestion that Herod had died in the meantime—Elisabeth duly conceived (1:24), and during her pregnancy addressed Mary as "the mother of my Lord", which surely implies that Mary too was pregnant at this time (1:42–43).

3. Schürer 1973, pp. 317, 416n, 417n. Appeal has been made to a register of the resources of the whole empire which Augustus, as a careful financier, compiled. Tacitus tells that it recorded "the strength of the citizens and allies under arms, the number of the fleets, protectorates and provinces; the taxes, direct and indirect [tributa aut vectigalia]; the needful disimbursements and customary bounties" (Annals, i, 11, Loeb library translation). Apologists have seen in this not only evidence for an imperial census, but even evidence that Augustus held censuses in the territories of client kings. In fact, however, the passage shows only his concern for sound financial administration (cf. Schürer, as cited, pp. 407–08 and n36 on p. 408).

4. Attempts by Christian apologists to make Quirinius governor of Syria in Herod's lifetime include adducing an inscription from Tivoli, which does not state any name, but records the career of "a legate" with the words: "[legatus pro praetori] divi Augusti iterum Syriam et Ph[oenicem optinuit]." This does not mean that the unnamed man was twice legate of Syria, but that his second legateship was that of Syria (Schürer, 1973, p. 258). Feldman quotes scholars who think the man was Lucius Calpurnius Piso, who was governor of Asia and later of Syria (1984a, p. 713). Syria was governed from 10/9 to 7/6 B.C. by Sentius Saturninus and from 7/6 to 4 B.C. by Quintilius Varus. This leaves no room for a governorship by Quirinius during the last years of Herod's reign, when Matthew and most probably Luke too require Jesus to have been born.

   Vogt supposes that not only the inscription from Tivoli but also "the short biographical sketch" which Tacitus gives of Quirinius suggest that he had been imperial legate in Syria in Herod's time, and "in this position had conducted a war against a tribe in the Taurus mountains" (1971, p. 5). Although no details are given of the "short biographical sketch", the reference can only be to *Annals*, iii, 48, where Quirinius is said to have subjugated the Homonadenses (Cilician brigands on the southern border of the province of Galatia). It is not said that he was legate of Syria at the time; indeed the war was presumably conducted from the north, from Galatia, not from Syria in the south; and according to Feldman (1984a, p. 712) it has been "convincingly shown" that he was governor of Galatia at the time.

5. Some have argued, for instance, that Josephus had in mind a *second* census, made only after Herod's death. That leaves us asking why he omitted such a notable event as the alleged census in Herod's lifetime. Others have tried to reconcile Luke with Josephus by suggesting alternative translations for Lk. 2:2. Instead of "this was the first enrolment, Quirinius being governor of Syria" (it was the first, and at the time Quirinius was governor), they propose: "This census was earlier than the one under Quirinius", or "This census was

before the governorship of Quirinius". Feldman has commented that these renderings necessitate an unparalleled
use of the Greek word *prōtos* ('first'), and also that it does
not make much sense to say that the census took place
earlier than when Quirinius was governing Syria rather
than stating who was governor at the time (1984a, p. 712).
Robin Lane Fox, who discusses the birth and infancy
narratives in some detail, calls these alternative translations "attempts to evade the meaning of the third Gospel's
Greek", and declares that nobody has ever entertained
them for non-doctrinal reasons (1991, pp. 29–30). *Prōtos*
can mean 'before' if it governs a following noun or pronoun
(in the genitive case): for instance Jn. 1:15, "he was before
(prōtos) me", i.e. 'first of me'. Luke, however, follows *prōtos*
with a participle phrase grammatically quite independent
of this *prōtos*.

Another way out of the problem is to take Luke as saying,
not that Quirinius was governor of Syria at the time, but that
he was "in charge" or "in office" there, but not as governor,
so that the reference could be to some 'office' he held in
Herod's time. The Roman Catholic scholar Fr. R.E. Brown
regards this as an "unlikely hypothesis", and as "another
ingenious attempt to save Lucan accuracy" (1979, p. 395n).
Also, in the updated 1993 edition of this book, he reviews
recent discussion of the proposals that Quirinius was twice
governor of Syria and that there were two censuses, and
concludes that they are "better given up" (p. 668).

Another argument has been that the relevant census took
place in two stages: the first in late B.C. will have consisted in
drawing up the electoral roll by requiring all persons to
register; the second followed only in A.D. 6, and consisted in
the official tax assessment. These two stages, it is claimed,
are distinguished by Josephus as *apographē* (registration)
and *apotimēsis* (assessment), and it is only the second that he
reports, whereas Luke is referring to the first. Unfortunately
for this view, Josephus uses these two terms to refer to
different aspects of the same situation: Quirinius, he says,
came to Judea to make an *assessment* of the property of the

Jews, who in consequence submitted to the *registration* of their property (*Ant.* 18:1–4).

6. J.T. Sanders (1966, p. 339)—a colleague of the E.P. Sanders to whose work I refer frequently in this book—explains the discrepancy between the two episodes in this way. But does it suffice to account for what R.M. Price calls "the stubborn fact" that "in Galatians Paul tells his readers that what he preached to them when he founded their church was not taught him by human predecessors", whereas in 1 Cor. 15:3 "he is depicted as telling his readers that what he preached to them when he founded their church was taught him by human predecessors" (1995, p. 78)? Price believes this verse to be a post-Pauline interpolation which represents Paul in the manner in which he is depicted in Acts, namely as subordinate to earlier Christian leaders—a dependence which the real Paul repudiates at Gal. 1:20 in the strongest terms as a distortion of the truth. In his carefully argued article, Price even sets aside the whole pericope of 1 Cor. 15:3–11 as interpolated. J.C. O'Neill had already called it "a later credal summary not written by Paul" (1972, p. 27 n6). It is admittedly included in all extant manuscripts, but, as Price points out (p. 71), none of these is earlier than the third century. Commentators often adduce 'lack of any shred of manuscript evidence' as sufficient to dispose of a hypothesis. They perhaps forget that, while there is, for instance, no manuscript evidence whatsoever for the omission of Chapter 21 of the fourth gospel, the view that it was written by the author of the other twenty is—in Haenchen's words—"as good as abandoned in today's critical scholarship" (1980, p. 594).

7. I discuss in detail the problems arising from what the NT says of the twelve in chapter 5 of *DJE*, and have also covered them briefly in *WWJ*, pp. 36–37. They are addressed briefly but persuasively by P. Vielhauer (1965, pp. 68–71). Guenther (1985) has restated the whole case for regarding the gospel twelve as unhistorical.

8. H. Conzelmann presses this point in his article 'Auferstehung Christi', in Galling (editor), 1957, (volume 1, p.

699). C.F. Evans discusses the matter in detail, saying: "There are passages in the New Testament which virtually ignore resurrection and pass straight to an exaltation to God or to his right hand". They give the impression that "exaltation is the primary and inclusive concept" and that "resurrection is subordinate and contained within it". Other passages, however, derive Jesus's lordship from his resurrection, while in yet others "the two conceptions of exaltation and resurrection jostle one another". Only when we come to Acts are the two firmly distinguished: "There the resurrection has the character of an interim, limited in purpose to providing visible proofs that Jesus is alive and a programme for the future, and limited in time to forty days, when it is succeeded by exaltation in the form of a further visible and describable event, the ascension, which brings the temporary resurrection period to a close" (Evans 1970, pp. 135–37). See also, more recently, the chapter 'Resurrection, Exaltation, and Ascension in Early Christianity' in Zwiep 1997, especially pp. 129–130, 143.

9. In the fourth gospel there is only one woman visitor to the tomb; in Matthew there are two, in Mark three, while Luke writes of "they" (24:1), referring to numerous women who had followed with Jesus from Galilee (23:49), identified earlier as three named persons and "many others" (8:2–3). Mary Magdalene is the only name common to all these empty tomb traditions.

10. Luke emphasizes, by means of repeated references to timing, that Jesus commanded his disciples to stay in Jerusalem on the same day as, according to the gospels, his tomb was discovered to be empty. The women make this discovery early in the morning (24:1–3); the Emmaus road appearance to two disciples occurs "that very day" (verse 13), and at supper on that day Jesus disappears from their sight (verses 29, 31). The two return to Jerusalem "at that same hour" (verse 33) and tell the eleven what they had experienced. Jesus then appears while they are giving this report (verse 36) and concludes his speech to them with the injunction to stay in the city.

11. M. Goulder, 'Did Jesus of Nazareth Rise from the Dead?', in Barton and Stanton 1994, pp. 65–66.

12. P. Baelz, reviewing the above symposium in *Theology*, 98 (1995), p. 305. What he has in mind is perhaps illustrated by Robert Morgan's contribution to it, which states that "most theologians have long since learned to distinguish between the reality of God's Yes to Jesus articulated in the metaphors [sic] of exaltation and resurrection, and the historicity of particular Easter traditions" (*The Resurrection*, as cited in the previous note, pp. 8–9). It seems good to Morgan "to call God's vindication of Jesus a mystery, like God's identification with Jesus in the incarnation, and to insist that how the disciples became convinced of it is a secondary question that cannot be answered for sure" (p. 12).

13. For example 'Erstvision' is 'first vision' (not 'first visit', p. 11); 'Rüsttag' is 'preparation day' (not 'day of rest', p. 19); 'Bestattung durch Juden' is 'burial by Jews' (not 'burial by James', p. 22). John Bowden, the translator, has been working himself too hard.

14. Linking Jesus's resurrection with a very uncritical evaluation of his ministry is now not uncommon. Thus J.A. Baker (formerly Bishop of Salisbury) maintains that the resurrection matters because of the kind of moral person Jesus was—a man who "went about doing good and healing all that were oppressed of the devil" (Acts 10:38). This was the person whom "God raised up the third day" (verse 40). According to Baker: "The nature of existence is such that the only credible God is one whose values are those exemplified in Jesus. If Herod the Great had risen from the dead, this would not have been tolerable to reason as a testimony to God. For a God who ratified monstrosity might explain the evil in the world; he could never satisfy us as a source of goodness" (1970, p. 278). John Barton comments, approvingly: "Thus the resurrection is evidence for what God himself is like. It shows that God is like Jesus. And that is very good news indeed" (*The Resurrection*, as cited in note 11 above, p. 113).

15. *Did Jesus Rise From the Dead? The Resurrection Debate*. Gary R. Habermas and Antony G.N. Flew, edited by T.L. Miethe, San Francisco: Harper and Row, 1987.

16. This theory was not published by Reimarus himself, in 1778 as Ladd (1979, p. 134) alleges, for he died in 1768, and parts of his manuscript were published only posthumously by G.E. Lessing as 'Fragments of an Unnamed Writer' between 1774 and 1778. Knowing that there would be a furore, Lessing withheld the author's name from consideration for his family.

17. I discuss the 'swoon theory' in *Religious Postures*, pp. 36–37, and Schonfield's *The Passover Plot* in *JEC*, pp. 325–28.

18. For instance, in Acts 2:26 Peter 'proves' Jesus's resurrection by quoting, as a prophecy of it, the Greek (Septuagint) of Psalm 16, where both the wording and the sense differ from the Hebrew. In this latter, the Psalmist says "my flesh shall dwell in safety", meaning that he will not die prematurely. Only in the Greek version does he speak "in hope" of deliverance from the corruption of death. Similarly, at Acts 13:34 the "men of Israel" are regaled with the Septuagint of Isaiah 55, where the Hebrew would not give the required sense. An even more striking example is Acts 1:19–20, where Peter, addressing 120 Aramaic-speaking Jewish Christians in Jerusalem, refers to Aramaic as "the language of the inhabitants", and goes on to elucidate, in Greek for their benefit, one of its words, before presenting them with a proof from prophecy taken from the Septuagint, the wording of which has been adapted so as to make his point. In Acts 15:13ff James appeals to Christian Jews of Jerusalem by quoting a Septuagint distortion of the Hebrew original. And his purpose is, by such means and with such an audience to justify the mission to the gentiles. In the original, Yahweh promises to restore the Davidic kingdom to its former glory, so that his people may then possess what is left of the neighbouring kingdom of Edom, and also "all the nations that were once named mine" (Amos 9:12). In the Septuagint this promise of conquest is transformed into a universalist

message: Yahweh declares that the kingdom's restoration will enable "all the gentiles upon whom my name is called" to "earnestly seek me". F.F. Bruce calls this "a complete spiritualization of the passage" (1988, p. 294). It is in fact a flat contradiction of its original anti-universalistic implications and, as Haenchen justly notes (1968b, pp. 389, 401), betrays that the real speaker where it is quoted in Acts is not James, the Jewish Jerusalem Christian, but Luke, the Hellenistic gentile. Haenchen's commentary shows how heavily these speeches in Acts rely on the Septuagint, and how frequently they need to distort the text even of that, as well as to interpret it arbitrarily, so as to extract the required meaning.

19. That this is the case was clearly stated by Fridrichsen (1972, p. 35); cf. Wrede 1907, p. 91, and as quoted in note 26 to chapter 1 above.

20. Peter declares that "whoever shall call on the name of the Lord shall be saved," and urges his audience to "be baptised in the name of Jesus Christ" (Acts 2:21,38). Speaking the name summons the deity (as it would a man), and so elicits his protection. Cf. the still valuable Heitmüller 1903 and—for similar ideas in ancient Egypt—Budge 1899, p. 157. See also Wells 1993, pp. 129–130.

21. Gibbon notes (1910, I, 458–59, chapter 15) that the "awful ceremony" of expelling the demon "was usually performed in a public manner, and in the presence of a great number of spectators; . . . and the vanquished daemon was heard to confess that he was one of the fabled gods of antiquity, who had impiously usurped the adoration of mankind." This idea that pagan cults were demonic naturally encouraged persecution of them once Christianity had gained ascendancy.

22. I.M. Lewis 1970, pp. 294, 296, 308–09; cf. p. 296.

23. In 1987, some readers of the *Biblical Archaeology Review* wrote to its editor expressing dismay that the journal had published a review of H.D. Betz's 1986 English translation of the Greek magical papyri. One such letter warned: "The

realm of the supernatural is very real. Don't be deceived. And don't offer it to your readers as something that needs to be understood and studied" (Quoted in Garrett 1989, pp. 1–2).

24. 2 Samuel 24 tells that the Lord, angry with the people, ordered David to number them, then punished him for doing so by sending a plague which killed seventy thousand of them, and finally "repented him of the evil". 1 Chronicles 21 recasts this story so as to exonerate Yahweh. Here it is Satan who "moved David to number Israel". This seems to be the one instance in the whole of the OT where Satan figures as a power that tempts man to sin; and he is clearly given this role because it had come to be felt unbecoming to assign it to Yahweh. Elaine Pagels's 1991 article gives an informative account of the origin and role of Satan.

25. Angra Mainyu (alias Ahriman), the powerful counter-deity of Zoroastrianism, "commands a host of demons who spread sin, death, disease, and every kind of affliction among the human inhabitants of this earth." These beings are "incessantly at work to ruin the ordered universe which Ormazd"—the good spirit—"struggles to uphold" (Cohn 1970, p. 5).

3. Teachings and Non-Miraculous Actions of Jesus Ascribable to the Early Church

1. France (1971, p. 141), however, supposes Jesus at his trial to be speaking not of his second coming to Earth, but of a coming to God (as specified in Daniel 7:13) to receive power and glory; and this can only mean his exaltation at his resurrection. But if this were so, one would expect the 'sitting' of Mk. 14:62 to *follow* the coming: Jesus would first come to God and only then sit at his right hand. Possibly France is trying to avoid the difficulties which arise from Mark's statement that the Sanhedrists would witness Jesus's parousia. Difficulties there are, as we cannot suppose that

Mark thought him deluded and yet faithfully recorded his delusion. Luke was conscious of the difficulties, and reworded the saying so that the Sanhedrists are not told they will see anything (Lk. 22:69 reads: "But from henceforth shall the Son of man be seated at the right hand of the power of God"). As for Mark, he may have felt that the setting he gave to the saying is not inappropriate, in that the Sanhedrists will have 'seen' Jesus in power when the veil of their temple (a curtain which screened off the Holy of Holies from view) was rent as he died (15:38), making their holy place no longer holy. Matthew built on this by giving them even more to see on this occasion: the earth is shaken, rocks split, and the dead within them raised.

The reconstruction of the history of the Son of Man tradition remains one of the most controversial subjects in NT studies. A useful survey of the history of the discussion is given by Adela Yarbro Collins in J.J. Collins's 1993 commentary on Daniel in the Hermeneia Series (pp. 90ff). Mildly amusing is her unease with the phrase 'Son of man'—problematic, she says, "with regard to the issue of gender-inclusive language". She thinks that in "contexts involving the proclamation of the gospel", an alternative such as 'Child of Humanity' might be preferable.

2. Wright adumbrates these views in his 1992b, and states them fully in his 1996. Obvious predecessors in this thinking are Hoskyns and Davey and G.B. Caird (on whom see my *Belief and Make-Believe*, pp. 112–13). This whole argument fails to do justice to the development of Jewish thinking (outlined in chapter 6 of *WWJ*) from the OT prophets to the book of Daniel, and further to the kind of apocalyptic literature typified in 1 Enoch. On all this see Schürer 1979, pp. 492ff, and D.S. Russell 1961. J.J. Collins 1997 also gives a very helpful survey.

3. It was the Scythian monk Dionysius Exiguus who, in the sixth century, introduced the B.C.–A.D. dating, replacing the system that had been established by the pagan emperor Diocletian. In the eighth century the Venerable Bede did much to establish the new system.

4. Käsemann, for instance, thinks it "quite impossible to extract from our Gospels anything resembling an historical sequence or even a biographical development." The "individual sayings and stories" served religious, not historical interests, and so "the overwhelming mass" of the tradition "cannot be called authentic" (1964, p. 59). "While we can say with certainty that the great bulk of the tradition does not enable us to lay hold of the historical Jesus, equally we can say that even the most highly perfected procedures of historical science permit us to make on this point only very approximate estimates of probability" (p. 98). The material is replete with crass contradictions: "It is incomprehensible to me how anyone can reconcile the eschatology of the Fourth Gospel with that of Revelation" (p. 102). And some of the material is obviously worthless: "What kind of tradition is it which can quite happily allow canonical authority to Jewish legends about the fight between Michael and Satan for the body of Moses . . . ?" (p. 103, with reference to verse 9 of the epistle of Jude).

5. Schmiedel, art. 'Gospels', para. 139 in Cheyne and Black.

4. The Earliest Non-Christian Testimony

1. Chapter 3 of *The Jesus Legend* where I show that it is doubtful whether Thallus referred to Christianity at all, and whether, if he did, he was writing early enough to do more than merely reproduce what he found in Christian tradition. This is conceded in France 1986, p. 24.

2. Origen, *Contra Celsum*, i, 47; repeated in his *Commentary on Matthew*, 10:17.

3. P. Winter, 'Josephus on Jesus and James', in Schürer 1973, p. 432.

4. On p. 158 Stanton suggests "led astray" many Jews as an alternative rendering. He is perhaps prompted by Charlesworth, who suggests the rendering "stirred up many Jews" and claims that the Greek verb here (*epagō*) "has a pejorative

innuendo" (1989, pp. 91, 100 n26). Liddell and Scott's *Greek-English Lexicon* does not bear this out, but translates the middle voice used here as 'bring to oneself', 'bring in as allies', 'bring over to oneself, win over'. When used in the sense of 'to bring something (often something bad) upon someone', the 'something' has to be specified (for example bring grief, danger, destruction, blood, persecution upon someone.) There is no such specification here in the Greek of the *Testimonium*, and to supply it, by introducing the word 'trouble' in the English rendering, is gratuitous.

5. Zeitlin 1931, pp. 62–64; Eusebius, *Ecclesiastical History*, iii, 33.

6. The extract from H.G. Wells occurs at the point in his account of world history where he is dealing with religious development under the Romans and so could not avoid giving his opinion of Jesus. He does not accord him any supernatural status, but simply echoes the kind of eulogy that has been formulated again and again both by Christians and by many others. The extract from Einstein is no more than an almost indignant repudiation of the suggestion that the Jesus of the gospels might be a mythical personage; and this is not unlikely from a non-Christian. Indeed, apologists commonly stress how few, even of those outside the faith, have denied his historicity. The passage from Rousseau does suggest that Jesus was more than human, but Rousseau was not altogether outside Christianity. Brought up as a Protestant, he converted to Catholicism in 1728, but reverted in 1754. He held that all who do not believe in God or in a future state with rewards and punishments should be banished, or killed if after professing these doctrines they behaved as if they did not believe them (Morley 1886, I, 220–21; II, 176). Hume, who knew him well, characterized him as having "a hankering after the Bible" (Quoted by Wollheim in the Introduction to his 1963, p. 28). Finally, the statement by Napoleon was made in St. Helena where, as Pieter Geyl has reminded us, he "set about the task of shaping his reputation for posterity" and gave a self-portrait

with "nought but unblemished beauty, endearing humanity, greatness and virtue" (1964, p. 23). He did not wish to go down as sympathetic to atheism, and had two priests come to the island where mass was said every Sunday. Two days before he died he received extreme unction. His will begins: "I die in the Catholic religion in which I was born", and goes on to express the hope that his son would become a good Christian (Lührs 1939, pp. 7, 19, 23–24).

I can but repeat that if Josephus had believed all that the *Testimonium* represents him as saying about Jesus he would not have restricted his remarks to this paragraph of some ten lines. The same is not true of the almost obbligato hat-doffing from H.G. Wells. Einstein's words about Jesus's "personality" accord with other statements he made about him. Rousseau was obsessed with religion and was not outside Christianity; and Napoleon at the end a professed Catholic.

7. I discuss the views of both Bammel and Charlesworth on the *Testimonium* in *Belief and Make-Believe*, pp. 143–48. See *Ibid.*, pp. 107–09 for the Koran's denial that Jesus was put to death. This denial derived from aberrant Christian teaching, according to which suffering of any kind involves change and so implies imperfection, and therefore could not have been experienced by Jesus.

8. See, for instance, Morton Smith's review of Pines: "That Josephus could have said Jesus 'was perhaps the Messiah' is hardly credible. The confused reports of shady sources that precede (and also follow) the passage in Agapius do not inspire confidence, nor does the attribution of the passage to Josephus's work *On the Governance of the Jews*; 'governance' has to be explained [by Pines] as a corruption of a mistranslation of 'antiquities'. The process of citation from memory and of multiple translation—from Greek to Syriac and from Syriac to Arabic—that Pines supposes (p. 23) could occasion incalculable errors. . . . The passage . . . is the sort of thing that might have been written by a fourth-century (Jewish?) neo-Platonist or Manichean, trying to fit both

Jesus and Judaism into some universal religion" (1972, pp. 441–42).

9. The best known of the forgeries is a Latin correspondence between Seneca and Paul, first attested by Jerome and held by him and by Augustine to be authentic. Details in Hennecke 1965, pp. 133ff.

5. Ethics in the New Testament and in the History of Christianity

1. Jesus threatens great misery to those who do not receive his missionaries (Mt. 10:14–15) and, in the appendix to Mark, damnation to those who do not believe his gospel (Mk. 16:16). He declares that all who "blaspheme against the Holy Spirit" shall never be forgiven (Mk. 3:29). Acts 3:23 has it that a Jew who is not converted to Jesus "shall be utterly destroyed". Cf. Acts 13:39–41. No wonder Jews have been persecuted in Christendom!

2. See, for instance, McBrien's exposition of Catholic teaching (1994), p. 1176: "What the New Testament says about hell is to be interpreted according to the same principles which govern our interpretation of apocalyptic literature. Apocalypticism is too individualistic, too much oriented to worlds beyond this one, too elitist or Gnostic in its approach to revelation and salvation, and too fascinated with the esoteric and the ominous. Hence what the New Testament says about hell is not to be taken literally". McBrien quotes a 1992 *Catechism of the Catholic Church* to the effect that the "chief punishment" of hell is no more than "eternal separation from God".

3. General Synod 1995, p. 199.

4. Arnobius adds: "Since to accept the accounts as they stand is shameful and disgraceful, recourse is had to this expedient, that one thing is substituted for another, and a more becoming interpretation is squeezed out of something disgusting" (Quoted from *Adversus Nationes*, 5, 33, in Ramsey 1993, p. 201).

5. See, for instance, the protest by the Jewish scholar C.G. Montefiore (1910, pp. 53, 91) against this way of contrasting Judaism and Christianity. Some Christian scholars nevertheless continue to endorse this same contrast. J. Riches, for instance maintains that the term 'kingdom of God' was traditionally associated with "the destruction of God's enemies", whereas for Jesus, "God is not a God of battles, a warrior destroying his enemies but a Father who forgives and commands his children to forgive" (1980, pp. 103–04). Jesus, then, "reworked and renewed the religious traditions which he inherited", which were in a "relatively impoverished state" (pp. 106, 108). Against this, it has been shown that "the non-retaliatory ethics of the New Testament stand solidly in the tradition of the non-retaliatory ethics in early Judaism" (Zerbe 1993, p. 294; cf. Räisänen 1997, pp. 184f and the references to relevant early Jewish literature in his n71 on p. 283). Those who contrast Christianity with the truly hateful elements in the OT are apt to overlook the fact that eminent Christians have appealed to them in order to justify their own hateful conduct. When Calvin had Servetus burnt, he pointed to Deuteronomy 13. Riches's view of Jesus does not do justice to the fact that, in the gospels, although he is nice enough to those who accept his message about the kingdom and his own role in it, he rejects in God's name those who do not: "He that denieth me in the presence of men shall be denied in the presence of the angels of God" (Lk. 12:9). "Whosoever shall deny me before men, him I will also deny before my Father which is in heaven" (Mt. 10:33). Räisänen comments: "As so often happens, love seems to be converted to threats if the message is not accepted" (1997, p. 184).

6. Quoted from Tertullian's *De Praescriptione Haereticorum*, 7, by Ramsey (1993), p. 210. Ramsey adds that Jerome and Augustine likewise inveighed against learning, or were at least suspicious of it, even though all three were intellectuals. Cf. Gibbon, 1910, I, 465: "The acquisition of knowledge, the exercise of our reason or fancy, and the cheerful flow of unguarded conversation may employ the leisure of a liberal

mind. Such amusements, however, were rejected with ab-
horrence, or admitted with the utmost caution, by the
severity of the fathers, who despised all knowledge that was
not useful to salvation, and who considered all levity of
discourse as a criminal abuse of the gift of speech". The
severity of the Fathers is well documented in Ingvild Saelid
Gilhus's 1997 study of laughter in the history of religion.

7. In *After the Deluge* (1987), a volume of essays by various
hands and introduced by himself, the Anglican priest (as he
then was) and broadcaster Dr. William Oddie deplores the
view that man's understanding of himself and of his place in
nature depends entirely on his "unaided observation and
reason" (p. 25). He believes that, without faith as the starting
point, "the achievements of autonomous reason are void".
Reason is to be made "subject to the authority of the
Christian revelation", subject to "God's own self-disclosure
conveyed by Holy Scripture" (pp. 9, 32). In the same
volume, Roger Beckwith, "widely regarded as a leading
spokesman for the Evangelical wing of the Church of
England" (p. vii), contrasts "self-sufficient human wisdom,
which is really foolishness", with "the divine wisdom of
revelation, known only to humble faith" (p. 106). There is
little humility in what is said in this volume of the views of
Christians who are less beholden to scripture and have less
faith in faith. Oddie has recently transferred his allegiance to
the Roman Catholic church.

8. "Metropolitan Nikolaj, the highest-ranking church official in
Bosnia, has publicly endorsed the architects of the ethnic-
cleansing policy as followers of 'the hard road of Christ', . . .
and Serbian priests have blessed militias on their return
from kill-and-plunder expeditions" (Hays 1997, p. 318).

9. Details in Morton Smith's 1988 paper. Margaret Davies finds
the Pastoral epistles particularly offensive on this matter:
"They exhibit complete complacency to the cruelty of
slavery and to the dangerous moral and physical conditions
in which slaves might be forced to live". They "endorse the
cruelty of Graeco-Roman society without reflection.

Through many centuries this teaching supported Christian slave owners and merchants in their inhuman and irreligious practices" (1996b, p. 89).

10. Trevelyan 1944, p. 495. Hugh Thomas emphasizes the important contribution of the Quakers, once they were converted to the movement for abolishing the slave trade. They had earlier "participated in the trade, and so knew exactly what it was they were up against" (1997, p. 798).

11. Hugh Thomas's detailed study (1997) shows that the slave trade was repeatedly defended also on the ground that the economic prosperity of a port such as Liverpool depended on it, that its abolition would result in mass unemployment, and that its critics were fanciful idealists with no first-hand experience of conditions on the vessels which transported slaves or on the slave plantations of the New World. He illustrates the ethics of the trade with the example (pp. 488–89) of the Liverpool slaveship *Zong*, which sailed in 1781 with 442 slaves from São Tomé. The ship lost its way, water became short, and slaves, confined in the usual appalling conditions, were falling sick and dying. The captain told his officers that, if the slaves died naturally, the loss would be suffered by the owners, whereas if on some pretext they were thrown into the sea, the underwriters would be the losers. 133 slaves were duly thrown overboard, even though the water shortage had not become acute, and was being alleviated by rainfall. In the upshot, the insurers refused to pay up, and were then sued by the owners. The right to kill the slaves was not in question, and the issue before the court was whether it had been done from necessity. The Solicitor-General deplored what he called any "pretended appeal to humanity" from outsiders to the case.

Thomas adds (p. 787) that Turner exhibited his painting *Slave Ship*, depicting slavers throwing overboard dead and dying slaves, in 1840. The Atlantic slave trade was by then nearly at an end, but slavery itself survived until the late nineteenth century.

12. Bruce argues that America still has a strong religious culture because it is a society made up of immigrant groups, each one of which has retained the religion it brought with it, initially as a means of easing the strains of transition to a new environment (since religion is one of the few sources of cohesive identity for a migrating people) and subsequently as a means of sustaining group solidarity in the face of other groups in the new territory. The large size of the United States and the relative autonomy of each State allows a good deal of freedom to an individual religious group to dominate a particular area, even to create there a 'ghetto' strongly critical of the culture of neighbouring areas. The liberal mainstream churches, on the other hand, are much more open to contact with secular forces, and as a result the children of their members tend to become so secularized as to defect; whereas the children of the highly conservative groups are brought up in relative isolation from what is secular, and so are much more likely to remain within the faith. Hence the present strength of these conservative groups, and the weakness of the liberal churches (Bruce 1996, particularly chapter 6, 'America and God').

Conclusion: Reason and Tolerance

1. John Bowden, Appendix to his English translation of Gerd Lüdemann, (1997), pp. 146, 151, 160.

2. G.N. Stanton, 'Jesus of Nazareth: A Magician and a False Prophet Who Deceived God's People?', in Green and Turner 1994, p. 165n.

3. See E.P. Sanders's well-argued account: 'Paul as Apostle of Christ and Member of Israel', in Sanders 1983, pp. 171ff.

4. For details, see Courcelle 1963.

5. Kümmel mentions Wrede's "influential little book on Paul" of 1904 as "the first to draw the consequences of a radically historical representation of the apostle". He quotes Wrede as saying that "the moral majesty of Jesus, his purity and his

piety, his ministry among his people, his manner as a
prophet, the whole concrete ethical-religious content of his
earthly life, signifies for Paul's Christology—nothing
whatever . . . Paul's faith had been achieved through a 'revelation', and in consequence he was able to apprehend and
interpret the vision of Jesus by means of ideas about Christ
whose origin was quite independent of Jesus the man"
(Kümmel 1973, pp. 295, 296, 298. Cf. note 26 to chapter 1, p.
268 above).

6. For trenchant criticism of the Bible's accounts of David and
Solomon, and of the "woeful record" of Biblical scholarship
in taking these accounts at face value, see Redford 1992, pp.
300–311.

7. P.R. Davies has defended his views much more fully in his
1995.

8. The rubric under which J.A.T. Robinson discusses critical
views in his 1977 is "the cynicism of the foolish". He writes
dismissively of what he considers to be unduly sceptical
"assumptions" which have "tended to dominate some of the
most widely read paperback commentaries" (p. 25), but
does not name Dennis Nineham's *Mark*, which is the work
he obviously had principally in mind. He shows no such
reticence towards less critical members of the theological
fraternity: C.H. Dodd and Joachim Jeremias are named in
the index of his book, with numerous references to pages of
his text where their views are represented. In commenting
(pp. 13–15) on two of my books (*JEC* and *DJE*) he avoids
naming either me or them, and so gives readers no opportunity to consult them. He does not even specify what he
designates my "chief source", which he calls "an old encyclopaedia published some seventy years earlier, which even
in its day could hardly be said to represent a particularly
balanced judgement and which no student would now
dream of consulting as an authority". The reader will
naturally suppose that I had based my case on out of date
editions of *Chambers* or *Britannica*. What I actually did was
to draw extensively (not 'chiefly') from certain articles in

Cheyne and Black's *Encyclopaedia Biblica*—articles written
with commendable candour by theologians who believed
that they were serving Christianity by clearing away what the
evidence had shown to be indefensible positions. One can
safely ignore the scholarship of the past if one is quite sure
that what is worthwhile in it has been fully assimilated in the
present. That is certainly not the case apropos of the virgin
birth, the resurrection, and other key issues discussed in
relevant articles of the *Biblica*. A pleasing contrast to Robinson's technique is Professor Kenneth Grayston's good-
natured quip in his generous review of *JEC* in *The Methodist
Recorder:* "The *Encyclopaedia Biblica* rides again".

Bibliography

ABBREVIATIONS

ABC	*Anchor Bible Commentary*
ABRL	*Anchor Bible Reference Library*
ANRW	*Aufstieg und Niedergang der römischen Welt*
ATR	*Anglican Theological Review*
CBQ	*Catholic Biblical Quarterly*
ET	*Expository Times*
HTR	*Harvard Theological Review*
JBL	*Journal of Biblical Literature*
JHC	*Journal of Higher Criticism*
JSOT	*Journal for the Study of the Old Testament*
JTS	*Journal of Theological Studies*
NCB	*New Century Bible*
Nov Test	*Novum Testamentum*
NTS	*New Testament Studies*
PAPS	*Proceedings of the American Philosophical Society*
SCM	Student Christian Movement
SJT	*Scottish Journal of Theology*
SOAS	*School of Oriental and African Studies* (University of London)
SPCK	Society for Promoting Christian Knowledge
Th R	*Theologische Rundschau*
VC	*Vigiliae Christianae*
ZNW	*Zeitschrift für neutestamentliche Wissenschaft*
ZPE	*Zeitschrift für Papyrologie und Epigraphik*

Aland, K. 1961. The Problem of Anonymity and Pseudonymity in Christian Literature of the First Two Centuries. *JTS* 12, 39–49.

Alexander, L. 1993. *The Preface to Luke's Gospel.* Cambridge: Cambridge University Press.

Alexander, P.S. 1986. Incantations and Books of Magic. In Schürer, 342–379.

Alexander, W.M. 1902. *Demonic Possession in the New Testament.* Edinburgh: Clark.

Allison, D.C., Jr. 1982. The Pauline Epistles and the Synoptic Gospels: The Pattern of the Parallels. *NTS* 28, 1–32.

Anderson, H. 1976. *The Gospel of Mark* (NCB). London: Oliphants.

Arnold, C.E. 1989. *Ephesians: Power and Magic.* Cambridge: Cambridge University Press.

Aune, D.E. 1980. Magic in Early Christianity. *ANRW* II, 23(2), 1507–1557.

Baker, J.A. 1970. *The Foolishness of God.* London: Darton, Longman, and Todd.

Barnes, T.D. 1994. Pagan Perceptions of Christianity. In *From Eusebius to Augustine* (Aldershot: Variorum); 232–243.

Barr, J. 1981. *Fundamentalism.* Second edition. London: SCM.

———. 1988. 'Abba' and the Familiarity of Jesus' Speech. *Theology* 91, 173–79. A less technical version of Barr's 'Abba isn't "Daddy"', *JTS* 39 (1988), 28–47.

———. 1992. *The Garden of Eden and the Hope of Immortality.* London: SCM.

Barrett, C.K. 1963. *The Pastoral Epistles.* Oxford: Clarendon.

———. 1970. *The Holy Spirit and the Gospel Tradition.* Fifth impression. London: SPCK.

———. 1974. Pauline Controversies in the Post-Pauline Period. *NTS* 20, 229–245.

Barton, S., and G. Stanton (editors). 1994. *The Resurrection: Essays in Honour of Leslie Houlden.* London: SPCK.

Bauer, W. 1972. *Orthodoxy and Heresy in Earliest Christianity.* English translation. London: SCM.

Beare, F.W. 1955. The Ministry in the New Testament Church. *ATR* 37, 3–19.

———. 1964. *The Earliest Records of Jesus.* Oxford: Blackwell.

Berger, K. 1988. Neutestamentliche Theologien. *Th R* 53, 354–370.

Bernhardt, R. 1994. *Christianity Without Absolutes.* English translation. London: SCM.

Bernheim, P.A. 1997. *James, Brother of Jesus*. English translation. London: SCM.

Bettenson, H. 1956. *The Early Christian Fathers*. London: Oxford University Press.

Beversluis, J. 1985. *C.S. Lewis and the Search for a Rational Religion*. Grand Rapids: Eerdmans.

Blackburn, B.L. 1994. The Miracles of Jesus. In Chilton, 353–394.

Blaiklock, E.M. 1983. *Jesus Christ: Man or Myth*. Homebush West, NSW (Australia): Anzea.

Bockmuehl, M. 1994. *This Jesus*. Edinburgh: Clark.

Borg, M.J. 1994. *Jesus in Contemporary Scholarship*. Valley Forge: Trinity.

Boring, M.E. 1991. *The Continuing Voice of Jesus: Christian Prophecy and the Gospel Tradition*. Louisville: Westminster.

Bowden, J. 1988. *Jesus: The Unanswered Questions*. London: SCM.

Brown, R.E. 1971. *The Gospel According to John* (ABC). London: Chapman.

———. 1979. *The Birth of the Messiah*. Garden City, NY: Image Books.

———. 1993. *The Birth of the Messiah*. Reprint of the above, with a supplement on post-1979 discussion (ABRL).

———. 1994. *The Death of the Messiah* (ABRL). 2 volumes with continuous pagination. London: Chapman.

Bruce, F.F. 1952. *The Acts of the Apostles: Greek Text With Introduction and Commentary*. Second edition. London: Tyndale.

———. 1988. *The Book of Acts*. Revised edition. Grand Rapids: Eerdmans.

Bruce, S. 1990a. *The Rise and Fall of the New Christian Right: Conservative Protestant Politics in America, 1978–1988*. Oxford: Clarendon.

———. 1990b. *Pray TV: Televangelism in America*. London: Routledge.

———. 1995. *Religion in Modern Britain*. Oxford: Oxford University Press.

——. 1996. *Religion in the Modern World*. Oxford: Oxford University Press.

Buchanan, G.W. 1965. Jesus and the Upper Class. *Nov Test* 7, 195–209.

Budd, Susan. 1977. *Varieties of Unbelief: Atheists and Agnostics in English Society, 1850–1960*. London: Heinemann.

Budge, E.A.W. 1899. *Egyptian Magic*. London: Kegan Paul.

Burckhardt, J. 1989. *The Age of Constantine the Great*. English translation. New York: Dorset.

Cadbury, H.J. 1933. The Summaries in Acts. In *The Beginnings of Christianity*, volume 5, *Additional Notes*, edited by K. Lake and H.J. Cadbury. London: Macmillan, 393–402.

——. 1951. Mixed Motives in the Gospels. *PAPS* 95, 117–124.

Caragounis, C.C. 1990. *Peter and the Rock*. Berlin and New York: De Gruyter.

Carnley, P. 1987. *The Structure of Resurrection Belief*. Oxford: Clarendon.

Chapman, C. 1988. *Christianity on Trial*. Tring: Lion.

Charlesworth, J.H. 1989. *Jesus Within Judaism*. London: SPCK.

——. (editor). 1992. *The Messiah: Developments in Earliest Judaism and Christianity*. Minneapolis: Fortress.

Cheyne, T.K., and J.S. Black (editors). 1899–1907. *Encyclopaedia Biblica*. 4 volumes. London: Black.

Chilton, B., et al. (editors). 1994. *Studying the Historical Jesus*. Leiden: Brill.

Cohn, N. 1970. The Myth of Satan and His Human Servants. In Douglas, 3–16.

Collins, J.J. 1977. *The Apocalyptic Vision of the Book of Daniel*. Missoula: Scholars.

——. 1992. The Son of Man in First-Century Judaism. *NTS* 38, 448–466.

——. 1993. *Daniel*. Hermeneia series. Minneapolis: Fortress.

——. 1997. *Apocalypticism in the Dead Sea Scrolls*. London: Routledge.

Conzelmann, H. 1971. *Geschichte des Urchristentums*. Göttingen: Vandenhoeck and Ruprecht.

Courcelle, P. 1963. Anti-Christian Arguments and Christian Platonism: From Arnobius to St. Ambrose. In Momigliano, 151–192.

Cranfield, C.E.B. 1988. Some Reflections on the Subject of the Virgin Birth. *SJT* 41, 177–189.

Cullmann, O. 1962. *Peter*. English translation of second edition. London: SCM.

Dancy, J.C. 1972. *The Shorter Books of the Apocrypha*. Cambridge: Cambridge University Press.

Davies, Margaret. 1996a. *The Pastoral Epistles* (Epworth Commentaries). London: Epworth.

———. 1996b: *The Pastoral Epistles* (New Testament Guides). Sheffield: Academic Press.

Davies, P.R. 1995. *In Search of 'Ancient Israel'*. Second edition. Sheffield: Academic Press.

———. 1997. 'Ancient Israel' and History. *ET* 108, 211–12.

Davies, W.D., and D.C. Allison. 1988 and 1991. *A Critical and Exegetical Commentary on the Gospel According to St. Matthew*. 2 volumes. Edinburgh: Clark.

Davis, S.T. 1993. *Risen Indeed: Making Sense of the Resurrection*. London: SPCK Grand Rapids: Eerdmans.

Day, J. (editor) 1995. *Wisdom in Ancient Israel*. Cambridge: Cambridge University Press.

De Jonge, M. 1966. The Use of the Word 'Anointed' in the Time of Jesus. *Nov Test* 8, 132–148.

———. 1988. *Christology in Context: The Earliest Christian Response to Jesus*. Philadelphia: Westminster.

Dibelius, M. 1956. *Studies in the Acts of the Apostles*. Edited by H. Greeven, English translation. London: SCM.

———. 1971. *From Tradition to Gospel*. English translation. Cambridge: Clarke (reprinted 1982).

Dihle, A. 1971. The Graeco-Roman Background. In *Jesus in his Time*, edited by H.J. Schultz. English translation. London: SPCK, 10–18.

Dingle, H. 1931. *Science and Human Experience*. London: Williams and Norgate.

Dodd, C.H. 1952. *According to the Scriptures: The Sub-Structure of New Testament Theology*. Welwyn (Herts): Nisbet (fourth reprint 1961).

———. 1968. *The Interpretation of the Fourth Gospel*. Cambridge: Cambridge University Press.

———. 1971. *The Founder of Christianity*. London: Collins.

Doherty, E. 1997. The Jesus Puzzle: Pieces in a Puzzle of Christian Origins. *JHC* 4(2), 68–102.

Douglas, Mary (editor). 1970. *Witchcraft, Confessions, and Accusations*. London: Tavistock.

Dunn, J.D.G. 1989. *Christology in the Making*. Second edition. London: SCM.

———. 1994. Jesus Tradition in Paul. In Chilton, 155–178.

Ehrman, B.D. 1993. *The Orthodox Corruption of Scripture: The Effect of Early Christological Controversies on the Text of the New Testament*. Oxford: Oxford University Press.

———. (editor). 1995. *The Text of the New Testament in Contemporary Research*. Grand Rapids: Eerdmans.

Ellegård, A. 1993. Theologians as Historians. *Scandia* 59, 169–204.

Elliott, J.K. 1994a. Review of C. Thiede's *The Earliest Gospel Manuscript?* (Exeter: Paternoster, 1992) in *Nov Test* 36, 98–100.

———. 1994b. Review of B.D. Ehrman 1993 (as cited above) in *Nov Test* 36, 405–06.

Elliott, J.K., and the late I. Moir, 1995. *Manuscripts and the Text of the New Testament: An Introduction for English Readers*. Edinburgh: Clark.

Ellis, E.E. 1957. *Paul's Use of the Old Testament*. Edinburgh: Oliver and Boyd.

Esler, P.F. 1987. *Community and Gospel in Luke-Acts*. Cambridge: Cambridge University Press.

Evans, C.F. 1970. *Resurrection and the New Testament*. London: SCM.

———. 1971. *Is 'Holy Scripture' Christian? And Other Questions*. London: SCM.

———. 1990. *Saint Luke*. London: SCM/Philadelphia: Trinity.

Feldman, L.H. 1984a. *Josephus and Modern Scholarship, 1937–1980*. Berlin and New York: De Gruyter.

———. 1984b. Flavius Josephus Revisited. *ANRW* II, 21, 2, especially pp. 821–838: Josephus on the Origins of Christianity.

Feldman, L.H., and G. Hata (editors) 1987. *Josephus, Judaism, and Christianity*. Detroit: Wayne State University Press.

Feldman, L.H., and G. Hata (editors) 1989. *Josephus, the Bible, and History*. Detroit: Wayne State University Press.

France, R.T. 1971. *Jesus and the Old Testament*. London: Tyndale (reissued in paperback, Grand Rapids: Baker Book House, 1982).

———. 1986. *The Evidence for Jesus*. London: Hodder and Stoughton.

———. (editor) 1993. *Evangelical Anglicans*. London: SPCK.

———. 1995. *Women in the Church's Ministry*. Carlisle: Paternoster.

Fridrichsen, A. 1972. *The Problem of Miracle in Primitive Christianity*. English translation (from the French of 1925). Minneapolis: Augsburg.

Fuller, R.H. 1972. *The Formation of the Resurrection Narratives*. London: SPCK.

———. 1994. *Christ and Christianity: Studies in the Formation of Christology*. Edited by R.Kahl. Valley Forge: Trinity.

Furnish, V.P. 1968. *Theology and Ethics in Paul*. Nashville: Abingdon.

———. 1989. The Jesus-Paul Debate: From Baur to Bultmann. In Wedderburn, 17–50.

———. 1993. *Jesus According to Paul*. Cambridge: Cambridge University Press.

Galling, K. (editor) 1957–1965. *Die Religion in Geschichte und Gegenwart*. Third edition in seven volumes. Tübingen: Mohr.

Gamble, H.Y. 1995. *Books and Readers in the Early Church*. New Haven: Yale University Press.

Garrett, Susan R. 1989. *The Demise of the Devil: Magic and the Demonic in Luke's Writings*. Minneapolis: Fortress.

General Synod. 1995. *The Mystery of Salvation*. Report by the

General Synod of the Church of England. London: Church House.

Geyl, P. 1964. *Napoleon: For and Against*. London: Cape.

Gibbon, E. 1910. *The Decline and Fall of the Roman Empire*. Everyman edition in six volumes. London: Dent (This work was first published 1766–1788).

Gilhus, I.S. 1997. *Laughing Gods, Weeping Virgins*. London: Routledge.

Golb, N. 1995. *Who Wrote the Dead Sea Scrolls?* New York: Scribner.

Grabbe, L.L. 1987. Fundamentalism and Scholarship: The Case of Daniel. In B.P. Thompson, 133–152.

Grant, F.C., and H.H. Rowley (editors). 1963. *Dictionary of the Bible*. Edinburgh: Clark.

Grant, M. 1994. *Saint Peter*. London: Weidenfeld and Nicolson.

Grant, R.M. 1952. *Miracle and Natural Law in Graeco-Roman and Early Christian Thought*. Amsterdam: North Holland Company.

———. 1963. *A Historical Introduction to the New Testament*. London: Collins.

———. 1986. The Christ at the Creation. In *Jesus in History and Myth*, edited by R.J. Hoffman and G.A. Larue. (Buffalo: Prometheus), 157–167.

———. 1988. *Greek Apologists of the Second Century*. London: SCM.

———. 1990. *Jesus after the Gospels: The Christ of the Second Century*. London: SCM.

Green, J.B. et al. (editors) 1992. *Dictionary of Jesus and the Gospels*. Leicester: Intervarsity.

Green, J.B., and M. Turner (editors). 1994. *Jesus of Nazareth: Lord and Christ*. Carlisle: Paternoster/Grand Rapids: Eerdmans.

Grünbaum, A. 1994. In Defense of Secular Humanism. In *Challenges to the Enlightenment*, edited by P. Kurtz et al.; (Buffalo: Prometheus), 102–129.

Guenther, H.O. 1985. *Footprints of Jesus' Twelve in Early Christian Traditions*. New York: Lang.

Haenchen, E. 1965. Schriftzitate und Textüberlieferung in der

Apostelgeschichte. Zum Text der Apostelgeschichte. Both in the volume of Haenchen's essays, *Gott und Mensch* (Tübingen: Mohr), 156–171, 172–205.

———. 1968a. *Der Weg Jesu.* Second edition. Berlin: De Gruyter.

———. 1968b. *Die Apostelgeschichte.* Sixth edition. Göttingen: Vandenhoeck and Ruprecht.

———. 1980. *Das Johannesevangelium.* Edited from Haenchen's papers by U. Busse. Tübingen: Mohr. (There is an English translation in the Hermeneia series, Philadelphia: Fortress, 1984.)

Hagner, D.A. 1973. *The Use of the Old and New Testaments in Clement of Rome.* Leiden: Brill.

Hammond Bammel, Caroline P. 1982. Ignatian Problems. *JTS* 33, 62–97.

Hanson, A.T. 1982. *The Pastoral Epistles* (NCB). London: Marshall, Morgan and Scott/Grand Rapids: Eerdmans.

Hanson, R.P.C. 1985. *Studies in Christian Antiquity.* Edinburgh: Clark.

Hanson, R.P.C., and R.H. Fuller. 1948. *The Church of Rome: A Dissuasive.* London: SCM.

Hare, D.R.A. 1967. *The Theme of Jewish Persecution of Christians in the Gospel According to St. Matthew.* Cambridge: Cambridge University Press.

Harnack, A. 1961. *History of Dogma.* Volume 4. English translation. New York: Dover.

Harries, R. 1987. *Christ is Risen.* London: Mowbray.

Harris, M.J. 1983. *Raised Immortal.* London: Marshall, Morgan, and Scott.

———. 1985. References to Jesus in Early Classical Authors. In *Jesus Tradition Outside the Gospels,* edited by D. Wenham (Sheffield: JSOT. *Gospel Perspectives,* volume 5), 343–368.

Harvey, A.E. 1982. *Jesus and the Constraints of History.* London: Duckworth.

Hawthorne, G.F. (editor) 1993. *Dictionary of Paul and his Letters.* Leicester: Intervarsity.

Hays, R.B. 1997. *The Moral Vision of the New Testament*. Edinburgh: Clark. (First published by Harper Collins, New York, 1996.)

Head, P.M. 1993. Christology and Textual Transmission: Reverential Alterations in the Synoptic Gospels. *Nov Test* 35, 105–129.

Head, P.M. 1997. *Christology and the Synoptic Problem*. Cambridge: Cambridge University Press.

Heitmüller, W. 1903. *Im Namen Jesu*. Göttingen: Vandenhoeck and Ruprecht.

Hennecke, E. 1963 and 1965. *New Testament Apocrypha*. Edited by W. Schneemelcher. English translation. London; volume 1 (1963): SCM; volume 2 (1965): Lutterworth.

Heyer, C.J., den. 1996. *Jesus Matters: 150 Years of Research*. English translation. London: SCM.

Hoffmann, R.J. 1994. *Porphyry's 'Against the Christians'*. Amherst: Prometheus.

Hood, J.Y.B. 1995. *Aquinas and the Jews*. Philadelphia: University of Pennsylvania Press.

Houlden, J.L. 1976. *The Pastoral Epistles*. Harmondsworth (Middlesex): Penguin.

———. 1996. The Resurrection and Christianity. *Theology* 99, 198–205.

———. 1997. Review of Lüdemann 1996, in *Theology* 100, 219–220.

Houston, J. 1994. *Reported Miracles: A Critique of Hume*. Cambridge: Cambridge University Press.

Hull, J.M. 1974. *Hellenistic Magic and the Synoptic Tradition*. London: SCM.

Hylson-Smith, K. 1988. *Evangelicals in the Church of England, 1734–1984*. Edinburgh: Clark.

Joad, C.E.M. 1952. *The Recovery of Belief*. London: Faber and Faber.

Joly, R. 1979. *Le dossier d'Ignace d'Antioche*. Brussels: Éditions de l'université.

Jones, A.H.M. 1963. The Social Background of the Struggle Between Paganism and Christianity. In Momigliano, 17–37.

Käsemann, E. 1964. *Essays on New Testament Themes*. English translation. London: SCM.

Kenny, A. 1986. *A Stylometric Study of the New Testament*. Oxford: Clarendon.

Kent, J. 1987. *The Unacceptable Face: The Modern Church in the Eyes of the Historian.* London: SCM.

Kenyon, F.G. 1912. *Handbook to the Textual Criticism of the New Testament,* Second edition. London: Macmillan.

Kittel, G., and G. Friedrich (editors) 1964–76. *A Theological Dictionary of the New Testament.* English translation in ten volumes. Grand Rapids: Eerdmans.

Klingberg, F.J. 1926. *The Anti-Slave Movement in England.* London: Oxford University Press.

Kloppenborg, J.S. 1996. Egalitarianism in the Myth and Rhetoric of Pauline Churches. In *Re-imagining Christian Origins.* Edited by Elizabeth A. Castelli and H. Taussig. Valley Forge: Trinity, 247–263.

Knight, G.W., III. 1992. *The Pastoral Epistles.* Grand Rapids: Eerdmans/Carlisle: Paternoster.

Kümmel, W.G. 1973. *The New Testament: The History of the Investigation of its Problems.* English translation. London: SCM.

———. 1975. *Introduction to the New Testament.* English translation of the revised 17th German edition. London: SCM.

Küng, H. 1976. *Christ Sein.* Zürich: Ex Libris.

Ladd, G.E. 1966. *Jesus and the Kingdom.* London: SPCK.

———. 1979. *I Believe in the Resurrection of Jesus.* London: Hodder and Stoughton.

Lampe, G.W.H. 1965a. Miracles in the Acts of the Apostles. In Moule, 165–178.

———. 1965b. Miracles and Early Christian Apologetic. In Moule, 203–218.

———. 1966. *The Resurrection: A Dialogue Arising from Broadcasts by G.W.H. Lampe and D.M. Mackinnon.* Edited by W. Purcell. London: Mowbray.

Lane Fox, R. 1991. *The Unauthorized Version: Truth and Fiction in the Bible.* London: Viking.

Lapide, P. 1984. *The Resurrection of Jesus: A Jewish Perspective.* English translation. London: SPCK.

Lawlor, H.J., and J.E.L. Oulton (translators). 1927. *Ecclesiastical History* by Eusebius. London: SPCK.

Lewis, C.S. 1940. *The Problem of Pain.* London: Centenary.

———. 1947. *Miracles: A Preliminary Study.* London: Bles.

——. 1974: *Miracles: A Preliminary Study*. Revised edition. London: Fount.

——. 1979. *God in the Dock*. London: Collins.

Lewis, I.M. 1967. Reply to Wilson. *Man* (2), 626–27.

——. 1970. A Structural Approach to Witchcraft and Spirit Possession. In Douglas, 293–309.

Lindars, B. 1972. *The Gospel of John* (NCB). London: Oliphants.

——. 1990. *John* (New Testament Guides). Sheffield: Academic Press.

——. 1991. *The Theology of the Letter to the Hebrews*. Cambridge: Cambridge University Press.

Lindsey, H., with C.C. Carlson. 1971. *The Late Great Planet Earth*. London: Marshall Pickering. (First published, 1970 in U.S.A. by Zondevan.)

——. 1974. *Satan is Alive and Well on Planet Earth*. New York: Bantam.

Linfield, A.M. 1994. Sheep and Goats: Current Evangelical Thought on the Nature of Hell and the Scope of Salvation. *Vox Evangelica* 24, 63–75.

Lowther Clarke, W.K. 1937. *The First Epistle of Clement to the Corinthians*. London: SPCK.

Lüdemann, G., in collaboration with Özen, A. 1995. *What Really Happened to Jesus: A Historical Approach to the Resurrection*. English translation. London: SCM.

Lüdemann, G. 1996. *Heretics: The Other Side of Early Christianity*. English translation. London: SCM.

——. 1997. *The Unholy in Holy Scripture*. English translation. London: SCM.

Lührs, M. 1939. *Napoleons Stellung zur Religion und Kirche*. Berlin: Eberling.

Luz, U. 1990. *Matthew 1–7. A Commentary*. English translation. Edinburgh: Clark.

Macgregor, G.H.C. 1936. *The New Testament Basis of Pacifism*. London: Clarke.

Mack, B.L. 1991. *A Myth of Innocence: Mark and Christian Origins.* Philadelphia: Fortress.

———. 1993. *The Lost Gospel: The Book of Q and Christian Origins.* Shaftesbury (Dorset): Element.

Macquarrie, J. 1990. *Jesus Christ in Modern Thought.* London: SCM/Philadelphia: Trinity.

Mason, S. 1992. *Josephus and the New Testament.* Peabody (Mass): Hendrickson.

Mayhew, P. 1989. *A Theology of Force and Violence.* London: SCM.

McBrien, R. 1994. *Catholicism. Third revised edition.* London: Chapman.

McCown, C.C. 1941. Gospel Geography: Fiction, Fact, and Truth. *JBL* 60, 1–25.

McDowell, J. 1990. *Historical Evidences for the Christian Faith,* British edition in 2 volumes. Amersham-on-the-Hill (Bucks): Scripture Press Foundation. (First published in U.S.A. in 1981 by Here's Life Publishers, San Bernardino.)

McKenzie, J.L. 1965. *Dictionary of the Bible.* London: Chapman.

Meier, J.P. 1990. Jesus in Josephus. *CBQ* 52, 76–103.

Metzger, B.M. 1981. *Manuscripts of the Greek Bible.* New York: Oxford University Press.

Metzger, B.M., and M.D. Coogan (editors). 1993. *The Oxford Companion to the Bible.* Oxford: Oxford University Press.

Meynell, H.A. 1994. *Is Christianity True?* London: Chapman.

Miller, M.P. 1995. 'Beginning from Jerusalem' . . . Re-examining Canon and Consensus. *JHC* 2, 3–30.

Mitton, C.L. 1975. *Jesus: The Fact Behind the Faith.* London: Mowbray. (First published in U.S.A. by Eerdmans, 1973).

Moehring, H.R. 1972. The Census in Luke as an Apologetic Device. In *Studies in the New Testament and Early Christian Literature,* edited by D.E. Aune (Leiden: Brill), 144–160.

Momigliano, A. (editor) 1963. *The Conflict Between Paganism and Christianity in the Fourth Century.* Oxford: Clarendon.

Montefiore, C.G. 1910. *Some Elements of the Religious Teaching of Jesus.* London: Macmillan.

————. 1927. *The Synoptic Gospels*. Second edition, volume 1. London: Macmillan.

Moody Smith, D. 1986. *John*. Second edition. Philadelphia: Fortress.

————. 1995. *The Theology of the Gospel of John*. Cambridge: Cambridge University Press.

Morgan, R., with J. Barton. 1988. *Biblical Interpretation*. Oxford: Oxford University Press.

Morley, J. 1886. *Rousseau*. 2 volumes. London: Macmillan.

Mosley, A.W. 1965. Historical Reporting in the Ancient World. *NTS* 12, 10–26.

Moule, C.F.D. (editor) 1965a. *Miracles*. London: Mowbray.

————. 1965b. *The Gospel According to Mark*. Cambridge: Cambridge University Press.

Murray, G. 1946. *Euripides and His Age*. Second edition. Oxford: Oxford University Press.

Neil, W. 1967. *The Letter of Paul to the Galatians*. Cambridge: Cambridge University Press.

Neill, S., and T. Wright. 1988. *The Interpretation of the New Testament 1861–1986*. Second edition. Oxford: Oxford University Press.

Neirynck, F. 1986. Paul and the Sayings of Jesus. In *L'Apôtre Paul*. Edited by A. Vanhoye (Leuven: Leuven University Press), 265–321.

Nickelsburg, G.W.E. 1981. *Jewish Literature Between the Bible and the Mishnah*. London: SCM.

Niederwimmer, K. 1967. Johannes Markus und die Frage nach dem Verfasser des zweiten Evangeliums. *ZNW* 58, 172–188.

Nineham, D.E. 1963. *The Gospel of St. Mark*. Reprinted 1992. London: Penguin.

————. 1993: *Christianity Mediaeval and Modern: A Study in Religious Change*. London: SCM.

Oddie, W. (editor) 1987. *After the Deluge*. London: SPCK.

O'Neill, J.C. 1972. *The Recovery of Paul's Letter to the Galatians*. London: SPCK.

Pagels, Elaine. 1991. The Social History of Satan. *HTR* 84, 105–128.

Parker, D. 1997. *The Living Text of the Gospels.* Cambridge: Cambridge University Press.

Parrinder, G. 1970. *Avatar and Incarnation.* London: Faber and Faber.

———. 1993. *Son of Joseph: The Parentage of Jesus.* Edinburgh: Clark.

Pearson, B.A. 1997. *The Emergence of the Christian Religion.* Harrisburg: Trinity.

Pines, S. 1971. *An Arabic Version of the Testimonium Flavianum and its Implications.* Jerusalem: Israel Academy of Sciences and Humanities.

Polkinghorne, J. 1983. *The Way the World Is: The Christian Perspective of a Scientist.* London: Triangle.

Potter, H. 1993. *Hanging in Judgment: Religion and the Death Penalty in England.* New York: Continuum.

Price, R.M. 1995. Apocryphal Apparitions: 1 Corinthians 15:3–11 as a Post-Pauline Interpolation. *JHC* 2(2), 69–99.

Räisänen, H. 1987a: Römer 9–11: Analyse eines geistigen Ringens. *ANRW* II, 25(4), 2891–2939.

———. 1987b. *Paul and the Law.* Second edition. Tübingen: Mohr.

———. 1990. *Beyond New Testament Theology.* London: SCM/Philadelphia: Trinity.

———. 1997. *Marcion, Muhammad, and the Mahatma.* London: SCM.

Rajak, Tessa. 1983. *Josephus the Historian and his Society.* London: Duckworth.

Ramsey, B. 1993. *Beginning to Read the Fathers.* London: SCM.

Ranke-Heinemann, U. 1994. *Nein und Amen.* Munich: Knaur.

Redford, D.B. 1992. *Egypt, Canaan, and Israel in Ancient Times.* Princeton: Princeton University Press.

Reumann, J. 1991. *Variety and Unity in New Testament Thought.* Oxford: Oxford University Press.

Richards, G.C. 1941. A Note on the *Testimonium Flavianum. JTS* 42, 70–71.

Richards, J. 1974. *But Deliver Us from Evil: An Introduction to the Demonic Dimension in Pastoral Care*. London: Darton, Longman, and Todd.

Riches, J. 1980. *Jesus and the Transformation of Judaism*. London: Darton, Longman, and Todd.

———. 1990. *The World of Jesus*. Cambridge: Cambridge University Press.

Rignano, E. 1923. *The Psychology of Reasoning*. English translation. London: Kegan Paul.

Roberts, C. 1953. An Early Papyrus of the First Gospel. *HTR* 46, 233–37.

Robertson, J.M. 1927. *Jesus and Judas*. London: Watts.

Robinson, J.A.T. 1976. *Redating the New Testament*. London: SCM.
———. 1977. *Can We Trust the New Testament?* London: Mowbray.

Robinson, R. 1964. *An Atheist's Values*. Oxford: Blackwell.

Romer, A.S. 1949. *The Vertebrate Body*. Philadelphia: Saunders.

Ruef, J. 1971. *Paul's First Letter to Corinth*. Harmondsworth (Middlesex): Penguin.

Russell, D.S. 1961. *The Method and Message of Jewish Apocalyptic*. London: SCM.

Sanders, E.P. 1969. *The Tendencies of the Synoptic Tradition*. Cambridge: Cambridge University Press.

———. 1983. *Paul, the Law, and the Jewish People*. Minneapolis: Fortress (also London: SCM, 1985).

———. 1985. *Jesus and Judaism*. London: SCM.

———. 1991. *Paul* (Past Masters Series). Oxford: Oxford University Press.

———. 1993a. *The Historical Figure of Jesus*. London: Lane.

———. 1993b. The Life of Jesus. In *Christianity and Rabbinic Judaism*, edited by H. Shanks (London: SPCK/Washington, DC: Biblical Archaeological Society), 41–83.

Sanders E.P., and Margaret Davies. 1989. *Studying the Synoptic Gospels*. London: SCM/Philadelphia: Trinity.

Sanders, J.T. 1966. Paul's "Autobiographical" Statements. *JBL* 85, 335–343.

Scheidweiler, F. 1954. Das Testimonium Flavianum. *ZNW* 45, 230–243.

Schmithals, W. 1971. *The Office of Apostle in the Early Church.* English translation. London: SPCK.

———. 1972. *Jesus Christus in der Verkündigung der Kirche.* Neukirchen: Neukirchener Verlag.

Schoedel, W.R. 1985. *Ignatius of Antioch* (Hermeneia Series). Philadelphia: Fortress.

Schürer, E. 1973. *The History of the Jewish People in the Age of Jesus Christ.* New English version revised and edited by G. Vermes et al., volume 1. Edinburgh: Clark.

———. 1979. Volume 2 of the above revised edition.

———. 1986 and 1987. Volume 3 (in two parts) of the above revised edition.

Schweitzer, A. 1954. *The Quest of the Historical Jesus.* English translation of the third edition. London: Black.

Shaw, G. 1987. *God in Our Hands.* London: SCM.

Sim, D.M. 1996. *Apocalyptic Eschatology in the Gospel of Matthew.* Cambridge: Cambridge University Press.

Smith, J.Z. 1990. *Drudgery Divine: On the Comparison of Early Christianities and the Religions of Late Antiquity.* London: SOAS.

Smith, M. 1972. Review of Pines 1971. In *JBL* 91, 441–42.

———. 1988. On Slavery: Biblical Teachings v. Modern Morality. In *Biblical v. Secular Ethics,* edited by R.J. Hoffmann and G.A. Larue, (Buffalo: Prometheus), 69–77.

Spencer, H. 1885. *Principles of Psychology.* Second edition, volume 2. London: Williams and Norgate.

Spong, J.S. 1993. *This Hebrew Lord: A Bishop's Search For the Authentic Jesus.* San Francisco: Harper.

Stanton, G.N. 1974. *Jesus of Nazareth in New Testament Preaching.* Cambridge: Cambridge University Press.

———. 1995. *Gospel Truth? New Light on Jesus and the Gospels.* London: Harper Collins.

Strauss, D.F. 1997. *The Old Faith and the New.* Reprint of the English translation of 1874, with Introduction and Notes by G.A. Wells, Amherst: Prometheus/Oxford: Westminster College.

Talbert, C.H. 1976. The Myth of a Descending-Ascending Redeemer in Mediterranean Antiquity. *NTS* 22, 418–440.

Taylor, V. 1966. *The Gospel According to St. Mark*. Second edition. London: Macmillan.

Telford, W.R. (editor) 1995. *The Interpretation of Mark*. Second edition. Edinburgh: Clark.

Theissen, G., and A. Merz. 1998. *The Historical Jesus: A Comprehensive Guide*. English translation from the German of 1996. London: SCM.

Thiede, C. 1990. *Jesus: Life or Legend?* Oxford: Lion.

———. 1995. Papyrus Magdalen Greek 17 (Gregory Aland P^{65}). A Reappraisal. *ZPE* 105, 13–19.

Thiede, C., and M. D'Ancona. 1996. *The Jesus Papyrus*. London: Weidenfeld and Nicolson.

Thomas, H. 1997. *The Slave Trade*. London: Picador.

Thomas, K. 1973. *Religion and the Decline of Magic*. Harmondsworth (Middlesex): Penguin.

Thompson, B.P. (editor) 1987. *Scripture, Meaning, and Method: Essays Presented to A.T. Hanson*. Hull: Hull University Press.

Thompson, M. 1991. *Clothed With Christ: The Example and Teaching of Jesus in Romans 12:1–15:13*. Sheffield: JSOT.

Trevelyan, G.M. 1944. *English Social History*. London: Longmans.

Tuckett, C. 1996. *Q and the History of Early Christianity*. Edinburgh: Clark.

Tyler, R.N. 1996. *Was There A Real Jesus? Twenty Questions*. London: Minerva Press.

VanderKam, J.C. 1994. *The Dead Sea Scrolls Today*. London: SPCK/Grand Rapids: Eerdmans.

Vermes, G. 1973. *Jesus the Jew*. London: Collins.

———. 1983. *Jesus and the World of Judaism*. London: SCM.

———. 1993. *The Religion of Jesus the Jew*. London: SCM.

———. 1998. *Providential Accidents: An Autobiography*. London: SCM.

Vielhauer, P. 1965. Gottesreich und Menschensohn. in *Aufsätze zum Neuen Testament* (Munich: Kaiser), 55–91.

Vogt, J. 1971. Augustus and Tiberius. In *Jesus in His Time*. Edited by H.J. Schultz. English translation (London: SPCK), 1–9.

Wachtel, K. 1995. Fragmente des Matthäusevangeliums aus dem ersten Jahrhundert? *ZPE* 107, 72–80.

Walker, D.P. 1981. *Unclean Spirits: Possession and Exorcism in France and England in the Late Sixteenth and Early Seventeenth Centuries*. London: Scholar.

Walsh, J.J. 1991. On Christian Atheism. *VC* 45, 255–277.

Walter, N. 1989. Paul and the Early Christian Jesus-Tradition. In Wedderburn, 51–80.

Watson, F. 1986. *Paul, Judaism, and the Gentiles*. Cambridge: Cambridge University Press.

Watts, M. 1995. *Why Did the English Stop Going to Church?* London: Dr. Williams's Trust.

Weatherhead, L. 1951. *Psychology, Religion, and Healing*. London: Hodder and Stoughton.

———. 1967. *The Christian Agnostic*. London: Hodder and Stoughton.

Wedderburn, A.J.M. (editor) 1989. *Paul and Jesus: Collected Essays*. Sheffield: Academic Press.

Wells, G.A. 1971. *The Jesus of the Early Christians*. London: Pemberton.

———. 1982. *The Historical Evidence for Jesus*. Buffalo: Prometheus.

———. 1986. *Did Jesus Exist?* London: Pemberton.

———. 1988. *Religious Postures: Essays on Modern Christian Apologists and Religious Problems*. La Salle: Open Court.

———. 1989. *Who Was Jesus? A Critique of the New Testament Record*. La Salle: Open Court.

———. 1991. *Belief and Make-Believe: Critical Reflections on the Sources of Credulity*. La Salle: Open Court.

———. 1993. *What's in a Name? Reflections on Language, Magic, and Religion*. Chicago: Open Court.

———. 1996. *The Jesus Legend*. Chicago: Open Court.

Wenham, D. 1995. *Paul, Follower of Jesus or Founder of Christianity?* Grand Rapids: Eerdmans.

Whybray, R.N. 1996. What Do We Know about Ancient Israel? *ET* 108, 71–74.

Wilckens, U. 1974. *Die Missionsreden der Apostelgeschichte.* Third edition. Neukirchen-Vluyn: Neukirchener Verlag.

Wiles, M. 1965. Miracles in the Early Church. in Moule, 221–234.

———. 1967. *The Making of Christian Doctrine.* Cambridge: Cambridge University Press.

———. 1974. *The Remaking of Christian Doctrine.* London: SCM.

———. 1976. *Working Papers in Doctrine.* London: SCM.

———. 1986. *God's Action in the World.* London: SCM.

———. 1991. Orthodoxy and Heresy. In *Early Christianity,* edited by I. Hazlett (London: SPCK), 198–207.

Wilson, I. 1996. *Jesus: The Evidence.* London: Weidenfeld and Nicolson.

Wilson, P.J. 1967. Status Ambiguity and Spirit Possession. *Man* 2, 336–378. (The same volume includes a response to this article by I.M. Lewis, 626–627).

Wilson, S.G. 1995. *Related Strangers: Jews and Christians 70–170 C.E.,* Minneapolis: Fortress.

Wollheim, R. (editor) 1963. *Hume on Religion.* London: Collins.

Wrede, W. 1907. *Paul.* English translation (from the German of 1904). London: Green.

Wright, N.T. 1992a. *The New Testament and the People of God.* London: SPCK.

———. 1992b. 1989. *Who Was Jesus?* London: SPCK.

———. 1996. *Jesus and the Victory of God.* London: SPCK.

———. 1997. *What Saint Paul Really Said.* Oxford: Lion.

Young, Frances. 1994. *The Theology of the Pastoral Epistles.* Cambridge: Cambridge University Press.

Zeitlin, S. 1931. *Josephus on Jesus.* Philadelphia: Dropsie College.

Zerbe, G.M. 1993. *Non-Retaliation in Early Jewish and New Testament Texts.* Sheffield: JSOT.

Zwiep, A.W. 1997. *The Ascension of the Messiah in Lukan Christology.* Leiden: Brill.

Index of New Testament References

Matthew

1:16	218	33	289
23	268	34	232
23–24	120	39	24
2:1	117	11:2–11	147
3	120	11	77
8–11	119	19	266
16	154	20–22	151
19–20	117	12:15–16	144
3:2	77	24–28	187
4:1–11	178	46ff	229
14	268	13:35	268
17	77	36–43	26
18	218	41	181
24	205	41–42	23, 226
24–25	144	47–50	26
5:3	31	58	20
9	232	14:33	210
17	22	15:24	21
18	21	16:16–18	210
32	20	17–19	262
39	232	18	53
39–40	224	27	181
44	65	17:27	147
46	266	18:15–17	21
46–47	22	17	19
6:7–8	22	19:9	20, 266
9–13	60	17	20
19	229	27–28	184
25–26	224	28	182
26	229	20:21–23	184
31–32	22	21:4	268
34	229	18–22	146
7:1	65	31	61, 266
21–23	23	43	22, 26
8:10–12	26	22:2–14	24f
25	20	6–7	25f
9:10	61	10	26
10:5–6	24, 60	37–39	64
6	21	23:13ff	224
8	21	24:9	22f
13	24	11–12	23, 26
14–15	288	25:31	182
18	22	31–46	226
21	229	41	182
21–22	24		
23	23f, 60		
26ff	24		

General Index

Cadbury, H.J., d. 1974, American NT
  scholar, 144, 192, 194
Calvin, J., 289
Capital punishment, 237f
Caragounis, C.C., 53, 262
Carnley, P., 125, 129, 137f
Cassian, J., d. ca. 435, monk, 162
Celsus, 2nd cent. pagan philosopher,
  199
Cephas (Aramaic equivalent of 'Peter'),
  53ff, 59, 69, 124ff, 262
Chapman, C., 172
Charlesworth, J.H., 73, 109, 207f, 214,
  216, 285, 287
Christ: Jesus recognized as, 210, 262;
  meaning of the term, 103, 109, 200,
  207, 217
Christmas, date of, 115
Chrysostom, J., St., d. 407, 162
Church order, 85ff, 92
Churchill, W., 74
Circumcision and early Christianity,
  59, 78
Claudius, Roman emperor A.D. 41–54,
  15, 197
Clement of Alexandria, St., d. ca. A.D.
  215, 114, 220, 259
Clement, first epistle of, xix, 15, 38,
  68, 88, 95, 143, 258, 271
Cohn, N., 283
Collins, J.J., 107f, 123, 148, 180ff, 261,
  284
Conditioning, 174
Conzelmann, H., d. 1989, German NT
  scholar, 257, 269, 278f
Courcelle, P., 292
Cranfield, C.E.B., 116, 120f, 273f
Crucifixion, pre-Christian, 57, 99, 264
Cruelty, 161
Crusades, 235
Cullmann, O., 14, 53

D'Ancona, M., 8
Dancy, J.C., 260
Daniel, book of, xviii, 17, 30, 123,
  180ff, 261
David, King, d. ca. 970 B.C., Jesus as
  son of, 58, 106, 115, 274
Davies, Margaret, 63f, 83f, 88f, 90,
  269f, 290f
Davies, P.R., 248f, 293
Davies, W.D., 24, 119
Davis, S.T., 129
Day, J., 99
Dead, raising of the: in Daniel, 123; by
  Jesus, 40, 145f, 148, 159, 193; in lat-
  er Christianity, 50, 170; promised in
  NT (See also First Fruits.), 60f, 178

Dead Sea Scrolls (See also Qumran.),
  64, 100, 106ff
Decapolis, region of league of ten cit-
  ies, 260
De Jonge, M., 70, 109
Demons (See also Exorcism.): activity
  of, 56f, 100, 123, 151ff, 162ff, 236;
  when conquered by Jesus, 143, 156,
  158; do not recognize Jesus, 156ff;
  and the wilderness, 152, 154
Deuteronomy, book of, 153, 289
Devil, the (See also Satan), 151f, 162,
  178f, 182
Dibelius, M., 130, 144f, 269
Didache, the, 89
Dihle, A., 99
Dingle, H., 175ff
Dio Chrysostom (= Dio Cocceianus),
  d. after A.D. 112, Greek orator, 83
Dionysius Exiguus, 6th cent. monk, 284
Disciples of Jesus: and apostles, 54;
  authority of, 184; differently por-
  trayed in different gospels, 20, 30
Divorce, Jesus on, 4, 20, 63f, 266f
Docetists, 114
Dodd, C.H., d. 1973, English NT schol-
  ar, 135f, 179, 187f, 209, 293
Doherty, E., 57
Domitian, Roman emperor A.D. 81–96,
  212
Dornseiff, F., 207
Dunn, J., 49ff, 75ff, 97f, 110, 265

Ebionites, 103
Ecclesiasticus, book of, 96, 98
Ecumenical movement, 242
Ehrman, B.D., 5, 162, 192, 255ff
Einstein, A., 208, 286f
Elders, 86ff, 90, 127, 256
Elijah, 137, 194, 248
Elisha, 146, 248
Ellegård, A., 104
Elliott, J.K., 9, 10, 255
Ellis, E.E., 92
Emmaus, appearance of risen Jesus at,
  132ff, 279
Enlightenment, supposed prejudices of
  the, 131
Enoch, book of, 96, 102, 181ff, 284
Ephesians, epistle to, 60, 151, 157f
Ephesus, 54, 66, 88, 90, 256
Epistles of NT, relation to gospels,
  xvii, xix, 67, 246f
Eschatology (doctrine of the last
  things): Jesus on, 28, 95, 193f, 209,
  234; Jewish, 137, 156, 179f, 182,
  184; in John, 41f; in Pastorals, 81; in
  Q, 102f; 'realized', 187